The Growth of Music

A STUDY IN MUSICAL HISTORY

The Growth of Music

A STUDY IN MUSICAL HISTORY

By H. C. COLLES

Fourth Edition

LONDON
OXFORD UNIVERSITY PRESS
Oxford New York
1978

Oxford University Press, Walton Street, Oxford OX2 6DP

OXFORD LONDON GLASGOW
NEW YORK TORONTO MELBOURNE WELLINGTON
IBADAN NAIROBI DAR ES SALAAM LUSAKA CAPE TOWN
KUALA LUMPUR SINGAPORE JAKARTA HONG KONG TOKYO
DELHI BOMBAY CALCUTTA MADRAS KARACHI

ISBN 0 19 316115 X (*limp*)
ISBN 0 19 316116 8 (*boards*)

First Edition 1912
Second Edition 1939
Third Edition 1956
Fourth Edition 1978

Printed in Great Britain
at the University Press, Oxford
by Vivian Ridler
Printer to the University

Preface to the Fourth Edition

'Most of the artistic insincerity of the present day comes from the ability to talk about things without actually hearing their effect.' Those words, written over sixty years ago by H. C. Colles, remain substantially true today. It is a trap into which anyone may fall. Yet the danger seems to have loomed larger at the start of the century than it does at present. Histories of music and pedagogical studies of that vintage had their virtues but sometimes give a curiously abstract impression, as if sheltered or even sheltering from the actual sound of music.

Colles made no such mistake, and in *The Growth of Music* he presents himself as the first, or one of the first, of a new wave of communicators who introduced music not merely as a living art but as a *lively* art. Others would include Sir Walford Davies, whose broadcasts achieved an immense popularity, and Percy Scholes. Their aim, though conveyed in differing ways, was to make music accessible to the layman. That aspiration shines all the way through *The Growth of Music*, furthered by Colles's command of a literary style at once elegant and vernacular. Always easy to read, he neither patronizes nor pontificates, nor, save on the rarest occasions, does he air any prejudices.

Writing about music was of course Colles's trade. A product of Oxford and the Royal College of Music, he spent his life on *The Times*, reigning for over thirty years as its august chief music critic. As a scholar with a special interest in Brahms, he was responsible for the seventh volume of *The Oxford History of Music* and also edited two editions of *Grove's Dictionary of Music and Musicians*. Also he was a Professor of the History of Music at the Royal College of Music. Although the publication of *The Growth of Music* preceded some of these activities and appointments, Colles was well equipped for his task. In particular, his experience as a critic, initially as assistant to Fuller Maitland, exposed him to a wider range of music than might have come his way in some other branch of the profession.

Nevertheless, for all Colles's erudition and verbal fluency, he set himself a difficult job. He had to make an orderly, coherent progress through about seven hundred years of music-making. In his 'Note on the Use of this Book' he explains his policy. 'So far from taking each master or masterpiece, [the book] merely makes a small selection of a few of the salient works by a few of the greatest men, and tries to trace the growth of musical technique by means of them. No apology is offered for the many omissions of even great names of men and works. The whole object has been to discuss as far as possible those works which people are likely to hear at concerts, in church, or on the radio, television [an interpolation by a later editor, Eric Blom], or gramophone; which they play or hear played at home.'

There are, then, limitations to the scope of *The Growth of Music*, but they are for the most part deliberate ones. It is the measure of Colles's success that within the outlines of his curriculum it is hard to better his choice of topics or his method of dealing with them. Details of emphasis or lack of emphasis in the text may be queried from time to time, but its perspectives and value-judgments stand up to modern scrutiny remarkably well. Its strong point is obviously its discussion of Classical and Romantic music, not to mention Bach and Handel. His commentaries on Haydn, Mozart, and Beethoven are excellent, as too are those on Schubert, Brahms, and Wagner. Was Colles therefore, like many British musicians of his generation, German-orientated? Not necessarily. He devotes a lot of space to Lully, in an era when the chance of hearing or seeing any of his stage works was even rarer than now, though he may be considered to have undervalued Rameau. Berlioz is most handsomely treated—more handsomely, most of Colles's contemporaries would have thought, than the composer deserved. (Clearly, the writer ranged himself in the embattled pro-Berlioz lobby, along with Ernest Newman and Beecham.) By contrast, the music of Liszt appears to have interested him rather less, and, like many another, Colles holds reservations about the symphonies of Mahler. How well did he know them? How much opportunity indeed had he had to study them? (The cult of Mahler in this country began some years after Colles's death in 1943.)

Previous editions of *The Growth of Music* ended with a chapter, little over twenty pages long, called, simply, 'The Twentieth Century'. This has been dropped. It is unrealistic. So exciting and so multifarious has been the evolution of music in the present century that it cannot possibly be contained within the boundaries of one short chapter. Fortunately, there is considerable information available in guides to modern music of one sort or another.

The earliest chapters have however been retained. In their case, readers are reminded that our experience and understanding of medieval, renaissance, and baroque music have been transformed since Colles's day. Even a baroque composer as prominent as Vivaldi is scarcely mentioned in the text. Such neglect may seem odd to us but would have seemed reasonable to our grandparents. The Vivaldi boom is of relatively recent origin, encouraged by a mixture of musicological research, the development of the long-playing record and the appearance of expert groups specializing in the performance of baroque music.

It is Chapter 1 that has to be treated with caution. Were Colles writing today, he would no doubt have completely reshaped it into two or even three chapters, which would reflect contemporary scholarly and popular interest in music of the distant past. This is the one part of the book that shows its age. By modern standards it is insufficient, but to leave it out would cause even graver problems.

The 'Suggestions for Further Reading and Listening' printed at the end of every chapter make no claim to comprehensiveness. The criteria have been quality, availability, and suitability. The ideal is an up-to-date study by a recognized authority, which is in most libraries and is also available for purchase in paperback form. Occasionally, out-of-print books are recommended, but only if they are of acknowledged calibre and still to be found on library shelves. Very specialized volumes lie outside Colles's term of reference. Thus Westrup's *Purcell* is recommended, but not, for instance, Schjelderup-Ebbe's *Purcell's Cadences*. Some series crop up very frequently, notably the 'Master Musicians' volumes (J. M. Dent) and the 'BBC Music Guides', and although *Grove's Dictionary* is not in fact listed it will be helpful if readers can consult it.

Record sleeves also represent a valuable source of information, more especially those of pre-Classical music, which are usually written by specialists. As to recordings themselves, it is not worth while making specific recommendations, save in an occasional case. He would be a bold man who laid down which version of a Beethoven symphony was the best. The only possible advice one can offer is familiar: 'When in doubt, ask.' Readers are reminded however that those public libraries which include a gramophone section usually take considerable care over the stocking of their shelves of records.

Finally, everyone who reads this book might like to own a more modern general music reference book. For a larger book I would recommend *The Oxford Companion to Music*, and, for something shorter and cheaper, either *Everyman's Dictionary of Music* or *The Concise Oxford Dictionary of Music*.

CHRISTOPHER GRIER

The publishers are grateful to Christopher Grier for his assistance in revising the 'Suggestions for Further Reading and Listening' at the end of each chapter.

Contents

A Note on the Use of this Book

MUSICAL history cannot be learned from a book. It is the uninterrupted record from the work of unknown composers in a far-away age to those of famous men who are living today. All that a book can do is to help the study of the music by pointing out what influence helped to mould the work of each master and what resources were added to the art with the birth of each masterpiece.

This book undertakes a still humbler task. So far from taking each master or masterpiece it merely makes a small selection of a few of the salient works by a few of the greatest men, and tries to trace the growth of musical technique by means of them. No apology is offered for the many omissions of even great names of men and works. The whole object has been to discuss as far as possible those works which people are likely to hear at concerts, in church, or on the radio, television, or gramophone; which they may play or hear played at home. In the first two chapters, however, it has not been possible to do this entirely, and that is why these chapters contain fuller musical quotations in the text than it has been necessary to make in the later ones.

If this book is used for reading in school, teachers will find that each chapter is divided into sections, one or more of which may be made the basis of a lesson, according to the capacity of the pupils. But the one thing which the teacher must remember is that the contents of the book should always be made tributary to the music itself. Most schools nowadays have a gramophone and some sort of a record library, and this must be used as extensively as possible to illustrate and reinforce (or controvert) the argument of the book. There are notes at the end of each chapter suggesting what music can most usefully be played in this way (do not forget to make frequent breaks: listening can be an exhausting activity). But even when this is done it should be constantly borne in mind that the only real music is 'live' music. If the teacher can do so, he should persuade a pianist, or violinist, or better still an ensemble of some kind, to come and play to his pupils as often as possible, though not for long at any one time. And of course, if his pupils can themselves make music, that is so much the better.

Pupils should be made to follow scores whenever possible. It is very little use to attempt mere paper analysis, which is peculiarly boring to young minds. When works are being studied by sound and sight at once it will be a useful plan to make pupils number the bars in their scores so that attention may be called to any point without waste of time.

The ordinary reader should also find the notes on suggested listening useful. He must find out for himself, however, whether, and where, records of the suggested material are available. No references to actual issues can be made here, for various reasons, the most obvious being that such references could not be relied on to remain up to date for more than a few months. Not only are new records constantly issued, but unfortunately old ones are almost as constantly withdrawn from the market. The best thing to do is thus to map out what records it is desirable to use for illustration, and then to seek the aid of a good record shop or library to ascertain which of them are obtainable at any given time. Many famous or popular works are, of course, to be had several times over, performed by different artists; but the choice of the interpreters, which is not so very important where it is mainly a question of making the first acquaintance of this or that work, may safely be left to the reader's taste or opportunity.

Also included at the end of each chapter are suggestions for further reading. The books referred to naturally tend to be somewhat more technical and advanced than this one, but they should help readers to follow up points not fully dealt with here.

The plan of the book requires little explanation, but one detail, the use of the numerous cross-references which it contains, may be here explained. It is part of the scheme to show that the great men who gave us our music were not isolated phenomena, each one working out his own salvation without reference to his neighbour, but that they have all been links in a chain and mutually dependent. No one of them therefore must be studied alone. Purcell must at one point be referred back to Tallis and at another to Lully; Bach again was influenced even more widely by Italian and French music as well as by his German predecessors, and there was even a Toccata by Purcell among his manuscript copies. The influences upon Handel were equally numerous, and the farther we go the more deep seem to be the roots of the art, so that when we come to modern composers we find a whole range of historical development in their work. Nor does this in the least damage originality. Bach's French Suites are not less unmistakably Bach because the composer learnt something from the style of Couperin, nor Handel's arias less Handel because he met Alessandro Scarlatti as a young man and studied his methods. Each man added something of himself to what he found already existing, and not the greatest revolutionary in the world ever succeeded in shaking himself free and making an entirely fresh start. It is equally important to see what the great men have discarded as it is to see upon what they have built, and as the revolutionaries, of whom Monteverdi is an outstanding example, have always retained a certain vein of conservatism, so those who most held to tradition, such as Palestrina, have yet had their share of reform.

Moreover, since these men all live now in their works, it is often helpful to explain the earlier by the later. Handel is a good preparation for the study of Corelli, and Bach for Palestrina (or indeed for practically anybody), and so the more modern composers are constantly repaying the debt which they owed to their predecessors at first by securing fuller appreciation for them afterwards. One finds the process going on among our concert audiences; people learn to appreciate Beethoven through the more obvious attractions of Tchaikovsky, while the love of Puccini secures sympathy for Gluck. And so an occasional reversal of chronological order may illuminate a lesson in musical history.

These and kindred points will be best realized if in addition to reading the book in its chronological sequence the corresponding sections in the various chapters are taken together, so as to illustrate different musical strata, such as the development of church music from the medieval forms to the Protestant types of England and Germany as shown in Purcell and Bach, or that of harpsichord music (which eventually became piano music) in the work of the English Elizabethans and later Domenico Scarlatti in Italy, Couperin in France, and Bach and Handel. The number of lines which can be followed out is indeed almost inexhaustible. The sectional headings with the references, and perhaps some of the remarks under those headings, may prove helpful to this kind of study.

Most of the artistic insincerity of the present day comes from the ability to talk about things without actually hearing their effect. For this reason the usual tabulated treatment of sonata form has been purposely avoided. Its principles have been discussed solely in connexion with examples, from C. P. E. Bach to Beethoven, which show it to be continually undergoing change with each accession of material, and so, like the fugue, never able to be defined according to any code of rules. The method may lose something in clearness, but it gains more in truthfulness. Its use may help to dispose of the old superstition which regards sonata form as a sort of magic formula, having mysterious virtues of its own and conferring a special prestige upon composers who write in accordance with it.

For a somewhat similar reason the customary division of Beethoven's works into three periods has been ignored. It is easy to learn the classification and to think that one knows something about Beethoven on the strength of having learnt it. But the first object must be to get some notion of Beethoven's musical character, which remained essentially the same from Op. 1 to the Ninth Symphony, but became more and more strongly delineated as time passed. The distinctions are valuable only when the consistent lines of his personality have been realized.

The question of opera is the most difficult one to deal with, but if the musical life of this country is ever to develop fully, a definite course of education in opera, comparable with that which is being undertaken in pure music, will have to be established. Opportunities will have to be provided for young people to see the operas which count in the making of artistic history, just as they are given for them to hear the symphonies, quartets, and sonatas. Opportunities for hearing opera are now rather frequent, and in London at least Mozart is especially familiar, and all his greatest stage works are the mainstay of the repertory at Glyndebourne. Nevertheless the majority of English people have to get their operatic experience in the reverse of the historical order, forming their acquaintance with opera through Puccini, Wagner, and Verdi, and gradually extending it towards works of an earlier date. With this in view a little knowledge of modern opera has been assumed in order to explain the older opera and to suggest principles which underlie that of every time. It may be worth while to urge here that parents and teachers should encourage the intelligent appreciation of opera by taking young people regularly to the best things available, and to remind those who live in London that there are matinée performances by the English National Opera which amply satisfy educational demands.

The treatment of the nineteenth century is less chronological, less technical than that of the earlier periods. The reasons will be obvious. The great composers of the nineteenth century consist practically of two generations: those born in or about the first decade of the century, and those born in or about the fourth and fifth. But here we get a cross-division, for while some members of the first generation, such as Mendelssohn and Chopin, had completed their work and died by about the middle of the century, others, such as Berlioz and Wagner, only began to exert their greatest influence in the latter half of the century, and so appear as the artistic contemporaries of the younger generation. This complicates the task of the chronicler to some extent, but does not much affect that of the student. For the fact is that the majority of the leading musical spirits of the last century were only incidentally affected by their contemporaries. Antipathies were more apparent than affinities, and it is often only when their courses have been traced independently that we can discover the underlying affinity, such as that which undoubtedly exists between the melody of Brahms and Wagner. The plan, therefore, has been to follow out the development of a particular form of art through the century, and that has entailed returning upon the tracks in point of time more than once.

CHAPTER I

From the Troubadours to Monteverdi

We take so many things for granted in our music that it is often difficult to realize how long it took musicians to discover the use of them, or that music of a different kind existed long ago, music as valuable in its way as that with which we are familiar, though without certain features that now seem indispensable to us.

The errand boy who whistles a tune as he goes from door to door makes the accents fall in with the regular tramp of his feet on the pavement, because his tune is naturally divided into a number of equal measures. We say he has a sense of **Rhythm,** and unconsciously he illustrates one of the great principles of modern music, **Time.**

The two things are not the same, for rhythm expressed to the ear in sound and to the eye by movements of the body, either marching or dancing, seems to be one of the first instincts of human beings, whereas time in the musical sense took hundreds of years to develop. In order to see the difference look at this tune by Haydn:

Ex. 1

The phrases bracketed '*a*' and '*b*' are in the same rhythm and time, though the notes are different. Beat out either of them with raps on the table and you will find that the result is the same. But the larger phrases, bracketed 'A' and 'B', are in quite different rhythms, as you will feel at once if you beat them, although they are in the same time. They take an equal time to play, and they are divided into measures, or bars, of equal length, having accents falling regularly at the beginning of each one. If a savage were so fortunate as to make up a tune in the rhythm '*a*', he would go on repeating it till he was tired of it, and then he would make up another rhythm which probably would represent a quite different time. Indeed, the power of joining many rhythms together by making them conform to one time is almost a new thing considering for how long people have loved and studied music, and a great deal of fine music has been written by composers who had little or no idea of time and who had to rely on their sense of rhythm to give shape to what they wrote. When the music was written to be danced to, the steps of the dancers would suggest the musical rhythm, and as we trace out the progress of music we shall find that dancing in particular helped tremendously in the development of musical rhythm and time.

There is another part of music which we all take for granted but which is even newer than time, namely, **Harmony**. Many people who can scarcely play the piano at all can 'vamp' an accompaniment to a song, and if you play them the tune you mean to sing they will immediately put a few simple chords to it which suggest that it belongs to a certain **Key**. Suppose the song to be the old English one, 'Early one morning'; if the accompanist is not very clever he will use some such chords as those shown at A (Ex. 2), that is, three common chords of which F, B flat, and C are the bass notes. These are chosen unconsciously because they are most representative of the key of F, since between them they use all the notes of its diatonic scale and no others. But if the accompanist were a little more clever he would give more variety to the harmony, introducing other chords with notes which are not members of the diatonic scale, as at B. Here the three main chords are the same and occur on all the accents (except in bar 6), but others are used between them where the asterisks are placed. The notes E flat and B natural do not interfere with the key, the harmonization is just as clearly in F as before, but it is richer and more varied.

Many people who know nothing about harmony can make up an accompaniment of this kind at the piano. They have no idea why they choose certain chords rather than others, but they have an instinct for **Tonality**, i.e. the grouping of chords together around a key-note. These people, like the whistling boy, do quite easily what clever musicians only four hundred years ago achieved with the utmost difficulty, and what one hundred years before that they never thought of doing at all, and yet at that date very beautiful music was being written.

While we are on the subject of harmonizing tunes there is one other distinction to be made clear as to the ways in which it may be done. If you play a hymn-tune as it is written in *Hymns Ancient and Modern* you are really playing what the composer intended should be sung by four voices: treble, alto, tenor, and bass. Take, for example, 'All people that on earth do dwell' (A. & M. 166); the tune itself is written for the treble voice or right hand of the pianist, and you feel this to be the most important part of all. If you cannot play well enough to grasp all the notes you at least make sure of playing all that belong to the tune. Next in importance come the bass ones, the lowest in the left hand, and many people play hymn-tunes fairly well when they can play the notes of the treble and the bass quite correctly and merely fill in as many of the inner ones, alto and tenor, as their hands can reach conveniently. It is imperfect but quite passable because we listen most to the tune, next to the bass which makes it fairly clear what the harmonies are to be, and all that the inner parts have to do is to complete the chords which the bass suggests. If you play the alto or tenor parts alone the effect is scarcely like music at all, for they have very little tune of their own; sometimes they repeat the same note over and over again if it happens to agree well with the treble and the bass (cf. alto lines 2 and 3, tenor lines 2 and 4).

This way of writing music is called **homophonic,** which means 'like-sounding', that is to say, the voices are all made to agree with one set of sounds which is called the tune and contains the chief beauty. The other parts taken together must produce a beauty of harmony, but they may have little or no beauty of melody when taken singly.

We are so used to this style of harmony in hymn-tunes, in partsongs, and in pieces for the piano that it seems to us the simplest one, and it is hard to realize that another style which is more difficult to understand was actually perfected by composers long before they had learnt to use the homophonic one at all successfully. That style is called **polyphonic**, which means 'many-sounding', and when a piece of music is written in this way each one of the parts, treble, alto, tenor, and bass, sings a tune so that if you heard it alone you would say that it had distinct musical beauty. Of course the parts have still to agree with one another: if they do not, but sound ugly when they are put together, the result is not polyphonic but 'cacophonic', which means 'bad-sounding', just as when a brass band and a barrel-organ play different tunes in the same street. But though the several parts of polyphonic music must agree, their agreement is not the chief point, but rather their differences both of melody and rhythm.

The simplest form of polyphonic music is a 'catch' such as 'Three blind mice' in which the voices all sing different portions of the same tune at once (see 'Sumer is icumen in', p. 29). But it need not be the same tune, nor need all the parts be equally interesting at once; the only essential feature of polyphonic music is that each must have a separate existence of its own, as it were, besides what it contributes to the harmony of the whole.

MEDIEVAL SONGS AND DANCES

If we consider that all music began with the making of tunes we see how men learnt to write polyphonic music, for in the process of finding out how their tunes might be made to fit together they discovered that certain notes sounded simultaneously make harmonious chords and others inharmonious ones. But the medieval notions of what is harmonious were not the same as ours: major thirds were not at once felt to be so, and minor thirds even less, nor were their inversions as minor and major sixths regarded as consonant.

It would be impossible to find a time when tunes of some sort were not made up and sung to poetry or used as dances, and as both poetry and dance steps suggest strong rhythm most of the early tunes were more remarkable for their rhythm than for any other feature. In the thirteenth century we find the Troubadours and Trouvères of France, the Minstrels of England, and the

Minnesinger of Germany all busily engaged in composing and singing both tunes and poetry; and besides these there were the songs of the people, that is to say, songs made by unknown authors which were passed from mouth to mouth and altered and often improved in the process, some of which have lasted to the present day and are generally called 'folk-songs'.

There was also the music of the church which we know very much more about, because the monasteries were the chief seats of learning, and the monks took more trouble than the secular musicians to find a way of writing down music accurately, so that their work is much better preserved now, with the result that we are apt to think that there was less, or less important, secular music in the Middle Ages, compared with the music for the church. We are also apt to suppose that it was church music which contributed most to the evolution of polyphonic music, merely because so much of it is preserved, and because it did in the course of time take much the largest share in its advance. The curious fact is, however, that from about the tenth to the twelfth century it retarded rather than promoted polyphonic writing in free parts, and on the other hand established a habit of singing in vertical block chords and so pointed towards homophonic music. For a custom arose of singing plainsong in two or three parts by a device known as *organum*. This was due in the first place simply to the different pitches of the alto, tenor, and bass voices of the church choirs, each of which sang the plainsong melody in the register most suited to it, but in parallel lines, not in independent parts. It was found that the intervals most satisfying to the medieval ear at which this could be done were fifths if two voices were singing, and superimposed fourths and fifths if three were engaged. Rigid block chords, such as these, where the plainsong melody of 'Dies irae' is in the middle part:

Ex. 3*a*

taught later composers the value of this kind of effect used as contrast against other textures, and it still survives in its primitive form in such a passage as this in Debussy's *La Cathédrale engloutie*:

with the only difference that the medieval fourths and fifths, which are still present, are here filled in with thirds.

The parallel progressions of the *organum* gradually began to be felt as being too stiff, and small changes were introduced which, for instance, permitted an interchange between fourths and fifths at certain points. Then thirds and sixths began to creep in occasionally, still as dissonances; but once this had begun to happen, there was no reason why composers should not experiment with more varied combinations, and thus chords of different kinds established themselves in their own right, and no longer merely as incidental clashes where polyphonic parts converged to produce contrasts of consonance and dissonance. Counterpoint and harmony met half-way, establishing the modern approach to musical composition which no longer dictated that music should be either purely polyphonic or purely homophonic, but permitted it to use freely a mixture of both these procedures according to the composer's choice.

The most important contribution to medieval music was made by France, inside the church by the great twelfth–thirteenth century Notre-Dame school, and outside by three different classes of people: (1) the quite untaught populace that cultivated folk-song; (2) the southern Troubadours, who included princes and kings such as Guillaume, Duke of Guienne, and Richard

Cœur de Lion; and (3) the northern Trouvères, among whom was Adam de La Halle.

From its earliest days French poetry has been very clear and definite in form, and French musicians took care to make the music fit the words closely, so that their tunes took character from the poetry and were written in neat little phrases finished with cadences. Moreover songs and dances often went together in France, and plays in which the characters both sang and danced soon became very popular.

Among the first of these, and the one from which we will take an example, was a pastoral play by Adam de La Halle called *Robin et Marion* which was played in 1285. Here is one of the songs in which Robin is courting the love of Marion, and he does it just as in so many English folk-songs, such as 'The Keys of Canterbury', by offering her presents. In this verse he invites her to eat a *pâté* with him; then the dialogue goes on and he asks her if she wishes for anything more. She replies most emphatically that she does, and so he sings again to the same tune offering her a 'capon' (*chapon*). It is all very artless, but what we have to notice is the perfect neatness and crispness of the tune, partly suggested by the lines of verse and partly by the need of carrying on a rhythm to which the actors could dance:

Ex. 4

Notice too that all the elements of a song are in place: the first phrase repeated to give balance, then another ('Que nous mangerons') carried on in the way called a 'sequence', that is by repeating it on other notes ('bec à bec'), and then the refrain made out of the repetition of the words and tune with a cadence added. The whole is so perfect and suggests to our ears such simple harmony that it is hard to believe that it was written without thought of harmony, or that, if Adam de La Halle did think of harmony, it would have been unlike what we imagine. When he and his contemporaries wrote music for two or three voices to sing in harmony they brought chords together which seem to us most incongruous, because as we have already seen in the case of *organum* they merely calculated what intervals would go well with each note of the tune and did not think of the result in chords at all. Their ideas of what would go well, moreover, were very different from ours, since they regarded fifths, fourths, and octaves as the most consonant intervals. In our first harmony lessons we are taught to avoid these because of their bareness; we have learnt that thirds and sixths are sweeter, and if you try to 'sing seconds' to a tune you generally follow it in a series of thirds below, thus:

Ex. 5

using a major or a minor third according to which fits in best with the scale, in this instance G. But the old writers would not have agreed with you. They would have added their harmonies probably above the tune, consisting of fifths and fourths, and they would have used only perfect intervals, not taking any account of the notes of the key as we do. It was only gradually that a taste grew for other intervals, and a desire for each separate chord to be harmonious. It was a long time before what we now know as the triad and the chord of the sixth became acceptable. All the process of making harmonized music, therefore, began by adding parts or tunes to one which had been already composed without regard to effects of harmony, but rather as something which might be sung quite by itself.

CHURCH MUSIC

What men like Adam de La Halle began to do in the way of supplying songs with harmony, monks and churchmen did much more consistently, so that for nearly three hundred years the main development of polyphonic music was carried on by these faithful workers whose business it was to supply the daily offices of the church with music.

The tunes which they first had to work upon were the old 'plainsong' melodies which had been handed down traditionally and sometimes altered and improved upon by the singers in churches much in the same way that the folk-songs were being treated by the people, so that these melodies became the basis of church music just as folk-song became the basis of secular song.

But the two kinds of melody were not long kept distinct. It is often difficult to tell whether an old song originally belonged to the church or the world, for the musicians of each borrowed from one another. Tunes which the people heard in church would be used for secular words and turned into popular songs, while the monks often deliberately adopted popular tunes, and, so to speak, wrote their masses round them. Here is a very famous French folk-song called *L'homme armé* ('The man at arms') which was taken as the basis or, as it was called, the *canto fermo* (fixed song) of a great many masses written by the Flemish composers of the fifteenth century:

Ex. 6

Notice that the tune itself has very strong rhythm and a clear form. Though the first part is never exactly reproduced in the sequel, the downward phrases are copied to some extent and are really the same phrase written on different parts of the scale. If it were a modern tune we should say that it modulates into the key of G and then returns to that of C major; but that is not precisely the case, for according to the principles of what was called *musica ficta* it was left to the singer to put in the F sharp or not, and it is now uncertain how far it was a question of taste or a matter of unwritten rules to make these changes at sight. But be that as it may, musicians never thought of a change of pitch as meaning a change of key. Still, the placing of the same phrase in different positions shows that the unknown composer had a strong feeling for contrast of pitch.

What composers did was to take this tune instead of the plainsong of the mass and set one voice to sing the sacred words to it while the others sang the words to free and flowing melodies which were quite independent. Ex. 7 is a short extract from a 'Sanctus' by JOSQUIN DES PRÉS (born *c.* 1450), one of the distinguished composers of the Netherlands, who carried the art to Italy when he, like many of his countrymen, went to Rome and became a member of the papal choir.

You see that the tune is buried among the other parts. It is not set at all as though it were the most important thing to be heard, as we should set it; it is put into very long notes so that its merry rhythm is lost, and this was done partly that it might have

Ex. 7

some of the solemn dignity fit for church music, and partly in order that the other voices, which take no account of it except to agree with it in consonant intervals at the principal accents, might move the more freely. There is something incongruous between the tune (or *canto fermo*) and its counterpoints (i.e. notes or 'points' written against it); the tune would be more expressive without the elaborate counterpoints, and the counterpoints would be more beautiful without these stiff-sounding long notes held on amongst them. Nevertheless, though this way of composing seems clumsy to us, Josquin was a very great composer who wrote most beautiful-sounding passages for the voices.

Two things, however, which we consider essential to music are quite absent from this and from most of the church music of

† The part is sung an octave lower than it is written.

the fifteenth century; they are **rhythm** and **key**, which we saw at the outset are now felt instinctively by every one who is at all musical. The early folk-songs and troubadour songs show that the old musicians had the feeling for rhythm equally with ourselves, but in seeking out the art of writing counterpoint the church musicians lost sight of rhythm to a considerable extent. It was natural enough, for the very conditions of their work took it away from the influences of dancing and poetry and it became more and more contemplative and less spontaneous.

The feeling for key on the other hand had never been reached, and could not be reached until chords and their relations to one another were more fully understood. A modern musician would consider the first phrase of *L'homme armé* as used by Josquin to be in the key of B flat, or possibly F, and either view would shut out the chord of E minor (marked *); but Josquin merely considered that the tune was written on a certain series of notes called the **mode**, and that any notes which were consonant with these and with each other could be made effective. He had no conception of what we call the **tonic chord** as a centre and other chords supporting it and contrasting with it as the dominant and subdominant do in Ex. 2.

A definite feeling of key is bound up with the modern major and minor scales, and chromatic alterations are permitted within these by the use of accidentals to a much larger extent than *musica ficta* allowed. These alterations in turn can effect modulation from key to key (thus F sharp in the key of C major turns it towards G major and B flat towards F major), whereas there was no such thing as modulation from mode to mode. But although the modes did not permit modulation, which is one of the great resources of the key system, it must not be thought that they were inferior makeshifts for something that was eventually to bring about a great improvement. As the predecessors of tonality they have their own perfection and obey laws as valid artistically as those which govern the major and minor keys. The old church modes have their roots as far back as ancient Greek music—hence their Greek names, which are, however, differently applied to the various modes—and the four authentic modes (let us disregard the plagal ones which merely have their final tonic on a different degree of the scale) are as follows, if played on the white keys of the piano:

D—D Dorian mode,
E—E Phrygian mode,
F—F Lydian mode,
G—G Mixolydian mode.

To these were added in the sixteenth century:

A—A Aeolian mode,
C—C Ionian mode.

The last is identical with our major scale; the Aeolian with our minor scale in its descending form.

The work of Josquin and the others of his time strikes modern ears—but modern ears only—as though a great deal of beautiful material were in need of sorting out and arranging in a more definite order than the composers themselves understood. A gradual process of achieving orderliness in a way that comes nearer to the procedures to which the 'classical' era of music has accustomed us was undergone by music in the hands of composers of the fifteenth and sixteenth centuries.

THE MADRIGAL

Though one can trace this process in their church music, it was even more strongly forwarded in their settings of secular words to be sung by several voices in the polyphonic style which were called **Madrigals**.

Again we find the influence of poetry exerted to recall musicians to the fact that rhythm is the true basis of their art, and that however attractive the sound of many voices singing many melodies may be they must conform to some common standard of rhythm in order to produce an effect of unity. Such men as WILLAERT and ARCADELT, who, like Josquin, were northerners, but who lived in Italy (both were masters of the choir of

St. Mark's in Venice), wrote both church music and madrigals, but the latter are the more famous. In their madrigals the counterpoints became simpler, and in the best of them the length of the musical phrase was regulated by the length and accents of the poetic lines. Often a single note was used to each syllable as in the old songs, or if more were used for the sake of expression, they were grouped together into a clear phrase instead of wandering vaguely and holding on a single syllable until the words and sense became unrecognizable.

In their work and in that of ORLANDE DE LASSUS (1532–94), the last and greatest of the northern school, the music became divided into phrases by distinct and beautiful **cadences**, which have the same effect in music as good punctuation has in literature. If the stops are left out or badly distributed in a book even the wisest words become nonsense, for there is nothing to show where one idea ends and another begins, and similarly the division of musical sentences is shown by the use of certain chords which make an ending and separate one idea from another, and these are called cadences.

Ex. 8

This opening of a graceful little French song for four voices by Lassus shows how closely he could make his music follow the metre of words. Notice the cadences (marked †) at the ends of the lines, and also the fact that although the counterpoint is very simple each voice moves quite freely at the words 'et prend' without destroying the rhythm of the verse.

Both in his madrigal and in his church works (Masses, Magnificats, and the famous settings of the Penitential Psalms) Lassus used the same means for giving order and clearness to his ideas, but in his church music he was not so closely bound by the rhythm of words as he was in setting secular poetry. Where, as in the Penitential Psalms, he had great and deep feelings to express, he naturally thought more of beauty of melody and of making the voices join in rich and varied harmony, but even in these the rhythmic form is not disregarded as it was in the church music written before the rise of the madrigal.

PALESTRINA

The man who put the crown on the whole method of polyphonic writing for voices was an Italian, GIOVANNI PIERLUIGI DA PALESTRINA. The name Palestrina is that of the small cathedral town in the hill country near Rome where he was born about the end of 1525. He lived most of his life in Rome, holding appointments in the papal choir and working with untiring devotion to compose some of the loveliest and most purely religious church music which has ever been written.

Most of the Italian church composers in the early part of the sixteenth century had not reached anything like the simplicity of style which the settlers from the north had acquired in their madrigals and imported into their church music. There is a well-known story that polyphonic music was in danger of being banished altogether from the services of the church by the reforms of the Council of Trent (1562) on account of its elaborateness which made the words of the liturgy unintelligible, but that Palestrina saved it by writing some masses which were so pure and expressed the devotional feeling of the words so aptly that the Council decided not to destroy the good with the bad. The story itself is not true to facts, but like most stories of the kind, it was based upon a certain truth, and shows where the strength of Palestrina's music lay. He began where Josquin left off, writing masses on *L'homme armé* and other *canti fermi* of a more or less mechanical kind. He soon outgrew the mechanism and found well-ordered forms for his musical thoughts inspired solely by the words which he set.

Let us take two instances from the famous *Missa Papae Marcelli* (Mass of Pope Marcellus), the work with which his reform of church music is generally associated—the beginning of the 'Kyrie eleison' (Lord have mercy) and the beginning of the 'Gloria'. In the first instance each one of the six voices sings the same beautiful fragment of melody—'Kyrie' on a long sustained note, the music rising by the interval of a 4th on the second syllable of 'eleison'. The phrases are very simple and yet exactly express the aspiration of the prayer, and the passage shows how perfectly Palestrina was able to make each voice move in an independent and gracious flow of melody, while at the same time they unite in expressing the one idea. But the beginning of the 'Gloria' is quite different. Here, instead of the voices all singing independently, they are grouped together into strong and dignified chords. The first phrases hardly seem to be polyphonic music at all, but rather homophonic, so smoothly do the parts move in harmony and rhythm. Soon, however, the independence of the voices makes itself felt in such beautiful figures as the tenor sings to the words 'laudamus Te' (We praise Thee). Each clause of the words 'We praise Thee, we bless Thee' has some such musical feature to give it distinction, but it is not till the climax is reached 'Fili unigenite, Jesu Christe' (O only begotten Son, Jesu Christ) that the voices spread out into the full splendour of the polyphonic style.

In reading Palestrina's music it is well to remember that he did not write it with bar lines as it is printed now, and so the bar lines are no indication of accent. There is rhythm in his music, but not time in the sense explained at the beginning of this chapter. Again, there is no clear notion of key, though the cadences, first on G, then on A, then on C, in this 'Gloria' show him feeling his way in that direction.

One more example of Palestrina's music will impress these points about time and key still more strongly. It is the first phrase of his exquisite setting of the Latin hymn 'Stabat Mater' which he wrote quite near to the end of his life, about 1590:

The music gives the 'quantities' of the verse exactly, but the bar lines, if they had any effect upon the rhythm, would throw out the accents of the second line. Further, the example shows that Palestrina fully understood the beauty of contrasted chords, but his use of chords of A, G, F, at the outset, and of both the major and minor form of the chord of G, proves that his chords are not connected by a key system such as ours. To understand and enjoy the music of Palestrina we have first to rid our minds of the principles of time and key which modern music has engrained, but the more familiar one is with it, the more one can realize the wonderful variety which he obtained from simple contrasts such as have been remarked.

A REVOLUTION

Although after Palestrina's death in 1594 the same serene and beautiful style of writing for voices in church music and madrigals was carried on by composers such as Victoria, Ingegneri, and Soriano, an entirely new influence soon made its appearance which overturned the art of composition to such an extent that it seemed to be establishing just the opposite principles to those which had guided the great choral composers.

This was nothing less than the beginning of **Opera**, that is to say the performance of stage plays in which the characters sing their words to an accompaniment played by instruments instead of speaking them. It would be difficult to say quite how old the idea was. We know that songs and acting had gone together in the 'mystery' and 'miracle' plays of the Middle Ages as well as in the secular plays of the French (see p. 8). But now in the year 1594, the very year of Palestrina's death, a number of artists, both poets and musicians, assembled in the house of a nobleman of Florence, not to revive the musical plays of the Middle Ages, which they heartily despised as belonging to an age of superstitious folly, but to copy the drama of the Greeks by setting musical notes to poetry in such a way as both to express the meaning of the words and to preserve their metre and accent accurately. There was a distinct difference between their object and that of the medieval songs which often kept close to the feeling and metre of the words, because the first object of these songs was always to make a beautiful tune, whereas the Florentine experimenters did not want to write tunes at all, but only to express the words in musical notes rising and falling as the voice of a reciter would rise and fall. And so they eventually established the kind of singing which we now call **recitative**, because it reproduces the expression of a reciting voice and has no definite rhythm or tune apart from the words.

One of the earliest operas of the kind which has been preserved is a setting of the story of *Euridice* by Jacopo Peri, which was performed at Florence in 1600. The old and beautiful legend of the musician, Orpheus, who so loved his wife, Eurydice, that he brought her back from death, became at once one of the most popular subjects for opera, and other settings appeared almost immediately, notably one by Giulio Caccini, who was a singer and the writer of some beautiful songs.

But these early efforts were comparatively amateurish, and the man who really proved what tremendous possibilities this kind of music possessed was CLAUDIO MONTEVERDI (born 1567), the first of the great revolutionary composers whose stories we shall tell in studying the growth of modern music. The date shows that Monteverdi was not a very young man at the time when the Florentine musicians began their experiments in opera. He was over thirty when Peri's *Euridice* was produced, and he had been educated by his teacher, Ingegneri, in the strict tradition of the old choral music and himself wrote a number of madrigals and continued to write then after he had taken to writing operas in the new style. But his madrigals show his love of trying experiments and they contain a number of curious harmonies which make them less smoothly perfect of their kind than similar works by his predecessors.

We shall generally find that the men who discovered new ways of making music have begun by writing less fluently than others in the older styles because they could not be satisfied with what had been already done, and they could not find a new way without beginning by spoiling the old. Handel complained that Gluck knew no more of counterpoint than his cook, Waltz; Mendelssohn shook his head over technical blunders in Wagner's *Tannhäuser*; and fifty years ago people blamed Richard Strauss because some of the sounds which his orchestra makes are crude in comparison with Wagner's orchestra. They are all right in one sense, but people only make great discoveries by risking a good deal, and that is the way in which music grows.

The first of Monteverdi's operas which has been preserved and the most celebrated of all his works is *Orfeo*, a setting of the same story as Peri's *Euridice*, though called by the name of the hero instead of by that of the heroine. It was produced at the court of the Duke of Mantua in 1607, for at that time there were no such things as public opera houses, and works of the kind could only be performed for the pleasure of rich people who chose to pay for the entertainment. The one and only rule which Monteverdi followed in writing *Orfeo* was the determination to make every part of his music express the feelings which the words of the play described.

THE ORCHESTRA

In the first place, since the voices sang separately he had to form an orchestra to accompany them, but he was not content with just a few instruments to support the voices; he needed them to take part in the descriptive effects of the opera, and so he gathered together practically all the kinds of instruments then existing in order to have the advantages of their different sorts of tone.

Organs had been in use in churches for some time, and besides the big ones which were fixed in their places, small chamber organs, which were something like small harmoniums, were in use. Monteverdi decided to have two of these in his orchestra. Then there were instruments rather like a grand piano in shape, but in which the strings were plucked by a quill instead of being struck by a hammer; they were called by the Italians *gravicembalo*, our name for them is 'harpsichord'. Lutes of various sizes, the strings of which were plucked by the fingers as in the modern guitar, and the harp had been used to accompany voices in songs, and Monteverdi included all these.

No instrument in which the strings are plucked makes a very sonorous effect, because however sharply the plucking is done the tone stops at once, just as when the violin is played *pizzicato* (that is, with the fingers). Although these instruments seem a pretty large force, and most of them were so bulky that they must have taken up a great deal of space, the actual musical result from them would be so small that we should probably think it weak in comparison with one modern piano.

But Monteverdi was not content with only these. He also required twelve instruments of the violin family in various sizes, 'two little violins of the French kind', three bass viols, two recorders, some trumpets, two *cornetti* (wind intruments made of wood with a trumpet mouthpiece), and five trombones.

If he had set these to play all at once he would have had a fairly powerful orchestra, but as a matter of fact the wind instruments and even the strings were not allowed to be heard constantly with the voices, and some of the wind instruments were so imperfect that they could only play a few notes. The piece of music for orchestra which begins the opera, called 'Toccata', is merely a sort of 'fanfare' on a single chord of C, evidently so written in order that the trumpets which, like the modern military bugle, could only play the notes of the common chord, might take part in the opening whatever happened afterwards. It is followed by a quiet passage for strings in five parts which reminds one very much of madrigal music, for the parts move in the same smooth way which is natural to voices. All through the early music for viols and violins we find passages which recall the old choral music, for musicians had to discover the scales, arpeggios, and other special kinds of figure which sound so well on stringed instruments but which voices cannot sing. Nowadays we can often tell by glancing at a piece of music what instrument it is meant for, but at the beginning of the seventeenth century not only was this impossible, but it is often difficult to tell whether a given piece was intended to be sung or played. Monteverdi scarcely wrote any notes even for the 'little violins' which a high soprano voice could not sing easily, but nevertheless some of the things which he made the players do must have seemed amazing to people whose ears were accustomed to pure choral music. For example, the effect got by drawing the violin bow rapidly to and fro on a single note thus:

Ex. 10

was a thing which Monteverdi found out and which is quite impossible on any instrument but one played with a bow. Even now that we are all quite used to it it has an exciting effect when a large mass of violins tremble in this way. Imagine how impressive it must have been to unaccustomed ears, and this was only one new effect among innumerable other ones which Monteverdi gained from his orchestra. He was not the first to make an orchestra. Some of his contemporaries, notably Andrea and Giovanni Gabrieli, uncle and nephew at Venice, were at this time writing independent pieces for groups of instruments, strings and wind, which may be called the remote ancestors of that kind of orchestral music which we call 'symphony'.

In his later operas, which were written to be performed publicly at Venice, Monteverdi used a much simpler method of instrumentation, with fewer instruments than those of *Orfeo.* This was partly due to what he had learnt from the Venetian composers and partly a practical economy (cf. Scarlatti, p. 56).

THE VOICES

Let us turn now to the vocal side of the music. Here is a passage which shows at once how different his method was from that of the polyphonic writers. The main story of the opera is that Eurydice dies and Orpheus mourns for her so passionately that at last he determines to go and seek for her among the dead and by his love and his music to draw her back to life. A shepherd asks him for whom he weeps in this beautiful phrase:

Ex. 11

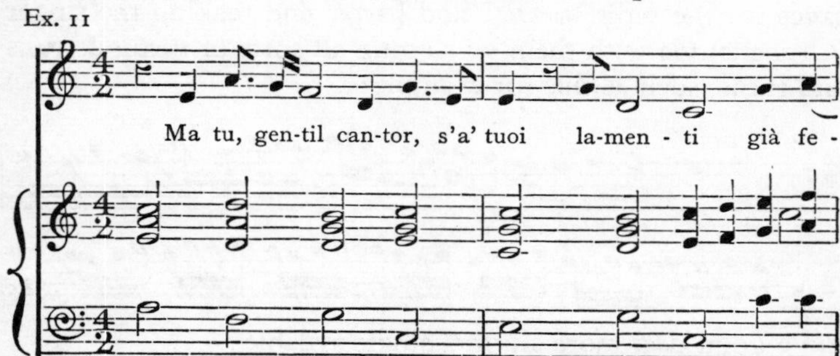

The voice is not singing a melody with any shape or rhythm of its own, it merely rises and falls with the syllables of the words, accentuating them as perfectly as possible, and their expression is reinforced by the harmonies. For example, in the third bar the words 'festi lagrimar' ('madest weep') lead him to use grinding discordant harmonies (chords of the seventh following one another chromatically) to convey the poignancy of grief. To the ears of people used to the smooth common chords of the madrigals they must have sounded more violent than any of the strange chords with which modern composers startle us.

The scene in which Orpheus visits the lower regions and demands that Eurydice shall be restored to life is another marvellous piece of writing of a quite different kind. Monteverdi was here determined to produce something weird, strange, and unearthly, and he did it by writing wild scale passages for the viols, *cornetti*, and harps, and making the singer (Orpheus) vie with them by singing all sorts of tortuous runs and turns, such as this for example:

Ex. 12

and a good deal more all on a single syllable.

Such a musical effect was of course a direct contradiction of the principle laid down by the Florentines that the words should be strictly preserved; it distorted them as much as the old church music of Josquin and others had done, and it did so for the very same reason, namely, in order to make the music more telling. These passages were in fact given the name of 'coloratura' because they were supposed to give colour to the situation. Monteverdi, of course, used them for that purpose, but they soon became very popular for their own sakes both with the singers and with the people who heard them. Singers liked to show off how cleverly they could execute the runs and shakes and other ornaments, and audiences thought them very wonderful and applauded the performance without stopping to think whether it was at all appropriate. Composers of operas soon discovered that they had a great many things to take into account besides the purely artistic effect of their works, for they had to satisfy the vanity of singers by giving them music which would show off their voices, and they had to amuse the grand people who were looking on by giving them scenes which made a great effect, and so it has happened that showy 'coloratura', fine scenery, and gorgeous dresses have often made an opera successful when both the play and the music set to it were very poor and had nothing to do with each other.

Monteverdi, however, was much too good a musician to give in to such nonsense, and like Gluck and Wagner in later ages he spent endless trouble in trying to make his music dramatic and appropriate at all points.

As far as the voices were concerned his chief means were (1) the simple recitative which the Florentines had invented, (2) beautiful fragments of melody growing out of the recitative to give effect to the more expressive words, and (3) 'coloratura' for special effects, such as the scene in the infernal regions and the one at the end of the opera, where Apollo and Orpheus ascend to heaven.

Orfeo, then, shows the beginning of many different kinds of music since in it there are at least three distinct kinds of solo song besides dramatic choruses and a great deal of instrumental music. The modern orchestra had its birth as it were in this opera. While Monteverdi was far from being the first composer of opera, he was the first who so combined the resources of voices and instruments in such a way as to make of opera a great form of art.

HARMONY

The new way of writing for a single voice with instrumental accompaniment had another very important effect: it brought about much clearer ideas of harmony. For when one voice sang alone it naturally became the most important part, and the instruments had rather to agree with it than to play independent music on their own account. Their parts became grouped together in chords which supported the voice exactly in the homophonic style which we explained early in the chapter as that of the hymn-tune.

Moreover, the frequent use of these chords, especially those of the tonic, dominant, and subdominant (cf. Ex. 2) which came so often to form the cadences helped to establish their relations to one another in a **key**. When once the existence of the key was recognized all the wonderful effects got by changing from one key to another and contrasting passages in different keys could be gradually discovered, as in fact they soon were by the composers of the next generation.

All this was not done by Italian opera alone, though it was without doubt the strongest influence at the beginning of the seventeenth century. Songs for single voice with an accompaniment for the lute or harpsichord were written by various composers, foremost among them Caccini (see p. 20), who in the year 1600 brought out a volume of them which he actually called by the name of 'The New Music'. Everywhere, too, instruments were soon more freely used. In the private houses of wealthy people both in Italy and France music for instruments alone (viols, harpsichords, and lutes) was cultivated and cantatas for a single voice accompanied by one or more instruments became popular. In those parts of Germany where the Protestant reformation had turned the old music out of the churches the use of organs to accompany the simple hymn-tunes had much the same effect in helping to establish a clear system of harmony (see p. 85).

The new music did not make itself felt so soon in England, and before going farther in tracing its course we must go back and see what had actually taken place in our own country.

Suggestions for Further Reading and Listening

THIS chapter spans an enormous period, about four hundred years, no less, and one which has come increasingly into focus over the last few decades. This has been brought about both by musicological research and by the proliferation of ensembles which specialize in the music of the fourteenth, fifteenth, and sixteenth centuries. In the half-century or so since Colles wrote *The Growth of Music* the situation has thus altered entirely. Radio, recordings, and recitals alike delight in revising the idioms of the distant past so that, for instance, the love songs of the trouvères, the sophisticated music-making associated with the Burgundian court, or the madrigals of Marenzio have become easily accessible.

For general purposes, with regard to this particular chapter and its successors, any reading list could begin with Grout's *A History of Western Music*, prosaic but informative, to which should be added *Man and his Music* by Harman and Mellers. A further recommendation is Paul Henry Lang's *Music in Western Civilisation*, not least because of its comprehensive view of music in its social and artistic context. Handier and of course infinitely cheaper are the appropriate volumes in the paperback *Pelican History of Music*, and Arthur Jacobs's *A Short History of Western Music*, also in Pelican.

Such books take a bird's-eye view of the period under discussion, and it is probably wiser to begin with them than with more specialized studies. These would include Volumes II, III, and IV of *The New Oxford History of Music*, and also *Music in the Middle Ages* and *Music in the Renaissance*, both by Gustave Reese. In the same way Einstein's two-volume study of the Italian madrigal is a classic, but, to begin with, Roche's *The Madrigal* will be much more helpful. Denis Arnold's *Marenzio* too is excellent. There is an ever-increasing amount of literature about Monteverdi, a composer whose stock rises continually, but the best buy is again Denis Arnold's critical biography in the 'Master Musicians' series, which could be supplemented by *The Monteverdi Companion*, edited by Denis Arnold and Nigel Fortune.

As indicated earlier, there are nowadays very many recordings of old music on the market, most of which can be recommended for their expertise, scholarship, and interpretative relish. Be adventurous. Explore widely and see what periods and styles attract you most. In recent years English groups have been pre-eminent: recordings by the late David Munrow and the Early Music Consort of London cover much of the territory surveyed by Colles, and so too do those of Musica Reservata and Anthony Rooley's Consort of Music. The best continental ensembles tend to be German, Dutch, or Swiss. David Munrow's *Instruments of the Middle Ages and Renaissance*, a lavishly illustrated book with accompanying records, is a good introduction to its subject.

CHAPTER 2

Music in England up to the Beginning of the Seventeenth Century

So far we have left England out of count, not because its music was unimportant but because it is so important for us that it is necessary to study it in a separate chapter. We have seen that most of the work of discovering how voices could be combined in choral music was done by composers who sprang from the northern provinces of Europe, who carried their achievements into other countries, Italy in particular. But at an earlier date it seemed almost as if this would be done by English composers. In the Middle Ages the English were great makers of ballads and songs, especially of the kind which, like the famous Agincourt Song, celebrated victories and gave voice to patriotic sentiment. Moreover, one example of early English polyphonic music survives which is such a marvellously perfect thing that it still remains a mystery how it could possibly have been written at so early a date, about the year 1240, that is to say about the time that Adam de La Halle was born. It is the famous 'round' called 'Sumer is icumen in'. Four treble (or tenor) voices sing the delightful, lilting melody in succession, just as in a modern 'round' or 'catch', and two bass voices maintain a constant refrain of 'Sing cuc-cu', making beautifully pure and rich harmony with the melodic parts. Since it was possible to make voices sing together so perfectly in the thirteenth century it is strange that progress later should have been so slow.

One composer, JOHN DUNSTABLE (born about 1390), stands out as a person of special importance, for he was contemporary with the early Netherland composers, a full generation before Josquin des Prés (see p. 11), and he was evidently quite famous all over the Continent. In 1437 one Martin Le Franc wrote a poem in French in which he compared Dunstable favourably with the only other two great composers of the time, both of them Flemings, Gilles Binchois and Guillaume Dufay, who were about ten years younger than he. He wrote, chiefly for three voices, both church music and secular songs, and from the collected edition in vol. viii of *Musica Britannica* it is easy to see that it must have been his skill in making the voices move smoothly without producing harsh harmonies which earned him his reputation.

Musicians in other countries certainly looked up to him as a leader, and that fact in itself is remarkable because between his time and the present English composers were distinctly lacking in the power of initiative. Most of their best work has been done when the way has been pointed out by others. There have been no great pioneer musicians, like Monteverdi, for example, who led the way to new and unexpected kinds of music which influenced the art of the whole world.

CHURCH MUSIC (FIFTEENTH AND SIXTEENTH CENTURIES)

We get an immediate example of this in the fact that, though church music was cultivated seriously in England from the time that Henry VII ascended the throne (1485) after the Wars of the Roses, nothing of much practical importance to us now was accomplished until the work of the Netherlandish composers had become known to musicians in this country in the reign of Henry VIII. As soon as they were shown the way a splendid group of Englishmen came forward, and wrote masses, motets, and other service music which rival the best done elsewhere.

The first of these men was CHRISTOPHER TYE (born about 1500), who was brought up as a chorister in the choir of King's College, Cambridge, and was afterwards organist of Ely Cathedral as well as holding a place in the Chapel Royal of both Henry VIII and Edward VI.

The part that the Chapel Royal has played in the history of music in England is very important, for most of the best composers up to the end of the seventeenth century held the appointment of 'gentleman' of the choir, which meant that while they were engaged as singers they were able to devote time to composing music which was sure to be sung by the choir. They had every inducement to do good work and every chance of judging of the result when it was done, and that is the best encouragement a musician can have.

One of Tye's early works was a Mass for four voices which was written round an old English folk-song *Westron Wynde*, just as the Netherlanders used to write church music with their popular songs as a *canto fermo* (see p. 10). Though in this instance Tye copied a bad principle from his teachers, he learnt all that was good in their manner of writing. His great work was a Mass for six voices called by the name *Euge bone* (probably an allusion to an antiphon on the text 'Well done, good and faithful servant') and it is splendidly written on simple and stately themes for the most part composed for the words to which they are set, as were Palestrina's melodies in the *Missa Papae Marcelli*. The themes are often repeated and closely imitated by all the voices in turn, so that the whole effect is as strong and clear as it can be. The only fault is that it is so strictly written that it is apt to sound rather stiff. There is not the grace and freedom of melody which one finds in Lassus or Palestrina or indeed in some of the best works of the Englishmen who followed Tye. It is possible that this Mass was the one which Tye was required to compose when he took his degree of Doctor of Music at Cambridge in 1545, and this would account for its strictness. Tye and his companions wrote music which expressed deeper religious feeling and showed a finer sense of musical beauty than this Mass, though nothing could surpass its technical skill.

One of the greatest of these was THOMAS TAVERNER, organist of Cardinal Wolsey's College (now Christ Church) at Oxford, who wrote half a dozen fine settings of the Mass including one on the *Westron Wynde* tune. Another was ROBERT WHYTE, a pupil of Tye, whose daughter he married. But far more famous is THOMAS TALLIS, most distinguished of all the members of Henry VIII's Chapel Royal.

What remains of Whyte's work is so fine and like Tye's in style that one cannot help suspecting that there was more of it which has been lost. But the large quantity of Tallis's music shows that he was one of those great minds which gain more power the more they use it. It is possible to trace his growing strength through a long series of works from an early Magnificat and a Mass for four voices, in which he seems to be feeling his way as the earlier polyphonic composers did, to the beautiful series of Sacramental Motets of which *O sacrum Convivium* is the most celebrated. Both he and Whyte composed settings of the Lamentations of Jeremiah which were part of the service of 'Tenebrae' sung in Holy Week, and both are full of the tender and plaintive feeling of the words which Lassus caught so perfectly in his Penitential Psalms.

THE REFORMATION

While all these men were still young the personal quarrels between Henry VIII and the Pope were fermenting, and none of them had gone far in their careers when it became clear that the quarrel was not to remain a personal one between King and Pope, but that it would produce drastic changes in the church in this country, though no one could tell how drastic those changes would be. The first which really affected the musicians seriously was the suppression of the greater monasteries (1539–40). This event deprived Tallis of his place as organist of Waltham Abbey, and besides merely individual losses of the kind did away at one stroke with nearly all the centres at which music had been most faithfully cultivated for generations. In fact it amounted to the destruction of the principal musical colleges of the country. Still the musicians were undaunted. The King was a friend to music; he was a performer and possibly a composer himself, though the music ascribed to him may have been revised, finished, or even written altogether by his court musicians; his chapel was maintained as fully as before, and Tallis soon found a place in it which he held through the three reigns that followed until his own death in 1585. The cathedral services too remained unchanged, and Tye continued his work at Ely without check.

But no sooner was Henry dead and his young son Edward VI on the throne than matters began to press more hardly on the church musicians. The issue of the First English Prayer Book in 1549 must have caused consternation to composers. All their lives had been occupied in setting Latin words to music, and now English was to take its place. Their work must be lost altogether except in so far as they could adapt it to the new language. They were fortunate indeed that the new Prayer Book did not for the most part introduce new services but was rather a translation of the old liturgy considerably simplified.

It is wonderful how close the English translation of the words of the Mass keeps to the sense and to the rhythm of the Latin, but the differences in the two languages offered many problems for musicians. The great difficulty lay in the number of little words (particles 'a', 'an', and 'the', which do not exist in Latin, as well as the greater quantity of prepositions in English) which are so troublesome to set to music in a dignified way worthy of the traditions of church music. Take the example of the 'Gloria' in the Mass:

'Gloria in excelsis Deo,'
'*Glory be to God on high,*'
'et in terra pax hominibus bonae voluntatis.'
'*and in earth peace goodwill towards men.*'

In the first clause the Latin requires only one preposition, the English two and the verb 'be'; the second makes use of the clumsy word 'towards'.

This is sufficient to show that the process of making music

already written suitable to the new conditions was an exceedingly difficult one, and the fact that it was done, and well done in so many cases, is in itself a proof of the genius of the sixteenth-century composers. No sooner was the First Prayer Book authorized for use than a remarkable man, JOHN MARBECK (or Merbecke), set to work to adapt the ancient plainsong to the English words, and he published his 'Booke of Common Praier Noted' (i.e. set to notes) in the following year (1550). At the present day arrangements of the Te Deum and Communion Office called by his name are often heard in churches, but they are rarely given as he wrote them. For he added no harmony to his melody, old or new; his only care was to adapt it so as to show that the traditional music could still be made use of, and he certainly proved his point.

Had the change of language been the only way in which the reformation of Edward VI affected musicians they might very soon have suited themselves to its needs and gone on writing anthems instead of motets, Communion Offices instead of Masses, in the style to which they were accustomed. But this was not all. Protestants clamoured for a simpler kind of worship altogether. For them the music like the ritual was too elaborate, because it required trained musicians for its performance. They longed to sweep it away as the Lutherans in Germany had done (see pp. 27 and 85) and to put hymns and psalms in its place in which the congregation could take part. Each one of the musicians we have been discussing met this demand in a characteristic way.

Marbeck showed once for all that the old plainsong music at least was worth preserving since it consisted solely of melody which could be learnt and sung by the people, and having done so he made no further practical contribution to the question but gave up his time to preaching and writing violent pamphlets against the Pope. He therefore drops out of musical history.

Tye, like Marbeck, sympathized with the Protestants on religious grounds, and he set himself to try to satisfy the desire for a popular form of sacred music by making a very curious experiment. He made a rhymed version of the first fourteen chapters of The Acts of the Apostles in such a way that each verse of the text became a four-lined stanza of poetry. Then he wrote a simple piece of music for each chapter which he called a motet, thus keeping the old name. Each motet was long enough to cover two of the stanzas and was to be repeated like a hymn-tune to the remaining stanzas of the chapter. Ex. 13 is part of the one to the third chapter.

Not only is it very like the homophonic hymn-tune style,

Ex. 13

but in later years a popular hymn-tune, *Windsor*, was in fact arranged from this motet (cf. Hymns A. & M., 43). At the time when Tye made this attempt he was in a position of some influence at court. It is generally supposed that he was music master to the young King, Edward VI, and he offered his Acts of the Apostles to the King with a dedication. But they do not seem to have become very popular, probably because they were a compromise between two styles. The second stave of the example shows the voices separating into independent melodies in something like the old polyphonic style, and this occurs so often that though the motets are comparatively simple, they still needed a trained choir such as that of the Chapel Royal for their performance, so that they did not start the congregational kind of church music in England which came in a generation later when the Psalms were similarly put into verse and sung to tunes. Tye in fact after one honest effort failed to establish a Protestant form of church music, and later in the reign of Elizabeth he gave up music altogether and became a clergyman.

With Tallis the case was quite different. His own principles underwent no change; he went on writing as he had begun, only influenced to a limited extent by the outcry for simple music. He wrote an English 'Service' in D minor in which the voices all move together in plain chords instead of in separate lines of melody so that the words might be more distinctly heard than was possible in the old style, and this way of writing started what is known now as the 'Cathedral Service', which is quite as unlike popular congregational music as is the older style.

Incidentally, however, this shows us that the Protestant movement in England helped to establish the idea of harmony as consisting of series of chords as the operatic and instrumental movements in Italy did, though it worked with a very different object. Underlying both, however, was the same wish to make music conform more closely to the words (see pp. 19 and 24).

Nevertheless it soon became clear that the Protestants were

not to have it all their own way as they had in many parts of Germany. In the short reign of Mary the pendulum swung back in the direction of Roman Catholicism, and though the bigotry of the Queen and her ministers produced a distaste for Romanism from which the country has never recovered, yet after her death, when a settlement was made under Elizabeth I, Englishmen still resisted the extreme views of the strict Protestants. The outlines of public worship were preserved much as they had been determined in the Second Prayer Book of Edward VI, the cathedral foundations were maintained, and Elizabeth certainly desired that her Chapel Royal, as far as the music was concerned, should be continued with as much importance as it had had under her father. Everything was to be sung in English, but there was no check upon the elaborateness of the music. Motets by Tallis were translated into English anthems, and anthems new and old by Tallis, Whyte, and Tye written in the polyphonic manner were welcomed. Church music had weathered the storm raised against it and its future seemed bright. Yet it had suffered sorely. Tye and Marbeck had, as we saw, abandoned it for other things; Tallis's sympathies were too strongly with the Latin ritual for him to take kindly to the English one, though he remained a 'gentleman' of the choir and still wrote for it.

Curiously enough the same is true of another and a younger man, WILLIAM BYRD (1543–1623), although he was quite a little boy in the days of the First Prayer Book of Edward, and was only about sixteen years old when Elizabeth came to the throne. He, therefore, was not brought up like Tallis in the older tradition, but still he clung to it devotedly. He wrote Masses for three, four, and five voices, and many beautiful motets published under the titles *Cantiones Sacrae* and *Gradualia*, partly in conjunction with Tallis, for the Latin liturgy. For the English he composed the Great Service, as majestic in style as anything in his Latin music, and many beautiful anthems. In his short services, however, he accepted the simpler methods initiated by Tallis. A passage from an English service and a corresponding one from the Latin Mass (five voices) will show this at a glance. It is the opening of the 'Sanctus':

Simplicity is the only advantage which the English has; the expressive beauty of the long slurred notes on the word 'sanctus' could not be reached in any kind of music which required the voices to keep to the same movement.

With Byrd, it may be said, Catholic church music reached its apex in England and at the same time Anglican music made a beginning the majesty of which it was never quite to match in later ages, though several of the Tudor composers came near it. For Byrd is at once one of the three or four supremely great English composers and one of the great masters of his time regardless of nationality, the equal of Palestrina in Italy and Victoria in Spain.

THE MADRIGAL IN ENGLAND

The name of Byrd brings us to another instance of the way in which foreign music suggested a new outlet to our composers. In the year 1588, that in which the Spanish Armada was defeated, a certain Nicholas Yonge published a collection of Italian madrigals with the words translated into English under the title *Musica Transalpina* ('Music from across the Alps'). Previously madrigals had been known in England only through manuscript copies brought privately from abroad, and a few attempts of native composers to write in the same style, such as the well-known partsong 'In going to my naked bed' ascribed to Richard Edwards. From this time onward every composer of repute turned his attention to writing them. They were freely published and sung everywhere; so great was their popularity that the singing of madrigals became an accepted part of social intercourse, and an educated gentleman or lady would take part in a madrigal then as readily as most young people today can join in a game of tennis.

Consequently we have a host of exquisite works in which all the skill composers had gained in writing polyphonic church music was turned to account to illustrate secular poetry. No time was so rich in poetry as the reign of Elizabeth I. It was poured out in abundance by poets great and small, from geniuses such as Shakespeare and Spenser, from courtly versifiers such as Sir Philip Sidney, and from the lesser men whose verses might have been lost or forgotten if composers had not given them life by wedding them to beautiful and lasting music. This poetry had a strong effect upon musicians, wearied as they were by the endless quarrels and restrictions which had gathered round church art. It set them free again to follow their fancy, to see how music could heighten the fancy of the poet and enforce his meaning, and in doing so they learnt to use the voices more lightly, to introduce greater varieties of rhythm suggested by the language and the poetic metres.

Some of the earlier madrigals of Byrd, who published a collection called *Psalms, Sonnets and Songs of Sadness and Piety* in the same year as *Musica Transalpina* appeared, are elaborate and rather like church music in style, but such a one as his 'This sweet and merry month of May', which was said to be composed 'after the Italian vaine', is quite different. The little phrase of quavers which always goes with the words 'merry, merry' is as light-hearted as anything could be, and the broad passages to the words 'O beauteous Queen' bring the main idea of the poetry (the praise of Queen Elizabeth) into strong prominence.

Poets loved to make the Queen the subject of their verse, and musicians vied with them in this, eventually producing in 1603 (dated 1601) the most famous collection of English madrigals existing to this day, which was called *The Triumphs of Oriana*. It consists of madrigals by many of the most eminent men of the time, and the series was edited by one of the greatest of them, Thomas Morley. Whatever the subjects of the poems might be, whether they had to do with the loves of shepherds and shepherdesses or with nature and spring-time (the most favourite subjects), all had one feature in common: each one ended with a refrain such as

Then sang the Nymphs and Shepherds of Diana.
Long live fair Oriana.

A glance at a few numbers will both tell us who were the principal composers and give some idea of their work. The series opens with a fine madrigal by Michael East beginning 'Hence stars too dim of light' in which the poet fancies that the stars must pale before the beauty of his Queen, and the dignity of the whole music, especially the majesty of the two broad chords with which it opens, contributes to the splendid notion. In many cases we can see a direct attempt to illustrate the idea of the words, as in John Mundy's 'Lightly she tripped o'er the dales' which begins by four voices singing the same tune after one another with very dainty effect, or in John Benet's 'All creatures now are merry minded'. The last is more modern in sound than many, for the voices seem less independent of one another, and their movement is more clearly controlled by the use of certain chords:

Ex. 15

This passage from it, for instance, in which the voices twine round a single chord of A to express the idea of hovering is unusual, and more like the later style of Purcell and Handel, when the parts were all made to conform to a definite key of which one chord was the centre and chief.

Thomas Morley's 'Arise! awake!' gives a good example of the way in which composers were beginning to make their tunes more permanent. Most of the earlier madrigalists did not treat their first idea as of special importance, and after the first words had been sung they did not reproduce the same musical figures. But here Morley brings the figure marked '*a*' into almost every line except the refrain, and its charming lilt pervades the whole and gives it a feeling of continuity:

Ex. 16

John Willbye's 'The Lady Orianna' and Thomas Weelkes's 'As Vesta was from Latmos hill descending' (the latter is one of those most often sung at the present day) are two particularly fine madrigals for six voices, and the works of their composers are surprisingly varied. The frank simplicity of Weelkes's 'Lo country sports' and the delicate charm of Wilbye's 'Adieu sweet Amarillis' contrast wonderfully with these stately madrigals in the *Triumphs*. Probably Weelkes's 'Vesta' gets its present popularity from the close way in which the words are illustrated throughout. Vesta descends and the 'maiden queen' ascends, and both are realistically pictured in the downward and upward movement of the music. Moreover the line 'then two by two, and three by three together' is sung by two voices on the first phrase, three on the second, and all six on the word 'together', and this quaint way of depicting the words never spoils the flow of the music. It is managed with perfect artistic skill.

ORLANDO GIBBONS

One composer who did not contribute to the *Triumphs of Oriana* must be noticed specially. ORLANDO GIBBONS (1583–1625), whose brother Ellis Gibbons wrote two fine madrigals for the *Triumphs*, belonged to a musical family, and, like Tye, was educated as a chorister at King's College, Cambridge. He became organist of the Chapel Royal, and finally, only two years before his death, he was appointed organist of Westminster Abbey. These two appointments may be taken as a sign of the increasing importance of instrumental music in churches, for in the case of the Chapel Royal the position itself was a comparatively new one. There had been no organist in Tye's day.

Of Gibbons's madrigals, 'The silver swan', 'O that the learned poets', and 'Ah! dere heart' are still very popular, and they and others have a thoughtful, plaintive character which is quite Gibbons's own. He alone of the composers of his time seems to have cared deeply what words he set. Nymphs and shepherds and light-hearted verses with 'fa la' refrains had no attractions for him. Almost all his words are serious and many are sad. He certainly had a wonderful way of expressing melancholy sentiment in the melodies he found and in the way in which he combined them. For example, nothing could convey more thoroughly the idea of a questioning unrest than the beginning of the madrigal, 'What is our life' (Ex. 17).

His serious nature is no doubt the reason why he alone of his generation was able to write new and really valuable church music, suitable to the needs of the English liturgy and filled with the dignified and lofty spirit of the older Latin music. His service in F and certain of the anthems are truly polyphonic, in that all the voices have melodious music to sing, and yet the parts do not overlap in such a way as to hide the meaning of the words. In this respect he seems to have brought back the experience of the madrigalists to the service of the church.

Another new thing in Gibbons's church music calls for attention. He sometimes wrote important parts for instruments, especially viols, with the chorus or, more remarkable still, an accompaniment to a solo voice. A case in point is the anthem

'This is the record of John' (John i. 19) in which the questions and answers are sung by an alto voice (now generally by a tenor) and the answers are reinforced by the full choir. It is true that the music for the viols is not very different from that for the

Ex. 17

voices; in the solo passages the instruments merely weave a quiet background to the carefully accentuated words, but still the contrasts between solo, chorus, and orchestra show that Gibbons's mind was moving in a direction similar to that of the Italian operatic composers.

INSTRUMENTS AND THE VOICE

The fact is another sign of the increasing interest in instruments. Composers would often publish their madrigals with a note on the title-page to say that they were 'apt for voices or viols', which meant that they might be played as we would play a string quartet, as pieces of pure music without words, or with one voice singing the words and the other parts played on viols. They also composed 'Fantasias' or 'Fancies' originally written for the viols. Some of the best of these were the work of Gibbons himself. His fantasias include passages which would be most inapt for voices, but which are perfect on the instruments, so that it is clear that in a quieter and less enterprising way Gibbons and other Englishmen were going through some of the same experiences which Monteverdi and the Italians had had.

Again the habit came into fashion of writing partsongs so that it was possible to perform them either by several voices or by one voice accompanied on the lute. They were generally called 'ayres' to distinguish them from the more complex madrigals, and of course the single essential voice was given more important music than the others which might be left out in favour of a lute. Numbers of charming 'ayres' of this kind were written by John Dowland, Robert Jones, Thomas Campion, and Philip Rosseter. Look at this beautiful one by Campion:

Ex. 18

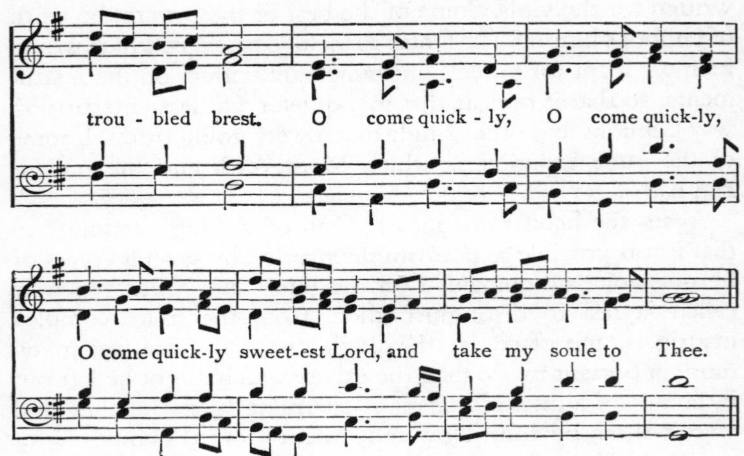

The tune of the treble voice is the all-important part of it; the chords underneath can be sung by three other voices or thrummed upon a lute with equal ease. The tune has the simplicity of the old folk-songs; it fits its words as beautifully as the early song by Adam de La Halle (see p. 8), but it is also clearly harmonized according to its key in a way which was quite beyond the powers of the medieval composers, and this power was the result of the polyphonic style being applied as a means of accompaniment.

The composers who wrote these songs, which very strikingly show, in comparison with the madrigals, the entirely different flavour of the Stuart school, were not always skilled musicians like Byrd and Morley and Gibbons. Dowland, indeed, was famous as a lute player, and had travelled to many of the courts of Europe, but others were rather poets who had enough musical knowledge and feeling to make tunes to go with their poetry. During the reign of the Stuarts and even under the Commonwealth the development of solo songs went on, and songs were joined with dances and instrumental music connected with plays and 'masques' (cf. p. 61). Lawes's music to

Milton's masque of *Comus* is the most well-known instance and one which you may still sometimes hear performed. The care which Lawes gave to the accurate accenting of words was rather like the Italian recitative of Monteverdi, but Lawes was in no other respect comparable to Monteverdi, for he had none of his commanding musical genius.

KEYBOARD INSTRUMENTS

We have already seen music for sets of viols growing up into independent life and organs being used with the voices in churches. Needless to say, organists exercised themselves in composing for their instrument alone, and another sort of keyboard instrument had come into use in private houses and filled the place that the piano holds now. It was called the 'virginal' and is perhaps best described as a small kind of harpsichord (see p. 21). It is not always easy to tell whether the early English keyboard music was written for the organ or the virginal, and probably a great deal of it was played indifferently upon either, but nearly all the great composers of the time, Tallis, Byrd, Morley, Gibbons, and others wrote quantities of music for keyboard instruments. Much of it took the forms of dance-tunes such as 'Pavans' and 'Galliards', and these would naturally be for the virginal rather than the organ.

Fantasias and preludes, pieces which were a mixture of the style of choral music with scales and turns such as were found to lie well under the fingers, were also popular. But perhaps the most important kind of piece was the 'Air with Variations'.

Sometimes a folk-song, sometimes a church tune was taken as the air, and the composer would then add ingenious figures and new harmonies. The practice of writing variations led to the discovery of what we now call 'thematic development', that is to say, the power of carrying on and increasing the interest of a tune by placing its figures and rhythms in a number of new relationships.

The cleverest of the English writers for the organ and virginal was Dr. John Bull. He was considered a very brilliant performer both at the court of Elizabeth I and on the Continent, and certainly his pieces show more of a genuinely instrumental style than most of the music of the time; scales, arpeggios, and broken chord passages, such as we often find in modern piano music, frequently appear in his variations, and sometimes he tried truly marvellous experiments in harmony, modulating through a number of keys. The most wonderful of these is a set of variations on an ascending scale of six notes (Ut, Re, Mi, Fa, Sol, La) in which the scale begins a tone higher each time, and so passes through modulations which seem strange even to modern ears.

If Bull was the cleverest, others wrote with more intimate feeling for what was really beautiful in music; Byrd's variations on 'Jhon come kisse me now' and Gibbons's on 'The woods so wilde' are lovely specimens of the style. We have seen the folk-song taken as the basis for church music and used in a quite unsuitable way (see pp. 10–11 and 31); in these and other pieces collected together in the Fitzwilliam Virginal Book the songs are set forth and expanded in a way which is natural and beautiful, since instead of hiding their origin the variations emphasize and enlarge it.

A truly original and thriving school of music for keyboard instruments was thus founded in Elizabeth's reign and carried on after it. Probably the Civil Wars and the Puritan rule did actually check its further growth, but it is unsafe to give political reasons for artistic changes. The art of the madrigalists was certainly exhausted, and the wave of musical enthusiasm in England was receding long before the trouble came. Once again England had to wait for a new impulse to come from abroad before her music could spring forth in fresh and still more varied forms.

Suggestions for Further Reading and Listening

All the general books suggested as supplementary reading for Chapter 1, which omitted English music, are also suitable for the present chapter. Nevertheless, for surveys of the course of English music from the time of Dunstable to that of Bull, Ernest Walker's *A History of Music in England* and Fellowes's *English Cathedral Music* (both revised by Westrup) are recommended. Other books worth consulting are Peter le Huray's *Music and the Reformation in England 1549–1660*, and Kenneth Long's *The Music of the English Church*. Students of the earlier part of the period will find Frank Harrison's *Music in Medieval Britain* (from the eleventh century until the Reformation) illuminating.

As far as individual biographies are concerned, both Paul Doe's *Tallis* and David Brown's *Wilbye* are excellent; Fellowes's studies of Byrd and Gibbons (though written over fifty years ago) are still very valuable, and his books *English Madrigal Composers* and *English Madrigal Verse* have not seriously been challenged. The standard study on Dowland is by Diana Poulton.

For a contemporary view of music and music-making in about 1600, turn to Thomas Morley's *A Plain and Easy Introduction to Practical Music*, a pedagogic work with a light touch, put across in the form of dialogue between master and pupil.

All the major composers mentioned in Chapter 2 are represented on record, some very handsomely. There are also, as mentioned earlier, a great many ensembles which specialize in the sort of music under discussion. Readers are also reminded that 'in quires and places where they sing' English church music of the fifteenth and sixteenth centuries can often be heard.

CHAPTER 3

Music in Four Countries at the End of the Seventeenth Century

ITALY

WE saw that Monteverdi's operas were only one sign, though the most striking one, of the revolution which spread over the whole of the art of music in the seventeenth century. Before that time all music for voices was written in practically one style, that of the Church, since the secular madrigals were only a variation of the same type. Monteverdi's *Orfeo* suggests at least three ways of writing for the solo voice, recitative, expressive aria or melody, and coloratura (see p. 25), and also shows some of the wonderful things which instruments can do, both as a contrast to the voice and by themselves, as a means of illustrating the dramatic situation (e.g. the descent of Orpheus to the nether world).

ORATORIO

In Italy the development of these different styles went forward very rapidly. GIACOMO CARISSIMI, who was born near Rome in 1605, did notable work in writing a number of oratorios on Old Testament subjects, such as *Jephte*, *Judicium Salomonis*, and *Baltazar*, which consist of recitatives, arias for solo voices, and choruses with, however, a much more slender instrumental accompaniment than the early composers of opera used. As they are not dramatic works the story which on the stage would be acted has to be told by the singers, and this is the most important difference existing between opera, or music with acting, and oratorio in which there is no acting. Let us take a modern example to make the difference quite clear. When Wagner in the last scene of *Götterdämmerung* wished to depict

Brünnhilde and her horse leaping into the flames which surround the funeral pyre of Siegfried he was able to do it by means of a very few bars of descriptive orchestral music, because the audience could see the whole thing acted on the stage, before their eyes, and all that the music had to do was to impress the meaning of it upon them by recalling the ride of the Valkyries and the fire music. But when Mendelssohn wanted to tell in oratorio how Elijah was taken up by a whirlwind into Heaven he had to write a great chorus on the words, 'And when the Lord would take him away to Heaven, Lo, there came a fiery chariot with fiery horses and he went by a whirlwind to Heaven'. The singers have to tell what is going on, and the rushing, excited character of the music has to picture the whole scene to the mind since it is not visible to the eyes.

Carissimi generally met the difficulty by making a tenor voice labelled 'Historicus' tell the story in recitative. At some of the more exciting parts of the story, however, he did just what Mendelssohn did in his *Elijah* and made the chorus take up the part of the historian. The principal characters are represented by solo singers as in opera, and in the dialogues between the characters Carissimi used the recitative very beautifully. He made his voices move by smoother intervals and arranged his harmonies much better than Monteverdi usually did, so that though his effects were less striking they were more genuinely beautiful. There is a splendid instance where Jephthah has told his daughter that she must die, and she has asked leave to go to the mountains and mourn with her companions. The daughter sings (Ex. 19). See how clearly the cadences at the end of each

Ex. 19

'Weep O hills, mourn O mountains!
And in the affliction of my heart lament!'

phrase mark the key. The first in A minor, the second in D, the third in E, and the fourth coming back to A with a lovely echo refrain to round it off. Then notice how genuinely pathetic the voice part is. The use of B flat in the cadence and the little turn on the second syllable of 'ululate' (lament) is perfectly expressed, and the whole, besides being true to the spirit of the words, is a beautiful bit of melody.

OPERA

Carissimi's works are more important for what they taught his pupils than for their own sakes, and of his followers the one who had greatest effect upon music as a whole was ALESSANDRO SCARLATTI (born 1659), who is said to have studied with him. This is just possible, but Carissimi died when Scarlatti was fifteen.

By the time that Scarlatti got to work the new kinds of music were being heard in all the big towns of Italy, but especially at the courts of princes and cardinals. Although the latter were churchmen by profession they often supported opera and other forms of secular music more ardently than the strictly church kinds of art, and the houses of some of the wealthy cardinals, usually members of the nobility who did not always serve the church for strictly religious reasons, were the resort of musicians anxious to secure the patronage of these great men for the performance of their works. It must be remembered that as soon as music left the church and ventured into the world at large, it had to depend for success upon its popularity, so that the style of music has been influenced at every time and at every place since the middle of the seventeenth century by the taste of the people for whom it was written, and consequently we must take this fact into consideration and try to find out the degree of importance which music had in the lives of these people. Opera had a particularly good chance of success in Italy at this time because not only were there princes, like Ferdinand III of Florence, who maintained private opera houses at their palaces, but public ones began to be opened in the principal towns, beginning with Venice (1637), which any one who could afford to pay for a seat might attend, and at which composers could get their works performed. The first public opera house in Rome was opened in 1671, and though the popes who were the reigning sovereigns of Rome did not always approve (and with some reason) of the conduct of the opera house, and this one was suppressed for a time by Innocent XI, such mishaps were merely a temporary check. So we find Scarlatti trying his fortune in various places, at one time sending an opera to Ferdinand de' Medici with a long letter to assure him that the music was 'pleasant and tuneful rather than learned', at another living at Rome under the patronage of Cardinal Ottoboni, or again setting off to Venice to direct the performance of a new opera there, or producing operas in Naples where he spent a great part of his life. The chances for composers were indeed many, but still they had to learn what sort of music would please their patrons, as Scarlatti's letter to Ferdinand shows. A great dramatic scheme, carried on with a huge, unwieldy orchestra, such as Monteverdi had used in *Orfeo*, was not likely to be very acceptable. Grand people who patronize opera, as well as people who pay for it, like to be entertained with 'pleasant and tuneful' music and gay and brilliant scenes on the stage, and often care much more to compare the performances of singers and to applaud their efforts than to follow the story of the drama or to consider whether the music is really appropriate. This was what Scarlatti found out, and that no doubt is the reason why, although he could write brilliant musical dialogues and did so in comic operas, his serious operas are mainly a series of songs joined together by recitative.

This defect, however, had its compensation, for Scarlatti learnt to write songs of a certain pattern more perfectly than any one had done before him. In doing so he had to establish certain laws of contrast, which now that they have been used over and over again seem so simple to us that it is hard to think that they were not always understood. It seems natural enough to us if a song in C major has first a tune in that key, then one modulating, as we say, to the key of G, and then repeats the first one in C. It is the simplest kind of ternary (threefold) form, and 'The Bluebells of Scotland' is a well-known instance of it. You can find plenty of others among hymn-tunes and old songs. Even the early song *L'homme armé* (see pp. 10–11) comes very near to being in a simple ternary form. Scarlatti did not invent the idea, but by writing hundreds of songs in operas and cantatas on this plan he taught himself and his successors several important facts: (1) that a great deal of variety and charm can be given by changing the key at the moment when a new melody is begun; (2) that the repetition of the first melody after the variety has been given helps to avoid any feeling of vagueness which the change of key alone would produce; (3) that in order to contrast one key with another it is necessary to make each key quite clear in itself, and the chords which do this most of all are the tonic and dominant. The type of song cultivated by Scarlatti and his successors, including Handel, is known as the '*da capo* aria', from the direction *da capo* ('from the beginning') shown at the end of the middle section to indicate that the first part is to be repeated.

Probably Scarlatti's songs did more than any music of their time to spread the new plan of writing in accordance with a key system which, as we saw, was quite foreign to the ideas of the old church composers. Scarlatti has been blamed for using the same pattern so constantly, and the fact that he did so would make any of his operas tedious to listen to nowadays if the music as such were less magnificent and the songs, though they belong to the same pattern, did not have tunes of very different characters. There are smooth and pathetic ones, bold and martial ones, lively and florid ones. The canzonetta 'O cessate di piagarmi' is quite a perfect little example of the form. The words ('O cease to wound me, O leave me to die') are very mournful, and the tune with its constantly repeated note, its lovely, drooping cadence, and the contrast between the principal minor key and the major one in the middle expresses their feeling beautifully. Another, 'Rugiadose, odorose, graziose violette' ('Dewy, scented, graceful violets'), is as light and dainty as a song can possibly be. You must hear them sung and played in order to realize how perfectly they are written, simple as they are, and to note how clearly the key of each phrase is marked by tonic and dominant cadences.

Since Scarlatti had practically given up all attempts to illustrate the dramatic ideas of his operas by the instruments of his orchestra, he used fewer instruments than Monteverdi. Their chief duty was to accompany the voice, but nevertheless he sometimes found out new and beautiful ways of combining them. He discarded the clumsy lutes and organs and used the harpsichord chiefly to accompany the recitative, so that the stringed instruments of the violin family became the basis of the orchestra, and they have kept their position to the present day. Sometimes he added effective parts for flutes, oboes, horns, and trumpets in the arias or in the overtures and other pieces for the instruments alone which occur in the course of an opera.

INSTRUMENTAL MUSIC

Scarlatti must have found out a good deal about the use of stringed instruments from ARCANGELO CORELLI, whom he met at the house of Cardinal Ottoboni. Public concerts such as we have now were unknown in Italy at that time, but musicians, poets, and other artists often met together to perform and to listen to each other, and perhaps the most celebrated society of the kind was that called 'Accademia Poetico-Musicale' (the Poetic and Musical Academy) which met in the palace of this cardinal at Rome.

Corelli (1653–1713), the first great violinist of history, was a few years older than his friend Scarlatti. He devoted his whole life to playing his instrument and composing music for it and other stringed instruments, so that he gained a special knowledge of this kind of art from which men like Scarlatti, who were busy composing in every known form, must have learnt a great deal. Corelli's works are of two kinds. There are **sonatas** for one or two violins with a bass part to be played both by a violoncello and a harpsichord (the harpsichord player adding chords to fit with the other parts according to his discretion), and **concertos**, in which three solo players (two violins and a violoncello) play together accompanied by a band of violins, violas, violoncellos, and double basses, always supported by a harpsichord. Some of the sonatas, his earlier works, used to be played at the meetings of the 'Academia', of which both Scarlatti and Corelli became members in 1706. In the same year a young German, George Frederick Handel, visited Rome and attended some of the meetings. Since he listened to Corelli's work and learnt much from it, it will certainly be worth while for us to do so.

The sonatas generally contain four movements, a quick one and a slow one alternately, and each movement is divided into two sections. The first section gives out a melody which modulates into some other key at the cadence, and the second, beginning in that key, returns to the one from which the first started, using some fragments of the melody given out by the first and adding others. The form is called **binary** (twofold), and the difference between it and the **ternary** one of Scarlatti's songs is very important. The well-known hymn-tune by Thomas Tallis called 'Tallis's Ordinal' (Hymns A. & M., 78, &c.) is as simple an instance of the form as could possibly be found, for it consists merely of two musical sentences, the first of which modulates into the dominant key, while the second returns to the first or tonic key. It is interesting to remember that 'Tallis's Ordinal' was written about a hundred years before Corelli used the same principle for his sonatas. It allows space for a great deal of contrast, and yet the shape of the piece is perfectly clear without requiring any actual repetition. It was usual to play each section through twice, but that was only a matter of custom. Although the bare outline is the same in each case, there is plenty of change in the character of the pieces. This will be seen if we look particularly at one sonata—Op. 5 No. 8, in E minor (Chrysander's edition). This is one of the best-known of the solo sonatas. It begins with a prelude, a beautiful, slow melody in 3/4 time. Then follows a very lively one called

'Allemanda' (i.e. in the German style), of which we must quote the first phrase:

Ex. 20

You see at once that it is violin music. No voice could jump about in so sprightly a way, and it would be hard even to play such a tune on the piano because the hand would have to move such a long distance. But it is perfectly written for the violin, since a little movement of the bow reaches from the E string to the G string and back again quite easily. It shows how well Corelli understood the character of his instrument. Next there is a smooth and expressive tune called a 'Sarabanda' (a kind of Spanish dance), and finally there is a lively one called 'Giga' (we should call it a jig), in which again there are many passages which leap over long intervals and could only be made really effective on the violin. The movements are very short, for one of the things which composers had not yet learnt to do was to carry on the tunes and sustain the interest through long movements, but you will find that each of the four belongs clearly to the binary pattern, and each one has a strong, rhythmic character.

There is rather more variety of form in the concertos, for where many instruments played together it was possible to get more contrast between the solos and the full band, so that the same phrases of melody could be repeated by different instruments, much as they used to be in the old choral music of the madrigals. On the other hand Corelli's writing is less distinctly instrumental in the concertos, and sometimes one finds passages which remind one very strongly of choral music. An example is the opening of the eighth concerto, which looks and even sounds quite like a piece of contrapuntal church music of the old style. Such passages, however, are the exception in Corelli, and his music marks a turning-point in the life of instrumental music, for he gave it a stronger character than it had possessed before. Corelli did further service to his art by founding a great school of violinists who, as we shall see, carried on his principles in playing and composing for their instrument through the next century. Meanwhile his music was a model for his contemporaries, and it remains a delight for us today because of its lovely melody and its purity of design.

Alessandro Scarlatti certainly benefited by Corelli's work to this extent, that after he had heard his sonatas he wrote passages in his own works which were more exactly suited to the instruments than was his earlier music. Even the form of the overtures to his operas was to some extent affected by Corelli. Scarlatti generally wrote his overtures in three movements, an allegro, a slow movement, and a rhythmic dance to finish with. It is in the last movements that he seems to have been so delighted by the 'giga' of Corelli that he was forced to try to copy it. Scarlatti himself wrote some concertos for strings with a few wind instruments, as well as some sonatas, but in pure instrumental music his most important work was for the harpsichord. His pieces called 'toccatas' for this instrument are very fluent and brilliant, full of rapid passages which do not halt just at the moment when they are becoming interesting, as is so often the case in the older harpsichord music. Some of the toccatas are followed by fugues, and occasionally a dainty minuet, *corrente*, or other dance tune is added to complete the scheme.

No doubt these works, which are carefully fingered by Scarlatti, were written partly for the education of his son, Domenico, who became a great player and composer for that instrument. DOMENICO SCARLATTI was born in 1685, a year to be remembered by all musicians, since in it were also born G. F. Handel and J. S. Bach. He devoted himself to the harpsichord and wrote over five hundred extremely characteristic sprightly and beautiful pieces which he called *Essercizi* (exercises), which is precisely what they are, although at the same time they are in an early form of sonata, and they are now always so described. But the term 'sonata' which Corelli used, is only an instance of the rather puzzling fact that different things in music are often called by the same name. Domenico's 'sonatas' are generally in one movement, and the form is only like Corelli's in that it is binary. They are not made out of dance tunes, 'sarabandes' or 'gigues', but are rather more like toccatas (that is to say pieces written for the display of the player's skill), only they are written in the regular order of key which belongs to binary form. They are almost all quick movements, requiring the utmost skill and neatness of execution, and full of a brilliant gaiety and high spirits which was quite new to the music of the time. People who were used to the solemn beauty of church music or to the pomp of operatic overtures or arias must have been taken by surprise when young Scarlatti poured out these pieces full of glitter and humour, or possibly they did not think very much of them.

Nowadays we can see that these sonatas were far in advance of anything which had been written for the harpsichord, and their only fault is that they are so much in the same vein of feeling. Each one is quite perfectly worked out. Domenico modulates from one key to another with even more ease than his father had been able to do, and indeed often with an audacity that seems quite 'modern' even today. The musical ideas are more consistently carried out, and the ideas themselves are always fresh and frank. So, although they are ideally written for the harpsichord, pianists delight to play his sonatas on the piano at the present day, just as violinists delight in those of Corelli. A certain thoroughness seems to belong to both Scarlattis, father and son. They worked in narrow limits, but within those limits their work was wellnigh perfect.

FRANCE

We saw in the first chapter that the French people were early in the field as makers of songs, and that they had special aptitude for setting music to poetry, so that the rhythm of the music should agree well with the metre of the verse. Towards the end of the seventeenth century the music of France became of importance to all the world, for the French people have the power of incorporating with their own what is pleasing to them of the art of other nations, and yet not losing their special characteristics. So when an Italian composer, Francesco Cavalli, who had been a pupil of Monteverdi, came to Paris in 1656 and performed operas of his own composition the French were pleased, but on the whole they thought that their own composers might do better than the Italians, and certain of them set to work to try.

Plays with music were no new thing to the Parisians, for, as we have seen, songs, dances, and acting had been companions ever since the days of Adam de La Halle, and at the court of Louis XIII *mascarades*, in which the actors danced and sang, were so fashionable that members of the court and even the King himself took part in them. But the idea of a whole play set to music in which all the words were sung instead of spoken was unfamiliar to the French people, and when they heard Cavalli's work they were not at all sure that they thought it an improvement on their own simpler songs and rhythmical dance-tunes.

OPERA

However, the movement in favour of regular opera was too strong to be resisted, and even before Cavalli's appearance in Paris the Abbé Perrin, who had heard some of the works of the early Florentines, wrote a pastoral play, which Robert Cambert set entirely to music, and which was therefore the first French opera. It is known as *La Pastorale d'Issy*, from the country house at Issy near Paris where it was first performed in 1659, but as it is lost we do not know whether it originally had another title, as seems probable. What the Parisians seemed to have disliked about the Italian opera was the recitative, which with its lack of definite rhythm seemed to them like a sort of church plain-chant. Cambert adopted the style of the Italians to some extent, but in the works by him which have survived the recitative is certainly more melodious than theirs. Perhaps the actual style of the music mattered less to the grand people of the court than the subjects of the drama and the way in which they were presented. Here Perrin was very successful, for his plays were a mixture of classical fables, in which gods and goddesses, nymphs and fauns, shepherds and shepherdesses sported and made love in groves and silvan scenes. He made use of the same kind of imagery that one finds in the words of English Elizabethan madrigals, but he used it much more elaborately, and this was just the kind of thing which appealed to his audience. For if there was one thing more than another which was characteristic of the court life under Louis XIV, *le grand monarque*, as he was called, it was the pompous ceremony that was carried on. The very furniture which is nowadays called by the name of 'Louis Quatorze', the chairs and tables and escritoires with their bulging lines and heavy ormolu ornaments, show the grandeur amongst which people lived. But when people live constantly in an artificial atmosphere they sometimes like to play at leading a simple life, just as people who live very quietly like to read stories of princes and millionaires, or criminals and detectives, and to go to see royal processions. And so the court of Louis XIV would pretend to admire the beauties of quiet country life, and Watteau painted his celebrated pictures of grand ladies and gentlemen sitting on the grass under the trees, and Perrin's and Cambert's later operas, *Pomone* and *Les Peines et les Plaisirs d'Amour*, included scenes which were supposed to represent primitive life, but were really highly artificial, with troupes of dancers and brilliant scenery. There seemed to be every prospect that a poet and a composer who could hit the court taste so well, and who at the same time had genuine artistic powers, would make a permanent reputation, especially since in 1669 they had been granted the sole right of producing operas in French. But another man was destined to supersede them.

Giovanni Battista Lulli (born 1632) was, as his name shows, an Italian by birth, but he became a Frenchman in the course of his remarkable career. Not only did he spend all his working life at the French court, where he managed to secure the monopoly which had been granted to Cambert, but he wrote work after work for the French stage completely in the French style. It is not surprising, therefore, that his name is better known in its French form as Jean-Baptiste Lully. To him belongs the credit of firmly establishing the kind of work which Cambert had begun, but unfortunately at the same time he must bear the discredit of having treated Cambert and other French artists exceedingly badly. Perhaps the fact that he was himself treated rather badly in early life may be some excuse for him, for he was brought to the household of a great lady, Mme de Montpensier, on account of his musical talents, and once placed there, his music seems to have been forgotten, and he was put to wash plates and do the duties of a scullion. Then he seems to have been turned out of the house because he had the impudence to make up sarcastic verses about his mistress. So it is not surprising that when he was about fifteen years old and had the luck to get a place in the King's band, he determined to work his own way up, and used even unscrupulous means of doing the best for himself. He had had no education in fair and honourable dealing. He was conscious of his lack of musical education, and did everything in his power to make this good by getting harpsichord lessons, and composing songs, dances, violin solos, and church music assiduously. However, he never felt his lack of moral training, but went on acting meanly towards other people whenever he could gain an advantage for himself. He remains one of the few men in the whole of musical history who wrote good music and were themselves despicable. In 1661–2 he received various appointments as musician to the King, and in 1664 he married the daughter of a court musical official, which seems to have been a profitable alliance for him.

The first event of artistic importance in Lully's life was his acquaintance with the great dramatist Molière, which began soon after his marriage. Lully provided incidental music for several of Molière's most brilliant comedies, such as 'Le Mariage forcé' and 'Le Bourgeois Gentilhomme', and thereby proved his skill as a composer of stage music. He also wrote a number of 'ballets', that is, sets of dances of various kinds for performance in the theatre, and gradually increased his popularity with the King and court, so that eventually he persuaded the King to transfer the patent in opera from Cambert to himself. From 1672 to 1687, when he died, he composed opera after opera, which were admired partly for their very genuine merits, and partly because by getting the right of producing operas entirely into his own hands he ousted all rivals. Poor Cambert had to leave the country, and he came to England and died here; but he was not the only one who was damaged by Lully's intrigues, for even Molière suffered by not being able to command sufficient music for his comedies. One would have expected that a man of Lully's stamp, having gained the public ear and successfully disposed of other competitors, would have merely produced what in the slang phrase are called 'pot-boilers', worthless works which thoughtless people enjoy for the moment; but though all his operas have too much of the court artificiality to be tolerated now, they were really important productions in their time. With the aid of Quinault, an admirable poet, Lully found subjects for his works of much more real dramatic power than those of Perrin and Cambert. Some were stories from Greek dramas very much modernized, such as Alcestis or Theseus; others were medieval romances such as Roland and Armida. Whatever their source, the stories were set much in the same way, and Lully was particularly successful in combining a really dramatic treatment of the story with the necessary dances, songs, and spectacular effects which were dear to the audience.

Like Alessandro Scarlatti he adopted certain fixed forms for various parts of his works, but they were different from those of Scarlatti. For instance, instead of the Italian overture in three movements like an instrumental concerto (see p. 59), Lully adopted a very concise form; a slow introduction led straight into a quick movement in which the various parts imitated one another in the manner of a fugue, ending up with a short coda in the slower time. This form, with or without the slow coda, became known as the French overture, and was very widely used by composers of many countries outside Italy, as we shall see later. It is very effective, for the solemn opening movement arouses the attention of audiences, and the quick movement,

Ex. 21

1st time.
2nd time.
Quick.

even when it is carelessly written, as Lully's sometimes were, is exciting and stimulating to the senses.

After the overture Lully always had an elaborate prologue, as Cambert had done, before the beginning of the opera proper, which was a kind of greeting ode to the King. In *Armide*, from which the overture is quoted above, and which we may take as an example of Lully's style, two women singers, each attended by a chorus, represented 'La Gloire' (glory) and 'La Sagesse' (wisdom); they sang in praise of Louis, calling him 'the august hero' and many other flattering names. This was followed by a ballet of three dances—an 'entrée', 'menuet', and 'gavotte en rondeau'. It was largely as a writer of dance tunes that Lully had made his success early in life, and when one plays those which appear in *Armide* and the other operas it is easy to see why they were so popular. They have nothing like the fluent grace of the Italian tunes such as Corelli wrote in his sonatas, but they are very compact, neat, and simple: the sort of thing one could hum as one went home, and yet rarely quite commonplace and never actually vulgar. The 'gavotte en rondeau' is a very good specimen with its precise rhythm, its strong

harmonies, and the clear feeling for balance of form which makes it always return to the first little tune after each of the contrasting ones.

The story of Armide and Renaud (or Armida and Rinaldo, as they were called by Tasso) has been as popular with opera composers as that of Orpheus and Eurydice, and as so many great men have used it, we will describe it in detail. The story dates from the time of the Crusades, and is the legend of a Syrian sorceress who was supposed to live in an enchanted palace and to lure knights to her, where they became so captivated by her charms that they forgot everything else. In the first act of Lully's opera the sorceress is seen in her palace; she receives a visit from Hidraot, the prince of Damascus, and together they plot to decoy Renaud, a very powerful knight. The entrance of Hidraot and his suite is accompanied by a spirited march rather like those of Handel (e.g. the march in *Scipione*), and there are of course dances performed by the suites of Armide and Hidraot. But all this is suddenly interrupted by a messenger who, in a truly dramatic recitative, tells how Renaud has rescued the prisoners of Armide, whereupon the sorceress and Hidraot vow vengeance on him, and the scene ends. In the next act Renaud, overcome by the spell, falls asleep by the water's edge; and here there is a descriptive piece of music for stringed instruments muted which is rather remarkable, for it suggests the effects of musical colour which have become so frequent in modern opera but which were rarely used in Lully's day. Then follows a pretty ballet of water-nymphs who sing and dance round Renaud, and finally Armide enters and sings a song of triumph at the capture. However, in Act III Armide discovers that she in turn is in love with Renaud, and she summons 'Hatred', who appears with all the passions of cruelty, vengeance, and rage; they dance and sing and call out 'non, non' (Ex. 23) on two detached chords with an effect which is rather like Elgar's demons in *The Dream of Gerontius*.

In Act IV two friends of Renaud's come armed with a magic

shield of diamonds and a golden sceptre to rescue him, but they meet with various difficulties, and only in the fifth act succeed in breaking the spell and tearing Renaud away. In this last act in the enchanted palace the attendants of Armide are seen dancing before Renaud to an elaborate Passacaglia, that is a

dance in which one phrase is repeated constantly in the bass, while all sorts of variations of melody and rhythm are played by other intruments over the various repetitions of the bass (see Purcell, pp. 80–82).

Lully took for his bass the first four notes of the descending scale of G minor, a very simple phrase which other composers used in the same way, and wrote a remarkable number of variations which get more and more interesting as they proceed. The scene is very effective, and he evidently intended it to be something like what Wagner wrote much more graphically in later years in the Venusberg music of *Tannhäuser*. When Renaud is finally rescued, Armide sings a lament which opens with a vigorous piece of recitative that actually sounds like a cry of pain and horror:

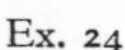

and so the opera ends.

Lully's airs are shorter and less developed into definite form than those of Scarlatti and the other Italians, and they have scarcely any variety of modulation or contrast of one key with another; but they fitted better into the operatic scheme than those of the Italians did, for the course of the story was never long interrupted by a single song. The beautifully smooth melody, 'Bois épais', from the opera *Amadis*, is an excellent example of Lully's vocal style.

Lully's selfish methods of dealing brought musical matters in France very much to a standstill when he died in 1687, for only one or two of his own pupils had had any practical experience in stage music at all, so that all his successors could do was to try rather feebly to copy his work. Not that it would be fair to blame Lully entirely for this. If any one of the court musicians had been a man of genius the death of Lully would have been his opportunity; but there was no genius ready to take up the work, and it was certainly Lully's doing that there were so few capable craftsmen. Jean-Philippe Rameau, the man who was destined eventually to carry on French opera and break through some of the formal traditions which hung round it as a court entertainment, was at this time only a baby of four years old. We shall see what he did later. Meantime there was only one branch of music which was cultivated with any important result, and that was music for the harpsichord or *clavecin*, as the French called it.

MUSIC FOR THE HARPSICHORD

François Couperin (born 1668) was a member of a family of French musicians, many of whom held good positions as organists, though they did not, like Lully, fight for high places. A few years after Lully's death François obtained the appointment of organist in the private chapel of the famous palace at Versailles. Of course he, like all other Parisians, was thoroughly acquainted with Lully's music, and in fact he arranged a number of Lully's most famous ballet dances for his favourite instrument, the harpsichord, to which he devoted himself as faithfully as did Domenico Scarlatti (see p. 60). Couperin's most valuable work includes sets of dances called *ordres*, in which a number of tunes in various styles are placed together so as to make very effective contrasts. *Ordres* are in fact suites.

Though these dances were founded on the style of Lully, yet they are much more delicate and intimately beautiful than his. This is natural, not only because Couperin was by far the greater genius, but also because Lully's were written to be danced to and Couperin's to be listened to. Moreover, instead of being written for an orchestra they were written for one instrument, and that the one which he loved and had studied very closely. Couperin knew that every little turn of phrase and rhythmic figure would be heard when played on his harpsichord, whereas Lully knew that only the general effect of his tune would be noticed when people in glittering dresses were dancing to it on the stage. Couperin was an imaginative man who was not merely content to make graceful tunes or even satisfied to make his music for the harpsichord perfect in design, as Domenico Scarlatti his contemporary in Italy was. He liked to connect his pieces with ideas that could describe their character. So besides calling them by the name of the dance to which they belonged, such as courante, sarabande, gavotte, menuet, or gigue, names which belonged alike to every composer, he often invented special descriptive titles. In his first *ordre* the sarabande is called *La Majestueuse*; it uses large and dignified chords and some very bold discords. That in the second, called *La Prude*, is much less enterprising, and a very beautiful one in the third *ordre* is called *La Lugubre*. At other times he would leave the recognized dance rhythms altogether and write pieces with all sorts of fancy titles, some of which seem really appropriate, such as the *Cuckoo*, whose double note can always be heard running through the pieces called by his name, or *Les Petits Moulins à vent* ('The Little Windmills'), whose perpetual movement is figured in a graceful little piece in flowing semiquavers. There is a remarkable set of little pieces called *Les Folies françoises, ou Les Dominos*, each of which represents some side of human nature, such as modesty, ardour, hopefulness, fidelity, perseverance, languor; and while some seem to have very little connexion with their subject, others, like *La Coquetterie*, in which the time changes no less than six times in sixteen bars, are full of delightful humour and insight. The idea underlying *Les Folies* is very like that of Schumann's *Carnaval*, in which each number pictures some particular character in a whimsical way.

Couperin, therefore, pointed out another direction to which music could turn, the illustration of ideas and subjects not connected with it by words sung or scenes acted, and this direction, which we now call 'programme music', is of immense importance to us at the present day.

ENGLAND

When Charles II returned from his 'travels', as he called his exile during the Commonwealth, he brought a complete change of life and manners into London which had many undesirable features and some good ones. There can be no doubt that his coming was good for music, for the Puritan rule had forbidden theatres and suppressed cathedral services, so that the grand old church music of Byrd and Gibbons had been long silenced, and the new music of the theatre, which was developing in Italy and France, had made no strong mark here. Charles had spent some time at the French court, and though in 1660, when he returned to England, the opera of Lully had not begun, he had enjoyed the gay dances and ballets and *mascarades* of the French, and heard the early church music of Lully, which was scarcely less secular in rhythm and spirit than his theatre music. The services of the Chapel Royal were again reopened, and a choir was brought together under the mastership of Captain Cook, a musician who had got his military title by serving in the army of Charles I against the Parliamentary forces. It is not wonderful that the efforts of Cook and the other musicians who had survived the Commonwealth seemed old-fashioned and dull to the light-hearted king. Their music seems dull enough to serious musicians nowadays, for all they could do was to copy the form and manner of the older writers, and there was no real genius among them.

English music required a fresh stimulus from without, and

this was given to it in various ways by the restoration of Charles II. He tried to bring it about directly by sending one of the choristers of the Chapel Royal to France to study music under Lully. This was Pelham Humfrey, a very clever boy, who picked up the manner current in France, and returned to England 'an absolute *monsieur*', as Samuel Pepys tells us, and very proud of his achievement. But he only lived until the year 1674, seven years after his return, and though he wrote a good many anthems and songs, his music is chiefly important because it helped to show the new way to his successors. Captain Cook seems to have been very shrewd in finding boys of real musical talent for his choir, since apart from Humfrey a great many of his choristers distinguished themselves as composers.

The three most important of them were MICHAEL WISE (born 1648), JOHN BLOW (born 1649), and HENRY PURCELL (born 1659), who was the greatest musician of his time and with whom this chapter must be chiefly concerned. All these must have profited more or less by the experience of Humfrey in France, for Wise and Blow were his contemporaries in the choir, and when Cook died and Humfrey succeeded him for a few years, Purcell was a chorister under him. But Purcell was less indebted to Humfrey than were the two older men, for by the time that he was growing up French music and even Italian music was becoming fairly well known. Though King Charles was determined not 'to go on his travels again' he was determined also not to be cut off from continental life, and the coming of visitors from abroad and the constant intercourse with France did good service to art and music in particular, however injurious the connexion might be from a political point of view. Blow succeeded Humfrey as master of the children of the Chapel Royal in 1674 when Purcell was still one of the 'children'. He also therefore was Purcell's teacher, and when his distinguished pupil grew up he seems to have given up the post of organist of Westminster Abbey, which he held together with that of the Chapel Royal, to Purcell in the year 1680. However, Purcell died in 1695, and then Blow returned to the Abbey and held the position there as organist till his death in 1708. Wise held hardly less distinguished appointments as a member of the Chapel Royal choir both as a boy and as a man, organist for some time of Salisbury Cathedral and afterwards master of the choristers at St. Paul's Cathedral in London.

All the music which you are likely to hear either by Blow or Wise is contained in their church anthems. Blow's 'I was in the Spirit' and 'I beheld and lo a great multitude', and Wise's 'Prepare ye the way of the Lord' and 'The ways of Zion' are some which you may often hear in cathedrals. They are quite different from the old church music of Gibbons, for example, for he, even when he used instruments, made them behave like voices, but Blow and Wise often made their voices behave like instruments. They sing runs and rhythmical tunes and especially figures containing this curious jerky rhythm (A):

Ex. 25

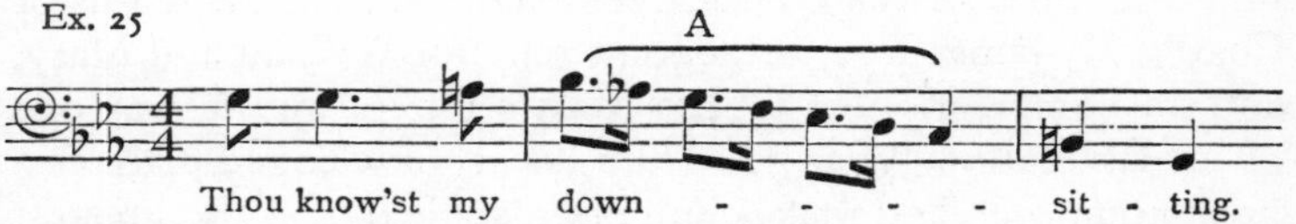

in Blow's 'O Lord, Thou hast searched me out', which is almost like a comical imitation of a heavy man sitting down suddenly. Altogether, the restraint and solemnity of church music seems to have given way to a kind of music which could express much more than the old, but often expressed ideas and feelings which do not specially belong to church music. Still there are fine and noble passages in their music, ranging from Blow's dignified 'God is my hope', a solid piece of work for a choir of eight parts or voices, to Wise's pathetically beautiful anthem, 'Thy beauty O Israel', the lament of David for Saul and Jonathan. Often one feels that their music does not continue long enough in one mood. Their anthems are broken up into a number of little movements of various kinds, and no sooner is one idea fairly started than the movement ends and another begins. This scrappiness seems characteristic of all the Restoration composers, Purcell as much as any of them, and no doubt it came from the fact that these composers were finding out how to express feelings and thoughts which were new to music in this country, and they had scarcely time to consider principles of artistic arrangement very closely.

Purcell does not seem to have had any special advantages in life which Blow and Wise did not share, except the advantage of being ten years younger and so profiting by their experience. He came of a musical family, however; both his father and his uncle were appointed as gentlemen of the Chapel Royal at the restoration of the King, and he had several brothers, the youngest of whom, Daniel, made quite a reputation as a composer. Henry Purcell, like Blow, lived all his short life as a London musician, with few events of importance to mark it except the productions of his very numerous compositions and the one fact of his appointment as organist of Westminster Abbey in 1680. His career extended over the reigns of Charles II, James II, and the joint reign of William and Mary, and the composition of Queen Mary's funeral music was one of his last duties. What gives him his acknowledged place as a great composer, and makes him often spoken of as the greatest of English composers, is the extraordinary readiness with which he seized on every known form of composition and wrote fine work in it. He did not specialize in any one branch, but wrote quantities of music for the church, for the theatre, for the concert-room (which now first became an established institution in London), and chamber music (that is, music for performance in private houses), songs, dialogues, and instrumental works; and whatever he touched had a certain strong, fresh individuality which marked his work as distinct from that of any other man. The influence of older and of contemporary composers is often clear, and the fact that he made use of so many influences is not the least part of his skill. The old English church composers make themselves felt in the best of his church music. Lully's methods appear in his theatrical overtures, dances, and songs, and he acknowledged that his sonatas for stringed instruments were built on Italian models, and yet he never seems to be copying or writing at second hand; he builds up his own style upon the work of his predecessors.

The Englishman whose work seems to have influenced him most directly was MATTHEW LOCKE (born about 1630), the composer who wrote the processional music with which Charles II was brought back to London at the Restoration. Locke was also the composer of suites for violins which Mr. Pepys tells us in his Diary that he loved to play. Still more important, Locke composed certain operas which were given in London theatres, and he stoutly maintained in a preface to one of them that if only English musicians were given the opportunity they could excel in the production of operas equally with their fellows in Italy and France. His pioneer work for English opera was an incentive to Purcell, who wrote an 'Elegy on the Death of his worthy friend Mr. Matthew Locke' (1677) which begins with the words 'What hope for us remains now he is gone?'.

PURCELL'S CHURCH MUSIC

Purcell wrote a large number of anthems for singing in church. It is generally supposed that those for voices with organ accompaniment only were written for the daily services of Westminster Abbey. Such are 'Save me, O God', 'Thy word is a lantern', and the eight-part chorus 'Hear my prayer', very beautiful pieces of choral writing but comparatively short. His longer anthems, partly accompanied by strings and with overtures and interludes for strings, were written for the Chapel Royal at Whitehall, where the King's band of string players took part in the service. Some of these are very splendid works and too rarely heard in their completeness now because we do not often have an orchestra to play in church, and they are difficult to fit into a choral concert, although splendidly effective there. One of the greatest of them is the anthem for the coronation of James II, 'My heart is inditing'.

Perhaps his most celebrated piece of church music is the festival setting of the Te Deum and Jubilate in D for voices, strings, trumpets, and organ. This great work sums up all the new characteristics which belong to the church music of the Restoration composers, and is so important that every one who wishes to understand the differences between their music and that of the older school of Byrd and Gibbons must study it. What strikes one at once is the wonderful variety of expression it contains. A few examples from the first few pages will show this, and others can be added.

First look at the theme of the instrumental introduction which is that sung by the voices afterwards to the words 'We praise Thee'. It is a march-like phrase, played by trumpets and violins alternately, as unlike as possible to the serene calm of Gibbons's Te Deum in F, or Byrd's Short Service, but giving the feeling of a great and moving procession. Next notice the way in which the voices mount up the notes of the chord of D proclaiming the word 'All' and finally sing it together on a brilliant sounding chord accompanied by all the instruments. Then at 'the Father everlasting' the voices for the first time move in smooth and flowing counterpoint as though those words brought the composer back to the more solemn thought which continually held the minds of the older writers. The big exclamations of the word 'Holy' by the whole choir while two treble voices repeat 'continually do cry', and the broad choral phrase to give the idea of 'Majesty', are further examples of Purcell's remarkable variety. Almost every page shows his keen sympathy with the spirit of the words, and perhaps the most striking part of the work is the alto solo 'Vouchsafe, O Lord'. This (in D minor) is in a kind of very free recitative. Its phrases are full of tender feeling. Notice especially the long phrase on the first 'O Lord', and the descending fifths on the repetitions of the same words. Coming as it does between two massive choruses in the major key this solo is particularly appealing.

One cannot fail to notice, however, how very little actual contrast of one key with another there is in this and in a great deal of Purcell's music. Where such changes are used they are generally from the major into the minor mode and back again, and the relation between the tonic and the dominant major keys is never used with the ease and mastery which the Italians, Scarlatti for example, acquired. But though the modulations are rather vague the harmonies are very rich, and the only fault in the spontaneous flow of the melody is the frequent use of the jerky rhythm (♩. ♪ ♩. ♪) which we remarked in Blow's anthem.

ST. CECILIA AND OTHER ODES

This Te Deum was written for the Festival of St. Cecilia, who was and is still regarded as the patron saint of music, and an interesting set of circumstances led to its composition. There was an old custom in many countries of celebrating the saint's day (22 November) with music, and in 1683 a scheme was started in London for holding a festival service in a city church on that day, and giving a public performance of an ode in praise of St. Cecilia and the art of music in Stationers' Hall. It was for the service eleven years after the first celebration that the Te Deum and Jubilate were written, but meanwhile Purcell had been connected with the secular part of the festival, and in fact wrote the first ode in 1683.

These performances mark the beginning of what has been the most important form of music-making in England for not far from three hundred years, the choral concert. It is interesting to remember that as Italy led the way in opening public opera houses, England can take credit for the first establishment of public concerts. The earlier odes were written on rather a small scale. Purcell set some doggerel verses, 'Welcome to all the pleasures', by a man called Fishburn, using a four-part chorus, solo voices, and stringed instruments. The work began with an overture, written in the manner of Lully's operatic overtures, and short songs and choruses were contrasted with artistic effect. The first ode was a great success, and in the following year Blow wrote one on much the same lines. These odes are really the beginning of secular cantata form in England which composers such as Parry and Elgar have cultivated. They were continued more or less intermittently until in 1692 Purcell wrote one which is on a much grander scale than any of the others. He had been gaining experience in this sort of work by writing numerous odes on other occasions, such as the birthdays of members of the royal family, and so being provided with an efficient libretto, 'Hail, bright Cecilia', a poem by Dr. Brady (who is celebrated for his part in 'Tate and Brady's Psalms'), he produced a work which surpassed all previous efforts. Besides the stringed instruments of the orchestra he used flutes, oboes, trumpets, and drums, and instead of the short Lullian overture he wrote a long one in several movements, more in the Italian sonata style. After the overture the bass solo declaims the words 'Hail, bright Cecilia' in a dignified recitative, and the chorus takes up the theme and carries it on in magnificent fashion. The strong, free writing for the chorus, the powerful harmonies in the recitatives, the vigorous airs for the solo voices, such as 'The fife and all the harmony of war', make this work a triumph of art in a direction which had not yet been attempted by the musicians of any country.

A comparison of 'Hail, bright Cecilia' with the Te Deum shows that almost the only difference of style between them is the fact that the individual movements of the ode are much longer and more fully developed than are those of the Te Deum. Let us see how he did this. The song 'The fife and all the harmony of war' will show us one of his means. The alto voice starts with a martial tune six bars long to the accompaniment of trumpets and drums, and after an instrumental interlude it is repeated and then carried on with running passages in the manner of the Italian 'coloratura' aria, till it reaches a cadence on the dominant (A). The song is continued by similar passages which keep up the general feeling of the original tune without ever repeating it, and cadences are made which touch on other keys without actually modulating into them or departing for any long passage from the principal key of D. In songs of this sort Purcell had no fixed plan to work upon as the Italians had in their ternary form, and so he had to rely more upon his own invention in each case. Sometimes he required a more definite plan, and then he often used the form known as the ground bass. The bass song 'Wondrous machine', a song in praise of the organ supposed to be St. Cecilia's own instrument, will show you what a 'ground bass' really is. The first two bars for bass instruments only make a sort of groundwork for the whole song. They are repeated over and over in the bass while the voice and the other instruments add melody and harmony above them. In the middle, however, the ground bass changes its key to that of G major, and then there is a repetition of the first part, so that this song is a combination of the ground bass with ternary form (see Lully, p. 70).

THEATRE MUSIC

Purcell got his first chance of writing for the theatre at about the time that he became organist of Westminster Abbey, but what he then wrote was not an opera, only incidental music to a play. Thenceforward he went on writing such music in large quantities, always hoping, like Matthew Locke before him, for the fuller opportunity which a well-equipped opera house with a company of singers and players to produce new operas would bring. That hope was never fulfilled, but none the less a play was hardly considered complete without the introduction of music and dances. When new plays were written authors would provide opportunities for music, and when old ones were revived, such as Shakespeare's *Midsummer Night's Dream*, they would be altered and even shamelessly rewritten to make room for the display of song and dance, generally called a 'masque' (cf. the *mascarades*, pp. 46 and 61). Purcell wrote a great quantity of this music, such as the incidental music with the charming masque in the last act of *Dioclesian* (1690), a version of a play by Beaumont and Fletcher, which was advertised as 'being in the manner of an opera', and also that to *The Fairy Queen* (1692), which was a version of *A Midsummer Night's Dream*. Most important among them was Dryden's play, *King Arthur*, which was written for musical treatment: Purcell's music to it is so elaborate and often so genuinely dramatic that it only requires continuity to be a complete opera. Overtures, dances, and songs flowed from his pen with amazing ease, and it is not surprising that he often repeated himself and often adopted a rather stereotyped form, but still the fertility of his invention is very remarkable, much more remarkable for instance than that of Lully, who was doing the same sort of work at the same time in Paris.

Purcell produced only one real opera, that is a work in which a whole play is set to music, and that was the beautiful *Dido and Aeneas*. Curiously enough this was written for performance in a school of young ladies kept by a man named Priest, a fashionable dancing-master, who also used to arrange the dances at theatres for which Purcell composed.

The story of the love of the hero Aeneas for Dido, Queen of Carthage, their separation by witchcraft, and her death, is told in wonderfully pure and moving music. The overture is so exactly in the form which Lully laid down that it should be compared closely with his overture to *Armide* (pp. 65–67). Notice the greater power of Purcell's harmonies in the slow movement. The little by-episodes, the choruses and dances of witches, who plot against the lovers, and the merry-making of the sailors, have any amount of point and character, and give the necessary stage contrast, besides fulfilling their original purpose of showing off the acquirements of Mr. Priest's pupils.

One song, 'Dido's Lament', is particularly worthy of study, since it is probably the most moving song that Purcell ever wrote, and it is unsurpassed by anything of the kind which had been written by composers of other countries at this date. Like so many of Purcell's best songs it is written upon a 'ground bass', in this case a wonderfully pathetic theme of descending semitones. Above the solemn repetitions of this the voice sings a broad melody. Notice especially the drooping fifths on the word 'trouble' wherever it occurs, and the words 'Remember me' sung pensively on a single note (D), which rises to the high G when the feeling becomes most intense just before the end.

The chromatic harmonies (the chord of the seventh, ninth, and inversions) are also very striking, for they show that Purcell realized what strength of expression such things give at a time when they were scarcely appreciated by musicians in general.

Dido and Aeneas is sufficient to show that he had a real genius for this sort of art, and if he had lived to write other complete operas the course of that form of music in England must have been a good deal more distinguished than has actually been the case. As it was *Dido and Aeneas* could make little more than a passing impression, and the patchwork system of plays with incidental music continued its vogue until quenched by the coming of Italian opera to London.

INSTRUMENTAL MUSIC

One more branch of Purcell's art must be noticed before we take leave of him, and that is his music for instruments alone. In the eventful year (1683) in which the Cecilian celebrations were started, Purcell published twelve sonatas 'of three parts', that is, for two violins, violoncello (or viol da gamba) with harpsichord accompaniment, in which he said he had 'faithfully endeavoured a just imitation of the most famed Italian models'. It is not certain what Italian works Purcell had seen, certainly not Corelli's, whose first book of sonatas was published in the same year, but when we take this fact into account his achievement in this direction is certainly very great. Ten others were published by his widow two years after his death, which are finer and richer in detail than the earlier ones. In neither do we find the intimate knowledge of what suits the stringed instruments which was so conspicuous in Corelli's works, nor is there the same grace of melody and definiteness of design, but they are full of fine writing, bold, sometimes crude harmonies, clever and humorous imitations between the parts, and strong contrasts between slow and quick, grave and gay movements.

Purcell's harpsichord music, too, consisting of suites and lessons, sets of clear, simple little pieces often in dance forms, show that the English musician was as much alive to the possibilities of keyboard music as were his companions in Italy and France (see pp. 60 and 71–73). It must have seemed as though Purcell could do everything for his art, and as though his genius were inexhaustible and untiring when all hopes of further achievement were suddenly cut short. He died after a short illness on 21 November 1695, the eve of St. Cecilia's Day, whose festival he had celebrated so often and so well, and he was buried in Westminster Abbey, where you may see his grave in the south choir aisle close to the organ.

GERMANY

So far the states of Central Europe collectively called Germany have had little of importance to add to the story of the growth of music, not because there was ever a time when the German races were unmusical, but because a number of causes kept them from taking the lead in the earlier artistic developments in which Italy, France, and England were all prominent in varying degrees. The geographical and political conditions combined to keep Germany back. It was a vast tract of country cut into innumerable states very much isolated from one another, and without acknowledged centres of culture such as Italy possessed in Rome, Florence, and Venice, or France in Paris. So although a great deal of music was composed by Germans, from the time of the Meistersinger and Minnesinger onward, the rest of the world heard very little of their efforts. Then, again, the religious disturbances in Germany checked the growth of church music at a time when that kind of work was at its best elsewhere. Luther published his famous protest against the teachings of Rome in 1517, that is some years before Palestrina was born, and those parts of Germany where Protestant doctrines prevailed had therefore no use for his complex and mystical style of choral music.

CHURCH MUSIC

They had to learn to write church music of quite another kind, to compose or adapt tunes such as ordinary people who were not skilled musicians could sing to the accompaniment of the organ. The Reformation in Germany was much more drastic than in England, for though English Protestants persecuted Catholics and Catholics burnt Protestants when they got the chance, in the end this country settled down to a compromise which laid down no hard and fast rules as to how the artistic side of worship should be conducted. But in the Lutheran churches the principle that the music like the words must be such as the people could understand and join in was so far insisted upon that almost all existing music except some of the old plainsong hymn-tunes became inadmissible. We must go back, therefore, and trace the advance of music in Germany from an earlier date than the latter part of the seventeenth century, which we have been studying in other countries. Composers, headed by Luther himself and his friend Johann Walther, began to write simple hymn-tunes called by the Germans *Choräle*, and to adapt old church tunes and folk-songs for the purpose. Some are well known in English churches, such as the one called Luther's hymn and translated as 'Great God, what do I see and hear' (A. & M. 52), which comes from a hymn-book of 1537, or the lovely tune sung to 'O sacred Head, surrounded' (A. & M. 111), the work of Leo Hassler, or the almost equally beautiful tune 'Innsbruck' (A. & M. 86), adapted from an old folk-song. These tunes and many like them became very dear to German Protestants, and their musicians would play them on the harpsichord and write variations upon them or add ornamental passages and counterpoints to the simple tunes, so that from them sprang both the vocal church music and the instrumental music of Germany as it appeared at the end of the seventeenth century in the works of J. S. Bach.

Hassler himself was a musician of the older school, and most of his work, such as the Mass for eight voices, was written in the polyphonic style like that of Palestrina, but the beautiful chorale mentioned above, though intended to be a secular song, became one of the very foundations of Protestant church music, when later it was set to a favourite Passion hymn.

A still more striking figure in early German music is that of Heinrich Schütz, who was born in Saxony in 1585, and lived to a great age. He was one of the first musicians who realized that it ought to be possible, in some way or other, to combine all the best characteristics of the various kinds of music which, as we have seen, were leaping into existence at the beginning of the seventeenth century. No doubt the fact that his father was a man of some social position, and that Heinrich was given the benefit of a university education, as well as the advantage of study in Italy under Giovanni Gabrieli at Venice and a certain amount of foreign travel, enabled him to take a broader view of music as a whole than the ordinary German musician was able to take. Schütz was able to study and admire both the choral music of Palestrina and the new dramatic ideals of Peri, Monteverdi, and others. He saw that it should be possible to use the vivid expression of the new style without sacrificing all the grandeur and dignity of the old. In 1614 he obtained the appointment of *Kapellmeister* (i.e. chief court musician) to the Elector of Saxony, whose court resided at Dresden; he was particularly required to reorganize the music both sacred and secular upon Italian models. This practically meant that he had to know the best music of every kind that had been written; it did not mean that in his own compositions he had to copy any one style slavishly. He wrote a great quantity of sacred motets for voices and instruments combined, and an oratorio on the subject of the Resurrection appeared not many years after his appointment, in which it is curious to see choruses of a severe and church-like type joined with realistic, descriptive passages for the instruments. The story is told in free recitative by a single voice just as in Carissimi's oratorios (see p. 51). Schütz also made experiments in purely secular opera with *Dafne*, set to a German version of the libretto of Peri's work, produced at a court performance at Torgau, and also wrote an Orpheus ballet on much the same principle. (Both these works are lost.) But most important were four settings of the story of the Passion according to the four Evangelists, which he wrote late in life.

The Catholic custom of singing the Passion story in Holy Week was one of the parts of the service that England lost at the Reformation and Germany kept, with merely the difference that the words were sung in German instead of in Latin as formerly. But whereas in the Latin Passions the story and words of the chief characters were intoned to the traditional plainsong, and only the words of the crowd were set to short dramatic choruses, in the German Passions of Schütz the words of the story and the conversations are set to free recitatives which are so well joined with the choruses that the whole becomes a complete work of art instead of a patchwork between traditional and original music. This is a very important difference, for it brought about an entirely new and very beautiful kind of church music which reached its highest point later on in the works of J. S. Bach (see pp. 111 et seq.).

The long series of wars, generally known as the Thirty Years War, between the Emperor and the Catholic cause on the one hand and the various Protestant interests on the other, are often put forward as one reason why German music developed slowly, but since Heinrich Schütz carried on his work in the midst of them, it would seem that battles and bloodshed are not a very effective bar to artistic work when a man of real genius is concerned. It was, however, more in the latter part of the century, when the country was settling down, that music became a definite part of the life of every German town of consequence, and the organists in the churches and the town musicians became important as composers and performers.

Many members of the family of Bach were notable town musicians in the small towns of Thuringia—Erfurt, Arnstadt, and Eisenach—and from them eventually sprang one of the greatest musicians of all time, JOHANN SEBASTIAN BACH. The names and doings of the various members of the Bach family have all been carefully recorded for the sake of the great man who belonged to it, but in many other parts of Germany, particularly in the north, there were families and individuals whose names are forgotten, but who did the same permanent and sterling work in cultivating the musical taste of their countrymen by their excellent playing on the viols and the organ. Reinken, the organist of St. Catherine's at Hamburg (1654), is remembered because J. S. Bach as a young man made frequent pilgrimages to hear his famous playing and to learn from him, and the Dane Buxtehude, who held a similar post at Lübeck, is of still greater note, for he was not only a fine player but a composer of consequence.

Dietrich (originally Diderik) Buxtehude (born 1637) was one of the composers who made use of the hymn-tunes or chorales and saw that these melodies, besides being the noblest form of congregational church music, could be introduced also into more elaborate forms of composition. When people hear a tune they know and love they are helped by it to understand that part of the music which is new to them, and so the practice of taking a familiar tune as the basis of new compositions has always been very popular from the time when church composers wrote masses upon *L'homme armé* and other favourite tunes to the present day, when we often hear music of various kinds based on well-known folk-songs and dances (cf. also p. 48). But the chorale preludes for the organ which Buxtehude and other composers wrote had a peculiar fitness, for the chorale tunes belonged to the churches in which they were played, and their use would call to mind beautiful and appropriate ideas. Buxtehude was particularly energetic in developing church music beyond the limits of the ordinary congregational service, for he carried on at Lübeck a kind of sacred concert in the church, called *Abendmusik* (evening music), in which motets and cantatas were sung by a choir with other instruments beside the organ; he composed a great deal of valuable work of this kind which was an example to J. S. Bach later on.

HARPSICHORD MUSIC

Outside the church, however, music did not progress so quickly. There was in Germany nothing comparable to the violin sonatas and concertos of Italy, or the harpsichord school of

Couperin and others in France. It is said, indeed, that Buxtehude attempted some suites in which 'the nature and character of the planets' were 'agreeably expressed', but this would seem to have been rather a quaint idea than a genuine piece of artistic expression. Pachelbel, one of the organists of the south of Germany who studied his art in Vienna, had written a number of variations and other pieces for the harpsichord, but nothing which remains of practical importance to modern music.

A very worthy man, Johann Kuhnau, who, in 1701, was appointed to the important post of Cantor at St. Thomas's School in Leipzig, the chief musical position in the town, realized how little German musicians had done to make music of this kind, and he set to work to write pieces for the harpsichord which he called sonatas. They differed from the sonatas of Domenico Scarlatti, which contained only a single movement, and were more like modern sonatas in that movements of various kinds were grouped together as in suites; but the movements were either quite independent ideas, worked out like those of D. Scarlatti, without reference to dance forms, or else they were written to illustrate a story. The most interesting of all are a set of six called 'Bible Sonatas'; they illustrate stories from the Old Testament, such as David and Goliath, the marriage of Jacob, and the campaigns of Gideon, and Kuhnau was particularly clever in finding musical phrases which would express the underlying ideas connected with the stories. For instance, he uses a heavy treading figure beginning deep down in the bass to suggest Goliath, which is rather like Wagner's theme for the giants in the *Rheingold*; again, the doubts of Gideon are suggested by phrases which first turn up and then down as though undecided what to do. Kuhnau tries to bring the whole story to the ears of his hearers, and sometimes he seems to imagine it performed on the stage, for he introduces passages almost like the recitatives and arias of opera. His musical descriptions are much more definite than those of Couperin, who liked to give character to his pieces by connecting them with fanciful ideas, but who did not always trouble to make the connexions clear to his audiences as Kuhnau did. If Kuhnau had had the opportunity he would certainly have left some remarkable contribution to German opera, but Leipzig offered none. Schütz's early introduction of opera at Torgau had made no permanent mark, and the only centre in Germany where opera took a firm hold at this time was Hamburg, which from its position in the extreme north could not much influence the musicians of Saxony.

At Hamburg, in the very end of the seventeenth century (1697), an opera house was opened by a remarkable composer named Reinhard Keiser, who, during the thirty years that followed, poured out one opera after another, producing altogether more than a hundred works of the kind. There is good reason to suppose that even J. S. Bach, who never wrote or wanted to write an opera, learnt a good deal from the fluent and varied arias of Keiser, and even copied their style in some of his cantatas; and since Handel came to Hamburg and first held a post in the orchestra of the theatre and produced his first opera there, Keiser's opera house certainly deserves to be remembered.

If you look up these towns on a map you will see how music was spreading through the centre of Germany at this time. The very fact that it could be illustrated by a map shows that the musical movement was far more widespread than in other countries. It would be absurd to draw a musical map of either France or England, for in those countries practically the whole of the musical culture was concentrated in the capitals, Paris and London. If we were to draw one of Italy it would be only necessary to put in half a dozen large towns. But in Germany music was spreading amongst the people of a great many small and little-known towns, and these people were not only practising music but creating it, and that fact accounts for the enormous strength of German music in the next generation, since so many earnest men contributed splendid work in different departments. It only required some supreme genius to arise in order to sum up the different lines of effort in his own life-work, and it so happened that two such men were born in the same year, 1685, whose lives and work we must now study in detail, though one of them was to forsake the country of his birth and leave no traces of direct influence upon German music.

Suggestions for Further Reading and Listening

CHAPTER 3 discusses aspects of music in what has come to be termed the baroque period. Though never neglected, least of all in its later phases, it has over the last fifty years been subjected to particularly intensive study. Not only has an enormous amount of its music been exhumed, revived, and discussed, but the whole question of the authenticity of performances has become very important. Further, some perspectives have altered: Colles made no mention of, for example, Vivaldi, an omission which no doubt seemed reasonable at the time, but appears strange to us today. (Vivaldi can now be studied in the critical biographies of Pincherle and Kolneder.) The literature on the whole multifarious subject is copious, but mostly for the serious student rather than the casual reader. As a start, readers should take note of Volume V of the *New Oxford History of Music*, covering 'Opera and Church Music 1630–1750'. The standard study, however, is Bukofzer's comprehensive *Music in the Baroque Era*, which could be profitably supplemented with Blume's collection of essays *Renaissance and Baroque Music*. Palisca's *Baroque Music* in the Prentice Hall 'History of Music' series is extremely useful, packs in a great deal of detail, and is lavishly furnished with examples.

This is perhaps the moment to introduce two books about performance, Robert Donington's authoritative *The Interpretation of Early Music* and Thurston Dart's short *The Interpretation of Music*, a lively investigation of musical styles from the Middle Ages to the eighteenth century. Since performance means, as often as not, instruments, this is also the moment to mention *Musical Instruments through the Ages*, edited by Anthony Baines.

Opera was the most spectacular and most influential art-form of the period. Accordingly readers are recommended to Grout's *A*

Short History of Opera, Robinson's *Opera before Mozart*, E. J. Dent's famous paperback *Opera*, and the *Concise Oxford Dictionary of Opera*. Second only in importance to opera was the concerto, and here Hutchings's *The Baroque Concerto* comes at once to mind.

As far as composers are concerned, Dent's book on Alessandro Scarlatti remains a classic of its kind. For Corelli, turn to Marc Pincherle. The expert, as scholar, performer, and editor, on Domenico Scarlatti is the American harpsichordist, Ralph Kirkpatrick. Lully, rightly, occupies an important place in all general histories of music, but there is no obvious full-scale biography of him to recommend. Rameau, by contrast, has had the advantage of an admirable critical biography by Girdlestone. Mellers is responsible for the best book in English on *François Couperin and the French Classical Tradition*. Purcell is covered by the authoritative study by Westrup in the 'Master Musicians' series, and by Franklin Zimmerman's *Life and Times of Henry Purcell*. Shares in Schütz are rising sharply, something demonstrated by the many public performances, recordings, and broadcasts. Moser's book on him has little competition at the moment.

As regards the development of German keyboard music, which concludes the chapter, Apel is the best guide in his *History of Keyboard Music*, though the chapter 'Early Keyboard Music' by Howard Ferguson in the Pelican *Keyboard Music* (edited by Denis Matthews) may prove more accessible.

The development of German church music is dealt with very fully in the appropriate chapters of *Protestant Church Music*, edited by Blume.

CHAPTER 4

The Lives of Handel and Bach

HALLE in Saxony and Eisenach in Thuringia are only about eighty miles from each other as the crow flies. In the spring of the year 1685 these two small towns were in reality, though no one could guess it at the time, the mainsprings of the whole musical world, for in February Georg Friederich Händel was born at Halle, and a month later Johann Sebastian Bach was born at Eisenach.

From the first the circumstances of the lives of the two children were very different. Handel, as we will now call him, and as he came to call himself, the son of a barber-surgeon who made up his mind that his son must be a lawyer, not only had no encouragement to become a musician but was kept away from music by every means which the zealous father could devise. He could only learn to play by stealthily practising on a small clavichord which a kindhearted relative had hidden for his benefit in an attic. On the other hand, music was the natural way of life for every member of the Bach family, and that Johann Sebastian should be thoroughly educated in it as far as his father and brothers could teach it was a matter of course. This difference of circumstance no doubt helped to mould the characters of the two boys; Handel's determination to carve out a career for himself and to convince the world of his power, no matter what the odds against him might be, was strengthened; Bach's pure love of music for its own sake without regard for its effect upon others was expanded by the early conditions. A change very soon came in Handel's case, however, for he was only seven years old when the Duke of Saxe-Weissenfels persuaded the father to withdraw his objection to his son's music, and after this time he was at least given regular teaching, even though he could not find practical help or sympathy at home.

He was still torn between his own passionate desire to devote himself to music and his father's demand that he should study the law, and he seems to have made a really noble effort to fulfil both requirements even after his father's death in 1697; but at last the struggle had to be given up, and when he was eighteen years old he said good-bye to his mother at Halle and set out to seek his fortune in Hamburg which, as we have already seen, was the greatest musical centre of North Germany.

In the meantime Bach's difficulties had been of another order. He had lost both his parents by the time that he was ten, and after his father's death he had gone to live with an elder brother who was good to him but evidently ruled over him with a strictness which elder brothers are apt to show. For there is a story that Johann Sebastian, anxious to learn all about music, copied out by moonlight the contents of a precious manuscript which belonged to his brother, and when the brother discovered it he not only took away the original but the boy's copy too. In spite of such small restrictions, however, he had plenty of opportunity of learning until he was fifteen, when it was thought to be time for him to begin to make his own way in the world, and so he entered the choir of St. Michael's Church at Lüneburg. The organist was an intelligent man who had been acquainted with the great Schütz in Dresden, and he no doubt made Johann Sebastian know and love that composer's motets and Passion music. At Lüneburg there was another musician, Boehm, who had been a pupil of Reinken, and thus Bach became indirectly acquainted with the works of two great masters, the one of choral music, the other of the organ. Naturally he was fired with an ambition to hear Reinken play. Lüneburg, as you will see from the map, is not a great distance from Hamburg, and Bach walked to Hamburg on several occasions to hear all the music that he could, and especially to hear the great organist. The latest of these visits may even have taken place in the year 1703 when Handel also came to Hamburg, not as a student to hear and learn, but as a young musician whose first business was to find out how he might make a living. This difference of object was quite enough to account for the fact that the two never met, for Handel secured a post as violin player in the orchestra of Keiser's opera house, and if Bach visited the opera, as he probably did, it was to occupy a place on the back benches and listen. He never came in contact with the people connected with the opera, and at this time his chief love was certainly given to church and organ music.

This time formed the turning-point in the careers of both young men; it decided their different lines of action, lines which diverged so far from one another that no two contemporary composers seem less alike in thought and feeling than Handel and Bach. Handel became entirely wrapped up in the attractions of an operatic career. He rose from the poor position of a secondary fiddler to the important one of player on the harpsichord, which was equivalent to conducting in modern opera, and then in January 1705 came the great moment when an opera of his own composition was performed, and *Almira*, as it was called, was pronounced to be an unqualified success. The love of the stage and the ambition to write music for the theatre took possession of him and he longed to visit Italy, the land from which dramatic music had sprung and where it still flourished more abundantly than in Germany. He only waited to find the necessary funds to take him there; in the year after the production of *Almira* this difficulty was overcome and he started on his travels.

Long before this Bach's training at Lüneburg was over and he had returned to the district of Thuringia to take up a comparatively small organist's post at Arnstadt and to put into practice in his own playing some of the wonderful effects which he had heard Reinken use. He must have longed to see more of the world and to hear more music, and once he did break away from his narrow surroundings and travelled up to the north again to hear Buxtehude's music at Lübeck. When he was there he was so fascinated by all that he heard that he could not bring himself to go back to quiet little Arnstadt at the appointed time, and he got into trouble with the church people for playing truant so long. They also complained of his playing, because they could not understand the way in which he would improvise new harmonies to the chorales, and make long and elaborate preludes before the hymns. They wanted a commonplace parish church organist, not a great genius whose one thought was to make his art as perfect as possible. The incident is a sample of Bach's life. It was all spent in a few comparatively small places where he held honourable but more or less humble appointments. No one suspected that he was more than a clever player and a learned musician, or that the works which he played on his organ or wrote for his choir to sing would come to be considered as the greatest among musical works by musicians all the world over. The actual incidents of his life are important to us now only because the various appointments which he held influenced the music he wrote. For example, in these early days when he was organist first at Arnstadt, then at Mühlhausen, and finally at the court of the Duke of Saxe-Weimar, his mind was naturally filled with the possibilities of his instrument, and many of the great organ works such as the famous Prelude and Fugue in D major, and the Toccata and Fugue in D minor were written at Weimar, as well as some of the church cantatas. Then, when Bach became *Kapellmeister* to the Duke of Anhalt-Köthen (1717) he had an orchestra to train instead of a choir, and as he had no organ he naturally played more on his harpsichord and clavichord, and wrote music for them. After 1723, when he succeeded Kuhnau as Cantor of St. Thomas's School at Leipzig, he began to write choral music again, and from this time onward works of almost every kind flowed from his pen, innumerable cantatas, the Passion music, the oratorios, of which the *Christmas Oratorio* is the most famous, the Mass in B minor, and instrumental music chiefly for the organ or for his favourite little clavichord.

The names of Weimar, Köthen, and Leipzig, therefore, can be made to stand for the three stages of Bach's career; Weimar for the time when he poured out all his youthful ardour in the massive effects of the organ and began to feel his way towards the special style of church music which he perfected later; Köthen for his activity in other kinds of instrumental music, especially the concertos for various instruments, the sonatas for the violin, the suites for violoncello, and a great part of the clavichord music; Leipzig for the full expression of all his powers, especially in large church works which include both voices and instruments.

The rest of his story is merely a record of quiet home-life broken only by occasional visits to other towns for business or pleasure or for both, since Bach's work was the delight of his life. He never left Germany except for a trip to Carlsbad when he was *Kapellmeister* to Prince Leopold. A visit to Dresden when he was living at Weimar, and the famous one in his old age when his son Carl Philipp induced him to visit the court of Frederick the Great at Potsdam were almost the whole extent of Bach's travels after he settled down to continuous work. He married early, when he was only two and twenty, and the fact of having a wife to care for and a family of sons to educate was another circumstance which kept him from moving far or indulging in large schemes such as occupied Handel's life. His first wife died just when the elder children were growing up and when the eldest son's talent for music was beginning to show itself. Bach had written a book of clavier pieces to teach this boy, Wilhelm Friedemann, in the same year that his wife, Maria Barbara, died at Köthen (1720). In the following year he was married again to Anna Magdalena Wilcken, who was evidently very musical, for soon after their marriage he wrote pieces and songs for her to sing and play, and throughout the years of their married life together at Leipzig, when Bach had to teach his boys at St. Thomas's School and superintend the music of no less than four churches, she helped him greatly in his busy life by copying out his music for performance.

We left Handel setting off for Italy in 1706 at about the time when Bach made the last of his youthful pilgrimages to visit Buxtehude. Bach could be scolded by churchwardens of limited imagination for staying away more than a certain time, but Handel was a free man. He was not bound by any times or appointments; he had saved sufficient money to make him independent for some time to come, he had made enough friends in Hamburg to secure him an introduction into the artistic circles of Italy, and although he was only twenty-one years old he had gained a reputation by his playing and by his composition, which made even the Italians respect him, though in general they were apt to think that no one but themselves knew anything at all about music. Handel was in fact most kindly treated by the Italians, by the wealthy patrons of art, by the musicians like the Scarlattis and Corelli, who made friends with him in Rome (see p. 57), and by the general public, who cheered him to the echo when his opera *Agrippina* was performed at Venice. Handel went from one place to another astonishing people by his powers, and yet he did not forget that he had come to Italy chiefly to learn. He certainly studied the music of the Italians very closely, for his own style became very like theirs. In his later operas and oratorios one can trace very clearly the influence of Scarlatti and even of Carissimi (though the latter was long since dead), while his later instrumental works are directly founded upon the style of Corelli (see p. 131). Altogether Handel's visit to Italy lasted until 1709. In spite of his success he seems to have had no thought of settling down to the life of an Italian opera composer in Italy itself. Probably he felt that the country was too crowded with musicians. He wanted to find a fresh field for himself, and possibly he thought that he would find such an opportunity in his own country. So in 1710 he accepted the post of *Kapellmeister* to the Elector of Hanover, and scarcely had he done so than he began to feel restless.

The court at Hanover was very unlike the brilliant courts of Italian princes. There was no chance of its providing any great occasion for a musician like Handel; there was no opera house to write for; there was nothing but a dreary round of services in the Protestant chapel, and small music-makings for the entertainment of the Elector and the court. Handel was not a man like Bach who could do great work in the most uninspiring conditions. He required the incentive of great opportunities, but he would not sit quiet and wait for great opportunities to come. If they did not come in Hanover he would go and seek them elsewhere. He had met some Englishmen in Italy and he had been pressed to visit London. He made up his mind to give London a trial, and so having obtained leave of absence from the Elector he came there in the autumn of 1710.

By this time the wave of musical enthusiasm which had filled London after the Restoration had dwindled down. Purcell had been dead for fifteen years, and with him had died the chance of any distinctive form of English dramatic music. Even John Blow, whose influence upon music outside the church was never very strong, was now dead. A few Italian operas had been tried in London just as at an earlier time Italian operas were tried in Paris before Lully took command of Parisian music. Now London required someone to take command, and Handel was certainly the man to do it. Not that he could do at the court of Queen Anne what Lully did at the court of Louis XIV. He could not wait and watch and find out what would please; it was not his nature to do so. On the contrary, he had spent his younger years in learning every detail of one kind of art, the Italian opera, and that was what he had to offer to the English. He did not come to consult their tastes or to find out what they had been used to in the stage music of their own country. If they liked what he gave them well and good, if not he would go back to Hanover. He had powerful friends who could arrange for the production of his operas in London, and he instantly set to work and wrote *Rinaldo*, which was first performed in the spring of the next year (1711).

Rinaldo was a version of the story of *Armida*, which we described in connexion with Lully's opera. It is recorded that the whole play was gorgeously put upon the stage and that everything that scenery and stage mechanism could do to make it effective was done, even to the flight of hundreds of birds on the stage in the scene of the enchanted garden. Whether because of these trivial details or because the English audience had never heard songs of such sustained power, beauty, and variety as Handel wrote, the result was a complete success, and Handel realized that London was his great opportunity. He had to go back to his duties at Hanover, however, but he evidently went with the determination to spend as little time there as possible, for in 1712 he was back in London again. Though he had only leave to come for a short time he soon got so involved in London life that he never went back to stay at Hanover. Meantime, he began to work with a most remarkable man named Heidegger, who was famous as a stage-manager and almost equally famous for his own personal ugliness. It seemed at first as if Handel were to continue through his life the brilliant success which he had met with everywhere, in Hamburg, in Italy, and in London. For not only was his new opera *Teseo* well received, but he began to be counted as the foremost man in London music. When the peace of Utrecht was proclaimed in 1713 Handel was invited to write the 'Te Deum' which was sung as a national thanksgiving, and after this the Queen granted him a small pension. With the Queen's death (1714) Handel's popularity received its first check, for the Elector of Hanover, whom he had really treated rather badly, came to England as King George I, and let it be seen that his *Kapellmeister* was in disgrace and that he had no business to be here. George, indeed, heard one of Handel's operas, but still ignored the composer, and it was not until Handel had composed the famous 'Water Music' to entertain the King on the river that he was taken back into favour, if the rather uncertain story is to be believed. He had to do penance by going back to Hanover with George and his suite in 1716, but after this one visit he was not troubled with Hanover any more. England became his home, and in future he only left it to make rapid tours either to Dresden or to Italy in order to engage opera singers, or to recover his health when he had been overworked.

Nevertheless, the apparent settlement of difficulties was really the beginning of Handel's troubles. From 1717 onward he settled down to his curious work of planting Italian opera in English soil. People sometimes speak and write as though Handel made the Italian operas to please the society people of London and English oratorios to satisfy his own ideals. This is quite untrue. Handel believed absolutely in the future of Italian opera. He went on in the face of every obstacle trying to make it thrive. The society people cared not one jot for the drama as expressed in music; nor could most of them understand Italian or appreciate great art when they heard it. All the majority cared for was to patronize one composer at the expense of another or to back one popular singer against another. Handel had to meet all the difficulties of keeping a company together, of persuading or more often compelling foolish singers to sing his music in a reasonable way, of reconciling the quarrels of rival singers, of competing with other operatic ventures which were started merely in order to injure him. If we were studying the history of Handel rather than the history of music we should have to tell the whole story in detail. As it is we need only say that an institution called the Royal Academy of Music was started in 1719, chiefly by the King and his household, for the production of Italian opera, and for this Handel worked assiduously for several years, producing one work after another. When it failed in 1727 Handel started a venture on his own account with his old colleague Heidegger, and struggled on through ten more years trying to convince people that there was more in opera than only singing and scenery. His antagonists (a rival opera house had been started by certain of the nobility) were too strong for him, that is to say, they ruined themselves and him too by their futile competition. Handel was broken down in fortune and in health in the summer of 1737, though never actually bankrupt, but in that autumn he returned to the charge and for several years afterwards he risked operatic ventures, though by this time he was finding out the capacities of oratorio as a means both of expressing himself and of suiting the more genuine taste of the English public.

During the early years of his career in England Handel had

plenty of inducements to leave opera for other forms of musical work. The Duke of Chandos, who lived in greater state than any other noble of the time, appointed him to be his chapel master on the same plan as that of the German rulers who kept musicians to supply them with music. The Duke had a large house with a private chapel at Canons Park, near Edgware; when Handel became a member of his household in 1718 he had enough to do to keep any ordinary man busy. But although he wrote some fine church music, now known as the Chandos Anthems, and produced *Esther* for the Duke's entertainment, he could not long be kept from his operatic efforts.

Esther was a kind of play founded upon the Biblical story of Queen Esther and King Ahasuerus. The music was set to English words, and Handel at first called it a 'masque', and intended it to be acted on the stage at the Duke's private house, just as the old English masques of Lawes and others had been acted (see pp. 46–47 and 81). *Esther* was simply a dramatic offshoot, and it was not until many years after, when Handel had written most of his best operas, when the Royal Academy of Music had failed and he was hard pressed to hold his own against the opera house of the nobility, that it occurred to him that music of this kind might be made genuinely popular.

In the year 1732 the choir-boys of the Chapel Royal got up a private performance of Handel's masque of *Esther*, and acted it in the presence of Handel himself and a small but distinguished audience. It pleased people so much that it had to be repeated in public, but since the Bishop of London objected to the practice of acting a biblical play in a theatre, it had to be given without stage action. He also rewrote an earlier work of his called *Acis and Galatea*, and gave it in the theatre with appropriate scenery, but without any action on the stage. In the following year in Lent, when the performance of opera was thought to be unsuitable, Handel made fresh attempts in this new kind of entertainment, half theatrical, half biblical. He used other Old Testament subjects, such as *Deborah* and *Athaliah*, evidently because their stories included great and stirring events which could be vividly illustrated in music. Though he had to give up the scenic effects of opera, the loss was more than balanced by the fact that he could make much greater use of the chorus and so gain massive musical effects which were out of the question on the stage (see p. 51). The new form gradually grew on Handel's imagination, and year by year he produced further works of the kind, which, with very few exceptions, such as *Israel in Egypt* and *Messiah*, are really operas in disguise, for their librettos contain no narratives and their plots are shown in direct action. The choruses, it is true, often provide comments, but so do those in ancient Greek tragedy. Handel also revived the performance of choral odes which had been so popular in Purcell's day (see pp. 79–81). In 1736 he set Dryden's ode, *Alexander's Feast*, to music, and in 1739 he set Dryden's *Ode on St. Cecilia's Day*, in which he actually seems to have copied Purcell's style to some extent.

Saul and *Israel in Egypt* appeared in the same year, 1738. *Messiah* was given first at Dublin in 1742, where Handel had been asked to go by the Lord Lieutenant of Ireland, and it and *Samson* were produced in London in the following season. The year 1745, when the Jacobite rising in Scotland had been suppressed by the battle of Culloden, was celebrated by the production of *Judas Maccabaeus*, of which the chief themes are war, bloodshed, and military glory; from this time until the end of his life Handel and his oratorio performances seem to have become a recognized part of London life, and he was able to carry them on regularly and successfully almost up to the time of his death in 1759.

Bach had died in Leipzig nine years earlier (1750). The two had never met, though once, when Handel had been paying a visit to his mother at Halle, Bach had made a special journey from Köthen in the hope of meeting him. But he had come too late. Though Bach stayed at home he was in close touch with the music of other countries, for he never lost an opportunity of studying such of it as was published. Handel's fame was very great, and probably Bach knew a good deal of his work, but on the other hand Bach can have been known to Handel only as a fine organist who had written some music. Very little of Bach's work was published during his lifetime, and that his reputation was local is shown by the fact that after his death his great choral works were laid aside and forgotten for nearly a hundred years.

Suggestions for Further Reading and Listening

A TASTE for picturesque narrative in the lives of composers was more widespread in the past than it is today. We have grown austere, preferring to dwell less on anecdotes than on those incidents, circumstances, and influences which have a direct bearing on the composers' music. In the case of Handel and Bach, born so close to each other, geographically and chronologically, there are obvious points of contrast. How different was the career of Handel, as a busy, fashionable operatic composer and entrepreneur in the turbulent context of early eighteenth-century London, from the relatively placid existence of J. S. Bach as a provincial kapellmeister and organist.

In both cases there is a good deal of biographical literature. As far as Bach is concerned, the basic biographies are by Forkel, Spitta, Schweitzer, Charles Sanford Terry, and Karl Geiringer. Further recommendations are *The Bach Reader*, edited by David and Mendel, in which the composer's life is related through letters and documents, and Percy Young's *The Bachs*.

The fullest biography in English of Handel is by Paul Henry Lang, though for general purposes readers may find the early chapters in Percy Young's 'Master Musicians' volume on Handel more useful. For reference rather than sustained reading, Otto Erich Deutsch's *Handel: a Documentary Biography* is invaluable.

CHAPTER 5

Vocal Music of Handel and Bach

HANDEL'S OPERATIC STYLE

IN all probability you will never have an opportunity of hearing an opera by Handel. He adopted the formal style of the Italians so completely that a modern performance can be attempted only in special circumstances for its historical interest. A vast amount of glorious music is thus wasted, but a style of opera in which there must be always six principal characters, each one of which must sing a certain number of arias in certain fixed styles and leave the stage at the conclusion of each, whatever the dramatic situation, is a kind of entertainment very difficult to revive. Each aria was complete in itself, and was generally worked out fully according to the ternary *da capo* form which Scarlatti had made fashionable (see p. 55), so that there could be no real progress of the drama in the course of an aria, since the singer had always to return to the point from which he started. Occasionally a piece of fine recitative would break through the monotonous scheme, and now and then a chorus was introduced, as at the beginning of *Giulio Cesare*, when the composer wished to gain a particularly impressive effect from the scene of Julius Caesar's camp on the Egyptian plains. Such departures are rare, however, and do very little to break the general rule.

Yet for half his life Handel put the best of his energies into composing operas of this kind, and they are full of splendidly free and flowing melodies, some of which you may hear in concert rooms, though many of the best of them are quite forgotten. A few are so well known that you may easily remember the operas in which they occur by means of them. 'Lascia ch'io pianga' is often played and sung, though most often with altered English words, and comes from his first opera in England, *Rinaldo*. The famous march from *Scipione*, which Gay introduced into *The Beggar's Opera* ('Let us take the road') will serve to remind you of one of the most famous operas of the Royal Academy period, and the lovely melody of 'Ombra mai fù', which for some reason is more often known as 'Handel's Largo'—as though he had not marked innumerable slow tunes of the same kind to be played *largo* (e.g. slowly)—comes from *Serse* (Xerxes), one of the latest operas (1738), produced with Heidegger after Handel had already begun to rely more on his oratorios as a means of reaching success.

Though you are not likely to gain a much closer knowledge of Handel's operas than a mere handful of the songs can give you, they have a great importance in musical history which has been too often forgotten. The long years of writing for the stage fixed Handel's method as that of a dramatic composer. Whenever he approached a subject, whether it was that of an opera, or an oratorio, or even that of a cantata like *Alexander's Feast*, it presented first to his mind a picture or series of pictures such as the stage produces to the eye. He saw before him the scene which the subject represented; he felt all the sensations which the events of the story would produce upon the minds of the people concerned in it, and his aim was to make his music convey the scene, the events, and the feelings of the people to his audience so that they might share them too. His famous exclamation about the Hallelujah chorus, 'I did think I did see Heaven opened and the great God himself', shows that even *Messiah*, which is less like his opera form than any one of the oratorios, was based to some extent upon a dramatic mental picture, though the picture in his mind's eye was the most sublime one possible.

HANDEL'S ATTITUDE TOWARDS ORATORIO

Many parts of the oratorios are simply operatic scenes upon Old Testament subjects, but the presence of a large chorus to take the place of the stage was a new factor which gradually led him away from the attitude of direct representation to a more reflective one. It will be easier to understand this if we look closely at one of his most representative oratorios, *Saul.*

After the overture the oratorio opens with a massive chorus, 'How excellent is Thy name', in which the Jewish people praise God for David's victory over Goliath. For this Handel used a particularly big orchestra in which trombones, trumpets, and drums were added to the more usual instruments, and it is quite evident that his main object was to present a scene of national rejoicing. A short soprano air exults in the prowess of David, and then 'the monster atheist' is described in a short trio, the orchestral music of which suggests his big and lumbering form by repeating a heavy unison phrase (cf. Kuhnau, p. 89). Another chorus tells in a bold theme how the courage of the Israelites was restored by the sight of Goliath overthrown, and how they 'headlong drove that impious crew', and then the chorus bursts into a repetition of the first hymn of praise and ends the scene with a ringing chorus of Hallelujahs.

The scene is dramatic, but it is not operatic, for it contemplates the story of David and Goliath, and does not try to give a direct representation of it. The following scenes of the oratorio are carried on in a strictly operatic way. All the principal characters make their appearance in turn. First comes Michal, the daughter of Saul, who loves David and sings a song in his praise. Then Abner, the captain of the host, presents David to Saul who promises him the hand of his elder daughter Merab in marriage. Merab, however, despises him, and sings a very vigorous song to describe her emotions; finally comes Jonathan, who greets David with friendship in music of a calmer kind than that given to most of the characters. Then a chorus of maidens, accompanied by a carillon (that is a peal of bells played from a keyboard), enters with the song 'Saul has slain his thousands and David his ten thousands', which rouses Saul's bitter jealousy. The well-known story of the evil spirit taking possession of Saul, of David's playing before him, and his attempt to kill David is told with characteristic songs and recitatives, and there is a harp solo to represent David's performance;

it is just as though the characters were enacting the whole before our eyes upon a stage. So much is this the case that Handel never troubles to tell his audience that Saul threw a javelin at David. He merely makes Saul sing an aria of burning hate and rage, and a rapid scale of demi-semi-quavers on the strings is meant to indicate the flight of the javelin, as though the composer were so completely wrapped up in the picture before his eyes that he had forgotten that the audience would not see it acted as he did in imagination. It is not until the very end of the first part that Handel seems to remember that after all his work is not an opera, for he then finishes off the part with a chorus which is not actually a part of the story but rather a comment on it.

The events of the second part of Saul are much less stirring than those of the first. The temporary reconciliation between Saul and David, the marriage of David with Michal, Saul's attempt to kill Jonathan, do not call out the same dramatic power or pictorial brilliancy which Handel bestowed on the first part. The marriage scene is passed over with a short love duet, and a conventional chorus follows to point the moral that love is superior to hatred. Handel seems less inspired by this part of his subject, although the opening chorus, 'Envy, eldest born of hell', is as bold and original as any number in the whole work, and the final chorus, 'O fatal consequence of rage', is another fine number. The events, and still more the emotions underlying the events of the third part, however, seized upon Handel's vivid imagination as forcibly as did those of the first part. Saul's visit to the Witch of Endor is treated most graphically. The witch's invocation is made to sound strange and unearthly by the violins playing a figure which continually falls and rises again by large intervals, and the hollow tones of the bassoons carry on the same feeling into the solemn recitative in which the spirit of Samuel speaks to Saul.

A very short orchestral interlude joins this to the scene after the battle when the Amalekite comes to tell David of the death of Saul. In a short but powerful song David condemns him for slaying the Lord's Anointed, and then follows the wonderful Dead March, which has become one of the most celebrated pieces in the whole range of music connected with the subject of death. After this the course of the oratorio turns completely away from anything like dramatic action until the end, when David is hailed as king by the people.

Immediately after the Dead March comes the lament for Saul and Jonathan, the point which shows us most clearly the difference between true oratorio, i.e. musical comment upon a dramatic subject, and opera, which is the direct representation of a drama in music. Handel carries it on by means of the chorus alternating with the solo voice of David. It begins with a beautiful choral number, 'Mourn Israel'. Then a recitative, 'O let it not in Gath be heard', is followed by arias, and a short chorus, 'Eagles were not so swift as they', made vivid by the rushing scales of the violins and the bass part moving continuously in rapid quavers. More arias and a fine number, 'O fatal day', in which both the solo and the chorus take part, continue the lament and lead up to the most imposing chorus in the oratorio, 'Gird on thy sword', which makes an inspiring climax.

This examination of *Saul* has shown us that almost everywhere the use of the chorus tends to make the oratorio less directly theatrical in style. There are some exceptions. The chorus of maidens singing the praise of David in the first part is one of them, for the maidens belong to the action of the story, and their music might be sung and danced to on the stage with even better effect than it has on the concert platform. But elsewhere it is in the great reflective parts, especially in the lament and the finale, that the chorus is most powerful. Handel realized this, and in the same year that he wrote *Saul* he produced *Israel in Egypt*, which practically is made up of indirect reflection upon the dramatic situation by means of huge choral numbers.

The first part of *Israel in Egypt*, dealing with the plagues of Egypt and the passage of the Israelites through the Red Sea, shows Handel's power of writing vivid descriptive music more than any other work, in spite of the fact that he used a good deal of his own and other people's earlier music as material for it. The second part, the song of praise for the delivery out of Egypt, is on a much larger scale, like the lament which is the culminating point of *Saul*, except that it is a song of joy instead of one of sorrow. It does not tell a story, but it dwells in an heroic style upon the great events which are past and the feelings of triumphant thankfulness which they call up. This is really the true business of oratorio, for it can never picture actions as well as opera can, but it can express the underlying thoughts and ideas far more thoroughly.

The mixture, however, of the direct, operatic style with the reflective one of oratorio is found in almost all Handel's works of the kind, and you may distinguish the two very clearly in *Samson*, *Judas Maccabaeus*, *Solomon*, and *Jephthah*, all of which were later than *Israel*. In only one of the works which follow *Israel* did he abandon the operatic manner altogether, and that was in the only Christian oratorio which he ever wrote, *Messiah*.

In *Messiah* he made no attempt to give a dramatic representation of the birth, life, and passion of the Saviour, and only in one instance, in the scene of the angels appearing to the shepherds of Bethlehem, did he give a description of events. He used both solo voices and chorus as a means of meditating upon the facts of the story, and consequently recitative, which was his usual means of relating incidents or conversations between the principal characters, is reduced to a minimum. It is partly because the subject is so much greater than the semi-barbaric stories which he usually set to music, and partly because it is so much more truly fitted to the method of oratorio, that *Messiah* has been judged universally to be Handel's greatest work. We may find choruses in the other oratorios which are finer than 'For unto us' or 'His yoke is easy', and solos which surpass 'Rejoice greatly' or 'Why do the heathen', but no oratorio is so consistent in aim as *Messiah*. His own remark about the 'Hallelujah' chorus shows that his strong dramatic sense guided his choice of a subject and directed his effects, but he had thrown off theatrical means of expression entirely, and he dwelt more upon the deeper meaning and the emotions aroused by the subject than upon its external features. *Messiah* naturally suggests a comparison with Bach's great choral works on the same subject, but before we can make such a comparison it is necessary to trace the growth of Bach's work in much the same way as we have traced that of Handel.

BACH'S CHURCH CANTATAS

Bach's style grew out of the church music of his own country just as Handel's grew out of Italian opera. We have seen that the basis of Lutheran church music was the hymn-tune or chorale, and that composers both in writing for instruments and for voices in church cantatas (which took the place of the anthems of the Anglican church) used both tunes and words of chorales as their groundwork (see p. 88). Bach followed their example in this as in other features of his work, but in the course of his life he borrowed ideas from many sources, and even incorporated some of the principles which Scarlatti and the Italians had discovered.

No sooner had Bach settled down to his life as a church organist than he began to compose cantatas which could take their places in the services of his church. Among those composed at Weimar is the beautiful one, *Gottes Zeit ist die allerbeste Zeit* ('God's time is ever the best time'), which gives a wonderful picture of the point from which Bach started. A very short instrumental movement written for two flutes, two *viole da gamba*, and basses with organ opens the work, and is described as a 'Sonata', though it is unlike any of the sonata forms of the day. It is followed by a chorus on these words:

> God's time is ever the best time.
> In Him we live and move and have our being
> So long as He wills.
> In Him we die at the right time when He wills,

which sets the subject for meditation. A composer who had not Bach's keen sense of what is beautiful and appropriate in music would have dropped into writing music which merely set forth the words without adding anything to the force of the idea. But Bach's mind was of a kind which saw the inner meaning underlying the conventional expression, and could make every feature of his music, the rise and fall of his melody, the rhythm and the harmony correspond closely to some phase of that meaning. For example, in this cantata the first chorus is full of confidence. Both its themes are made of strong rising figures:

Ex. 26

and he reserves more intimate expression for the numbers which follow. The words for these are drawn from various texts of the Bible. First, a tenor solo prays 'O Lord, teach us to number our days', and a bass solo answers 'Set thine house in order for thou shalt die and not live'. Then a remarkable chorus is sung by the three lower voices (alto, tenor, and bass), 'It is the ancient law; man thou must die', in which the music marches forward with a relentless tread, and at the end the trebles sing 'Yea come, Lord Jesus come' to an infinitely touching phrase which suggests the joyful acceptance of death by the Christian soul. An alto voice sings the psalmist's words 'Into Thy hand I commend my spirit', and a bass voice responds with those of Christ on the Cross 'Today shalt thou be with me in Paradise'. The way in which the bass voice breaks in with a sweeping downward phrase on these words is specially noticeable, and the reply of the alto singing a well-known chorale tune is very beautiful. The last chorus of praise is also built on a chorale, but it is very much ornamented both by the instrumental accompaniment and by the ending in which the voices expand into rich polyphony.

Soon after writing this cantata Bach came across various collections of sacred poetry, from which he drew the words for many of his later works of the kind. In setting poetry he developed his arias more fully than in the earlier biblical cantatas, and very frequently made use of the ternary form which Scarlatti and the Italians had devised for their operas. But in whatever form he worked, the actual music which Bach wrote was much more deeply thoughtful than that of the Italians; his melodies were more original, his harmonies were more striking, and his skill in weaving the voice part together with independent instrumental parts was a most remarkable feature of his solo writing.

For the choruses he adopted a great number of different designs. Sometimes he would write free contrapuntal choruses or fugues, such as the first chorus of 'O ewiges Feuer' ('O Light everlasting'), but very often they were founded on chorales. The two late cantatas 'Wachet auf' ('Sleepers, wake'), and 'Ein' feste Burg' ('A stronghold sure'), show the different ways of treating the chorale most perfectly. The first is a setting of a fine Advent hymn by Dr. Philipp Nicolai; in the first chorus the words are sung by the treble to the traditional tune in its simple form, while the other voices sing all kinds of free melodies in conjunction with it. In the other, a setting of Luther's popular hymn, the tune is treated as though it were a fugue subject, and all the voices take part in singing fragments of it in turn, and a tremendous effect of polyphonic sound is built upon it (see pp. 143–5, chorales for organ). The tunes, too, are used in the solos and duets of these cantatas. In fact, Bach used every device which could illustrate his subjects most fully. The subjects themselves of the cantatas are very varied, but generally are suggested by the thoughts put forward by the Sundays of the ecclesiastical year. Sometimes they touch upon incidents in Bible stories; for example, 'Bleib' bei uns' ('Abide with us'), which takes as its subject the scene of the disciples at Emmaus;

they do not attempt to tell a story but rather to meditate upon the ideas it suggests.

PASSION MUSIC

When we come to examine the large choral works by which Bach is best known, the two settings of the Passion, according to St. John and to St. Matthew, and *The Christmas Oratorio*, we find that the story takes a far more prominent place than in the cantatas, and that consequently they come very near to the kind of dramatic expression which was the life of Handel's oratorios. This is natural in the Passion, for the traditional object of Passion music was to recount the events of the Saviour's death, and however much it might be surrounded with other music which meditated upon the underlying thought, such ideas could never be allowed to obscure the story itself. In the Passions Bach secured the prominence of the story by setting aside one voice (a tenor) to sing all the words of the Gospel in recitative, with the exception of such parts as belong to conversations. A bass voice sang the words of the Saviour, and other individual voices were allotted to the words of Pilate, Peter, the High Priest, the witnesses, and others, while for any words which were originally spoken by a group of people (e.g. all the disciples together or the crowd who thronged into the Judgement Court) he used the whole chorus. This was the extension of the Roman Catholic plan adopted by Schütz (see p. 86). But Bach entered so much more deeply into the feelings of all those who took part in the tragedy of Calvary, and he had such a power of expressing himself in musical terms, that this part of the Passion music became a far more living thing than it had ever been before.

The *St. John Passion* shows him to some extent still feeling his way in this respect. The recitative is apt to repeat more conventional phrases than that of the *St. Matthew Passion*. The choruses representing the crowd are rather long and consequently not always very graphic. The scene of Peter's denial, however, is as perfectly carried out as anything in the later work. A recitative tells how Peter stood warming himself, and a little turn of four notes on the word 'warmed' suggests an attitude of affected carelessness. Then a short chorus of detached phrases makes a vivid picture of the chattering servants who accuse him of being one of the disciples of Jesus. Peter jerks out his denial with an evident effort in a phrase of three notes:

Then the cock crows: a little arpeggio on the violoncellos suggests its distant sounds. Peter remembers the words of Jesus, and his bitter weeping is described by the voice of the Evangelist in a long chromatic phrase in which all the pent-up feeling of the earlier part seems to burst forth in an agonized wail. No more perfect picture of weak human nature exists in music.

But while this scene is unsurpassable in the *St. John Passion* practically the whole of the narrative part of the *St. Matthew* is equally subtle. If the Passion music proper, according to St. Matthew, were performed without any of the chorales, songs, or choruses which comment upon it, it would sound like a wonderful sacred drama in music. Bach generally accompanied his recitative with the organ or harpsichord and merely the bass instruments in detached chords, but in the *St. Matthew Passion*, wherever the Saviour speaks, his words are accompanied by long sustained chords played by all the stringed instruments. They seem to surround his words with a reverent atmosphere like the halo of light which the old painters crowned their sacred figures. Throughout, the different characters are kept quite distinct. There is a serene dignity in every phrase of the music which belongs to the Saviour, and at times, more especially in the institution of the Sacrament, the recitative rises to the height of pure melody. When Judas speaks, it is generally in a phrase of rather harsh outline; Peter's short sentences in the denial are bolder than in the earlier Passion, and all the minor characters, the maid-servants, the glib false witnesses, even Pilate's wife, are carefully touched in. The choruses, too, are very graphic, from the frightened, questioning one in which the disciples ask who will betray their Master to the horrible clamour of the crowd 'Let Him be crucified', or the savage outburst of the single word 'Barabbas' which comes in answer to Pilate's question, 'Which then shall I release unto you?'

On the other hand, Bach continually broke through the progress of the Passion story to dwell in thought upon the meaning that each feature of it must have for the Christian. Sometimes he did this with a chorale in which all the congregation could take part. Very often he did it by means of a solo aria, generally when the incident on which it comments calls up intimate, personal feeling, such as the story of the penitent woman who bathed the feet of the Saviour, or the sorrow of Peter which calls forth the aria 'Have mercy Lord on me'. Occasionally the whole chorus has to be used to express the strongest emotions; for example, after the Saviour has been taken prisoner the two choirs burst out into a chorus of indignation at the outrage.

Both the Passions are begun with great choruses which take the place of the instrumental overtures to oratorios, and each ends with a wonderful choral lament which sums up the feeling in the most complete way.

THE CHRISTMAS ORATORIO

We see, then, that in the Passions Bach kept two lines of thought and feeling continually present, the one dramatic, the other reflective. In the earlier parts of *The Christmas Oratorio* he did the same, for the story of the birth of Christ at Bethlehem, of the angels and the shepherds, is told in the same way by a tenor voice representing the Evangelist, and the angelic chorus 'Glory to God' is among his finest inspirations. But the story itself does not take the commanding position which that of the Passion does, and the later parts of *The Christmas Oratorio*, intended to be sung on the various festivals following Christmas day, are more like the cantatas. The story is merely the text for religious contemplation.

The Christmas Oratorio contains some specially remarkable numbers. For example, in the first part after the Evangelist has told of the birth of the Saviour 'Wrapped in swaddling clothes and laid in a manger', there is a duet in which bass recitative is combined with a chorale sung by treble voices. The trebles sing one phrase of the tune 'For us to earth He cometh poor', holding on the last note in a thoughtful way till the bass solo breaks in with the words,

> Who rightly can the love declare
> That fills our tender Saviour's breast,

and each phrase of the chorale calls out some fresh idea on which the recitative comments. Moreover, the whole is bound together into a perfect musical shape by the delicate instrumental music written for oboes and strings. Another is the lullaby sung by an alto voice, 'Slumber Beloved', one of the purest melodies Bach ever wrote, which, like several others, appeared originally in a secular cantata.

In the fourth part there is a treble song in which a second voice is made to reply in the manner of an echo, a quaint device which reminds one of some of the devotional poems of George Herbert, and in the fifth part a trio for treble, alto, and tenor represents a kind of movement which is very characteristic of Bach. The treble and tenor sing a melody full of ardent longing to the words 'Ah when shall we see salvation', and at the end of each musical sentence the alto stills their agitation with the words 'Peace, for surely this is He', set to quieter music. Bach had a special fondness for this kind of dialogue in music, and in several cantatas he introduced them to portray the communion between the soul and its Saviour.

HANDEL AND BACH COMPARED

A comparison of the Shepherd scenes in Handel's *Messiah* and in Bach's *Christmas Oratorio* will show us the differences in the thought and in the workmanship of the two composers. Each begins with a 'Pastoral Symphony', a piece of instrumental music of a peaceful kind supposed to represent the scene of the quiet countryside with the shepherds encamped upon the hill making music to beguile their watch.

Handel's is written for string orchestra only; its simple melody and artless style, the violin parts moving together chiefly in thirds, gives just the right suggestion and nothing more. Bach's is much more intricate. Oboes, flutes, and violins weave a wonderful pattern of picturesque sound; two themes are contrasted and combined, and the whole is worked out at much greater length. We may leave out of count the chorales and arias interspersed in Bach's work, and look only at the telling of the story which both have in common. In each case this is done with recitative. The two settings of the words 'And lo! the angel of the Lord came upon them, and the glory of the Lord shone round about them and they were sore afraid', shows all the different character of the two composers. Handel accompanies his with an excited figure for the violins which emphasizes the idea of the sudden light flooding in upon the darkness. Bach attempts no such picture, but a long downward phrase on the violoncellos makes one realize the fear of the shepherds very forcibly. Again, we see Handel's love of pictorial effect in the recitative and chorus 'And suddenly there was with the angel'. It is accompanied by a fluttering figure for the violins which suggests the innumerable wings of the heavenly host, and the chorus 'Glory to God' begins with the three higher voices only, as though he wished to give a feeling of sound gradually coming from the heights down to earth.

We have seen that Bach, too, could use realistic effects (see *St. John Passion*, p. 115), but he avoids them here. His recitative is studiously simple, and he saves all his forces for a glorious outburst of contrapuntal sound in the great chorus 'Glory to God'. If we place these two choruses side by side, Handel's seems small and almost trivial in comparison with the huge waves of sound which Bach produces. But Handel's is really immensely effective. It needs a skilled musician to hear all the parts of Bach's chorus; a child can distinguish everything in Handel's. Here we see the great difference between them. Handel knew exactly what would make the most telling effect upon a great number of people, and he never spent his strength on details which people could not appreciate. Bach lavished all his immense power upon producing the most perfect piece of art whether his hearers could understand it all or not.

BACH'S LATIN CHURCH MUSIC

We must not leave the subject of Bach's vocal music without a word upon quite a different aspect of it, his setting of Latin words, in particular the *Magnificat* and the Mass. The *Magnificat* was written to be sung at Christmas time in St. Thomas's Church at Leipzig, and except for the fact that the Latin words are used, it is practically a church cantata of the German kind. At the first performance chorales were sung between its several movements, and one such tune is actually introduced into the work itself, played by the oboe, while a trio of voices sing 'Suscepit Israel puerum suum, recordatus misericordiae suae' ('He remembering his mercy hath holpen his servant Israel'). Most of the words are set to solo arias, with great choral numbers at the beginning and end. In the middle the chorus is used twice, and each time for a special, realistic purpose. It breaks in with the words 'Omnes generationes' ('all generations') to give the effect of a multitudinous consent, and again, 'Fecit potentiam in brachio suo, dispersit superbos mente cordis sui' ('He hath showed strength with his arm, He hath scattered the proud in the imagination of their hearts'), is set in a most graphic way. The voices are literally scattered at the word 'dispersit'; 'superbos' is shouted disdainfully by all the voices on a powerful discord, and a solemn ending seems to meditate on 'the imagination of their hearts'.

Bach wrote several masses, and parts of them were sometimes performed in the Lutheran churches of Leipzig, but his great Mass in B minor is written on a scale which makes it altogether beyond the bounds of any church service, Catholic or Protestant. It was written at various times, and probably represented to the composer's mind an ideal of musical worship which he never expected to be fully realized in any church. Now it is only to be heard in concert performance.

As in the *Magnificat*, so in the Mass there are places where Bach deliberately illustrates the meaning of special words by some feature of his music. Such are the wonderful passages in the Credo, where the voices all sink down to low, soft tones on the words, 'Passus et sepultus est' ('He suffered and was buried'), and after a moment's pause break out again with an exhilarating ascending phrase—'et resurrexit' ('and rose again'), and the even more wonderful one near the end of the Credo which introduces the words 'et expecto resurrectionem mortuorum' ('and I look for the resurrection of the dead') by a series of chords passing boldly out of the key of D major to harmonies which are not clearly related to any single key-note, and which seem to give a glimpse of limitless eternity. But the chief splendour of the Mass does not consist in these flashes of imaginative insight, beautiful though they are, but in the power with which the interest is maintained through the long succession of great choruses, solos, and duets, amongst which the words of the liturgy are divided. In order to do so, Bach draws upon every known style of music in turn. The ancient church plainsong is introduced into two passages of the Credo, the opening and the 'Confiteor unum baptisma' ('I believe in one baptism'), and in these and other choruses, especially the 'Gratias agimus' ('we give thanks'), the older polyphonic style of Palestrina is used to a large extent. Again, in one instance—the 'Crucifixus'—an overwhelming effect of brooding sorrow is produced by the use of a ground bass continually descending in semitones (cf. Purcell, p. 82). The arias, on the other hand, are full of the influence of Italian composers in their definite ternary form and the frequent use of florid ornamental passages (see especially

'Laudamus te'), but the deep feeling underlying the form is all Bach's own, whether it be the gladness of the soprano aria just named or the intensely earnest prayer of the contralto, 'Agnus Dei'. All the florid passages are there to express something, not to show off the singer's voice, and in no case is the singer allowed to be the chief object of interest, since an equal share of the music falls to some special instrument, violin, oboe, or horn, which is of as much importance as the voice.

Many of the choruses are examples of Bach's extraordinarily varied use of fugal writing; and as it would be impossible to explain the elements of this in connexion with such huge examples of its use, we will not attempt to study them. We will consider fugue later in connexion with Bach's and Handel's purely instrumental works, which illustrate its characteristics more simply.

Before leaving the subject we must see how far the growth of music has reached since the Masses of Palestrina appeared. Not only has the use of instruments produced quite new forms and means of expression such as the ground bass and the Italian aria, but whereas the first instrumental writers often made their instruments move with the smoothness of voices, Bach makes his voices move with all the force of instruments. The 'Kyrie Eleison' No. 1 ('O Lord have mercy'), one of the greatest fugues ever written, shows this at once, for instruments and voices play and sing the subject alike, yet its strong rhythm and its difficult intervals evidently come from a mind which knows that all intervals and rhythms can be played with equal certainty by the instruments, and what they do the voices must do. The definite rhythms and use of harmonies which, though sometimes dissonant in themselves, are quite understandable, because they all are founded upon a key system, show the technical advance of Bach and of Handel beyond the limits of the old church composers, and we have seen that these things put an immense increase of expressive power at their disposal. Without a clear system of key such a passage as Bach's 'Et expecto' (see above) would be powerless, for it would have no starting-point, and without a measured rhythm so vivid an outburst as Handel's 'Hallelujah' chorus in *Messiah* had been equally impossible.

Palestrina's most beautiful visions were always rather vague, Handel's were strong and somewhat material. Bach linked the mystic beauty of the one with the strength of the other.

Suggestions for Further Reading and Listening

THE revival of interest in Handel's operas began in the 1920s. It was the work of a handful of enthusiasts in Germany and, in this country, of E. J. Dent. Though this brand of opera may still count as caviar to the general public and be considered of doubtful box-office value, it is successfully championed by, for instance, the Handel Opera Society and the more enterprising university operatic societies. The leading English authority on the subject is Winton Dean, whose *Handel and the Opera Seria* can be strongly recommended. Opera of course looms large in Dent's *Handel.*

Winton Dean's masterly *Handel's Dramatic Oratorios and Masques* is a major contribution to Handel scholarship, but it deliberately omits *Messiah*, unlike Percy Young's *The Oratorios of Handel*, much slighter in scope but worth consulting. As one would expect, *Messiah* has inspired a lot of literature; the most authoritative study is by Jens Peter Larsen, who discusses in depth its origins, composition, and sources.

Bach's church music is examined in considerable detail in all the best general histories of the period and of course by Schweitzer. Readers are, however, directed towards Whittaker's *The Cantatas of Johann Sebastian Bach, Sacred and Secular*, in two large volumes. By contrast there is the slim, succinct booklet by Westrup in the 'BBC Music Guides' series.

As far as recordings are concerned, Handel's operas and oratorios are fairly well represented nowadays and so too of course is *Messiah*. Generally speaking, it is always worth going for performances that promise a greater degree of authenticity, but in the case of *Messiah*, after hearing more authentic versions, it is well worth listening to the DGG issue of the Mozart version, conducted by Charles Mackerras. It tells you a lot about both composers. A glance through the gramophone catalogue indicates that J. S. Bach's church music is now very fully covered. The problem is one of choice rather than of availability.

CHAPTER 6

Instrumental Music of Handel and Bach

WHILE it is quite possible to compare and contrast the music which Handel and Bach wrote for voices, a similar comparison is out of the question with regard to their music for instruments alone. Handel never devoted his attention to music of this kind in a wholehearted way. It is true that he wrote works of almost every kind then existing for various instruments, but they were always rather the offshoots of his genius written either for some special occasion, to fill up a blank space in his concert programmes, or for the benefit of his fashionable pupils. Bach, on the other hand, began life as an instrumental composer, and much of his earlier time was devoted to composition for his own instrument—the organ. Then, as we have seen, when he was at the height of his powers during the time that he spent at Köthen (1717–23) he gave himself up to the composition of music for instruments alone, and produced a great mass of splendid works of every conceivable kind, and in doing so he formed a style of his own which was quite unlike that of any of his predecessors or contemporaries. Consequently his work for instruments marches far ahead of Handel's, and to try to compare the two would be very unfair to Handel, for viewed in the light of Bach's music, his appears much less significant. Nevertheless there are beautiful things in Handel's works of almost every kind, and if we consider that most of them were very rapidly written, thrown off as it were in the spare moments of his busy life, we can realize something of the strength of his genius from them.

HANDEL'S INSTRUMENTAL MUSIC

Handel's instrumental music can be divided for our purpose into three classes, and we shall look only at a few examples in each class. There is (1) music for the harpsichord alone which was equivalent to piano music, and is now often played on the piano; (2) chamber music, that is to say sonatas for two or three instruments intended to be played in private houses rather than in public, of which those for harpsichord and violin are now the best known; (3) music for an orchestra. This last includes a number of concertos for the organ accompanied by the orchestra which Handel used to play between the parts of his oratorios, as well as some concertos for orchestral instruments, and further, the overtures and other pieces which were included in his operas and oratorios.

HARPSICHORD MUSIC

The harpsichord music consists of suites, lessons, fugues, and other pieces, many of which were written for pupils. We have already mentioned the suites and lessons of Purcell and the *ordres* of Couperin, and Handel's were planned in much the same way except that he did not confine himself to dance-tunes at all to the same extent as they, and instead of having a great number of little pieces in one suite he generally preferred to have only four or five, and to make them longer than the older writers were able to do. The actual order of pieces in a suite was always a matter for the composer's own taste, but still there were certain arrangements which were the most usual; for instance the suite generally began with a movement called either Prelude (which means something that is played first) or an Allemande, that is a German piece in a quick and fluent style. A Courante, an old French 'running' dance, would generally follow, and after it a Sarabande would frequently come, since it was a slow dance which contrasted well with the quick ones that had gone before. Next would come one or more Minuets, a Gavotte, and possibly others, with a quick dance, preferably the Gigue, to make a cheerful ending. Handel's suites contain movements of all these kinds, but they do not appear at all in the accepted order. Several of them have both a prelude and an allemande, as the first has. The second begins with an adagio, the fourth with a fine fugue which, properly speaking, has no place in the suite form. Some of them contain airs with variations, such as the fifth suite, which ends with the tune known, for reasons quite unconnected with the composer, as 'The Harmonious Blacksmith'.

The main point to realize, however, is that Handel's suites are not planned on any fixed form; he wrote any set of movements which would group well together, and generally the best movements were not the allemandes, courantes, and sarabandes which were the common property of suite writers, but those which he imported, as it were, from other kinds of work, such as the fugues (Suites IV and VIII[1]), the presto which ends Suite III, in which two themes are contrasted in a highly original way. The gigues, however, are an exception, for Handel had a special fondness for their delightful rhythm which, like Scarlatti, he had probably caught from Corelli when he was a young man in Italy (see p. 58). Sometimes when he has started a really good gigue theme it seems as though his delight in it would never stop, and as though he were determined to show that the dancers would be exhausted long before his powers of invention would be. The gigue ending Suite IX in G minor is a splendid example.

There is another interesting peculiarity in several of Handel's suites. Instead of letting all the movements stand apart from one another as quite separate things having no musical connexion, he would use the same theme as the groundwork of more than one movement. This was quite opposed to the old idea of a suite, which was that the movements should be as unlike as possible. Compare the openings of

Suite IV. Allemande and Courante.
Suite VII. Andante and Allegro.
Suite IX. Allemande and Courante.
Suite XI. Allemande and Courante.

You see at once that the first few notes which form the theme

[1] The numbers shown here are those of the Peters edition.

are much alike in the outline of the melody in each pair, though the rhythm is altered, and this is remarkable, because the method of altering the character of a tune by changing its rhythm is one of which more recent composers such as Liszt and Berlioz became very fond.

The moment when we have Handel's suites before us is a good one in which to find out a little more clearly what a **Fugue** is.

To do so we must go back to the distinction which we discovered in the first chapter between polyphonic and homophonic music (see pp. 4–5). Now the dances of the suites all belong more or less to the second class, that is to say, they are harmonized tunes. But a fugue is like a 'catch'; there must be several voices or parts of which sings or plays a tune which agrees in harmony with the others. Let us suppose for the sake of clearness that the fugue is sung by four people: treble, alto, tenor, and bass. The idea is that each should begin by singing the same fragment of melody, a fragment which is to be the chief point of the whole of the fugue, as the text is the chief point of a sermon. Suppose that the treble sings it first, the alto will have to sing it on lower notes because his voice is lower, and probably it will be transposed into the key of the dominant for him, four notes down. While the alto sings the subject the treble goes on singing a new tune called the counter-subject, which harmonizes with the subject, but is quite distinct from it. Next the tenor enters singing the subject an octave below the treble while the alto goes on to the counter-subject, and finally the bass voice begins an octave lower than the alto. So far the fugue is very much like a catch, for all the voices sing the same music in turn, only they do not sing it upon the same notes. But they do not follow each other singing the same music through the whole work as the singers of a catch do, for after each has sung the subject and the counter-subject there is no strict rule as to what shall happen next. The voices return from time to time to the subject and counter-subject, singing them now in one part, now in another, sometimes changing to another key or from the major to the minor, sometimes altering them or singing them in longer or shorter notes, and then as the fugue draws near to the end one voice may begin the subject and another enter also singing it before the first has finished, so that they seem to catch each other up. (This device is called a *stretto*.) The whole must be planned so as to give all the prominence possible to the subject itself, and so it is exceedingly important that the subject should be a really fine bit of music which it is worth while to make prominent.

The treatment of a subject in fugue is perfectly natural when it is sung by different voices or played upon different instruments, each one of which carries on its own part, and as we have seen, all the earlier polyphonic music was written for a number of different voices and written in that way in order that each might bear an equal part in the interest of the performance. But when the fugue is played on a single instrument, such as the harpsichord or the piano or the organ, it requires a certain amount of make-believe on the part of the listener. You have to imagine that there are several voices or instruments carrying on the separate parts, and to follow their course with your ears in order to understand what is going on.

You can see quite easily how the fugue got transferred from the real human voices to the pretended ones of the harpsichord if you compare No. 5 of the Six Grand Fugues by Handel (Peters ed., Book III) with the chorus 'They loathed to drink of the river' in his *Israel in Egypt*. Both have the same subject, and in spite of a good deal of difference in detail the two are practically the same piece of music. In the oratorio the bold subject with its hard-sounding sevenths seems to picture the disgust of the people at the polluted river; in the harpsichord fugue it is just as striking in effect even though it is not connected with any particular story. Your ear is caught every time that great striding subject comes in, and you listen for its contrast with the theme in descending semitones which grows up out of the counter-subject as the fugue advances. Notice especially bars 31–33 where the bass starts the subject and the treble comes in with the same tune two octaves higher before the bass has finished it. This gives a perfect example of the way in which a subject stamps its character upon the whole course of a fugue. The one in G in Suite IV, with its repeated B's like three determined strokes of a hammer, and the one in F minor from Suite VIII, the subject of which marches up the scale with a dignified tread, are other capital examples. We shall consider this aspect of the fugue more fully when we come to those of Bach.

CHAMBER MUSIC

The most important things in Handel's chamber music are the sonatas for one or two instruments with harpsichord *continuo*, and those for a single flute, oboe, or violin are the only ones which we shall study here.

For the most part they follow the plan of Corelli's works of the same kind, having four movements, a slow one and a quick one alternately, and the last one is generally written in the characteristic rhythm (12-8 time) of the gigue. In writing them Handel followed the custom which all his predecessors had used, when the harpsichord was employed as an accompaniment either to another instrument or to the voice. Instead of writing everything that the harpsichord was to play he simply wrote the bass and put certain figures under it to show what chords the right hand was to supply. The Italian word *continuo* for such a part indicates that this bass continued uninterruptedly throughout and so did the upper parts improvised by the player, except in rare cases where a passage was marked *tasto solo*. The musical 'filling' thus depended on the taste of the player, but in modern editions of such music it has been filled in by a later musician in a style as much like that of the composer as possible. You see then that sonatas of this kind were thoroughly homophonic and not polyphonic, that is to say, the tune of the violin was the chief thing, the bass was only important because it made the harmony clear, and the middle parts were so much less important that it was thought unnecessary to write them down. This is not to say, however, that a *continuo* part was necessarily uninteresting; indeed, harpsichord players in the eighteenth century were specially trained in the art of playing from figured basses, and the best of them were capable of astonishing feats which often included fugal and other polyphonic passages. They also had to be well grounded in the art of ornamentation and were required to know the conventions governing the use of trills, especially at cadential points. The only written guidance, apart from the bass line, was the general outline of the harmony: the figures showed the basic chords to be used, and to these the player had to adhere.

Although Handel's style is generally larger and broader than Corelli's, one sometimes finds themes in these sonatas which remind one very much of Corelli. The beginning of the allegro in the Sonata in G minor (Peters ed., No. 3) is a case in point:

Ex. 28

You see the likeness at once if you compare this with the Allemande of Corelli's Sonata in E minor (Ex. 20, p. 58), and one can also see that in this instance Corelli's skill as a violinist led him to carry on the leaping intervals of the theme far more strongly than Handel did.

To see Handel at his best in these sonatas look at the first allegro of the one in A (Peters No. 1). It shows how firmly Handel had grasped the principles of contrasting one theme with another and one key with another, and by means of these twin contrasts he is able to carry on his music and to make it grow in intensity till it reaches a splendid climax at the close. The principal theme is a double one given out by the violin and the bass of the harpsichord (Ex. 29).

Handel in his finest moments could not bear to confine himself to a wholly homophonic style, and here, although the upper part of the harpsichord is mere added harmony, the bass and the

Ex. 29

violin continue to treat these two ideas in a free contrapuntal style almost like a fugue. After eight bars the two are reversed, the harpsichord playing the bold downward theme (*a*) and the violin replying with the more delicate upward figure of quavers (*b*). A little later on they come in again in the key of E (that is, the dominant), and then for a time they are left in order to develop a new theme which leads through various keys back to the return of the double theme in its original key of A. Here the violinist must play both parts of it at once on two strings in order that the harpsichord may enrich the interest with a new bass, and afterwards, if you trace it out, you will find that the harpsichord part is almost entirely made up of one or other of the themes (*a*) or (*b*), while the violin adds all sorts of decorative passages until it at last bursts in with (*a*), emphasizing its two prominent notes by strong chords, the harpsichord accompanying it with a rolling passage in quavers, and so the movement ends majestically.

ORCHESTRAL MUSIC

We saw how the elder Scarlatti and others gradually sorted out, as it were, the mixed collection of instruments which the first experimenters, Monteverdi and others, had used, and how they decided upon the stringed instruments, violins, violas, violoncellos, and double basses, as the best foundation for an orchestra. It became recognized that every orchestra must contain a certain number of these, but a great deal of diversity continued to exist as to the use of wind instruments. Handel relied upon oboes and bassoons as a permanent part of his orchestra, and in many of his overtures to operas he got striking effects by contrasting their thick reedy tone with the sharper and clearer tone of the violins, as here:

Ex. 30

The oboe concertos seem to have had this object in view, for the oboes are not sufficiently prominent in them to take the place as solo instruments which the organ holds in the organ concertos, but they add a good deal of variety to the tone.

Most of the other wind instruments which belong to the modern orchestra were perfectly well known in Handel's day, but what was not so well known was how to combine them with the strings. He frequently used trumpets and drums when he wanted big effects, for instance, in some choruses of *Messiah*, such as 'For unto us' and 'Hallelujah', and in the first chorus of *Saul*, and in the last case there are parts for all the instruments we have named and three trombones as well. The same work, which is particularly rich in orchestration, has flutes in the funeral march, and the harp in the scene of David's playing before Saul and in the song 'Fly, fly, malicious spirit'. Four horns make their appearance in the opening chorus of the opera *Julius Caesar*, and later on in that opera the harp, lute, and *viola da gamba* are introduced in order to give a luscious colouring to the scene of Cleopatra's court. It would be easy to go on piling up instances of Handel's use of instruments for special effects, but the only point of mentioning a few is to show that all the instruments of Beethoven's orchestra were familiar to Handel with one important exception—the clarinet. Nevertheless, his normal orchestra was much smaller; we may say that it consisted of strings, oboes and bassoons, trumpets and drums (used sparingly), and that flutes, horns, trombones, and harp were all extra instruments.

This gives some notion of the means which Handel had at his disposal. The next thing is to see how he used them. His works for the orchestra alone consist chiefly of concertos with a few additions such as the 'Water Music' (p. 100) and 'Fireworks Music'. There are several sets of concertos, those already mentioned in which oboes (and occasionally flutes) take part, and twelve 'Grand Concertos' for stringed instruments only, in addition to the organ concertos. These last are the only ones in which there is a single solo instrument, and since Handel was accustomed to play the organ part himself he never took the trouble to write them out quite fully, but used to trust largely to his memory or to his inventive power at the moment to make them effective. The other concertos, called *Concerti grossi*, all bear much the same relation to Corelli's works of the kind as his violin sonatas do to that master's: that is to say, their general plan is like his, but they are freer and finer both in their musical ideas and in their treatment of those ideas. Handel adopted the same plan of having a group of solo players and a stringed band as an accompaniment (see p. 57); the group of soloists in the oboe concertos were the oboe players and a violinist; in the 'grand concertos' they were two violinists and a violoncellist. We need not examine them in detail, since almost any page from among them shows how well Handel knew what kind of passages are most effective on stringed instruments, and what varieties of sound can be obtained from them by grouping them in different ways. But with the wind instruments his skill was far less complete; he had not found out what kinds of passages were especially suited to the oboes and bassoons, for example, and consequently we often find them playing exactly the same kind of passage as the strings, the oboes either in unison with the violins or playing alternately with them.

In speaking of the orchestra you may often hear musicians talk of 'colour': the tone of each instrument is compared to the colours on a painter's palette. The art of combining them is indeed very similar to that of the painter, for when the tones of the instruments are well blended they produce an almost infinite number of subtle lights and shades which you would never have suspected could be got from the few simple tones of the separate instruments. Now, to use this common simile, in most of his work Handel only reached the power of laying on colours in a few broad washes, as the early Italian painters of frescoes in tempera did; but in a few instances he achieved the intimate combinations of sound which correspond to the more delicate effects of colour later painters used in their oil paintings.

This is a point which no amount of explanation or even the

study of scores can make really clear. You would perceive it most quickly by listening to an overture by Handel and a symphony by Beethoven at the same concert, but we will illustrate the point by two short quotations here, and expand it further when we are studying the later developments of the orchestra.

The opening of the first Chandos Anthem already shown as Ex. 30 (p. 132) demonstrates Handel's customary way of contrasting oboe tone and violin tone. The music for each is just the same and the variety depends simply on the fact that the two are of different qualities; they contrast as simply as blue and red in a picture.

Ex. 31

On the other hand, the passage from *Saul* quoted in Ex. 31 combines the instruments much more closely, and is rather exceptional in Handel's work for that reason. Of course, the massing of the heavier instruments (bassoons, trumpets, trombones, drum, and strings) on the rhythmic figure (♩. ♬ ♩) is an obvious effect; anyone would have thought of that, but notice the way in which the oboes and the violins are dovetailed into one another in the first bar, how in the third bar where the two violins have an imitative passage the colour of the oboe is added to the second violin to give it distinction, and finally how in the last bar but one the trombones enrich the harmony of the strings by adding parts in the middle of them.

Ex. 31 (*continued*)

Apart from its point as an illustration of Handel's method, it makes a capital first lesson in the art of reading a full score.

BACH'S INSTRUMENTAL MUSIC

At this stage of our study it is tremendously important to realize the differences between the effects of the various instruments and to see that these different effects are brought about by the different ways in which the instruments are made. We have just been looking at some of them in Handel's work; now before taking up any of Bach's music we must look for a moment at the mechanism of the organ, the instrument on which he

Ex. 31 (*continued*)

played and for which he wrote so constantly in his younger years that all his life through his thoughts seemed to spring from the sounds of the organ, just as later Schumann's sprang from the piano and Wagner's from the orchestra.

In the first place the organ is by far the most complicated musical instrument that has ever been invented for one person to play upon. That, no doubt, is why people have called it 'the king of instruments', because it brings such a great number of sounds under the control of one player. This is how it does so. Suppose that the keyboard of the organ contains fifty-six notes (i.e. about four and a half octaves), then fifty-six pipes will be required in order to make each one of these notes 'speak'.

Ex. 31 (*concluded*)

When the player presses down the key, wind from the bellows passes into the pipe belonging to that key, and as long as the key is held down the escape of wind through the pipe continues, causing the vibrations which produce the note. So an organ note (unlike that of the harpsichord, in which the string is plucked, or the piano, in which it is struck by a hammer) can be sustained as long as the player chooses to hold the key.

An organ, however, with merely one pipe to each note of the keyboard, would be a very simple affair. As a matter of fact, every organ has a variety of sets of pipes called stops, which can be made to sound either together or separately on the same keyboard. In the case we are supposing, each of these sets would contain fifty-six pipes, a pipe to a key, and the great beauty in a fine organ is that each set of pipes (i.e. each stop) has a distinct quality of tone which all its pipes possess equally and which distinguishes it from the other stops. Some stops are loud, some soft; some, called diapasons, have a strong, rich tone which make them the groundwork of the organ as the stringed instruments are of the orchestra; others produce light and sweet sounds like flutes; others copy the sounds of orchestral instruments closely, such as oboes and trumpets, and all these may be made to sound the same note together when the player's finger presses the key, or any selection of them may be used. The great difference between the stops of the organ and the instruments of the orchestra is that the stops on one keyboard all sound the same notes when they sound at all. You cannot, for example, hold down a chord of C in which the oboe sounds the top C, the trumpet G, and the diapasons E and the lower C. If you had drawn those stops they would all sound the four notes. In order to get over this disadvantage to some extent the plan of building organs with two or three keyboards was invented, each keyboard having certain stops of its own, so that the organist could play with one hand on each, or pass quickly from one to another. By this means a diapason stop on one keyboard might be contrasted with, say, an oboe stop on another, and such an effect as Handel got in the Chandos Anthem (Ex. 30) could be reproduced almost exactly on the organ. Still this sort of contrast was, and still is, limited to what the player's two hands can contrive in passing from keyboard to keyboard, and it would be impossible to contrast the tones of the various stops with anything like the closeness of the orchestration in Ex. 31.

One more of the special resources of the organ must be borne in mind, namely, the pedals. The pedal-board is merely another keyboard, played by the feet instead of by the hands, but its notes only include about two and a half octaves, and so represent the bass part of the other keyboards. Its principal stops sound an octave below those of the hand keyboards (called manuals), just as the double-basses of the orchestra sound an octave below the violoncellos.

If you have been able to follow this description you will now see what the organ is capable of doing. First, it can produce as many different kinds of tone as there are stops, and it can combine them in many ways to produce fresh ones, just as a painter can mix blue and yellow and get green; but these combinations are limited by the fact that all the stops on one manual must play the same music. Secondly, in Bach's day the organist could only make his music louder or softer by using more or fewer stops, since each pipe always gives a constant amount of tone.[1] That means that no single stop was capable of any expression at all, since the only thing under the control of the player was the length that each note should last; he could not alter its loudness or its softness, or give any accent to one note over another. The organist has none of the power of the violinist, whose bow can both sustain a note perfectly and can at any moment produce an accent by a little more pressure. But then, on the other hand, a violinist can only play comparatively few chords, and can scarcely play polyphonic music at all, so that in such things the organist has a great advantage. His power of sustaining notes, and of playing with feet as well as hands, made him better at

[1] Nowadays this defect is partly remedied by the use of a 'swell'.

playing such music as fugues than even the harpsichordist, whose notes diminished rapidly in sound as soon as they were struck.

ORGAN MUSIC

We are now ready to illustrate the capacities of the instrument by means of some of the music which Bach wrote for it. It has been said already that the amount of his music in every form is very great, and so it would be quite impossible to give even the shortest summary of what he wrote. Instead, we shall try to get some clear knowledge of two or three works which will give a notion of his style.

First, take the Toccata and Fugue in D minor, which is one of the most wonderful things he wrote to play on his organ at Arnstadt. The Toccata is short, but it contains almost every kind of effect obtainable on the organ. Its very first note, that A with a little ornament of two notes upon it (played ), shows how well Bach knew his instrument. If he had been writing for strings there would have been no need for that little turn; the bite of the bow would have given the necessary accent (cf. Beethoven's second Symphony or Leonora Overture No. 3).

See what a force is added to the rapid descending phrases by the rests and pauses between them. These impressive silences make up for the lack of any accent on the organ, for they seize the attention as a good speaker does when he pauses before saying something of special importance. Then notice that massive discord (technically a dominant minor ninth on a tonic pedal) which is gradually spread out using all the big overwhelming sound of the instrument, and which finishes the phrase by sinking down into the quiet major chord. After this come long passages rolling up and down the compass of the instrument and again cut off by the same striking chord in a still fuller form. Notice also the repetitions and variations on this simple harmonic figure:

Ex. 32

which of course can be enforced by the use of different stops, and the brilliant running passages which lead up to the last powerful phrase for the pedals, accompanied by detached chords played by the hands. This toccata has no definite melodic idea, it makes no attempt to develop a subject by any of the ordinary processes, but it compresses into a small space almost all the noble effects of sound which the organ can produce.

The fugue, too, is very unlike the examples by Handel which we studied. There is extraordinarily little counterpoint or interplay of parts in it, and many of its passages are not polyphonic at all, but consist of rushing scales and arpeggios, which are very effective on the organ, and require none of the thinking power on the part of the listener which most fugues call for. The flowing subject constantly recurs but is never used in *stretto* (see p. 128), and at the end Bach breaks away from the fugue style altogether and finishes by recalling some of the features of the toccata in a magnificent coda.

It is quite impossible to understand how in face of such pieces as this (and there are plenty more of the same kind) people could ever imagine that Bach was merely a learned man who wrote things hard to enjoy; but they did in his lifetime, and there are even some unfortunates who think so now.

It is natural that as he grew older and thought more deeply his music should take a more serious turn, and that he should grow to care more and more for the greater kinds of expression, which come from the development of fine ideas of melody, rhythm, and harmony, and care less for mere brilliant combinations of sound. So in his other Toccatas, the larger one in D minor and still more in the huge Toccata in F major, there are far fewer surprises for the listener, but the music is much more splendid and rich in design. It would take too long to analyse the Toccata in F in detail as we have the shorter one in D minor; everyone should hear it and compare it with the other for himself.

You will realize how tremendous is the sweep of the first theme, played in canon by the two hands while one long impressive note is sustained on the pedals; next, how the pedals at last burst out with a new version of the theme, and how closely the rhythm of the theme is adhered to until a fresh idea, a series of chords in detached pairs, makes its appearance, to be afterwards combined with the rolling semiquavers of the principal theme. The whole is on a gigantic scale, and while it is full of characteristic organ effects, they are not the things which seize and hold the attention. Rather they serve to set forward the majestic musical conception.

We shall not attempt to study Bach's wonderful power of fugal workmanship in his organ music. What makes his fugues greater than those of any other composer is the fact that he never allowed the artificial requirements of the form to interfere with the expression of his ideas, but used only those artifices which helped to make his ideas clearer and stronger. We shall be able to realize this more fully, however, when we look at the fugues in his clavier music (see p. 150).

There is, however, one other phase of music for the organ which is too important to be passed by, namely, the chorale preludes. We have already seen how dear the chorales were to the hearts of German Protestants, how Buxtehude and others made them the groundwork of their compositions, and how Bach himself built his cantatas upon them. His intense love of the chorales, and his power of bringing out all the nobility and tender sentiment of the old hymns by the music which he added to the tunes, can be still better shown in the chorale preludes written to be played on the organ. Some of these were meant to be introductions to the hymns themselves when they were sung in church, others, the longer and more elaborate ones, are separate instrumental pieces, and some are actual arrangements of movements from his cantatas.

The following are examples of various methods of treatment: *Herzlich tut mich verlangen.* This is a setting of Hassler's lovely tune (p. 85) which Bach used so often in his Passion music. The way he treats it here is very remarkable, because the tune does not appear at all in its simple form after the first bar. But if you listen to it you will hear that though the tune is altered by the little groups of semiquavers which take the place of plain crotchets, its general outline is preserved, and those little ornaments as well as the rich harmonies impress the pathetic beauty of the tune. Another more extended instance of the same way of treating the tune is *O Mensch, bewein' dein' Sünde gross*, a tune also used in the St. Matthew Passion. Contrast with these the setting of the old Christmas carol, *In dulci jubilo*. Here two parts, the treble and the bass, play the tune in canon, and while they do so joyful triplet figures are added, like the pealing of Christmas bells.

Nun danket alle Gott shows yet another method. The tune is played in long notes in the treble and the other three parts lead up to each phrase by passages in quicker notes in the manner of a fugue, so that every time a bit of the melody appears in the treble it seems to explain the more complicated music which has just passed in the other parts.

One more example must be our last, and it is worthy to be, for Bach never in his whole life wrote anything more beautiful. It is *Wachet auf*, an arrangement of a movement in the Advent cantata of that name (see p. 113). Again, the chorale is played through in detached phrases, this time in a tenor part (it is the tenors who sing it in the cantata). But there is no complex fuguing to accompany it. Instead, the organist's right hand is employed in playing another beautiful melody which has nothing whatever to do with the chorale and does not seem to have any special descriptive purpose like the ringing bells of *In dulci jubilo*. It has, however, much to do with the words to which it belongs, for it overflows with the spirit of heart-felt joy expressed in

> Zion hört die Wächter singen,
> Das Herz tut ihr vor Freude springen.

There is one other point of view from which this melody must be studied. Its beauty depends chiefly on two features: (1) the rise and fall in pitch of its notes (e.g. the drop of a sixth in the first bar), and (2) the rate at which the notes move (i.e. the contrast of quavers with semiquavers), and the syncopations. Both pitch and rhythm are so perfect that the additions of accents on prominent notes or variations of loudness and softness are scarcely necessary to it. It is, therefore, like so many of Bach's best, a typical organ melody, in spite of the fact that he first wrote it for stringed instruments to play.

CLAVIER MUSIC

With the clavier music—that is to say, music for either the harpsichord or the clavichord—we come to matter which is a good deal easier to understand than some of the questions which the organ music raises. This is because both the instruments called by the name of 'clavier' are much simpler in construction, and therefore produce simpler effects of sound than the organ, and, moreover, their music is so easily transferred to the piano, and sounds so well upon it, that we can appreciate it better than we can the less familiar organ music.

Again, however, we must remember what are the characteristics which distinguish the harpsichord from the clavichord, and both from the piano. When we first mentioned the harpsichord as used in Monteverdi's orchestra (p. 21) we spoke of the short, sharp tone got by plucking the string, and since the plucking was done by the mechanical action of a quill, the player could not control its loudness or softness any more than the organist could control the force of one of his organ stops. In other words, he could not play louder by hitting the keys harder as the pianist can, and he could not hold on a note by holding down the key as an organist can perfectly, and a pianist can to a certain extent. In order to get some varieties of tone, therefore, harpsichords were often made with two manuals like an organ, one loud and one soft, and in some instruments other alterations of the tone were contrived by means of stops, and sometimes pedals were added.

The clavichord, on the other hand, was quite a little instrument which could be carried about easily and stood on a table. Instead of being plucked, its strings were pushed by a little piece of metal called a 'tangent', and though it always produced a very soft sound, so soft that if any one spoke or moved while it was being played you could hardly hear it at all, yet the player could vary the degree of sound by the pressure of his fingers, and so in this most important respect it was more like the piano than any other keyed instrument of the time.

One can see why Bach loved the clavichord. He did not want to play to large numbers of people who fidgetted and made noises as people in drawing-rooms and concert-rooms always do; he played for the love of music and for the pleasure of the few who would sit near him and listen. So he delighted in the gentle little clavichord, the only keyed instrument which could produce the delicate lights and shades of expression.

The pieces included in the two books which together make up the 'Forty-eight Preludes and Fugues' were written at a great many different times and collected together by Bach in two series. The first twenty-four were put together while he was at Köthen, that is, in the time when his energies were particularly concentrated upon instrumental music, and he only finished the second set of twenty-four quite late in life at Leipzig. They are therefore spread out over many years, and if we knew when each was written they would make a sort of musical diary of Bach's thoughts and feelings in the different circumstances of his existence, for they are so full of varied expression that there can be no doubt that they represent very strong personal feeling.

The order in which the pieces are placed depends neither upon the time when they were written nor on artistic considerations of contrast, but on the keys to which they belong. Bach's name for the first collection was 'Das wohltemperirte Klavier' ('The Well-tempered Clavier'), and each pair of pieces, prelude and fugue, is in a different key, major or minor, beginning from C major, followed by C minor, and so on in ascending semitones. The meaning of the rather curious term 'well-tempered' is a simple one. It alludes to the fact that an old-fashioned system of tuning instruments had survived from the time when very little change of key was used, and this system made the instruments beautifully in tune in certain keys, the more usual ones, and quite unbearable in others. A key would be tuned, for instance, to B♭ or F♯ in just intonation, but they would not serve for A♯ and G♭, as they do by the compromise of the tempered scale. Bach realized that such a plan barred the progress of instrumental music, for, as we have seen, much of its progress consisted in the gradual establishment of the key system, and the power which it brought to composers of passing from one key to another. Bach insisted in this work that all keys must be equally available for use, and that the instruments must be tuned or tempered in such a way as to make them so. Bach, then, asserts the freedom of the musician on the very title-page, and in his music he maintained the same attitude fearlessly. The form of each prelude depends solely upon the kind of ideas which have to be expressed; there is no fixed shape to which all conform, as there is in the sonatas of Domenico Scarlatti for example. Sometimes it is possible to analyse them into a number of component parts, e.g. Book I, No. 7, E flat major, which has an impressive introduction followed by a long movement worked out in the organ style of counterpoint, or Book I, No. 10, E minor, which begins with a sustained melody in the right hand, accompanied by a flowing semiquaver figure in the left, and which halfway through suddenly abandons the melody for the sake of developing the accompanying figure into a brilliant presto. Or again, most remarkable of all in point of form, there is the prelude in D major, Book II, No. 5, which is actually in the sonata form of a later age, that of Mozart and Haydn.

More constantly, however, the whole prelude is woven without a break. Bach's modulations are clear and strong, but when he passes to a new key he does not rest there, but his ever-moving melodies and rhythms force one's attention to go forward so that a total impression is left of something indivisible. The actual expression of the preludes is very rich and varied. In the first book, for example, No. 1, C major, is a dreaming succession of beautiful harmonies played with just enough rhythmic interest to give them vitality; No. 4, C sharp minor, springs out of a fragment of melody one bar long, very tender in feeling, which is treated polyphonically by the two hands and extended into a lovely song; No. 5, D major, is a 'moto perpetuo' for the right hand, its rhythm emphasized by the piquant staccato notes of the left hand; and No. 8, E flat minor, is a wonderful romance. Pay special attention to this one. Notice the persistent throbbing chords, three in the bar, and the beauty of the melody added above them. As the piece advances this melody becomes a duet in which both hands take part, and the feeling is made more intense by the use of some unexpected harmonies. Twelve bars before the end the piece seems to be about to close with a cadence, but it is interrupted with a powerful discord, and the melody is continued until four bars from the end a similar point is reached. Again, however, the close is avoided by a strong chord of the seventh, as though Bach could not bear to leave so lovely an idea. This way of expressing deep feeling by means of poignant harmonies was rare (cf. Purcell, pp. 82–83). It was undreamt-of by the older writers, and even Handel rarely tried it, but it is one which later writers, especially Chopin and Wagner, adopted with wonderful results (cf. Chopin's Prelude in E minor, No. 4, and Wagner's prelude to *Tristan*).

The relationship of the preludes to the fugues which follow them is remarkably interesting. In some cases it seems as though Bach wished to correct the impression made by the prelude, and so followed it with a fugue of different character; in other cases the fugue carries on the feeling of the prelude to a further point. As examples of the first look again at Nos. 1, 4, 5, and 8 of the first book; three of them, 1, 4, 8, have preludes which are rather sad and very full of sentiment. They all have fugues particularly strong and virile in style, packed full of devices which need keen thought for their appreciation. The prelude of No. 5, on the other hand, is light-hearted, and perhaps a bit frivolous; Bach gives it a fugue of very sturdy rhythm. This must not be taken to imply that the preludes were thought of first and the fugues after, but simply that he chose to mate these movements according to the law of contrast. The Prelude in E minor, No. 10, on the contrary seems actually to grow up to the fugue. We have already seen how its accompanying figure becomes the chief object of interest, and the fugue subject is only one more step in its development. No. 12 is another good instance of both prelude and fugue building upon the same kind of idea, in this case the effect of a pathetic tune in crotchets combined with semiquavers.

It would be a good exercise of the imaginative faculties to go through some of the fugues playing merely the subject of each in its right tempo and with proper phrasing, and trying to name its character by a single adjective; thus No. 1 is stately, No. 2 playful, No. 3 graceful, No. 4 thoughtful, and No. 5 we have already found to be sturdy. If we go a step farther and ask why they suggest these qualities we find that it is because of special features in their melody or rhythm. The measured rise and fall of No. 1 gives it its stateliness, the little pairs of semiquavers make No. 2 playful, the rise of the sixth after the turn gives grace to No. 3, and that peculiar interval of a diminished fourth, which is so hard to sing accurately, suggests thought in connexion with No. 4. You will find as you study the fugues that generally the character of the subject is thoroughly justified in the working out of the fugue, and that the fresh music added to the subject helps to emphasize the same qualities. The first fugue is so full of its subject that there scarcely seems to be anything else; there is hardly a moment where there is not one part playing it, and towards the end they intertwine so closely that from bar 14 onward all four are playing different parts of the subject at one time. No. 2, on the contrary, is too cheerful for any such serious process. There is no *stretto* at all; instead the subject gets broken up into little fragments which are bandied about between the parts, and added to them are some delicate running semiquaver passages which play hide and seek with the merry subject. Similarly, the grace of No. 3 might be spoilt if Bach indulged in elaborate fugal work, so he avoids it, and instead he presents the subject and the flowing counter-subject in all sorts of new and graceful figures. But with No. 4 he becomes very serious again, for not content with the solemn subject (*a*) with which he begins:

Ex. 33

he afterwards thinks of two more quite independent ones (*b* and *c*), which join with it and appear in a number of relationships.

These are a few indications of the types of variety to be found in the first numbers of the '48'; similar illustrations could be drawn from any other group in either series, and their most marvellous quality of all is the fact that, however well they are known, one can always discover some fresh beauty in them.

The many works by Bach in the form of the suite show us a very different side of his character. The principal ones are a set of six small works called 'French' Suites, another larger set known as the 'English' Suites, and six more called 'Partitas'. The first were written in the book which Bach compiled for his second wife, and they probably got their name from the fact that the pieces are all very concise and are written in the simple forms which Couperin and other French clavecinists had used so well (see pp. 71–73).

Bach did not treat the suite form with the same freedom that Handel did. We saw that except the gigues, which are full of the feeling of the dance, Handel's best pieces were the preludes, fugues, and overtures which he included but which, properly speaking, have nothing to do with the suite as a form. Bach wrote no fugues in his suites, and their beauty for the most part rests upon the characters of the dance-tunes. It was in this respect that he learnt much from the example of Couperin, as can be seen by comparing his 'French' Suites with the pieces of Couperin. Bach did not give his dances descriptive titles as Couperin did, but one cannot hear his suites played without realizing how much trouble he took to make the various pieces of the same name contrast with one another. Compare for example the dignified Sarabande in D minor ('French' Suites, No. 1) with the fairy-like melody of the one in C minor (No. 2), or the plaintive one in G major (No. 5). Again he frequently wrote two minuets in the same suite and always made them contrast very strongly with each other, e.g. the pair in the Suite in B minor, the first of which is light and fluent, the second more wayward and continually changing its key. But the six gigues, one of which ends each suite, show the greatest variety of any. One point in which they are alike is the fact that they all have the rhythm of alternate long and short notes, but this very simple rule admits of countless variations of design. If you look at the Gigue in D minor (No. 1) and then at the one in G major (No. 5) you would scarcely suppose that they represent the same dance. The one in E (No. 6) is most like the straightforward style which Handel learnt from the Italians, and several numbers in the 'English' Suites are like them, but the first three in the 'French' Suites all try rather new experiments in rhythm, and several are so polyphonic as almost to have the effect of fugues. Indeed, Bach's way of combining polyphonic parts with the dance forms is one of the beauties of his suites. Couperin had done this in some instances, but it was a part of Bach's very nature, for he loved the deep tones got by the interweaving parts more than any other type of instrumental effect. Consequently, however much he learnt from the Italians—and he did learn a great deal, especially in writing his concertos—he always gave greater depth of feeling to his work because his mind moved in many directions at once. It was not enough for him to express his musical ideas in clear melodies of definite and balanced form with a substratum of harmony; every detail of harmony was important to him, and every part contributed both to the rhythm and colour of the whole work, whether it were a simple dance-tune or the most elaborate fugue.

CHAMBER MUSIC

Bach's concertos for one or more harpsichords with accompaniment for strings and those for one or more violins might be included under the comprehensive term 'chamber music', for they were not intended for the big concert performances in which we now often hear them. But instead we will draw our examples from the six sonatas for violin and harpsichord, and the six for violin alone. His thorough treatment of details especially in the harpsichord part is perfectly seen in the beautiful slow movements which begin the Sonatas for violin and harpsichord in B minor and E major (Nos. 1 and 3), the two which are most often played. The chief feature of the one in B minor is a tender figure of quavers phrased in pairs. This begins in the right hand of the harpsichord part and is continued while the violin enters with a flowing melody above it. Later on the violin joins in the characteristic figure, playing it in chords. Such a movement would have been quite impossible in a composition in which the details of the harpsichord part were left to the player to devise, as Handel and the Italians left them. It gains all its expressiveness from the way in which the two instruments treat the figure on equal terms. The Adagio of the Sonata in E has another device. Here the two do not develop the same music together, but each has a theme of its own and the two are contrasted. That of the harpsichord consists of a short group of notes constantly repeated and afterwards extended while the violin plays a long free melody full of ornamental and decorative passages. A few places will be found in these sonatas where harmonies are indicated by figures below the bass and not written out in full, but they are so exceptional as to show how little Bach dared to trust to such a casual plan.

The general form of the sonatas is exceedingly free. The movements owe nothing to the traditional dance forms. They bear no titles except Andante, Allegro, &c., which of course are merely indications of the pace at which they are to be played. An exception to this is the movement beginning the Sonata in C minor, called Siciliano, that is to say a dance popular in Sicily, which was like the gigue in rhythm but slower and smoother. The Italian writers used it often in their sonatas, and Bach's use of it, enriching it with beautiful arpeggio figures for the harpsichord, shows how he would adopt their methods and improve upon them.

Nothing is more extraordinary in the style of Bach's instrumental music than the way in which his devotion to organ music affected his work for the violin alone. These two instruments have nothing in common except the power of sustaining tone. The organist, as we saw, cannot make any of the subtle variations of quality which are the chief resource of the violinist; and the violinist has very little of that power of playing in polyphonic parts and producing big chord effects which the organist can command, yet in these sonatas Bach transferred as much as was possible of the organ style to the violin. He could not forgo his rich effects of many moving parts, and he found that even though the violin cannot maintain them, a skilful player can suggest them by rapidly passing from string to string, and by playing on two strings at once. The most celebrated of all his works of the kind is the great chaconne which ends the Sonata in D minor. When this is well played the amount of polyphonic effect is amazing, and the force of the big chords in which the theme is announced, contrasting with the brilliant variations which follow, make it the most wonderful piece ever written for a single violin without accompaniment. The fugues are further examples of Bach's skill in making the effects of organ music adaptable to the violin. Another movement which is often played apart from the sonata to which it belongs is the Gavotte en rondeau from the Sonata in E. This is a French form (cf. Lully's gavotte in *Armide*, p. 68), and of course has nothing to do with organ music, but again the rich harmony which gives almost the effect of a whole band of violins is of the kind which only Bach would have attempted to convey by means of one alone, and the same is true of many of the dance movements in these works.

ORCHESTRAL MUSIC

It would seem that whenever Bach wrote for instruments with which daily use had not made him thoroughly familiar, he was apt to draw upon his experiences as an organist. In writing for the harpsichord or clavichord he was least inclined to do so, for he knew perfectly what they were capable of doing; we know that he played the violin, but he did not live with it as constantly as he did with the keyed instruments, and consequently the organ influence is strong in his solo music for it, and again it is very prominent in his music for the orchestra. This is not surprising since there is much in common between the organ and the orchestra, but the organ is so much more limited than the orchestra that the one is rather misleading as a preparation for the other. Bach had an even keener feeling for the varieties of tone-colour than Handel, and he used all the instruments which Handel used and tried many different ways of combining them. But he was constantly inclined to treat them like so many stops of the organ, and to write the same kind of passage for them all as though they were all played in the same way, and could all manage the same music equally well. It is a disadvantage which serves to show that even he who accomplished so much did not succeed in mastering quite all the problems of musical workmanship, but it does not cloud the glory of the music which he wrote for the orchestra. His chief works of the kind are the six 'Brandenburg' Concertos (so called because they were written for the Margrave of Brandenburg while Bach was at Köthen), and four overtures which are fine examples in the style of Lully's operatic overtures with groups of dances added.

It is most probable that Bach never heard the Brandenburg Concertos played since he presented them to the Margrave, who was one of those people who care more for collecting works of art than for using them when they have got them, and so they were put away in his library and forgotten.

The only feature of these concertos which is like those of the Italians is the fact that in three cases the instruments are divided into the groups of soloists and accompanists, called by the Italians the *concertino* and *ripieno* respectively, but even in this as well as in the choice of instruments for each group Bach allowed his fancy to have free play, and seems to have thought only of what arrangement would express his ideas best in each case. Thus the first is written for a rather large orchestra in which strings, three oboes, bassoon, and two horns take part all on more or less equal terms. The group of solo instruments in the second is very unusual; it consists of a trumpet, a flute, an oboe, and a violin, while a full band of strings form the *ripieno*. No. 3 is for strings only, divided into ten parts, i.e. three violins, three violas, three violoncellos, and a bass, and the contrasts gained between the groups are extraordinarily subtle and beautiful. No. 4 has as its solos a violin and two flutes; No. 5 a harpsichord, a violin, and a flute, both being accompanied by strings, and the last, like the third, consists of an uncommon arrangement of strings, since it is scored only for two violas, two viole da gamba (nowadays generally played as violoncello parts), violoncello, and bass.

The Brandenburg Concertos, as it happens, sound quite

complete without a supporting harpsichord *continuo*, and are usually so played nowadays. But the convention of the time was that all orchestral music of this type, and indeed much else, such as the arias in operas and oratorios for instance, should be supported by a keyboard instrument (in some cases the organ), whether a *continuo* part was provided by the composer or not, and whether he had figured his basses or not. Even where a solo keyboard instrument forms part of a work, as in the fifth Brandenburg Concerto, a supporting harpsichord was still used; and the habit was so strong that even where it was not actually wanted, as here, the *continuo* persisted. Orchestral works as late as Haydn's early symphonies still retained it.

Nos. 2, 3, 4, 5 are all frequently played at concerts, No. 6 more rarely, and No. 1 scarcely ever. Probably the elaborate writing for the horns accounts for the neglect of the first, for Bach seems to have considered that so long as he kept the parts within the possible compass of the instruments the horns should be able to play anything he chose to write for them, and so he requires them to run about with almost the agility of a flute. This concerto also differs from all the others in the fact that added to the usual three movements are some charming dances, a minuet, and *polacca* (i.e. a Polish dance), each with a trio scored for small groups of instruments; the trio to the minuet is for oboes and bassoons only, and that to the *polacca* is for horns and bassoons. They remind one of the kind of music of which Haydn and Mozart afterwards wrote so much as *divertimenti* and serenades.

Unlike the others which have three movements, a slow one between two quick ones, the third Concerto has only two, and both are full of joy and good spirits. The strong pulsing rhythm of the tunes and the way they are divided between the stringed instruments, which at one moment are spread out into ten parts, at another massed together into broad unison passages, gives the impression of bounding energy and happiness.

We will take the second Concerto as our chief example of Bach's orchestral music and look more closely at the score.

There is one point which must be explained at the outset, because it will be met with in all the later orchestral music of Haydn, Mozart, and Beethoven, so it had better be understood at once—i.e. the principle of writing for what are called the 'transposing' instruments of the orchestra. We get an example of it here in the trumpet part placed at the head of the score. The natural trumpets and horns for which Bach wrote are merely tubes without any keys such as oboes possess. All the different notes, therefore, have to be produced by the varying pressure of the player's lip, and the possible notes range over about two octaves, say, middle C to the C above the treble stave. But it is impossible to get all the notes lying between these extremes. In the lower octave only the notes of the common chord, and in the upper octave those of the diatonic scale, but not all the semitones between them, are available. Bach's trumpet part in the first pages of this Concerto shows clearly what notes the trumpet could play. But in order that the trumpets (and horns) might be used in different keys, pieces of tubing called 'crooks' were added so as to transpose this series of notes into the key of the work, in this instance F. In Bach's time, however, composers always wrote as though these instruments were playing in the key of C, since they had only to put on the proper crook at the beginning in order to make it sound in the right key. This was perhaps simpler for the players, but it is harder for us who have to read the score, since we have to remember that the trumpet is not playing the notes written, which of course would sound excruciating, but is really playing in F like the rest of the orchestra. So the first phrase of the trumpet part sounds as here:

Ex. 34

Having disposed of preliminaries we come to the music. All the instruments begin with a brilliant and lively tune of a rhythm which is unforgettable once it is heard. When this is completed the solo violin creeps in with a more gentle theme which becomes the principal one of the soloists, for they all play it in turn with constant interruptions from the string band who burst in with fragments of the first theme. The whole of the first movement consists of these tunes woven together in all sorts of relationships; sometimes the tunes of the four solo instruments are contrasted with one another, sometimes they are massed together to contrast with the strings; at one time the soloists are all rushing about in florid passages while the strings hold long chords, then the violins mutter the rhythm of their chief tune (*piano*) while the soloists play bits of it in a bold *stretto* (*forte*). The trumpet is left out of the tender little slow movement, and the three other soloists with the violoncellos to accompany them have it all to themselves. Here you can see how Bach treats his instruments as if they were organ stops, and indeed the violoncello part suggests the pedals very obviously. Flute, oboe, and violin all develop the lovely melody in the same way, sometimes combining in harmony, but more often in passages which imitate one another very beautifully. Especially notice the delicate effect of the simple phrases of three or four notes which in the latter part are passed from one to the other. The trumpet after being silent for so long leads off the last movement with a merry tune which the others take up and treat in a free fugal manner. The string accompaniment of this is all much lighter than in the first movement; there is little of the intricate weaving of parts, but for the most part the violins play short detached quavers which add sparkle and brightness to the solo music. The whole is full of the sense of fun and jollity carried on to the very last bars where the trumpet begins the tune afresh, the others harmonizing it as though it were going to modulate into the key of B♭, when the music stops abruptly and takes every one by surprise.

These surprises are perhaps the most fascinating things in Bach's music. He knew thoroughly all that other composers in Italy and France had done, and he often chose to work according to their methods, especially as regards the form of his music, but he never bound himself to follow the lead of any one. All through his music one finds these evidences of a fresh and unfettered spirit which are all the more delightful because he never introduced them unless he meant something by them.

Bach's nature was so many-sided that his music touches almost every phase of human feeling from the irresponsible gaiety of this movement or the comicality of *Phoebus and Pan* to the deep sorrow of the Passion music, or the majestic splendour of the Mass in B minor. That is why his music appeals to men of such widely different tastes and ways of thought, so that although musical people differ and even quarrel about the greatness or worth of almost every other composer the name of Bach unites them all.

Suggestions for Further Reading and Listening

THE subjects under discussion in this chapter are covered to some extent in a number of books that have already been mentioned. These include Bukofzer's *Music in the Baroque Era*, Palisca's *Baroque Music*, and A. J. B. Hutchings's *The Baroque Concerto*. To that list should now be added Volume VI of *The New Oxford History of Music*, 'The Growth of Instrumental Music, 1630-1750'.

This is also the moment to introduce R. O. Morris's *The Structure of Music*, pedagogic and admirably clear in its exposition of late seventeenth-century and early eighteenth-century procedures: its dissertation on fugue is excellent. Tovey's *Companion to 'The Art of Fugue'* remains a classic study of a masterpiece; Peter Williams's *Bach Organ Music* ('BBC Music Guide') is a useful account. The handiest modern study of Bach's Brandenburg Concertos is by Norman Carrell, while *Bach's Ornaments* by Walter Emery is essential reading for any performer.

Although this chapter is about instrumental music by two specific composers, the instruments themselves deserve some study. Two valuable paperbacks, one by Robert Donington and the other edited by Anthony Baines, have already been mentioned. They should be supplemented by *The History of Musical Instruments* by

Curt Sachs, a very full and handsomely illustrated volume, by Raymond Russell's *The Harpsichord and Clavichord*, and by Sheila Nelson's *The Violin Family*.

So much of Bach's and Handel's instrumental music is now available on record that recommendations are invidious. As a general rule, readers should concentrate on recordings made in the last ten years or so—since, in fact, the Baroque boom became a commercial as well as a scholarly preoccupation. This should not be construed too literally, however, else it would exclude Casals's playing of the Bach cello suites. On the whole, a great deal of trouble is taken today to achieve authenticity of style and of actual sound. There are indeed soloists, ensembles, and small orchestras who make a point of using baroque-type wind and string instruments. Nevertheless, such purism is not yet a *sine qua non* of Bach and Handel recordings.

On the other hand, it is now rare to find the keyboard music of these composers played on the piano, save, exceptionally by Glenn Gould and, of an earlier generation, Dinu Lipatti. As far as Bach's organ music is concerned, most recordings seek a certain degree of authenticity, either through the use of surviving original instruments or from modern reconstructions.

Although sleeve notes for gramophone records are by no means always above reproach, those intended for baroque instrumental (and vocal) music are generally written by specialists, and can be very helpful.

CHAPTER 7

The Age of the Sonata: a Bird's Eye View

If you compare the first movement of Bach's second Brandenburg Concerto, which we took as our last example of him at the end of the last chapter (pp. 156 ff.), or the first movement of the third Brandenburg Concerto for strings only, which is more often played at concerts, with the first movement of Mozart's Symphony in C called the 'Jupiter' you must be struck by the big difference between them. There is here not only the difference between the minds of two men who naturally express themselves differently, just as no two men, though they speak the same language, will use the same turns of expression and the same tone of voice, but one feels that Bach's concertos and Mozart's symphonies scarcely are the same language. Even when they come near to saying the same thing they say it in such a wholly different way that one exercises one's listening powers in quite another direction when one turns from the concerto to the symphony.

To realize this let us place the first few pages of the F major Concerto (Bach) and the C major Symphony (Mozart) side by side. They have something in common; each begins with a strong rhythm, and so appeals at once to one of the deepest instincts of human nature, the instinct which we took as our starting-point at the beginning of this book (see pp. 1 and 2). It is so strong an instinct that when a composer begins a work by beating out a strong rhythmic pattern he literally makes his audience sit up. They become alert and expectant, and such rhythm is sufficient to excite them even when, as in Mozart's case, it appears stripped of all harmony and without any particular grace of melody.

But now see the difference between the two. Bach is like a runner out for a long cross-country run. He starts with a strong, easy stride, not putting forward his utmost energy in the first bar, but giving the impression that he has plenty in reserve. When after eight bars the solo violin brings in the second idea of the principal theme it does not check the impetus of the rhythm in order to do so; it merely quickens the excitement a little more, and out of the rhythms begun in the first page of the score the four solo instruments (trumpet, flute, oboe, and violin) and the string orchestra shape the whole course of the movement. Look where you will, you cannot find a bar which contradicts the first impulse. This is possible because the first page, simple though its rhythm seemed to be, contained besides the rhythm a number of melodic ideas, each one of which Bach felt when he wrote them could be developed, combined in different ways, and played off against one another, producing all sorts of new situations, now tender, now humorous, or again frankly exulting in strength. Bach more than any other composer reminds one of the Psalmist's description of the sun rejoicing 'as a giant to run his course'.

Mozart, on the other hand, as we have seen, presents his rhythm without any beauty of harmony or grace of melody. The first two bars are merely an emphatic call to attention, and having made his call he breaks off abruptly to introduce quite another idea, a phrase of tender appealing melody played by the first violins and delicately harmonized by the other strings. So the whole basis of his symphony is a direct contrast of ideas. These two are his hero and his heroine, the strong man and the beautiful woman, and for a time they are heard alternately as though speaking in dialogue. Presently a long pause comes (bar 23); then the dialogue is taken up again, but now a third character has appeared. It is a whimsical melody played by the woodwind instruments rising an octave and then falling down the scale with a ripple of gentle laughter which adds quite a fresh line of interest. After these have had their say another scene opens (key G major) with melodies which at first seem to have nothing to do with what went before; one is just beginning to wonder what the connexion may be when the tune, which for the sake of illustration we have called the heroine, is heard moving quietly in the lower instruments, and so taking its part in what is going forward. It becomes more insistent, joining with the other figures which now crowd the score until at last the first rhythm of all, our hero, strikes in just at the climax, and, to carry on the dramatic simile, his arrival closes the first act with the cadence and double bar.

Indeed a comedy by Shakespeare, such as *A Midsummer-Night's Dream* or *Twelfth Night*, is a close parallel to this symphony of Mozart. In Shakespeare we get first scenes in which the different characters are outlined separately, then they are drawn together to produce the complications of the plot. In *A Midsummer-Night's Dream*, Puck making confusion between the pairs of lovers and disturbing with his pranks the actors of 'Pyramus and Thisbe'; in *Twelfth Night*, the complications arising out of the disguise of Viola and the joke at Malvolio's expense; and finally in each comedy come scenes of general explanation and the clearing up of the difficulties. So in Mozart, after the first statement of subjects already described, there comes a period, technically called the **development,** in which the ideas strike across one another, changing from key to key and following out a musical plot of intense interest. In this part of his work Mozart comes nearer to Bach's method than anywhere else, but the great difference is that whereas Mozart is gradually bringing his characters closer together, having shown us their differences first, Bach is gradually moulding his into separate existences from the common rhythmic source in which all share. Finally in Mozart there is what is called the **recapitulation,** in which, like Shakespeare's characters, all the melodies range themselves in their proper order again, all the misunderstandings are cleared away, and all are heard in the principal key of the symphony, C major.

Now that we have realized the big difference between the way in which these two great geniuses worked, we have to look into the history of the time to discover what influences were present to bring about this change in the attitude of the musician towards his art. There is more in it than can be accounted for merely by saying that Bach and Mozart were men of very different characters and that each expressed his outlook upon life in his music. That is true and accounts for much, but each of these men represents more than himself. Each is typical of the musical thought of a certain time, and when we compare their work we find that the current of thought had changed between the time when Bach wrote the Brandenburg Concertos at Köthen, about 1720 (see p. 155), and the year 1788, when Mozart composed the three greatest of his symphonies, of which the 'Jupiter' is the last.

These dates state the distance between Bach and Mozart more fairly than do those of their births and deaths. Bach died in 1750; Mozart was born in 1756, and he was a wonderful child who began to compose as soon as he was old enough to hold a pen. His youthful works came into existence, therefore, only a very few years after the last ones of Bach. But neither Bach's latest compositions nor Mozart's earliest represent their places in the musical history of their time. Bach lived so retired a life after he settled in Leipzig (1723) that his work became separated from the new tendencies which began to stir even in the first half of the eighteenth century, and these tendencies only arrived at maturity in the latest works crowded into the last few years of Mozart's short life. Three years after the 'Jupiter' Symphony was written Mozart died (1791); he was only thirty-five years old, yet his music stands as the pinnacle of the kind of musical thought which was wrought out in the eighteenth century, just as Palestrina's does of that in the sixteenth century. In Mozart's case, however, the achievement is the more amazing, partly because only a few years of life were allotted to him to work in, and partly because music had spread like a great tree into many different branches.

In Palestrina's day the art of making music was like a young sapling growing up straight and true, putting out small branches to the sun, but mostly occupied in developing a single stem, the combination of voices in a beautiful contrapuntal design.

The styles of masses and madrigals did not greatly differ, and their means of expression, normally voices combined without instruments, were the same. The means with which Mozart and his contemporaries had to work were so many that to try to enumerate them is bewildering. There is the combination of the many different kinds of instruments in the orchestra which we outlined when we were describing the music of Bach and Handel (pp. 131 ff); there are all the different kinds of solo instruments and the many ways of using them together, of which the string quartet (two violins, viola, and violoncello) became the most important at this time; there is the music for single instruments like the harpsichord and piano, and of concertos for solo instruments with the orchestra, to say nothing of voices and of all the possible ways of uniting them with instruments; and lastly there is that most puzzling form of art, the opera, in which not only all musical means but the resources of many other arts are brought together.

Mozart worked at all of these and left his stamp upon each of them in the space of about twenty years of active life. One is staggered at the thought of such many-sided achievement. It seems miraculous if we look at his life by itself, full of difficulty, distress, and disappointment as it was, or even if we study his music apart from its surroundings. Taken in conjunction with what was going on around him, however, we find, as we have already found with men like Palestrina, Bach, and Handel, that much of the ground was prepared for him, so that his genius was set free to move easily, and he had not to puzzle over questions of how to express what he had to say.

We are going to trace out in this part the work and the lives of the principal men who contributed to the main progress of the art which made Mozart's work possible, and to do this we must not merely go forward from the point at which we left off at the end of Chapter 6. We must go back a little and pick up some threads in the story which we left on one side in order to follow up the special work of Bach and Handel, and see what some other men were doing in other directions while these two musical giants were following their own courses. For example, we must see what followed upon the work of the Scarlattis and Corelli in Italy and that of Lully in France. We have already studied some of the results of the former in Handel's operas and instrumental concertos (pp. 105, 131 ff.), of the latter in Purcell's instrumental music (p. 83), but these show their influences spreading to the great minds of other countries, Germany and England, and the question arises: what was their effect at home in their own natural surroundings?

A number of great players on the violin and composers of music for it flourished in Italy at the beginning of the eighteenth century; some of them actually pupils of Corelli, while others, of whom Tartini was the most important, owed much indirectly to Corelli's example. The composition of operas, too, went on vigorously in Italy, and though that country did not produce many lasting works of art in the direction of opera, it cultivated the art of operatic singing to a surprising extent. We have already hinted (p. 71) that French opera found a new birth after the death of Lully in the works of J. P. Rameau (born 1683), and from the time when he for the first time produced a complete opera, 1733—that is to say, when Handel was just beginning his oratorio performances in London (see pp. 106 ff.)—Paris became a battle-ground for a series of extraordinary conflicts, in which not only musicians but literary men and artists of all kinds quarrelled desperately as to the best means of presenting opera. A generation later a still greater man, Christoph Willibald Gluck, a German probably of Bohemian origin, fought his fight against the supporters of purely Italian opera in Paris (see pp. 20 and 25), and at the end of the century, even while the terrible political revolution was seething in France, opera was seriously carried on in Paris by the works of Grétry, Méhul, and others.

So great was the commotion caused by the operatic struggles of Paris that we might easily make the mistake of supposing them to be the chief business of music at this time, and imagine Paris to be the centre of European musical life. But keeping

Mozart before us as the man who summed up the highest achievements of the time in his own music, we find that he was little affected by these doings. Their very nature prevented them from having any influence upon his development of the symphony which we have taken to be the culminating triumph of his career, and the greater part of Mozart's operas might, one feels, have come into existence much as they stand even if Gluck had never fought his famous battle for the freedom of dramatic expression in music. Gluck was really before his time, and the benefits which he won were not fully realized until the nineteenth century, so that though we shall describe what he did in this part, we cannot truly estimate him until we come to study the German opera of the nineteenth century, and particularly the work of Richard Wagner.

Meantime we must look elsewhere for the mainspring of those developments which made possible the 'Jupiter' Symphony and its companions, and we shall find it in and around Vienna, the Austrian capital, which was also Gluck's home, but by no means exclusively his musical home.

In tracing the growth of music it is very interesting to notice how the centre of activity changes from country to country at different times. In the seventeenth century most of the big events sprang from Italy; next we saw music spreading through the central states of Germany and reaching its culmination in the works of J. S. Bach, and now a movement begun by Bach's own son, Carl Philipp Emanuel, who lived in the north (Hamburg and Berlin), was carried south and brought to fulfilment in the string quartets, orchestral symphonies, and other works of Joseph Haydn and Mozart.

Nor did it even stop with them, for one of the greatest musicians the world has seen, Ludwig van Beethoven, inherited their way of composition, and some description of his tremendous personality, and of the way in which that personality dominated all that he learnt from them, must end this part of our story. In the third part we shall try to gain a notion of how Beethoven opened up a fresh vista of possibilities to the musicians of the nineteenth century, so that he proved himself to be both a Palestrina and a Monteverdi, a man great enough to bring one kind of thought to perfection and then to show the road which lies beyond its limitations.

Suggestions for Further Reading and Listening

THE composers and topics mentioned in this chapter have in some cases already been introduced or will be discussed—sometimes quite fully—later on. There is therefore little in the way of literature that needs particular mention here. Nevertheless Colles's 'Bird's-eye View' can be supplemented by two books which, because of their general nature, and excellence, may help readers to gain an added sense of perspective. One is Alfred Einstein's amply illustrated *A Short History of Music*; the other *An Illustrated History of World Music* by Marc Pincherle, even more lavishly supplied with pictures. As their titles indicate, their scope ranges far beyond that of the present chapter.

As for gramophone records, it is easy enough to find first-rate versions of, for instance, Bach's Second Brandenburg Concerto and Mozart's 'Jupiter' Symphony, though their use should if possible be backed by miniature scores. (If the bars are not already numbered, it saves time to pencil them in before any detailed study takes place.) If a piano is available, so much the better. It is usually easier and quicker to establish some particular point from the keyboard than from a record. Those who feel confident of their score-reading abilities need no advice. Others may feel happier with ready-made piano reductions. These can often be picked up quite cheaply second-hand, though the copies will probably date from before the era of the radio and the gramophone. The same applies to arrangements for four hands, once to be found in every cultivated household though nowadays in abeyance.

The more rigorous type of music-lover was apt to maintain that passive listening to even the best recorded performance ranked far below a home-made performance, solo or duo. So absolute a distinction is unrealistic. The two activities complement each other.

CHAPTER 8

Instruments

INSTRUMENTS, such as the violin and the piano, are the musician's tools, just as the hammer and the saw are the tools of the carpenter. It generally happens that people invent their tools in the course of their work. For example, thousands of years ago, when men were just beginning to learn to build, they would break a stone by knocking it with a heavier stone. Next they found that quite a light stone could break a heavy one if it was fixed on to the end of a strong piece of wood held in the hand, and so they made a hammer. Similarly someone must have discovered that a piece of iron with a rough edge could cut through wood better than a piece with a smooth edge, and so the saw was invented. But neither the hammer nor the saw was invented because a man set out to make a hammer or a saw, but because he wanted to make something else and found that the hammer and saw would help him to do what he wanted to do. It is just the same with musical instruments. The different ways of making them were discovered in the course of making music; a man would find that he could make better music than had been made before, either by altering his instrument in some detail or by using it in a different way.

THE VIOLIN

The violin, for example, which is one of the simplest and most perfect of instruments, was gradually shaped into its present form by people who found that certain kinds of wood produced a more beautiful sound than other kinds, that a narrow neck with only four strings could be fingered more nimbly by the player than a thick one with six strings, such as the older viols had (see p. 21), and that an instrument with thin ribs could be held more conveniently by the player's chin than the viols with thick ribs could be. By the time that Corelli (see p. 56) lived the best form for the violin was fairly decided upon, but even that great man did not find out all the best ways of using it by any means. For example, he did not use the highest notes of the instrument at all. All the high notes above  are produced by shifting the left hand along the finger-board and stopping the string with the fingers, so that the vibrating part of it becomes shorter and shorter till at last there is only an inch or two left to vibrate, like the very short strings which make the high notes on the piano. Corelli only shifted his hand a little way, generally to what is known as the third position, so that he hardly used the notes above  at all. Later violinists, some of them Corelli's own pupils, found that by altering their way of holding the violin they could reach all these high notes without difficulty, that they could play much more rapidly, and use the bow in the right hand much more freely.

One of the most important changes was recommended by GEMINIANI (1687–1762), a pupil of Corelli, who published a book called *The Art of Playing on the Violin* in 1740. This change was simply that the player should hold his violin on the left side of the tailpiece instead of on the right side. If you take a violin and try to hold it in both ways, you will realize at once what a difference that makes. Holding it on the right side the violin lies almost flat. You have to raise the right arm very high in order to reach the G string at all, and you have to bring the left arm round in a very awkward way in order to use the high notes on the first, or E string. But holding it on the left brings the violin to an angle which is much more practicable for the work which both arms have to do, and so is much less tiring. It was, therefore, a most important step forward in improving the technique of the violin, for it served to place all four strings equally at the command of the bow, and all parts of the strings equally at the command of the left hand.

Geminiani was a most successful teacher, and it is chiefly for what he taught that he is worth remembering now. He was a very great player, and he composed a large quantity of music for the violin; but though you may sometimes hear one of his sonatas played, his actual music is not very important in the history of the art, for it was mostly designed to show how well the instrument could be played, and so was apt to be like the carpentering of a boy who has just got a new set of tools and is more interested in cutting up wood than in making boxes or other useful things. It is a difference which one often finds between the great composers of music, who may, like Corelli and Bach, be great players as well, and the men who merely compose because they happen to be clever players.

Another great violinist who was a much more striking composer than Geminiani was GIUSEPPE TARTINI (1692–1770). He was not a pupil of Corelli, in fact he is generally looked upon as a sort of rival, for he founded a separate school of violin-playing, which set a different ideal before its pupils and cultivated a a different style. This difference of ideal is best understood if we contrast Tartini's most famous composition, the 'Trillo del Diavolo' (Devil's Trill) Sonata, with Corelli's sonatas. It is a work which everyone who goes to concerts may hear, for all the great violinists of the present day play it constantly. In its general shape, its division into four movements alternately slow and quick, even the binary (twofold) form of the first two movements (see p. 57), it follows the general plan which Corelli had made usual in violin sonatas, but there the likeness ends. The stuff of which the music is made is something quite different.

Corelli delighted in inventing graceful and beautiful ideas and then setting them out in a perfectly organized pattern, making the second part balance the first, so that the hearer takes pleasure in the feeling of orderliness which the whole movement gives. Tartini knew that there must be a certain amount of orderliness or arrangement in the plan of any good music, but he was not primarily interested in that. He cared more to make every phrase express the ideas which his mind held. He wanted to make people think and feel what he thought and felt, to hold them spell-bound by the chain of his own vivid imagination.

He told a story about this particular sonata which, even supposing that he made it up after or while he was writing, shows the fanciful working of his keen brain. The story goes that one night he had a dream. The Devil appeared to him and offered to do anything he commanded. Among other things Tartini handed his violin to the Devil and told him to play upon it, whereupon he played a sonata of such wonderful beauty that it surpassed all music which Tartini had ever heard or made. As soon as he awoke, he said, he strove to reproduce the music which he had heard, but he was conscious that what he composed could only dimly reflect the marvels of what he had heard in his dream. The part about the Devil does not very much matter except that Tartini took him, as many other artists from Milton to Goethe have done, as typical of everything which is powerful and lawless and independent. But the important and real thing in the story is that Tartini looked upon his music as an attempt to express something far bigger and grander than could be conveyed by the notes which he wrote. It was not enough for him that the movement should be carefully balanced and rounded off; every detail had to be eloquent and expressive. He made the last two movements, Grave and Allegro, alternate with one another so as to get a direct contrast of mood (cf. Beethoven, p. 327), and further his conviction spurred him on to the discovery of new kinds of violin passage. The trills or shakes in the last movement, the passages of double-stopping (i.e. playing with the bow on two strings at once), the brilliant scales, and other ornaments, are not merely there to show off how clever the player is; they have a purpose beyond that, they are devised to stamp the work with the composer's individuality.

It is with the bow that the violinist gets expression from his music, and consequently it was in the method of using the bow that Tartini most advanced the technique of the violin. His work called *L'arte dell' arco* ('The Art of Bowing') consists of fifty variations upon a gigue by Corelli, and was written to show the many ways in which varieties of phrasing could be got by different styles of bowing. There is also a famous letter which he wrote to one of his pupils in which he shows how all grades of tone from very soft to very loud may be obtained by altering the pressure of the bow upon the string.

This question of expression in violin-playing was very important to the whole advance of music in the earlier part of the eighteenth century because at that time the stringed instruments, of which the violin was the chief, were the only ones which could deal with it successfully. In the music of Bach and Handel we find very few directions about expression beyond the broad distinction *forte* or *piano*, loud or soft.[1] The wind instruments were not capable of making any other distinction, and the harpsichord, which took the place now held by the piano, was not sensitive to the player's touch (see p. 145). On the other hand, the clavichord which had this important capacity was too weak for public use. Only the violin and its companions of the stringed instruments, therefore, could cultivate the sense of intimate musical expression and spur on the players and makers of other instruments to discover ways of producing expressive music by their means.

THE PIANOFORTE

In the birth and development of the pianoforte during the eighteenth century we get the most striking instance of the need for musical expression gradually finding the right tool with which to produce it. It may seem at first sight as though the instrument came into existence before the need was felt, because

[1] The majority of the marks of expression, degrees of tone, and manners of phrasing, found in modern editions of Bach, Handel, and their contemporaries, are merely supplied as suggestions by editors.

it is a well-known fact that J. S. Bach, the greatest musician of the time, thought poorly of the new pianofortes which King Frederick the Great showed him when he went to Potsdam (see p. 97). Not only this, but his son, Carl Philipp Emanuel, who spent much of his life at the court of Frederick, and who, after his father, was for the moment the greatest writer of music for keyed instruments, always preferred the harpsichord to the piano. But we have to remember that a mind used by long practice to getting the very best results from one kind of instrument does not readily feel the need of any other. As a bad workman proverbially complains of his tools, so a superlatively good workman will sometimes prefer an imperfect tool to which he is accustomed. Moreover, the new pianofortes which the elder Bach tried were anything but perfect; they were only the idea of the pianoforte in the rough.

Even Mozart was brought up as a harpsichord player, and until the year 1777 when he happened to come across some of the latest pianos of the maker Stein, at Augsburg, he did not realize what new possibilities of expression they opened for the musician. Long before that date, however, other musicians had felt the need of an instrument which would respond to the pressure of the finger as the violin responds to the pressure of the bow, and it is noteworthy that the first attempts at one were made in Italy just at the time when Corelli's school of violin-playing was coming into prominence, that is to say, at the beginning of the century.

A harpsichord-maker of Florence, named Bartolomeo Cristofori, invented the pianoforte, or 'fortepiano' as it was often called at first, that is to say, an instrument which could play both loud and soft; and some of his instruments were to be found in the house of Ferdinand de' Medici at Florence in 1709. As Ferdinand patronized Handel when he made his youthful visit to Italy (see p. 98), we can have very little doubt that Handel then became acquainted with the new instrument, but probably he was not much impressed by it. At any rate he made no use of it later.

The main difference between the harpsichord and these pianofortes was that the strings of the latter were struck by hammers (those of the former were plucked by quills), so that the degree of tone depended directly upon the amount of force used by the finger in striking the key. And the main difference between them and the clavichord was that the striking hammer was not a part of the key itself as was the tangent of the clavichord (see p. 146). The tangent of the clavichord was just pushed against the string and remained touching it as long as the player's finger remained on the key. That accounted for the feebleness of the sound. But Cristofori's hammers rebounded off the strings, leaving them free to go on vibrating as those of the modern piano do, and so the sound was much fuller and richer.

But this produced several difficulties. In the first place, if the string is free to go on sounding, it will continue after the finger has been taken off the key, so that if you play a scale, all the notes will be sounding together at the end of it. You may easily prove this by playing a scale on the piano and holding down the pedal on the right. Not only do the notes of the scale create a jumble of sound, but the other strings vibrate in sympathy with them. So besides a hammer to make the note there had to be a 'damper' to stop it, a piece of soft cloth which came in contact with the string at the moment when the finger was lifted from the key. Cristofori had discovered this, and his earliest pianos had dampers. Then another requirement was a piece of mechanism to check the rebound of the hammer lest it should touch the key a second time with the force of one blow. Cristofori also devised this 'check', but only in his later specimens. His pianos were all shaped like the harpsichords, roughly speaking the shape of the modern grand pianos.

Other difficulties which had to be met came from the fact that it was necessary to use thicker strings and to stretch them at greater tension when they were to be struck by hammers than when they were to be plucked by quills. This meant the use of a stronger framework, leading eventually to the huge steel frames on which modern pianos are built. The question of how to make the most resonant sound-board, which is to the piano what the 'belly' is to the violin, was the subject of further experiment.

These things are mentioned merely to give a faint suggestion of the numerous questions which had to be solved before Cristofori's invention could be of practical service to artists. Many of them could not be settled finally until the nineteenth century; and even the use of pedals to raise the dampers was not attempted until 1783, when it was the invention of a maker named Stodart. The early actions controlling the hammers, dampers, and 'checks' were naturally imperfect; they gave an uneven touch and were very apt to stick.

It is not surprising then if some men thought the early pianos a clumsy substitute for the simpler and older instruments, and it is obvious that no great school of composition for the piano could come into existence until the preliminary difficulties of construction were cleared away. No ardent romantic spirit could find expression through the keys of the piano as Tartini did through his bow upon the violin until many years later, but when it was ready other features of musical art had been advanced much farther than they were in Tartini's day, so that eventually in the sonatas of Beethoven and in the music of Schumann, Chopin, and many others the piano became the vehicle for a wealth of romantic expression which almost eclipses that of Tartini.

THE STRING QUARTET

The backward state of the piano as a means of expression and the comparatively unsympathetic character of the harpsichord, and even of the organ, had, however, one good result; it forced composers to express their finest musical ideas through several instruments in combination instead of through one alone. The violin was perfect for melody, but obviously imperfect for harmony. It needed Bach's astounding genius even to suggest harmony and polyphony upon the four strings of a single violin (see p. 154), but many composers from Purcell's day onwards (see p. 83) wrote sonatas for two or three stringed instruments together, with or without harpsichord accompaniment. Two violins and a bass (violoncello) was a common choice, the violins playing a duet on equal terms, using similar figures of rhythm, and imitating one another, and the violoncello supplying a prosaic groundwork to the harmony.

Most of the great violinist composers wrote works in this style, but as the larger members of the violin family, the viola and violoncello, became better understood by players, a means of improvement became apparent. A fine player on the violoncello nowadays finds these sonatas dull work, although the violinists find plenty to interest them in their parts. The technique of playing on the violoncello was altogether in a backward state. There were no great solo players upon it in the time of Corelli, and it was not until a Frenchman, Duport (1749–1819), published an essay on the subject quite late in the eighteenth century, that such elementary matters as the best method of fingering and of holding the bow became settled once and for all. It was indeed high time that they should be settled, that the violoncello might take its place as the equal of the violin, for by the time that Duport's essay made its appearance composers were demanding great things of the violoncello. Joseph Haydn had written his early string quartets.

The cultivation of the string quartet was the great improvement upon the old sonatas for strings which has been referred to above. Haydn was not the first person to write a string quartet, but he was the man who made it into a great means of musical expression. It was he who discovered the infinite capacity of four solo stringed instruments of the same quality of tone playing together on equal terms.

The viola, which fills the space between the violins and the violoncello in the quartet, had long been in use in the orchestra. We have already met it in the scores of Handel, Bach, and earlier composers, but several reasons prevailed to keep it in a state of subjection. It is a larger instrument than the violin, but held in the same way between the chin and the left hand. Consequently it is more clumsy to handle, and until the technique of the violin was fairly advanced it seemed impossible to get much music out of the viola. Moreover, there was a good deal of difficulty in determining the size of the instrument, for the ones which produced the best tone with the strings tuned a fifth below those of the violin were altogether too big to be held violin-wise except by a player with unusually long arms. The difficulty led to a convenient compromise in favour of an instrument which is really too small to produce the best effect as a solo instrument, but still fills the place of a tenor violin in the quartet effectively.

We have seen how the homophonic style of harmony (pp. 4, 129) made the middle parts between the tune and the bass which supported it comparatively unimportant, and it followed from this view of music that the middle instruments of the orchestra, and the viola in particular, rarely had anything of great distinction to play. The birth of the string quartet improved its position. While it was buried amongst a number of instruments, and while the middle harmonies were filled up on the harpsichord or organ, composers could neglect it. But when it became one of four solo players much greater work had to be required from it. A quartet, like a racing boat, cannot afford to carry any passengers. The quartet had to be considered as a single instrument fully equipped in each of its parts, each member of it ready to contribute to the expression of the whole by becoming at any moment the leader.

Let us trace the development of the quartet as an instrument by a few examples from Haydn's early works. The long series of his quartets began when he was a young man of about twenty-three years of age and received a most fortunate invitation to visit a certain Viennese gentleman at his country-house at Weinzierl (see p. 192). It was customary for musical amateurs who could afford to do so to keep a small private orchestra of a few stringed and still fewer wind players, and Haydn found such an orchestra at Weinzierl and spent his time in writing music for it. Often these orchestras were so small that the modern distinction between concerted chamber music and orchestral music could not be applied. There might or might not be two or three players to each part. A complete set of strings and a few wind instruments were all the essentials, and it seems probable that Haydn wrote most of these works for strings only merely because the wind players were not very efficient, and he preferred to dispense with their help. Probably it was a matter of indifference to him whether his first quartets were played by four players or by more, the additional players doubling the parts, with double-basses playing the violoncello part an octave lower. He wrote eighteen such works there (now published as Opp. 1–3, i.e. three sets of six), and among them there is one (Op. 1, No. 5, in B flat) which originally had wind parts and ought therefore to be considered as his first symphony.

Any page of this work would illustrate the fact that the two violins have all the fun to themselves; the violoncello supplied an harmonic bass, the viola often plays in octaves with the violoncello or in thirds or tenths above it, and just occasionally, as if for a treat, it is allowed to play some more important figure in thirds or sixths with the second violin. But it never has anything to say which is quite all its own. The general style is well shown in the following example from the middle of the first movement, where the two violins toss a fragment of the first theme playfully from one to the other while the two lower instruments trudge steadily along with repeated quavers, which are necessary to the harmony, but have no interest of their own.

It might just as well have been written for two violins, bass, and harpsichord.

But in those works written for strings only, and which may therefore truly be called quartets, Haydn quickly began to make experiments which brought the true character of each instrument into prominence. When he denied himself the use of wind instruments he naturally began to seek for ways of getting variety of tone from the strings to compensate for the loss of that variety which oboes and horns give. One of the first things he must have realized was that the viola has a richer and 'reedier' tone than the violin, a tone more like that of the oboe on its middle notes. Consequently he began to use that tone as a point of contrast with the violin. Here (Ex. 36) is an extract from the minuet in C (Op. 1, No. 6, second movement), where the violins give out a melody (A), repeated by the viola (B), with the second violin playing below it as an accompaniment. As far as the compass of the instruments is concerned, he might just as well have set the viola to play the accompaniment while the second violin played the tune (B) above it. But he wanted the contrast of tone, or 'colour' as it is often called, which was to be got by the sombre viola echoing the bright first violin.

Ex. 36

And now, to give one further example, which contrasts with that taken from the Symphony in B flat (Op. 1, No. 5), look at these few bars of the Quartet in A (Op. 3, No. 6), where the viola and violoncello assert their freedom by repeating a fragment of the chief tune originally started by the two violins, while the first violin adds a new counterpoint above, and the second violin accompanies in syncopated crotchets.

The point of view has changed from the idea of a solo or duet accompanied by lower instruments to something more like that of the polyphonic writers for voices in which each one may at any moment take the lead. Haydn's quartet is a small commonwealth and not a monarchy.

He carried his development of style considerably farther in his later years, but we may leave it for the moment with a single reference to one work written about a quarter of a century later (1785), the delightful Quartet in D minor (Op. 42). Its Finale actually has many of the qualities of a fugue (see p. 127). The strongly marked subject, with its two long notes descending a fourth and followed by a lively little figure in quicker notes, is played by each instrument in turn, and bandied about between them with complete freedom. The subject itself has a likeness to that of Handel's violin and harpsichord Sonata in A (p. 131, Ex. 29), but its feeling is lighter and more gay. We saw how Handel was feeling after a polyphonic style even when the means at his disposal were one violin and a harpsichord bass. Haydn gradually reached it through his discovery that the string quartet, which he began by using homophonically, was perfectly adapted to the freer method. The two movements are worth comparing.

At the moment, however, we are primarily concerned with instruments, and this peep into Haydn's early quartets is taken to show how he chose out the four stringed instruments from a country orchestra and made them virtually into a new instrument, having a new kind of music all its own, and one of the most beautiful kinds which the wit of man has ever devised.

THE ORCHESTRA

We must end this chapter with a few general remarks about that larger instrument from which the quartet sprang, the orchestra.

All the most important developments of the orchestra up to this time had treated it as an accessory to other things. We have seen Monteverdi bringing together a large orchestra as a means of illustrating the ideas of his operas (p. 22), Alessandro Scarlatti and other operatic composers using it principally to accompany the singers, Corelli and other violinists adopting it as a background to solo instrumental performances, Handel and Bach following the same method in their concertos and adapting its operatic use to their oratorios, Passion music, and cantatas. Now in the hands of such men as Haydn and Mozart it was to inherit a life of its own, and, like the quartet, become an instrument, no longer a servant, but an independent citizen.

In their orchestral music, symphonies, serenades, divertimenti, and cassations (the titles, except the first, are not of great importance), they used the instruments which they found at their disposal, as Haydn did those which he found on his visit to Weinzierl, and as they were often writing either for the private orchestra of some rich patron of the arts, a prince or archbishop, they had, as the saying goes, to cut their coat according to their cloth. The coarser wind instruments like the trumpets and trombones would not be found in orchestras of the *salon*, and indeed, would not blend well with the small bodies of strings retained in these orchestras. The softer horns, which Handel used only for special effects in his theatre orchestra (see p. 133), imperfect though they were, would take the place of brass instruments more satisfactorily. Trombones and trumpets therefore, generally speaking, retired temporarily from the orchestra, and where the latter are found there is no such brilliant writing for them as we saw in Bach's second Brandenburg Concerto. Oboes and bassoons were fairly established as the basis of the woodwind; flutes, because of their soft and beautiful quality, took their places more regularly in the latter part of the century; and at last one more instrument, and the loveliest, was added to this group.

This was the clarinet, a wooden wind instrument in general appearance not unlike the oboe, but quite different in its construction and in its musical effect. It would be futile to try to explain the technical difference without practical illustration, but it may be said that the clarinet is played through a mouthpiece fitted with a single reed; the oboe has a double reed. It is more important to know the difference in sound between the two, and that is still more impossible to explain in words than the difference of construction. The clarinet has the smoother and more liquid tone and a larger compass, which is particularly rich on the lower notes extending to below 'fiddle G', the actual lowest note depending on the pitch in which the instrument is built.

It was known and apparently used for military music long before its introduction into the orchestra. Its invention—if indeed it can be said to have been invented rather than evolved from more primitive instruments of the kind—cannot be attributed to one particular person with any certainty. The clarinet dates from the first years of the eighteenth century and it was at Mannheim on the Rhine that it first became famous in the orchestra. Its world-wide fame began with the accident of its being heard there by Mozart on one of his youthful journeys (see p. 201). The court band of the Elector Palatine was one of the few great orchestras of the day. Its celebrity dated from the time when Stamitz, a famous violinist, was appointed as its leader in 1745, that is the year in which Handel composed *Judas Maccabaeus* to celebrate the battle of Culloden (see p. 110). The latter event is mentioned here merely to recall the fact that the dates which mark musical progress lie very close beside one another. It was only thirty-two years later that Mozart, charmed by the performance of the orchestra, and particularly by the clarinets, wrote a full account of it to his father. He spoke of ten or eleven violins 'on each side' (probably meaning that the total was ten or eleven, and that they were divided into firsts and seconds, sitting on each side of the conductor as in most modern orchestras), four violas, four violoncellos, and four double-basses. The last-named, the biggest kind of fiddle in use, generally played the same music as the violoncellos, but sounded an octave lower. The double-basses were, of course, too heavy to be suitable for chamber music such as the quartet, but are quite essential to give a good deep bass to the orchestra in which there are so many treble instruments.

Mozart's list of the instruments at Mannheim speaks of two flutes, two oboes, two clarinets, four bassoons, and two horns. The greater number of bassoons would be due to a feeling that more bass was needed since all the other woodwind were treble instruments. He also mentions trumpets and drums placed on separate platforms, so that they were evidently treated as extra instruments.

The whole plan serves to show that the ideal of orchestration had changed since the days of Handel and Bach. The players were no longer treated as separate individuals, a certain number of whom might be chosen to play in this movement or in that. They were now rather parts of a great whole, closely combined and dependent upon one another, each one ready to give the right *timbre* or tint of tone at any moment, no one holding the position of supremacy for long. The idea may be made clear by contrast with Handel's orchestration (p. 133), or Bach's (p. 154), and we shall discuss it in greater detail in connexion with the symphonies of Haydn and Mozart (pp. 246 and 257 ff.). We have given a sketch of the chief tools with which these great artists worked, and we may turn now to their lives to see what opportunities they had for using them and with what difficulties they had to contend.

Suggestions for Further Reading and Listening

ANY reasonably well-stocked library will have a number of books in English on instruments. Some of them have already been mentioned, notably Curt Sachs's *The History of Musical Instruments*, Robert Donington's *The Instruments of Music*, and *Musical Instruments*, edited by Anthony Baines. To that list can be added Francis Galpin's *A Textbook of European Instruments* and Anthony Baines's *Woodwind Instruments and their History*. Some twenty years ago, a series of studies of individual instruments was issued under the Ernest Benn imprint, and at the moment of writing a similar series entitled 'Yehudi Menuhin Music Guides' is coming on the market, all written by well known artists and angled towards performance rather than history.

For those interested in orchestration there are classic studies by Berlioz, Rimsky-Korsakov, and indeed Cecil Forsyth, but for general purposes Gordon Jacob's *Orchestral Technique* is still invaluable and so too, in its different but equally practical way, is Walter Piston's *Orchestration*.

The subject of this particular chapter is covered in Adam Carse's *The Orchestra in the 18th Century*. His concern is less with the technicalities of the various instruments than with the how, when, and where of their use.

At the end of the last chapter, a plea was made for illustrations to be given on the piano. That cannot apply to the present chapter, where it is essential to demonstrate 'real' sounds. Baroque music played on baroque instruments has become a recording commonplace, but now there is a growing interest in authenticity of sound in performance of mid and later eighteenth-century music. It is not just a matter of harpsichord, clavichord, fortepiano, and organ, but of strings, wood-wind, and brass as well.

At the same time, it is possible to be too purist. Though there is little to be said for playing the sonatas of Domenico Scarlatti on the piano or for using unsuitably large forces for early Classical and Classical symphonies and concertos, the normal repertory will no doubt continue to be performed, as it is today, on general purpose instruments.

CHAPTER 9

The Lives of Haydn and Mozart

In an earlier part of our story we found two great men born in the same year in towns of central Germany not far from one another; but they never met, and their lives presented a strong contrast both in their circumstances and in the kind of music which each produced (see Chapter 4, 'The Lives of Handel and Bach'). The pair whose names head this chapter give us a contrast of another kind. Haydn was a young man twenty-four years old by the time that Mozart was born, and not only did Mozart get acquainted with Haydn's compositions and admire them and learn much from them, but the two men met personally and each had the strongest respect for the other. Moreover, curiously enough, Haydn outlived Mozart by eighteen years, and in that time profited by what Mozart had done to advance the growth of the art, so that in a sense the elder man was both the master and the pupil of the younger.

In other matters, besides the fact that one had a long life and the other a short one, their careers were very different.

HAYDN'S EARLY LIFE

Joseph Haydn was born on 31 March 1732 at Rohrau, a little village near to Pressburg, almost on the border-line between Lower Austria and Hungary. In mentioning his birthplace we change our scene of action and visit a country which hitherto we have hardly named. The map at the end of Part I showed Vienna away to the south-east of those regions which were regarded as the mainsprings of music because they gave us both Handel and Bach, but meantime the imperial court at Vienna was the centre of a wide artistic culture to which the artists of Italy crowded, and in which the opera flourished under the patronage of the Austrian nobility. But more than that, the neighbourhood of Pressburg produced many notable musicians. The Bach family came from it originally, for Veit Bach, grandfather of Johann Sebastian, was born there. The population contained a great mixture of races, and particularly a large proportion of Croatians, one of the Slavonic races conquered by the Austrians, whose original home was on the eastern coast of the Adriatic.

All the Slavonic peoples have strong musical instincts. The Croatian folk-songs have been collected in recent years, as those of the British Isles have been, and the process has shown a wealth of melody revealing a fund of untaught musical genius, the existence of which was almost as unsuspected by cultivated musicians of the eighteenth century as our English songs were in the nineteenth. There is no doubt that the folk-songs of Croatia stamped their character upon the music of Haydn's later life, but the evidence brought together to show that his family came of Croatian stock is no longer regarded as trustworthy. He had plenty of opportunity, of course, to hear Croatian tunes.

His parents were poor; his father was a wheelwright, his mother had been a cook. Joseph was the second of a large family. One of his younger brothers, Michael, became a musician whose fame would have been wide enough to make the name of Haydn memorable even if Joseph had not lived to make it illustrious, and in a simple way both parents and children were musicians, for though they were not, like the Bach family, devoted to music as their work in life, they loved it as a recreation. Yet it was probably a surprise to Matthias Haydn, the father, when his relative Franck, the schoolmaster of Hainburg, a town not far from Rohrau, noticed little Joseph, then six years old, and declaring him to be exceptionally clever, insisted upon taking him into his school.

Here Haydn began his education, but schools, and especially country schools, in those days were not models of efficiency and care, and Haydn lived a hard life, from which he was rescued at the end of two years by a certain Viennese musician named Reutter, who chanced to visit Hainburg, and discovered that Haydn had an exceptionally pure treble voice. He was therefore carried off to become a choir-boy in St. Stephen's Cathedral in Vienna, and there he remained for eight years. The choir-school taught him to play upon two instruments, the harpsichord and the violin, as well as to sing, and though it gave him no teaching in composition, which was what he most loved, choir-boys necessarily get a good many opportunities of hearing music, especially since the services of a cathedral church in those days included much instrumental music beside that of the organ.

It was indeed as happy a chance as could be wished for which took him to Vienna, and his voice steadily improved until he became the leading solo-boy of the choir. When he had been in the choir for five years his younger brother, Michael, was admitted as a junior boy, but then came the time when Joseph's voice began to break, when the Empress Maria Theresa complained that young Haydn's singing was like the crowing of a cock, and soon Michael had to take his place as solo-boy, and Joseph knew that before long he would have to leave.

When he was sixteen years old the dreadful moment arrived, and was intensified by the fact that he left the choir in disgrace for a silly practical joke, and so lost that chance of friendly help from the choirmaster which he might have looked for in other circumstances.

To go back to his parents at Rohrau would have been to give up his cherished career as a musician, and they were too poor to support him in Vienna. He was therefore as much thrown upon his own resources as Handel had been when he set out for Hamburg. But he was not quite friendless. One friend lent him some money, with which he hired a room to live in, and an harpsichord to practise upon. Another, a bookseller, allowed him to borrow books to improve his education. He acquired a few pupils, and so by one means and another made shift to live. The most important means of self-education was a copy of some of the earlier sonatas for harpsichord by Carl Philipp Emanuel Bach, which came into his possession through his bookseller friend, and which he studied with great earnestness. We shall see presently in what way they guided his efforts (see pp. 223 ff.).

In the next few years his circle of friends was widened by his coming in contact with two men, both holding high positions in the artistic world. These were the Italian poet, Metastasio, who had settled in Vienna, and whose librettos were looked upon both by composers and by people of fashion as the ideal basis for musical setting in opera, and Niccolò Porpora, who was the admired composer of some thirty operas, who had trained many of the greatest singers of his age, and who now in his old age (he was born in 1686, the year after Handel and Bach) was still a fashionable teacher. Haydn happened to lodge in the humbler upper regions of the same house as Metastasio, by whose means he was introduced to Porpora, and though neither of them could be expected to appreciate the genius of a young fellow who as yet had accomplished little, and whose aims were far different from theirs, they were helpful to him in increasing his acquaintance. Porpora gave him employment as his accompanist. In this company he met many distinguished musicians, among them Gluck, who had already risen to popularity by his settings of the librettos of Metastasio for the Opera, and Dittersdorf, a violinist seven years younger than Haydn himself, who was afterwards distinguished as a composer of quartets and symphonies, which owe much to Haydn's influence.

With this society, with constant efforts at composition, and the constant necessity for earning a living, Haydn's time was fully occupied in the years which followed, until the fortunate invitation to visit Weinzierl (see p. 178) presented itself in 1755. It was there that Haydn had his first opportunity of putting his studies into practice by composing music for instruments and testing the result by hearing it played.

When he returned to Vienna in the next year his life became less of a struggle. He was winning for himself a position of his own among the younger musicians of the day; pupils were more anxious to take lessons from him, amateurs more ready to engage him as a player, and his prospects gradually brightened until in 1759 he was offered his first appointment as *Kapellmeister*, or musical director, to a certain Count Morzin. Such appointments, as we have seen in the cases of Bach and Handel, were generally considered to be the best means of livelihood which a musician in Germany or Austria could secure, and they were eagerly sought after. This one yielded only a small salary, but Haydn thought it sufficiently good to justify him in marrying, though, as events proved, it afforded him little security for an income.

His marriage in 1760 to Maria Anna Keller was not a happy event. It is said that he was persuaded to it by the lady's father rather than by his own affection, and it soon became evident that no real sympathy existed between husband and wife. There may have been fault on his side, but when we think how genial and kindly was Haydn's nature, we do not need to read stories of her ill temper to realize that the larger share of blame was hers.

The appointment as *Kapellmeister* to Count Morzin did not last long. The Count had to dismiss his musical retainers soon after Haydn's marriage, but another and better appointment offered in 1761 and proved to be the mainstay of Haydn's career. Prince Paul Anton Esterházy required a second *Kapellmeister* to assist in the direction of the music at his country seat at Eisenstadt, and Haydn was appointed. Though the Prince died in the following year this proved to be no real misfortune for Haydn, for he was succeeded by his brother, Prince Nicolaus, who was a genuine enthusiast for music, who cared for nothing so much as to live quietly in the country and pursue his love of the arts, and who in course of time raised Haydn to the position of chief *Kapellmeister* and gave him every encouragement to develop his powers as a composer.

A great deal has been justly said about the evils of a state of society in which great artists are treated as the domestic servants of men who in everything but worldly position are their inferiors. But the extent to which individuals suffer from the evil depends in the first place upon the outlook of a given period, and secondly upon the characters of the master and the servant. What Haydn wanted was to be left alone. He had a special kind of art to work out, a kind which did not, like the opera or the performances of great players, need to be spurred on by the applause or censure of the world at large. He wanted to find the best way of making instrumental music speak the dreams and joys of his heart; he wanted players always ready to let him hear what he wrote, complete release from the ordinary distractions of daily life, and a measure of sympathy from those with whom he came in contact.

All these things he had in the household at Eisenstadt and later at the large new estate of Esterház which the Prince created on the Neusiedler-See. The Prince was sometimes trying, as princes are apt to be; he required a greater number of pieces to play upon his favourite instrument, the baryton, than Haydn would have thought it worth while to write for anybody but his master, he made inept suggestions about the music for the Mass in his chapel, and he sometimes kept the musicians in the country when they wanted to go home to their families. But Haydn understood the principle of give and take which many artistic people ignore or despise. Where Handel would have raged and hurled his wig upon the floor, or where Wagner would have chafed and written bitter letters about the want or true perception in the wicked world, Haydn's easy temper remained unruffled. He wrote the baryton pieces as rapidly as possible, he answered the complaints about the chapel music with a skilful practical joke, and he gave a delicate hint that musicians sometimes want a holiday by composing the 'Farewell' Symphony, in which each instrument in turn was made to retire from the orchestra, until only two violins were left at the end.

There was little else to disturb him. The move to the palace at Esterház in 1766, short visits with the Prince to Vienna, a fire which burnt the private theatre at Esterház, and the occasional visits of great people requiring special musical celebrations, such as that of the Empress Maria Theresa in 1773, were the only events to break the quiet flow of work. He wrote quartets and symphonies for the Prince's concerts, Masses for the chapel, music for plays and operas in the theatre, and though much, especially in the last-named class of work, was merely directed to the needs of the moment, his pure instrumental music was becoming a treasure-house for a wider world than that of the court of Esterházy. Such contentment has its drawbacks; a nature which never raged could not write a 'Hailstone chorus', nor could one without complaint give us a *Tristan*, but it could and did give us the sunny glow and cheerful humour of the 'Salomon' symphonies.

MOZART'S EARLY LIFE

We may turn here to contrast the very different lot of Mozart. If Haydn in the year after he gained the appointment under Prince Paul heard anything of the little boy of six who then paid his first visit to Vienna as a brilliant child musician, who was watched over and educated by his father, himself a cultured musician, and who was spoken of as a 'little magician' by the Emperor, he must have thought of him as a lucky child, and contrasted such good fortune with the hard one of his own early years. For, as we have seen, at the same age Haydn had been packed off to a rough school and ever after had had to fight his way in life for himself. Later on, however, the position was reversed. We know that when he grew up Mozart made desperate efforts to obtain such an appointment as Haydn possessed under Prince Esterházy, that he was always struggling with poverty, and died worn out with the effort at the age of thirty-five, while Haydn lived to enjoy world-wide fame and an honoured old age.

Wolfgang Amadeus Mozart was born at Salzburg on 27 January 1756. Everything at first marked him out as a favoured individual. The tall and spacious house in one of the best streets of the beautiful town surrounded by mountains and washed by the river Salzach contrasts strikingly enough with the low cottage by the roadside which was Haydn's home.

The parents of the latter were as ignorant as they were well-meaning, but Leopold Mozart, Wolfgang's father, was a musician who not only held a post as violinist to the Archbishop of Salzburg, but who wrote an able treatise on violin-playing which to this day is quoted beside that of Geminiani (see p. 170). His wife was a woman of sound common sense, if no great intelligence. They had several children besides Wolfgang, but only one, a girl a few years older than he, lived to grow up, and the whole life of the parents was centred upon the upbringing of these two.

Leopold Mozart was determined from the first that both should be musicians, and carefully thought out and superintended every detail of their education. The girl was clever, but the boy was a marvel. Before he could write he was composing music. Nothing seemed difficult to him; he took to the harpsichord so readily that when he was only six years old his father determined to take the children on their first tour in order to display their abilities in the chief towns of Bavaria and Austria, particularly Munich and Vienna. At the latter, as has been said, they played to the delight of the Emperor and Empress, and Wolfgang was nicknamed by the one and kissed by the other.

The following year the father undertook a more ambitious scheme, starting through Munich, visiting the chief German towns on the Rhine, travelling westwards till he reached Brussels, and making Paris his ultimate destination. Such journeys in a time when travelling was done by post-chaise, or still more slowly by coach, over roads which we should think execrable, were not undertaken lightly. Nowadays any child who can be advertised as a prodigy is hurried from one European capital to another, to play in Vienna, Paris, London, and Berlin upon the smallest justification. It is one of the penalties which we pay for the existence of the aeroplane. Nothing but an overwhelming belief in the true genius of his children could have induced Leopold Mozart to incur all the danger and expense of such a journey. The children were delicate. In the previous year the tour had been interrupted by Wolfgang catching scarlet fever in Vienna.

The children played at the court of Versailles, were admired and petted in Paris, and it was there that for the first time some of Wolfgang's boyish compositions were printed. Having got so far, it seemed a natural thing to go on and conquer London, and so in the spring of 1764 they arrived and were received by King George III.

At this time music in London was at a low ebb, not so much from lack of good musicians as from lack of good audiences. Thomas Arne, whose songs to words by Shakespeare are still well known, was assiduously composing operas; William Boyce, organist of the Chapel Royal, was writing solid church music. Neither was strong enough to direct the taste of the public into any new channel. The memory of Handel, who had died five years previously, was held in great reverence; there was a general feeling that there never could be another composer to stand beside him, and one-half of the public headed by the King admired everything which at all reflected Handel's style, while the other half cast eagerly about for any new sensation from the Continent.

In this mood Johann Christian Bach, one of the younger sons of J. S. Bach, had been accepted as a shining light. No son of Johann Sebastian could help knowing good music from bad, but Johann Christian was not a genius, only a well-taught man of considerable talent. He gauged London taste accurately, and set himself to amuse it with skilful harpsichord pieces which he played admirably. He is credited with the saying that the difference between his elder brother Carl Philipp Emanuel (see pp. 213–20) and himself was that while Carl Philipp lived to compose, he composed to live. But London society placed a higher value upon him; he was the queen's music-master and the leader of fashionable taste.

Such a man as J. C. Bach could be a valuable friend to the Mozarts, and he seems to have been as genuinely impressed by Wolfgang's extraordinary gifts as were the less critical members of the public. But with the King they needed no advocate, for the two things which appealed most readily to the simple heart of George III were children and music, and the Mozarts gave him both. He was delighted by Wolfgang's playing on the harpsichord and organ, and particularly by his playing at sight of some pieces by Handel and his improvisation upon a bass by the same composer.

In appealing to the wider public Leopold Mozart did not despise the arts of advertisement nor forget in what mould English taste was cast. He worked up the excitement of the sensation-lovers by calling his children 'prodigies of nature', and asked for sympathy on the ground that Handel was their countryman, though the latter claim was to stretch a point from Saxony to Austria, to say nothing of the fact that apart from Handel's naturalization there was nothing German about his music. The design succeeded, London went into ecstasies over the children, and the father's pride was gratified.

Mere sensation soon dies; Leopold Mozart should have carried the children away while it was at its height. He probably mistook it for real appreciation, and it was sufficiently gratifying and lucrative to induce him to stay. Moreover, he presently fell ill himself, so that there could be no question of leaving for a time, and when he recovered he began to find how poor a thing the excitement of the London public was, for in the spring of 1765 it became increasingly difficult to work up an audience for a performance which people had flocked to hear the year before. At last in the summer of that year he determined to leave England, and they started on their return journey, stopping in Holland and at Paris and visiting certain towns in Germany and Switzerland on the way.

The tour had been a great experience for Wolfgang; it had taught him much of the conditions of life in several countries of Europe; he had met and been treated as a friend by distinguished musicians, and all the time he had composed ardently, writing his first symphonies during his father's illness in England. It was a severe tax upon the constitution of a delicate boy; he had been seriously ill on the return journey, and when he got home to Salzburg in November 1766 (he was then between ten and eleven years old), his parents were wise in deciding to relax the strain by keeping him at home in comparative quiet for a time. They projected no more big tours for the next three years, but during that time he made many essays in composition. One important event was the production of his little German opera *Bastien und Bastienne* at a private theatre in Vienna. Another was his appointment as *Konzertmeister* (a less important position than *Kapellmeister*) to the Archbishop of Salzburg, though the post brought him no salary.

His father naturally had his eye upon one country, hitherto unvisited, which, because of all that had come from it in the past, was still looked upon as the true home of music. It was Italy, and in the winter of 1769 he and the boy, aged nearly fourteen, took their way towards Rome. From this time we begin to hear more of Wolfgang as a composer, less of him as a performer. He was passing out of the age when he could be described as a 'prodigy of nature'; his precocity was remarked in his quickness of mind and remarkable feats of memory. One instance of the latter is well known. It was during Holy Week in Rome that he first heard Allegri's beautiful 'Miserere' sung in the Sistine chapel and afterwards wrote it down note for note from memory. You may hear it sung in St. Paul's Cathedral on any Friday during Lent. He also learnt from Martini, a great musical scholar, the art of writing pure vocal counterpoint, an acquirement which he put to splendid uses later.

An opera by him had a certain amount of success at Milan; he was given a taste of the same enthusiasm which Handel had experienced in Italy sixty years before (see p. 98), and on this journey he learnt all that there was to know about the Italian manner of writing fluent and brilliant songs for opera.

The journey closed Mozart's boyhood. He came back to Salzburg with a commission to write another opera for Milan and a reputation which surprised his countrymen. Anyone so sought after by the Italians must, they felt, be a person of consequence; the Empress gave him a commission to compose a work, and other opportunities presented themselves. These things and his service to the Archbishop filled much of his time, but the most important thing for us when we come to the study of his music is that in 1773 he chanced, when visiting Vienna, to meet with some of the quartets of Haydn, and that these so impressed him that he wrote six studies in the same style, and afterwards said that it was from Haydn that he first learnt to write a string quartet.

In the years which followed he composed the dramatic cantata *Il rè pastore* ('The Shepherd King'), the words by Metastasio, some violin concertos, a serenade for orchestra written for a wedding in the family of Sigmund Haffner, burgomaster of Salzburg, and other instrumental music, but his troubles were beginning. A new archbishop reigned at Salzburg, a man as unlike to Haydn's complaisant Prince Esterházy as any patron could be. In the conditions of Mozart's service to this man we see the principle of patronage exercised in the worst possible way. Ecclesiastical patronage is likely to be more pernicious than secular patronage, for the reason that an archbishop has the excuse of his church for making exorbitant demands upon his musicians, although he himself may have no genuine appreciation of their work. This was what happened in the case of Archbishop Hieronymus and Mozart. The former probably realized that he had got an exceptionally able man to work for him; he was determined to get the most out of him and to give in return as little as possible either in actual payment or by allowing him opportunities to pursue his career in a wider sphere than a provincial cathedral town could offer.

Mozart therefore lived in bondage, cut off from the larger interests of his art. There was no opera at Salzburg, no adequate orchestra. He had to content himself with composing Masses and other church music, and occasional instrumental works for the Archbishop's household. He caught eagerly at the chance of composing for the wedding of a burgher's daughter mentioned above, he hailed with joy the invitation to produce a light opera at Munich in 1775, and in the same year welcomed the chance of producing *Il rè pastore* in his own town.

We can imagine how irksome such constraint was to a young man just feeling the strength of his powers and who as a child had been petted and praised in all the courts of Europe. His father too was impatient for bigger successes on the part of the son, and at last both began to press for leave of absence. In 1777 the Archbishop yielded grudgingly, and it was arranged that Mozart should travel with his mother, the father remaining behind as he also was bound to the Archbishop.

Then began another important tour, but quite different in results from the childish ones of which we have written. In October Wolfgang and his mother reached Mannheim, a place which must be remembered as important in Mozart's career and in musical history, for it gave him many new experiences. We have already described the orchestra which he found there (see p. 186) and the enthusiasm over the musical arrangements of the electoral court, particularly the clarinets, expressed in his letter to his father. He made friends with many of the musicians, and particularly with the Weber family, of whom the father of several daughters was a musician at the Opera. It is little wonder that Mozart was attracted first by the singing, then by the person of one of the daughters, Aloysia, and soon found himself head over ears in love with her. It is still less wonder that his father was aghast at his wish to marry at the age of twenty-one, feeling that it would be fatal to the career which he had marked out for his son. Mozart stayed in Mannheim all the winter, but at last he was half persuaded and half compelled to continue his journey to Paris, where alone his father was determined there was fitting opportunity for his powers to display themselves.

Though, as it turned out, the father was right in separating the lovers, he was wrong in supposing that Paris was ready to fall at the feet of his son. Musical Paris was seriously occupied in discussing the rival merits of two operatic composers, Gluck and Piccinni, both foreigners, and had no use for a third. The question behind the discussion was no mere superficial difference of opinion as to which was the better composer, such as had moved the Londoners in the contest between Handel and his rivals (p. 101). It was based upon the question of whether opera in the French language and in a style which appealed especially to French people could hold its own against Italian opera transplanted, language, style, and all to another country (see p. 274). Gluck was the champion of French opera; Piccinni, who years before had written a work which attained to world-wide popularity, was brought by the opposing party to uphold the Italian tradition. The contest could only end in one way, in the triumph of the nationalist party, but until it was decided there was little hope that a third party could get a hearing, and all that this visit did for Mozart was to give him the benefit of studying the original principles of Gluck's operatic style (see p. 288).

He made some new friendships and renewed old ones; among the latter was Johann Christian Bach, who had supported his childish efforts in London. One important work, known as the 'Paris Symphony', of which more later (see p. 247), was written for and performed at the famous 'Concert spirituel'. Except for this one success, however, the record was depressing enough for a young man who was both crossed in love and burning to distinguish himself in art. It was made the more so by a personal grief, the death in Paris of his mother, who had accompanied him on this journey.

After this there seemed to be good reason for returning home, but though he left Paris he lingered on the journey, staying again at Mannheim, although for no particular reason, except that he had tender memories connected with the place, for the court had removed to Munich, and with it had gone the musicians including the Webers. The presence of friends there was instrumental a little later in securing for Mozart the commission to write a grand opera for the Munich Carnival

(*Idomeneo*), but meantime there was nothing for it but Salzburg again and composition, of which he did a great quantity.

When he was in Munich in the early spring of 1781, and *Idomeneo* had been produced and proved an undeniable success, Mozart received a peremptory order to join the Archbishop in Vienna. He had to tear himself away from his success and obey, though there was no clear reason for the order, except that the Archbishop chose to call his servant to him. It proved to be the end of his confinement at Salzburg, however, and that was an improvement of circumstance which was balanced by the fact that the Archbishop's personal behaviour to Mozart became the more insolent and overbearing. It was not long to be borne; a chain of petty refusals to allow Mozart to play in public or at the houses of the nobility, intentional slights put upon him when others admired him, as well as other circumstances, led to several interviews in which Mozart asked to be discharged. The Archbishop responded with abuse which nowadays would sound peculiarly unseemly in the mouth of a cleric, and the scene ended in Mozart's summary dismissal.

It is difficult to realize that a young man of twenty-five years with a brilliant record of musical successes in many countries, who had attracted the favourable notice of the Emperor, and who had been badly treated by a man whom the Emperor hated, could have any difficulty in making his way in Vienna where there existed the most artistic society of the time. Yet so strong was the system of patronage that a musician of the highest order who tried to live unattached to the service of one nobleman might find it difficult to procure a satisfactory living. The career of a public performer on harpsichord or piano (the latter was just beginning to be appreciated) did not command the high fees such artists are accustomed to nowadays; a composer found publication difficult, and to get a work performed at a theatre was almost as hard as it is for an English composer of the present day to get an opera accepted at Covent Garden.

Mozart did secure through the influence of the Emperor the performance of a comic German piece, *Die Entführung aus dem*

Serail ('The Elopement from the Harem'), at a theatre founded for the purpose of producing light opera in German a few years previously, but this corresponded more to the performance of a play with an uncertain future, without necessarily entailing a 'run' such as a modern light opera generally gets.

HAYDN AND MOZART MEET

It was in the winter following his discharge by the Archbishop that Mozart first met Haydn and their lives began to interact upon one another. Haydn had come to Vienna on leave from Esterház for the performance of some of his quartets, and the two great men probably met at the house of a nobleman who had engaged Mozart to play. Haydn was now in middle age; as we have seen, he had fought through the difficulties of youth and declined upon an easy and profitable way of life, in which he was pursuing his natural bent with little interruption. Mozart, after a youth in which his genius had blossomed freely, was feeling the hardships of the world acutely. The genial sympathy of the older man was balm to Mozart, and the more strenuous nature of the younger one was stimulating to Haydn. It may even have struck Haydn that in the quietness of his own life he had missed some of the finer and more sensitive qualities which he found in Mozart's music. Certainly he was humble enough to learn from one who in years might have been his own son, and Mozart was enthusiastic enough to hail with joy the master of the string quartet. They were ripe for an ideal friendship, the effects of which began to appear in their music. Neither could be unduly influenced by the other; each was too firmly established in his own ideals to become the copyist of the other, but both could advance some distance along the lines of the other.

In the following year another event was a spiritual stimulus to Mozart, although it added to his material cares. He tempted fortune by getting married. His wife was not Aloysia, his first love (she had long since shown that her love for him was not deep by marrying someone else), but the younger sister of

Aloysia, Constanze Weber, who was now living in Vienna. Mozart's marriage was another point of contrast with Haydn, for he and his wife were genuinely attached, they shared their joys and their troubles, and they had a large share of the latter. They were always poor, partly through the difficulties which have been described, partly because neither was clever at making the most of what money they had. They lived chiefly in Vienna, making a visit to Salzburg in the year after their marriage, in order that Constanze might get to know Mozart's father and sister, both of whom had played such important parts in his early success. Their life in Vienna consisted largely of the interests of his profession, particularly the subscription concerts which he undertook and for which he composed his concertos for piano and orchestra, one of the most important branches of his composition.

In 1785 Leopold Mozart paid a visit to his son and daughter-in-law, and was comforted for his disappointment for the lack of worldly success by meeting Haydn at their house and hearing the high opinion which he had formed of Mozart's genius. Haydn's words have often been quoted. He turned to Leopold and said, 'I declare before God that your son is the greatest composer that I know either personally or by reputation'. What more could a father want? He went back to Salzburg and never saw his son again, though before he died (in 1787) he had the pleasure of hearing again of Wolfgang's success as a composer in the following way.

In 1786 Mozart's opera *Idomeneo* was performed in Vienna, and made so strong an impression that a writer, Lorenzo da Ponte, asked leave of the Emperor to adapt Beaumarchais's comedy, *Le Mariage de Figaro*, as an Italian opera-book for Mozart. The comedy was a satire upon the habits of court life, which had stirred Europe, and indeed the acting of it by Marie Antoinette, sister of the Emperor Francis Joseph and Queen of France, was one of her daring escapades which helped to precipitate the French Revolution. The Emperor was unwilling to give his consent, but eventually did so, and in da Ponte's hands the play was shorn of a great deal of its satirical wit, and became rather an irresponsible piece of light-hearted fooling.

Le nozze di Figaro ('The Marriage of Figaro') was produced in Vienna with a success which in itself was strong encouragement to Mozart, whose opportunities for producing opera in the capital had been few. But this success was momentary, and as nothing in comparison with the reception which *Figaro* achieved at Prague later in the same year. Prague rejoiced in Mozart with an intensity which Vienna never displayed. It was the capital of an exceedingly musical people, whose taste was less overloaded by the influx of foreign artists than was the taste of the Austrian aristocracy, and that taste leapt up at once to greet the sparkling vivacity of Mozart's comedy.

Nor did the delight stop with *Figaro*. Mozart was a hero; his playing at concerts and especially his improvisation at the piano on themes from *Figaro* kept enthusiasm at a high pitch, and the Symphony in D which he wrote for these concerts, and which is still known as the 'Prague Symphony' (see p. 248), shows in its happy quality how his nature responded to the general influence.

He returned to Vienna since he could not afford to lose touch with its wider musical life, but Prague had not done with him. Another opera was commissioned, and in the autumn of 1787 his masterpiece, *Don Giovanni*, was produced there with equally great acclamation. The story of how the overture to *Don Giovanni* was composed during the night before the first performance, and how Mozart's wife sat by him plying him with hot punch and conversation to keep him awake is often repeated to show the rapidity with which he could compose. But such rapidity was almost common property amongst eighteenth-century composers. It was partly due to the fact that certain musical forms were accepted, and that a man who, like Mozart, had his musical ideas clear in his head, had much less trouble in deciding his means of conveying them to an audience than a modern composer has. The story is an interesting example, however, of a curious habit of mind in Mozart, of which there are many other instances. He would constantly set to work and write sufficient of a new opera to make the whole scheme clear to himself. He then left it, only returning to it just in time to hurry the remaining details on to the paper before the work was heard.

THE END OF MOZART'S CAREER

Don Giovanni was the herald of the most important period in Mozart's career. He had achieved his ambition in opera, he now in 1788 put the crown upon his work as a writer of symphonies. His three most famous symphonies, of which the 'Jupiter' (see pp. 1 ff. and 94) is one, were written in this year. In spite of all these achievements his position remained unsatisfactory. The small post of court composer given him by the Emperor was only sufficient to keep him attached to the Viennese court lest he should be tempted to betake himself elsewhere.

He had, in fact, serious thoughts of trying his fortune in England, of which he kept some happy memories from his youth, and in the next year, 1789, he actually accepted an invitation to visit Berlin, though when he got there and King Frederick William II made him a really generous offer, he could not bring himself to accept it at the price of banishment from Vienna. For us the most interesting experience of Mozart on this journey is one which links him with J. S. Bach. He stopped at Leipzig on the way, made the acquaintance of the cantor, Doles, a pupil of J. S. Bach, at the Thomas Kirche, and played upon the organ. Doles was greatly struck by his playing, and made his choir sing for Mozart's benefit J. S. Bach's motet 'Singet dem Herrn' ('Sing to the Lord') which, like the bulk of Bach's music, was then unknown to musicians outside Leipzig. Mozart, who had already made a study of some of Bach's works in Vienna, exclaimed 'Here is something from which one may still learn', spread out the parts of Bach's motets before him (no scores were to be had) and became absorbed in them.

The only tangible result of the visit to Berlin was a commission to write some string quartets. The rest of Mozart's career on his return to Vienna is merely the record of strenuous efforts in composition, particularly opera, difficulties about money matters constantly increased by the illness of his wife, his own breakdown in health, and finally his piteous death on 5 December 1791. These last years include the comic opera *Così fan tutte*, the performance of which was stopped by the event of the Emperor's death (1790), *Die Zauberflöte*, written for Schikaneder, the manager of a poor theatre in the suburbs of Vienna, and his last bid for public recognition. *La clemenza di Tito*, a grand opera written for the coronation of the new Emperor.

We cannot leave Mozart's life without a mention of the Requiem Mass, which occupied his last hours of work and haunted him in his illness. He had been commissioned to write it by a man who adopted an air of mystery, refusing to tell him from whom the commission came. The reason for the mystery seems to have been an attempt to secure Mozart's work and palm it off as that of someone else. But Mozart in his distraction and with illness upon him looked upon it as a supernatural warning of his own death, and spoke of the Requiem as composed for himself. He left it unfinished, though, according to his custom, he had written enough to show the main design, and he had discussed its detail with his pupil Süssmayr, who eventually finished it.

HAYDN'S LATER LIFE

The death of Prince Nicholas gave Haydn at last the opportunity of accepting the invitations to travel, which for some time past had been pressed upon him by the outer world. Haydn was famous by his compositions, which had spread over Europe though he had remained at Esterház. Several years before, symphonies had been commissioned from him for the famous 'Concert spirituel' in Paris, and he had been asked to compose for the cathedral at Cadiz and had replied in 1785 with the meditation upon 'The Seven Words from the Cross', written in the first place for a small orchestra, without voices.[1]

[1] Arrangements for chorus and orchestra and for string quartet were made later (see p. 264).

Again, in 1787, an emissary from England had come to try to tempt him to London, in order that his works and his person might be made an attraction to the concerts which were being given by the violinist Salomon. To such invitations Haydn gave the excuse that his Prince could not spare him, but when the Prince died and another succeeded him there was no further reason for refusing. The new Prince was not musical; he dismissed the musicians, treating Haydn generously, however, by giving him an enlarged pension.

On 15 December 1790, Haydn at the age of fifty-eight started out upon a new phase of his career. He left Vienna and came straight to England, arriving in London on New Year's Day, 1791.

He found much the same conditions prevailing as regards music which had influenced the career of Mozart as a little boy twenty-seven years before. Handel was enshrined as a great memory, and Londoners looked to the Continent for the continuation of his tradition. Haydn became the man of the hour; he was fêted in London, six of his new symphonies were produced at Salomon's concerts, he was taken to Oxford to be made a Doctor of Music, to Westminster Abbey to hear the oratorios of Handel, and it is reported that when he heard the 'Hallelujah' chorus he exclaimed, 'He is the master of us all'.

His 'Seven Words from the Cross' was performed in the Hanover Square rooms, and having heard it the English public could only hope to turn Haydn into a composer of oratorios.

It was on his return that he stopped at Bonn and first met with a young composer of that town who submitted some work to him for an opinion. The composer was Ludwig van Beethoven, and the acquaintance begun accidentally led to important results, for Beethoven following Haydn to Vienna studied counterpoint and composition with him in the interval between Haydn's first and second visits to London (see p. 302).

The second visit took place in 1794, when six more symphonies were produced by Salomon, when Haydn renewed his impressions of Handel's work, and eventually left London carrying with him an English libretto founded upon Milton's *Paradise Lost*, which had been intended originally for Handel but had been unused.

This was composed by Haydn in Vienna as *The Creation*, the work by which he attained his widest fame during his life, though looking back over the years which have passed since, we realize that it was in his instrumental music that he did his biggest service to his art. One more choral work followed, *The Seasons*, based on Thomson, which in England at any rate had almost as great a vogue at first; but in spite of these distractions Haydn remained true to the simple form of quartet music, and in the years when he was occupied with these things many of his latest and finest quartets (between Opp. 71 and 103) were written.

That is practically all Haydn's story. His old age was spent quietly in Vienna amongst friends who loved him and whom he loved. Unlike Mozart, he saw the full fruits of his labours; he had said his say, persuaded rather than forced the world to listen to him, and, whether he realized it or not, he had handed on the torch to another and a swifter runner, Ludwig van Beethoven. He left no unfinished Requiem behind when he died peacefully on 31 May 1809.

Suggestions for Further Reading and Listening

THIS is a biographical chapter and the emphasis here must fall on books dealing with the lives of Haydn and Mozart rather than their music. Nevertheless, readers should remember that, through the telescope of time, composers of such stature may stand out in almost too sharp relief from their backgrounds. We do well to spare a thought for their innumerable contemporaries, some famous, some unsung, who supply the context in which to evaluate the fortunes and misfortunes of the two masters. In that connection, a topical survey of music and music-making helps us to gain a sense of proportion. Dr. Burney's *Musical Tours in Europe*, for instance, records his fact-finding travels on the Continent in the early 1770s.

They are as readable as they are informative.

The best biographies of Haydn are by Geiringer, *Haydn, a Creative Life*, and by Rosemary Hughes in the 'Master Musicians' series. Those wishing to follow up the composer's non-musical writings are directed towards *The Collected Correspondence and London Notebooks of Josef Haydn*, edited by H. C. Robbins Landon. *Haydn, his Life and Times*, by Neil Butterworth, comes into the category of coffee-table books, but covers the ground comprehensively and is unusual in the amount of space it devotes to Haydn's operatic ventures.

The standard biography of Mozart was by Otto Jahn, subsequently heavily revised by Hermann Abert, but in English Alfred Einstein's *Mozart: His Character, His Work* has become a classic and is constantly referred to by other writers. Eric Blom's *Mozart* in the 'Master Musicians' series has done yeoman service, but over the decades it has become dated. For an insight into the workings of Mozart's mind—sometimes a disconcerting experience—consult *The Letters of Mozart and his Family*, edited by Emily Anderson.

CHAPTER 10

Sonata Form

WE first came face to face with the sonata at an early stage of our study when we were describing the style of Corelli's violin music (p. 56), but even then the name was not a new thing in music. We have had to use it constantly since then. Purcell, Domenico Scarlatti, J. S. Bach, Tartini, and practically all composers who were much concerned with music for instruments alone made use of it, but if you have heard or played a number of their works you must have felt a certain amount of confusion in the way they used the same name to describe a number of very different kinds of music. What is there in common, for example, between Purcell's 'Golden Sonata', Scarlatti's well-known harpsichord Sonata in A, the instrumental movement for flutes and *viole da gamba* called 'Sonata' (see p. 111) with which J. S. Bach begins the cantata *Gottes Zeit*, and Tartini's 'Devil's Trill' (see p. 172)? Nothing, save the fact that they are all music for instruments without voices or words; music, that is to say, which speaks with a voice of its own and cannot be explained by any poem or story or thought put into words, even though, as in the cases of Bach and Tartini, such thought was actually present with the composer when he wrote.

But this attitude in common is enough to explain the meaning of the word 'sonata'; it comes, of course, originally from the Latin (*sono*, to sound), and composers used it whenever they were most anxious to fix attention upon the sound itself, as though to say to their hearers, 'Set yourselves free from thoughts of language; live for the time being in pure sound, and let us join hands by its means'. So the sonata might, and still may, take any shape, so long as its shape is justified in the music, without reference to things which lie beyond music and need description in words to make them reasonable. Very often composers have used in sonatas ways of expressing themselves which they first found out in connexion with words or drama, but when they do so successfully it is because they have found that those ways have a musical power of their own and are therefore strong enough to discard the help of words and drama.

VOCAL METHODS IN SONATAS

Take, for example the case of Carl Philipp Emanuel Bach's Sonata in F, the first of the six which he dedicated to the King of Prussia. The slow movement is made up of an aria and recitative alternating with one another.

Ex. 38

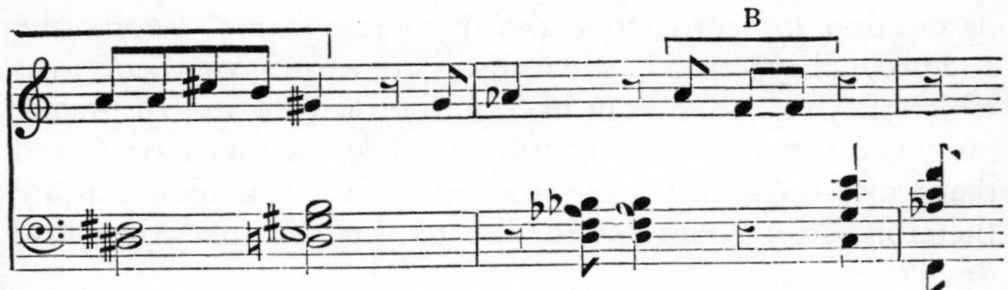

These few bars show the two types, and after the example given, the aria style of the first three bars is taken up again to be interrupted after three more bars by another passage of recitative. This recitative seems to be meant for a voice to sing, indeed at first sight the only sense of the repeated notes on the first beats of the bars (marked *) seems to be that the imaginary singer has two syllables to sing. The whole movement may be compared with the last but one in J. S. Bach's Passion Music according to St. Matthew where the solo voices sing phrases of recitative in contrast with the chorus corresponding to the aria part of this movement. Look at a fragment of recitative from that and you see the phrases taking the same shape for the sake of the words.[1]

Ex. 39

[1] English words are quoted here for the sake of clearness, but their accentuation is that of the German text which J. S. Bach set.

Or, again, compare the phrase marked A in Ex. 38 with J. S. Bach's 'Come then, our voices let us raise' in the *Christmas Oratorio* (Part II, recitative before the last chorale) and you find a very similar idea springing straight from the words.

Carl Philipp, then, was using merely a dead mannerism in his harpsichord sonata unless we can find that these recitative phrases have a rhythm and life of their own. The phrase A certainly has that, and even the repeated notes (marked with asterisks) help to keep a feeling of agitated movement, which would be lost if you played the passage as though they were crotchets. But the little cadence figure B, and still more his insistence upon it, at the end of the second passage of recitative,

Ex. 40

is inclined to be absurd except by reference to a voice.

One feels that he has not been able quite to rise above the association of ideas, but that does not make him wrong in bringing recitative into use as a part of the sonata. Haydn followed his example in more than one instance, in the symphony called 'Le Midi' and again in the slow movement of his Quartet in G minor (Op. 17, No. 5), which is planned on a precisely similar principle of alternating aria and recitative. A passage from that movement is so striking that it must be quoted here for purposes of comparison with Carl Philipp's recitative. In the rising phrases for the first violin (Ex. 41), each one beginning on a higher note than the last, that which was a copy of the voice is gradually driven out and its place taken by pure instrumental effect. The dramatic feeling is kept and even heightened, but there is no hint of artificiality.

Ex. 41

While we are touching on this subject of instrumental recitative it is worth while to turn also to Beethoven's piano Sonata in D minor (Op. 31, No. 2), where you will find him acting upon the same notion,[1] and doing it with phrases which have such complete eloquence in themselves that you need no memory of the singing voice to explain them.

[1] The instance which carries out the idea to its logical conclusion is, of course, that of the violoncellos and basses in the finale of Beethoven's ninth Symphony. There, however, the intention is that the instruments should, as it were, strain to reach the articulate speech of the human voice, which is consummated with the entrance of the bass voice singing 'O Freunde, nicht diese Töne'.

This, however, is a digression; the movement before us is a good illustration of the fact that Carl Philipp, who did more than any man to direct the free idea of the sonata into certain definite forms during the eighteenth century, could yet step out boldly in other directions when he had a mind to do so. We cannot get away from the fact that the broad idea of a sonata as an essay in pure sound became narrowed at this time to mean an essay of a particular kind and shape, and that the narrowing process was largely due to the influence of Carl Philipp.

C. P. E. BACH'S HARPSICHORD SONATAS

CARL PHILIPP EMANUEL BACH was born in 1714 (the year of Gluck's birth), when his father was organist to the Duke of Saxe-Weimar (see p. 96), and he had the immense value of J. S. Bach's training in music. The single example of his music given above (Ex. 38) is one out of many which show how strong was his father's influence upon him, but, unlike many sons of great artists, he was not overwhelmed by that influence. He had it in him to accomplish something which, though not at all as great as his father's work, was distinct from it and therefore of lasting value to the art. Indeed, so valuable was the music to the time in which he lived, and so little had people appreciated the magnificent genius of J. S. Bach, that for a time the son even seemed to be the greater man of the two.

When he was established at the court of the King of Prussia in Berlin (1738) he devoted himself very largely to playing upon and writing for the harpsichord, and it was here that he began to write his long series of sonatas. From the first he adopted the three-movement form as opposed to the old four-movement form (a slow and quick movement alternately), and the six published in 1742, from which our example above was taken, all have one slow movement standing between two quick ones.

The style of the music, in the quick movements at any rate, can be understood to some extent by turning back to the distinctions which we drew between binary and ternary forms in connexion with the sonatas of Corelli and the arias of Scarlatti (pp. 57 and 55). Most instrumental writing, in suites, sonatas, and other pieces not founded upon the fugue, had taken its shape from these simple ideas of balance, either one half of a movement being matched by the second half (binary), or one idea leading to a second which in turn was succeeded by a repetition of the first (ternary).

Carl Philipp's allegro movements in these sonatas were a combination of the two. An idea or chain of ideas is started at the outset in, let us say, the key of F (the key of the first sonata in this set). While this chain of ideas (short rhythmic figures scarcely long enough to be called a tune) is being followed out the music gradually changes its key to that of C (the dominant); the modulation is dwelt upon sufficiently to make it quite clear that the change is a definite one, the last link in the chain is altogether in the new key, and the music comes to a halt with a full cadence and a double bar in the printed score.

Now to complete the movement in a strict binary form the logical thing to do would be to pass over the same chain of ideas again, beginning with the first in the new key, in this instance C, and arriving at the last in the original key of F. But such a logical process would be terribly mechanical, and, moreover, the change of key back again could not be made uniformly. Carl Philipp begins his second half as though he were going to be as logical as possible, that is to say he gives us the first of his ideas in the key of C, but from that point he leads off to new and delightful ventures as regards both key and the rhythmic ideas. For instance, in the sonata in F he turns his first idea (Ex. 42 *a*) upside down and passes by means of its extension (Ex. 42 *b*) to the keys of B flat and D minor,

Ex. 42

giving a new middle section which brings us back again to the key of F.

From that point he proceeds to pass his chain of ideas before us again, generally rather compressing the first and chief of them because he has already dealt with that fully in the middle section, and hurrying on to the later ones, which before were emphasizing the new key of the dominant, but now re-establish the principal one, the tonic. The whole second part from the double bar to the end is therefore a good deal longer than the first part (from the beginning up to the double bar), because it contains both a middle section in which the chief theme is developed, and a recapitulation in which the other themes are passed in review and the principal key established to make us feel quite at home again after the journeys into foreign keys on which the composer has carried us.

Our feeling that it is a ternary form all depends upon how far we are taken both in new material and new keys in the middle, and so in Carl Philipp's earlier sonatas it is not always quite clear which scheme of balance (binary or ternary) is his real foundation.

Sometimes we feel that he attempts experiments which throw him off his balance. One very interesting one is found in the first movement of the third sonata, in E major, where he starts with a beautiful melody and indulges in a particularly expressive modulation into the key of G major. From this he has to recover in order to reach the dominant key (B major) which is the aim of his first part. When we look to see whether he will reproduce this G major modulation in the last part, or recapitulation, we find that he approaches it and then, apparently thinking that it will complicate matters too much, avoids it at the last moment, and so leaves us feeling that the beginning of the movement was finer than its ending, a serious mistake.

But it is an old saying that a man who makes no mistakes makes nothing, and Carl Philipp was making a new kind of music from which very great things were to come. The mistake in the plan of the E major Sonata is more instructive than many instances where the plan is perfectly carried out but is a less ambitious one.

It is easy to see that this kind of writing had great possibilities. In the first place the ideas themselves could be made far more distinctive than those of Carl Philipp's early work. Instead of a little two-bar phrase of no particular character like that of Ex. 42 (*a*), the first idea might be a tune of exquisite beauty like that of Mozart's Symphony in E flat (see p. 251), or a phrase of four incisive notes like the opening of Beethoven's Symphony in C minor (see p. 333), and these things were to come when the general scheme was sufficiently mastered for composers to be able to handle such ideas consistently.

Then also the questions arise: why should the first idea be of such paramount importance as to claim the middle section for itself, and why should not all the others be more than mere links in a chain, have an individuality of their own, and play some part in that important middle section? Carl Philipp himself answered that question, and we soon find him using the later ideas of his first part as matter for development in the middle, even though they did not appear very important on their first appearance. He does this in both the first and last movements of the sonata in E major already alluded to.

At the same time he often reaches farthest towards positive beauty of feeling when he is not working with the new form, but for the moment is writing more in the polyphonic style of his father. The slow movement of the Sonata in E, written like a trio for three instruments, is a perfect gem, woven out of one very simple theme in which continual variety is found in the way it is passed from part to part in a polyphonic style. It might have come from one of J. S. Bach's own concertos. Generally speaking, one may find the reflection of the father in the slow movements of the son, while in the quick movements, first and last, Carl Philipp gives rein to his own invention and enterprise. His music, then, shows us the transition of style described in the first chapter.

HAYDN'S EARLY QUARTETS

It was this spirit of enterprise which captivated Haydn when as a poor boy in Vienna he chanced to come across a copy of these sonatas. When we say that he took them as models for his own early works, in particular the Weinzierl quartets, we do not mean that he copied them in the sense of trying to write music like them. There is in fact no likeness between Haydn's quartets (Opp. 1–3) and C. P. E. Bach's sonatas comparable to the likeness existing between the recitative of the two Bachs quoted at the beginning of this chapter. That last may be called a family likeness in music.

Haydn was of a wholly different breed; different in character, nationality, and religion. He was quite untouched by the intimate and serious influence of Protestant church music which permeated the art of J. S. Bach and in which C. P. E. Bach passed his early days at Leipzig. Even his difficulties in life had done nothing to cloud his happy, sunlit nature, and at once it showed itself in his music, making his melodies flow with a suppleness which contrasts strangely with the more severe and sometimes angular style of C. P. E. Bach.

Haydn's first quartet (Op. 1, in B flat), written on the lines of a sonata for strings, brings us at once into a fresh atmosphere. At the beginning of its first movement all four instruments dance merrily up an arpeggio of the key chord (Ex. 43*a*), and the figure which crowns the phrase (marked A) is the mainspring of the whole movement. It is turned about in many ways and presently extended into the dashing downward arpeggio (Ex.

43*b*). Each phrase is so closely linked to its companions that one cannot mark any point of direct contrast. The music flows joyously along from first to last. Nevertheless, if we look close at the first movement and insist upon breaking it up into component parts, we see that it falls into the three sections, (1) statement of ideas modulating to the dominant key, (2) development from them, and (3) restatement ending in the tonic key, which we have seen was the groundwork of C. P. E. Bach's form.

Haydn brought one new feature into the scheme simply because he loved it. That was the **minuet,** a dance already familiar in the older instrumental suites. In Haydn's hands the minuet brought in an element of pure grace and delicate humour which was lacking in the three-movement sonatas of C. P. E. Bach.

At first he was lavish in his use of it. It was an old custom to write minuets in pairs, the second being followed by a repetition of the first (making together a sort of ternary form), and Haydn adopted this, designing the second as a contrast to the first, both in key and subject-matter, and calling it a **trio,** though the name, derived from older dance forms, the contrast sections of which were written strictly in three parts, no longer has clear meaning in this connexion. He was not content with one minuet and trio, but in the Weinzierl Quartets he generally wrote two, making five movements in all. In the first the order is: (1) Presto, (2) Minuet and Trio, (3) Adagio, (4) Minuet and Trio, (5) Presto.

Later, however, as the first and last movements grew in importance and length, he was content with one minuet and trio, at first placing it before the slow movement, but later on reversing the order when occasion offered. In a Quartet in C (Op. 20, No. 2), for example, a bold and restless slow movement in C minor ends, not with a complete close in the key, but with a cadence on its dominant (G), after which the smooth measure of the minuet in the major key steals in at once with indescribably beautiful effect.

Haydn never tied himself down to a fixed order of the movements. In the Weinzierl Quartets he made experiments, such as putting the slow movement first and saving the more vigorous feeling of the allegro for a later stage (cf. Beethoven's Sonata, Op. 27, No. 2, p. 326). The one in D major (Op. 1, No. 3) begins with an adagio, a duet for two violins with viola and violoncello accompaniment (we have already explained the prevalence of this manner of writing, p. 179), which in plan suggests a combination of the sonata form of C. P. E. Bach with a florid Italian aria. But probably Haydn felt the want of contrast in arranging five movements thus: (1) Adagio, (2) Minuet, (3) Presto, (4) Minuet, (5) Presto, for both minuets and presto movements were at this time very slight, and he had not yet discovered, as he did later on, how they might be elaborated in design without losing their crispness. Sometimes he would substitute an air with variations for the more customary sonata movement, and in one case (Op. 2, No. 3) he tried the curious plan of adding three variations to one of the minuets.

These things show Haydn keenly alive to the need for getting complete control of his material and ready to launch out into any scheme which would serve his purpose, although frequently he found that the normal plan of an allegro, a minuet, an adagio, and a final quick movement of lighter character than the first allegro offered all the scope he needed.

In the quartets written at about the time that he took up his service with the Esterházy family (Opp. 9, 17, and 20) we find that he made less attempt to vary the order of his movements, but concentrated more upon giving distinct character to the music, and particularly aimed at developing the features of the form more fully.

To see how far his art has matured let us look more closely into the first of the six quartets which make Op. 17 (in E major). Here three movements, all except the minuet, take their shape from the form which C. P. E. Bach designed in his harpsichord sonatas, but in each one there is much more melodic matter and the treatment of the detail is much fuller than anything in C. P. E. Bach's early sonatas or in Haydn's Weinzierl Quartets. The first movement begins with a little phrase of six notes (Ex. 44), which in itself is not more significant than that quoted from

Ex. 44

C. P. E. Bach's Sonata in F (Ex. 42 *a*). But see how perfectly Haydn has moulded it in six bars into a melody full of rhythmic beauty, rising to a climax where it reaches the higher E in the fourth bar, and completed with a cadence. What at first might have been a chance phrase by anybody has become in a small space something which is stamped with the character of its composer. The same phrase (Ex. 44) is used for a restart, but now with very different results, for instead of further emphasizing its prim shape, it is extended to freer forms till it is succeeded by another melody modulating to the dominant key (B major), the first violin part rising with excited shakes to a high note, E, from which it sinks in a scale passage, growing softer as it descends.

Here several new ideas follow, all in the key of B major. Haydn no longer felt it to be sufficiently interesting to pass from one key to another; the interest depends upon what happens when the passage has been made. To a child going in a train is sufficiently exciting in itself to make a journey good fun, but a grown-up person generally thinks it hardly worth while unless he has something to do at the end of the journey. Haydn's interest in musical modulation was by this time like that of the grown-up person travelling. He made his journey with distinct purpose, and so instead of coming at once to the double bar and beginning the return journey, he gives us a series of fresh impressions.

The most important in this case is the passage which rises steeply to a climax on a high note, stops short impressively, and then finishes with a light, soft phrase, like the laugh of a person who says, 'You thought me very serious, but I am not so really'. The laughter in Haydn's music is the most genial thing in the world. This is done twice, but not in the same way, for that would be as fatuous as to repeat a joke. The second time the ending is delayed by a passage which seems to be modulating back to the key of E, though it does not actually do so.

This part of a sonata movement has now earned the name of the second subject, because its ideas are intended to be a direct contrast to those of the first or opening subject. In the early works of C. P. E. Bach and Haydn there either was no such direct contrast, or else it was there merely incidentally and meant comparatively little in the scheme (see p. 218). The growth in the importance of the second subject was one of the most distinctive features of what Haydn and Mozart achieved in the sonata form.

Just before the double bar at the end of the exposition in this quartet there is some allusion to the rhythm of the first subject (Ex. 44) in order to prepare the mind for what is coming. In the middle section (or development) its rhythm is all-important. There is one very striking point where the music breaks off sharply on a chord of A, followed by a quiet modulating passage ending on the dominant of E, and then the figure of the first subject (Ex. 44) strikes in loudly in the original key. One might well think that now we have made the return journey and are back at the starting-point, beginning the recapitulation. But not at all: Haydn is fooling us. Instead of going on with the whole six-bar melody, he breaks off into further ramifications, using the figure of Ex. 44 as the basis. Only when another climax has been reached does the real return come.

He could not possibly have played this prank successfully if he had not given definite shape to the six-bar melody at the outset, so that we should not feel it to be a real return until the whole of it was played. The rest of the movement is all repetition, the second subject of course now coming in the tonic key of E.

Let us turn to another quartet in the same set (Op. 17, No. 6, in D major), because Haydn's treatment of the form there contrasts in an interesting way with the one we have been studying. It has been shown that the chief subject of the first movement of this work is a variation on a Croatian folk-song. It is a happy-hearted melody in 6/8 time, originally a spring song, which Haydn has made still more exhilarating by the additional notes and his phrasing for the bow of the violin.

One cannot say whether he consciously adopted it and the many other tunes of the same kind which one finds in his music, or whether without knowing it he naturally reverted to songs and dance-tunes which he had heard at home as a boy, but that does not matter very much. We can say that this tune was a part of his very being, for once he has started upon it he seems quite unable to leave it. Its rhythm pervades the whole movement from beginning to end. Even when he has modulated to a new key and one expects the contrast of a second subject, it pops up its head again in the key of A with almost impudent persistence. The fun is emphasized by the fact that Haydn takes an unusually roundabout way of getting from the tonic to the dominant, modulating first into A minor then into C major, as though he meant to shake the tune off by running far from the usual path, but it was too strong to be resisted. So he evades the obvious means of contrast in sonata form, but with a very distinct and wholly delightful purpose in view.

We must notice, too, in contradistinction to C. P. E. Bach's Sonata in E (see p. 219) that Haydn is quite equal to using this roundabout modulation consistently, for in the recapitulation he turns by way of D minor to F major and so back to the tonic key in place of the dominant, getting the perfect balance which C. P. E. Bach missed.

While we have this quartet before us a general word may be said about Haydn's finales. This one, like very many others, is a Presto in 2/4 time, with a very strongly marked rhythm of quavers and semiquavers. All the movements of this kind seem to be connected with a popular Slavonic dance called the 'Kolo', which must have been very familiar to Haydn from his memories of home and from its performance by the peasants colonized at Eisenstadt. Some of his finales take the actual tunes of this dance for their themes, but even when there is no evidence of this, the spirit of the dance is the motive power of the whole thing, and in these movements Haydn produced music which is unlike anything which comes from Western Europe. The rhythm is much more sharply cut than that of the gigue, which constantly had the last word in the suites of the time ranging from Corelli to J. S. Bach and Handel. It is so simple that some of the tunes seem almost childish, but they are never dull, for the spirit of health and frank merriment pervades them, and the themes are bandied about from one instrument to another with entrancing lightness and grace. Generally the form follows that which has been described in the first movements, but with less feeling of responsibility. Contrast is not so essential when the listener is caught up in the whirl of the dance, and there is no stopping for breath until all is over.

So far we have seen the special style, known from the eighteenth century onward as 'Sonata form', taking general shape in the first harpsichord sonatas of C. P. E. Bach and becoming more articulate in detail and more comprehensive in expression through the quartets of Haydn. If we never study the form as a thing apart from the music, we shall avoid the fatal mistake of supposing that the form governs the music, and that therefore all sonatas are very much alike. That is only true of bad composers or the inferior work of good ones. For when a man has nothing that he is very anxious to express he finds it convenient to take a recognized pattern and work in accordance with it. One finds the process continually going on in the work of poets who turn out sonnets, and painters who reproduce the subject of the Holy Family, as well as composers who write sonatas in quantities. Their work is bad because they put the cart before the horse and think of their form first and their matter afterwards.

But in the examples from the first and last quartets of Haydn's

Opus 17 we have seen, if we have studied intelligently, that the matter in hand changed the whole complexion of the form to suit itself, and that each new thought modified the form, so that it was by the need to get something said that the form became more pliable and fit to express the composer's feeling. Whenever an artist, be he musician, painter, or poet, finds that his form is governing his thought, he must break away from his associations and shape its expression in some other way if his art is to be true and living.

It is not necessary in order to place Haydn and Mozart on the pinnacles of fame to declare that their whole treatment of sonata form was of the ideal kind. On the contrary, we shall realize the height they reached all the better if we distinguish clearly between the things which placed them there and those which count for comparatively little in their development. Haydn's quartets, Op. 17, were probably the ones which Mozart first met with in Vienna, and which stimulated him to write on similar lines, but the ones which Mozart wrote as the immediate result of his experience were not destined to be famous, because they were chiefly essays in style. Later on, Mozart composed ten quartets, six of which he dedicated to Haydn as a sign of his gratitude, but they are much less recognizably like Haydn, because they are altogether like Mozart, and represent a quite different phase of quartet style and of the sonata form through which they are presented.

MOZART'S PIANO SONATAS

So many of us begin our musical experiences through the piano that it might seem more natural to trace the course of development through the piano sonatas of Haydn and Mozart than through their string quartets. But there were various reasons, some have been already mentioned, to make their piano music less truly representative of themselves. The transition from the harpsichord to the piano was going on at this time (see p. 173), the imperfections of both the new and the old instruments were being felt, Haydn had found his ideal elsewhere, and what he did for the keyboard was on the whole less truly his own than his discoveries on the strings.

Mozart's piano sonatas, although nearly all early works and thus less fully representative of their composer's personality than Haydn's, have nevertheless kept a greater hold on pianists, perhaps because they are so excellently written for the instrument. All his life he was a public performer. Playing, teaching, and writing music for himself and his pupils to play were his chief means of support, work which he did in order to set himself free for more important things. It would be surprising if we found him at his highest level here, and it is surprising that he never sinks below a certain standard of refinement and grace, never seems tempted to write music which is showy, purposeless, and consequently vulgar.

Still we shall find passages, especially when he is approaching the cadence at the double bar, or at the end of the movement, which are put there for their obvious utility, in other words, to make the form clear to the listeners. Look at one of the finest of his piano sonatas (that in C minor written quite late in his career, in 1784), which is generally placed with the great Fantasia written in the following year. The chief beauty of the sonata rests upon the use Mozart makes of the opening figure,

Ex. 45

which strides majestically through a great part of the development and contrasts splendidly with the delicate second subject in E flat. But if you count back eight bars from the double bar, you will find that at that point Mozart had reached a perfect cadence in E flat emphatically stated, when similar though less emphatic cadences had been reached at four and eight bars previously. Yet that was not quite enough to make the balance of key and rhythm sure. Four more bars were needed before Mozart could feel that the moment had come to reintroduce the first theme (Ex. 45). He filled those bars with two more perfect cadences, repeating subdominant, dominant, and tonic chords, the ones which define the key by covering the whole of its scale (see p. 3). The process is scarcely disguised by the triplet figure in the right hand, and the passage adds nothing to the musical interest of the piece. Mozart's treatment of it when he arrives at the corresponding point near the end shows that he felt it to be only a kind of punctuation. Now, when he felt it less necessary to emphasize the key, he improved the passage considerably by carrying it on into a fine *coda* based upon the principal theme (Ex. 45).

Many such places are to be seen in the piano sonatas, but there is not one in the richly imaginative Fantasia in C minor, where Mozart was free from formal impediments. There is no hint of concession to formality here, yet its form presents the ideas with crystalline clearness. If you examine the passages by which the various sections are linked together and the chief transitions of key are made, you will find that each one is the outcome of some rhythmic idea which is quite essential to the beauty of the music. The first, for example, is brought about by the impulsive statement of an exquisitely tender phrase in B minor (bar 22), which later on becomes the principal theme of the Andantino in B flat. Its three bass quavers are dwelt upon until the music settles down upon F sharp, and the repetition of this note gives rise to the lovely melody in D which follows. Again, when this has been unfolded, it is by dwelling reflectively upon one of its features that Mozart prepares the way for the bold contrast of the Allegro. Here the punctuation is as definite as anyone could wish it to be, but it is achieved without any musical sacrifice. The whole work shows Mozart making consummate use of the principle underlying sonata form, the principle which joins together a number of ideas presented in succession, without being bound by the strict order of ideas, the customary contrasts of tonic and dominant keys, the central development, and the restatement at the end.

C. P. E. BACH AND MOZART CONTRASTED

We may clinch the matter of the progress made by the Viennese composers, Haydn and Mozart, over that of C. P. E. Bach in northern Germany if we lay side by side two piano sonatas from these two sources which appeared at about the same time. We will take one by Mozart and one by C. P. E. Bach, in the same key (Mozart, piano Sonata in G, K. 283, 1774; C. P. E. Bach, Sonata in G, published Leipzig, 1779, No. 4 in the collection edited by Hans von Bülow, Peters edition).

Probably the first thing that strikes you when you look at the pages is that Mozart's sonata is much the easier to read and to play. C. P. E. Bach's, though marked *allegro moderato*, is full of rapid passages in very complicated rhythms. The page is black with semiquavers, demisemiquavers, and even semi-demisemiquavers; moreover, sometimes these are grouped in triplets (three in the time of two demisemiquavers, for example), and sometimes into quintuplets (five in the time of four). It means a good deal of mental and finger agility to divide a fairly quick crotchet beat accurately into four, six, eight, ten, twelve, or sixteen parts, especially when the musical figures lie by no means easily under the hand, and on the face of it the contrast between this elaboration of detail and Mozart's style which here never divides the beat into more than six parts (and that only by an occasional triplet figure in the development) is important.

Mozart's lifelong experience as a public player had taught him that such things are confusing to the minds of the player and his listeners, and so he kept them entirely for the slow movements where there was more time to appreciate them. Yet without resort to them he had plenty of means at his disposal for brilliant ornamentation of a kind which was to a certain extent the result of another experience, the florid arias of Italian opera. You will find that he has a habit of saying a thing twice; like Browning's thrush 'he sings each song twice over', but very often he adds decoration to the melody when he repeats it as the voice of the singer would, without disturbing its outline, but enhancing its 'first fine careless rapture'. Look at bar 23 of this sonata, where a new idea (second subject) begins. The four-bar melody in its simplest form would be this:

Ex. 46

but even on its first statement Mozart gives it a special lilt by throwing its accents on to the weak parts of the beats. Then he repeats it with tripping semiquaver figures, and if you glance at the passage just before the double bar (bar 45), you will find the same idea coming in again (though it begins a note higher, on B this time), and that this new version of it is immediately decorated with a figure in broken semiquavers.

The habit gives an extraordinary clarity to everything which Mozart says. C. P. E. Bach cannot touch him in this; on the contrary, the latter starts boldly upon his elaborate scheme, passing rapidly from one part of it to another, often indulging in the most abstruse detail at points where the harmonic movement is involved (see bars 16–20), and pouring out a wealth of ideas which are likely to escape all but the most diligent listeners. We feel that he is determined to say and do much more than Mozart in the same time. If we consider one of C. P. E. Bach's long bars as equal to two of Mozart's short ones, the passage from the beginning to the double bar is about equal in the two sonatas. C. P. E. Bach covers it in twenty-six bars, Mozart in fifty-three, but we come to Mozart's double bar with a much more accurate knowledge of what has taken place than we are likely to have when we reach C. P. E. Bach's double bar.

The middle sections, too, present a curious difference. Mozart's is not, strictly speaking, a 'development' at all. Its nineteen bars deal with an entirely new theme which has nothing whatever to do with anything already heard. C. P. E. Bach starts with his first subject in the dominant, just as he always did in the early sonatas (see p. 218), and deals conscientiously with the material also in nineteen bars (that is about twice the length of Mozart's nineteen). But it is so much in the same style as the first part that the development scarcely makes the matter clearer. When Mozart comes to his restatement the ideas are perfectly clear in our minds in spite of the digression. They are probably clearer than C. P. E. Bach's, although he has never digressed for a moment; we can follow the modifications of them required by the necessary changes of key with complete ease, and they are all the fresher for the relief which the middle section has given.

The comparison is all the more interesting because there can be no doubt that C. P. E. Bach's is the more earnest and deeply felt work of the two. Mozart's is a mere offshoot of his genius; he cannot have cared very much about it, and we need not, once we have realized the ease with which he modelled his material. When this is done we can pass on to the individual study of a few of the great works of the two Viennese masters, Haydn and Mozart, and try to appreciate some of their qualities over and above purely technical considerations.

Suggestions for Further Reading and Listening

SONATA form is studied by every music student. To the layman, however, the subject can seem bewildering, wrapped in jargon, and even, paradoxically, remote from the actual sound of music. Hence, no doubt, Colles's humane approach, concerning himself with the 'Prussian' keyboard sonatas of C. P. E. Bach, some of Haydn's early string quartets and, in passing, Mozart's piano sonatas. None of these three categories of music is of sufficient specific gravity to have engendered a whole book of scholarly comment, though they are often enough discussed in more general surveys—like Rosemary Hughes's *Haydn String Quartets* ('BBC Music Guides'). In the same way the Prussian Sonatas of C. P. E. Bach feature in Volume VII of *The New Oxford History of Music*, 'The Age of Enlightenment (1745–1790)'. For a general survey of musical design, written 'in simple terms and colloquial language', there is no more lucid book than Gerald Abraham's *Design in Music*.

To make the most of this chapter, copies of the music are essential, and a piano is desirable for experimental purposes. Ideally, any study of the layout of one of the Haydn quartets or quartet movements should be backed by examples on the piano, but it should not be forgotten that these and other examples represent not merely technical evidence cited to prove a point, but real music, which never expected to find itself quoted in this particular pedagogic context.

CHAPTER 11

Quartet and Symphony

HAYDN and Mozart naturally fill the foreground of our picture at this date, but to treat them as though they were the whole musical picture of the time would be to give a very distorted impression, and in the end to dwarf their stature. Even apart from the constant flow of operatic composers from Italy, musical activity was widely spread through the middle of the eighteenth century. The Viennese composers most fully represented a flowering time in which instrumental music in many kinds, from sonatas for one or two instruments to every sort of combination of wind and strings and symphonies for full orchestra, was poured forth with an exuberance which baffles strict classification. Haydn's preserved and recognized symphonies number a hundred and four, beside which Mozart's fifty-one (counting several incomplete ones) seems a comparatively modest output, and to them must be added in both cases quantities of other works for orchestra (cassations, divertimenti, serenades, &c.) considered to be too slight to be dignified with the name of symphony, but usually in sonata form.

LESSER COMPOSERS

Other composers vied with them in this. There were, for example, LUIGI BOCCHERINI (1743–1805), whose instrumental compositions, many of them unprinted, are computed to number something nearer to five than four hundred, and KARL DITTERS VON DITTERSDORF (1739–99), who, besides his many contributions to Italian and light German opera, was assiduous in the composition of string quartets and symphonies.

Many of the flowers of this musical spring-time were to fade without bearing any fruit, and the greater part of the work of these two men suffered this fate, but to mention them here is not merely to recall dead names. You may meet specimens of their music at concerts and catch a glimpse of their characters from them. Both were string players. Boccherini was trained by his father as a violoncello player, and passed much of his life touring as a performer. His sonatas and concertos for that instrument were famous, and remained popular after much of his other music was forgotten. One sonata (in A) is a favourite work with violoncellists at the present day because of the great effect with which the special capacities of the violoncello are used. There is remarkable vigour and freshness in its melodies, brilliancy and humour in its decorative passages, tender expression in its Adagio. In some ways its form is more like that of the older sonata types of which Tartini's violin music is an example, than like the style which the Viennese composers were pushing forward so vigorously. Boccherini's chamber music for strings is now chiefly remembered by one movement, a very graceful minuet in A from his string Quintet in E major, written, as most of his quintets were, for two violins, one viola, and two violoncellos. But this light, tuneful piece is not fully representative of his art.

Dittersdorf received his early training as a violinist in the orchestra of St. Stephen's at Vienna, where both the Haydns were choristers (see p. 191), and as we saw before, his friendship with Joseph Haydn in Vienna did much to mould the style of his compositions. Some of his string quartets are heard from time to time at modern concerts of chamber music, and as with the minuet of Boccherini, so with these quartets, the first impression that one gets from them is that they are rather like Haydn in his less adventurous moments. One finds many of the same turns of expression, harmonies, means of moving from key to key, and of filling in the details of accompaniment. One learns from them, in fact, to what extent Haydn's music was merely using the current language of the time, and when we have done so we can appreciate more easily how far Haydn went beyond the current language in the individual stamp of his melodies and particularly in the originality of his rhythms.

Nothing misrepresents Haydn and Mozart so completely as the attempt to explain them, and almost to apologize for them by reminding people that they lived in an age of formality, moved in the polite society of courts, and wore wigs and powder and ruffles. They did all these things, and the manners of their time are no doubt reflected in the more obvious characteristics of their music, just as they are in the music of their lesser contemporaries, such as those we have mentioned. But the true characters of big men stand out clearly, no matter what their manners or their dress may be. It is when we hear the music of the smaller men that we have to prepare ourselves by adopting a frame of mind which is in sympathy with the external conditions of their lives. We shall enjoy Boccherini's minuet the more for picturing to ourselves some courtly dance in an eighteenth-century ballroom; when we turn to the minuets of Haydn's later symphonies and quartets, the rhythms in the irregular number of bars (3, 5, 6, or 7 as contrasted with the ordinary 4 and 8 bar measures) seem calculated seriously to upset the usages of polite dancing. Indeed, his minuets have little more to do with the dance than have his first movements and adagios. It is the man himself, with his irrepressible humour and vitality, who stands up before us, and it is because both Haydn and Mozart put themselves into their works that they live, while their contemporaries have died, or only survive for the picture which they make of a time foreign to our own.

The impulse to make something new and self-existing with the orchestra was not confined to one local area. Stamitz, who founded the famous Mannheim orchestra (see p. 186), poured out symphony upon symphony for his players; C. P. E. Bach, whose harpsichord sonatas were, as we have seen, his most important contribution to musical literature, also developed the symphony in Berlin. But the few specimens by the latter which have been published give the impression that he was struggling with technical problems which made it impossible to express his ideas naturally and without restraint.

Those written about 1776, a date at which Haydn's style was fully formed and Mozart was just ariving at maturity, have some bold features of design, strong principal themes for the strings, occasionally interesting episodes for the wind (flutes, oboes, and horns, the bassoons generally reinforce the bass strings), and some striking passages of harmony—things which show the original mind of the composer. But between the flashes of inspiration there is a good deal which seems put there chiefly to keep up a busy movement.

One very interesting characteristic in C. P. E. Bach's symphonies is his fondness for linking the three movements together, and it is all the more remarkable because it was not his usual practice when writing sonatas for the harpsichord. He would follow the final cadence of a symphonic movement with a passage leading boldly out of the key, preparing the mind for what was to follow, such as the one which joins the Allegro and the Larghetto of his Symphony in F (Ex. 47). Since the slow movement is in the closely related key of D minor this passage has no mere utilitarian purpose of modulation. He could have gone straight from one key to another had he wanted to, but he interpolated this passage simply because of its big emotional power, akin to the 'et expecto' of his father's Mass in B minor (see p. 120). In his Symphony in D major there is a similar passage at the end of the first movement, but here it has an obvious usefulness, for the slow movement is in the key of E flat, and it was so unusual to place the slow movement in a key a semitone above the first that the composer may well have felt that it needed some justification in the way of a gradual modulation.

In each case, too, the slow movement passes directly into the bright Presto which ends the symphony, so that we see C. P. E. Bach determined to get away as far as possible from the old suite form and to ensure his symphonies being listened to as a whole (cf. Beethoven's later sonatas, p. 328).

COMPARISON OF HAYDN AND MOZART

In his early years Haydn's manner of handling the orchestra was almost as much behind his treatment of the string quartet as C. P. E. Bach's was behind his treatment of the harpsichord. But the quartet led naturally to the orchestra in a way a keyed instrument does not. A man who can handle four instruments in such a way as to respect their individuality and at the same time fuse them into his scheme of thought is in a fair way to be able to do the same with forty. The problem is really the same upon a larger scale. Just as we have seen Haydn learning that the viola was not to be treated as a mere make-weight to the general force of the quartet (p. 181), so in his early symphonies we find him gradually appreciating the special qualities of the wind instruments. The Symphony called 'Le Midi', composed soon after he took up his duties at Eisenstadt (1761), shows him enjoying the contrasts which can be gained between the pure tone of the flutes and the plaintive, almost human, cry of the oboes.

The bassoons were gradually freed from their subservience to the bass strings. He realized them as the appropriate bass to the oboes, or as the complement to the horns, whose scale was imperfect; and the horns too, though in the early symphonies they do a good deal of merely filling up obvious notes in loud passages, soon began to have moments when they supplied a touch of tender expression all their own. Yet it is quite probable that Haydn would never have arrived at that masterly treatment of the orchestral instruments found in his late symphonies written for Paris and London, had it not been for the example of Mozart, whose brilliant achievements appeared in the middle of Haydn's career before his own greatest symphonies were written.

The different temperaments of the two men account for the fact that Mozart, though so much the younger, and though he owed an immense debt to Haydn's initiative, as he himself declared, became during the few years of his grown-up life the leader. Haydn, overflowing with life and good spirits, in love with his musical ideas, and never at a loss to express them, had little inducement to rivet his attention upon details. Mozart's nature was more delicately poised and more sensitive to impressions. This quality must have been immensely quickened by all his early travel. He had moved among men of very different modes of thought, and the accounts given in his letters, when travelling in Germany, France, and Italy, show that nothing was lost upon him, but that every aspect of the thoughts and feelings of mankind, especially as expressed in art, made an instant appeal to him. He was by all the circumstances of his life far the more cultivated creature of the two, and this gave to his music a polish, a niceness of perception, and sometimes a fastidiousness of taste, which the other lacked.

We love Haydn at once for his robust simplicity and buoyancy of spirit; Mozart needs more knowledge before we can appreciate him to an equal extent. His was the kind of character which, when it is found in smaller men, is apt to fail by giving too much devotion to matters of style and good taste. Mendelssohn, for example, who half a century later brought the same characteristics to his art, just missed appealing strongly to men of all times because in the greater number of his works he was content to have expressed himself in the most perfect way possible. But with his sensitiveness to impressions, which Mendelssohn shared, Mozart had a depth of feeling which Mendelssohn, for all his charm, lacked. The struggles and distresses of Mozart's life emphasized the deeper side of his nature and made him turn his refinement of style to its true purpose, that of expressing his feelings with greater acuteness, and at times poignancy, than Haydn with his easier career could reach.

There is a Symphony by Mozart (K. 183, in G minor), written when he settled down at Salzburg in 1773, which is among the first by him to show his capacity for deep feeling in an unmistakable way. In its first movement there is a beautiful smooth melody for the oboe, dropping by wide intervals in which the diminished seventh is prominent, and contrasting with the strings, who play the same melody with agitated syncopations. Incidentally it is a remarkable instance of Mozart's sensitiveness to the opposed effects obtainable from the wind and stringed instruments, but one feels that he has arrived at the perfect balance between them because he had something which he very much wanted to say, and his highly cultivated perceptions found for him the most appropriate means.

We cannot contrast the natures of Haydn and Mozart more directly than by making a comparison between the string quartets which Mozart wrote and dedicated to Haydn and those of Haydn himself of about the same period. A very salient example is found in the minuet of the first of Mozart's set, in G major (K. 387), where, if anywhere, one might expect to find reflections of Haydn, who had stamped his personality more distinctly upon the minuet than upon any other type of movement. The best that most men, Boccherini for instance, could do in this direction was to produce a polite dance measure enlivened with some of the characteristics of Haydn's style of workmanship. Mozart's is an entirely new view of the minuet. It is true that the first two bars give a hint of the formal lilt of the dance, but that is done of set purpose, to act as a foil to the strangely accented chromatic passages which follow on the first violin copied in contrary motion by the violoncello. The charm lies in first setting a familiar pattern, then wiping it out, and finally re-establishing it at the cadence, as shown in the ten bars of Ex. 48.

Ex. 48

The whole movement must be played in order to grasp its originality. It is to be noted that its form irrespective of the trio is that of a regular sonata movement with a second subject, a development, and a recapitulation of both themes.

This chromatic melody resulting, where the instruments combine, in chromatic harmony, the imitations between the instruments and the minute, almost meticulous phrasing, are peculiarly Mozart's own, and, broadly speaking, we may say that to dwell upon chromatic intervals of melody (i.e. melody moving by semitones in place of the principal notes of the scale) is a sign of subtle thought and of a delicate brooding kind of emotion.

Haydn was generally too impulsive to think and feel in this way, and when his melody becomes chromatic it is usually so in order to give richness of colouring. Compare with this minuet the corresponding movement in Haydn's Quartet in G (Op. 33, No. 5)[1] written for his visit to Vienna, on which the two composers first met.

Example 49 gives its chief idea (also ten bars long), in which Haydn hustles the rhythm by contracting the phrase of three beats (A) into two (B), bringing unexpected accents upon the weak beats of the bar, but never resting until the fourth bar is reached. Mozart also gets crossed accents by the use of his *p's* and *f's*, but he does it through deliberate thought, Haydn through sheer impulse. Then when Haydn indulges in a chromatic passage for the first violin (C) he rushes through it as part of a wider sweep of melody, is pulled up short by a bar's pause, and, having made us hold our breath in expectancy, ends humorously with a soft cadence.

Look further into the movement and see what comes of it, and you find that the chromatic passage (C) was only a momentary flight of imagination. There is nothing to correspond with the intimate use which Mozart makes of his chromatic crotchets. The rhythms, A and B, crowd the short development, but C

[1] It is worth noticing that in these six quartets (Op. 33), generally called the 'Russian' because they were composed to greet a Russian archduke on his visit to Vienna, the name 'scherzo' is used in place of minuet. The name and its meaning is discussed in connexion with Beethoven (p. 325).

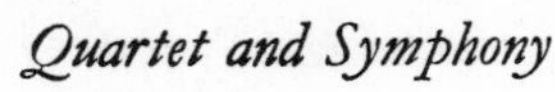

Ex. 49

Allegro.

f *sf* *p*

A B B B B

C

comes back only at the end, where the whole theme is repeated. Haydn was carried along on the wings of his first impulse; Mozart dwelt upon the inward significance of his idea.

MOZART'S STYLE IN CHAMBER MUSIC

While we have this quartet of Mozart before us, it is worth while to pay some attention to the Finale. It is a very quick movement begun by the second violin with a phrase of semibreves slurred together under one stroke of the bow. The other instruments imitate this phrase in the manner of a fugue. When all have played it new themes make their appearance; a running tune in quavers passed from one instrument to another, and a figure dropping by semitones for the two violins lead to the dominant key. From that point a new fugue subject is started by the violoncello, treated by all, and then combined with the first one, leading to the full close in D major and the double bar familiar in sonata form. One of Mozart's favourite chromatic figures introduces the development in which we are carried through various remote keys while the first fugue subject is combined with chromatic harmony. On reaching the key of C major (subdominant) the tune in running quavers makes its reappearance and leads to a recapitulation, in the course of which the two fugue subjects are heard simultaneously and all the diverse material is reviewed in a concentrated form.

The rapid sketch of the contents by itself can give no idea of the vivacity and variety of the music; it merely gives a few indications of how the movement may be analysed when it is heard and known. It points to the fact that here Mozart has woven together the means of interest supplied by two musical forms, the fugue and the sonata, which in their earlier stages seemed to be opposed to one another. We have seen that Haydn a good many years before, in the D minor Quartet, Op. 42 (see p. 183), had done something on these lines, but he had shown nothing like the same richness of design or facility of treatment which Mozart displays here. The Finale of Haydn's D minor Quartet is a very primitive affair compared with this movement. Mozart's contrapuntal style is extraordinarily easy. There is no hint that he is doing anything unusual or working out a design in which there are any incompatible elements. The fugal texture is as natural as that of J. S. Bach, the sonata plan as completely convincing as that of Haydn at his best. There is not a note or a phrase which seems put there in order to fill up a space in the design: every detail is necessary to the expression of his thought.

This contrapuntal ease was another element brought by Mozart to the partnership in which the two great men worked in their later years, and in his last symphonies and quartets Haydn caught fresh fire from it. Mozart has a captivating way of giving a free rein to his fancy in the invention of melodies which follow one another as though by accident, but as the music develops one finds that these melodies all have a connexion with one another. A fragment of one strikes across the path of another, they are heard simultaneously, they contradict one another or merge into each other.

A fascinating instance of this is the first movement of the beautiful string Quintet in G minor (1787) written when he was at the very height of his powers in the year that *Don Giovanni* was produced at Prague, and that town showed its good sense by going mad about him. Nothing could be more apparently unpremeditated than the wayward melody, half diatonic, half chromatic, which the first violin initiates above a simple accompaniment played by the second violin and first viola, or the little tripping downward figure which the violoncello copies from the first violin just before the second subject in B flat, yet presently we find these two being played off upon one another in the closest relationship, and the varieties of shape which the first tune assumes in the course of the development are almost bewildering to the senses and quite baffle analysis on paper. Even if we succeeded in making an analysis of every detail there would be still something missed, a fragrance, a delicate wit, and an underlying current of sadness which it is impossible to account for. And it is that unaccountable quality which is Mozart's self.

MOZART AND THE ORCHESTRA

Such a temperament as Mozart's, backed by that extraordinary facility in expressing itself aptly, was bound to exercise the strongest influence upon the development of the orchestra. The orchestra is, in fact, the most complex tool in the hands of the musician (see p. 184), and only a highly sensitive nature could discover its most subtle uses.

Mozart wrote symphonies from his childhood; but the first in which he spoke distinctly with his own voice, the G minor Symphony (K. 183), was also the first to give a strong indication of advance in the treatment of the instruments. Many of the works of subsequent years were less striking than this one.

Those which are most often heard are the 'Paris' Symphony in D (K. 297), the one work with which he was allowed to make an important appearance in Paris on his visit of 1778 (see p. 202), a Symphony in B flat (K. 319) for small orchestra without flutes, which may be taken as a fair specimen of his less inspired work, the Haffner[1] Symphony in D (K. 385), and the one also in D written for Prague (see p. 206). But all pale before the three masterpieces of 1788, the Symphonies in E flat (K. 543), G minor (K. 550), and C major, called the 'Jupiter' (K. 551).

The Paris Symphony is not among his most deeply-felt things; the circumstances hardly allowed it to be so. After waiting for months in Paris to get a hearing, hoping for the chance of producing an opera, the opportunity to write a symphony for the 'Concert spirituel' seemed to Mozart to be only a makeshift. Moreover, he was in a restless and unhappy frame of mind, caused by the uncertainties of his love for Aloysia Weber and his mother's death. He was hampered in its composition by being told that the players prided themselves upon their brilliant attack, and he was asked to give plenty of scope for the display of that quality, so that it was clear that they did not want so much to hear Mozart as to hear themselves. He gave them what they wanted. The Symphony opens with a brave flourish and then settles down to the discussion of a busily moving figure first played in unison. It is surprising how much interest Mozart gets out of not very promising material. Its three movements (there is no minuet) are scored with great variety of colour, and the opening of the Finale where the first violins give out a crisp tune against rapid staccato quavers played by the second violins is just the thing wanted to show off the skill of the players' bowing.

The 'Haffner' Symphony, written four years later, has something of the same arresting brilliance in its opening phrase, but here what seems to be a display of virtuosity at first (Ex. 50) is turned to extraordinarily fine musical uses later.

[1] A later work than the Serenade mentioned on p. 200.

Ex. 50

Through all the development of the first movement this phrase dominates the score; while one instrument is playing the long notes of its first two bars another is beating out the emphatic rhythm of its fourth. The Andante contrasts with the strenuousness of the first movement by the delicacy of its themes, and their ornamentation with passages in rapid notes which, like similar ornaments in the piano sonatas of Mozart (see p. 231), seem to spring to his mind as memories of the graceful *coloratura* of the opera. Here, too, we have a very charming minuet, not developed elaborately like that of the G major Quartet; but made of a few phrases of melody in which the instruments give strong contrasts of colour. The oboes and bassoons who lead the trio give a delightful relief from the more glowing tones of the strings in the minuet itself. But the Finale shows him in his most vivacious vein. There is something peculiarly piquant about its principal theme played *piano* by the strings in unison and the outburst of merriment which follows it. Each time that Mozart comes back to this tune he has a new way of gliding into it, so that every time it seems to take us unawares and produce a fresh feeling of playful mystery.

The Prague Symphony does not begin straight away with the Allegro, but opens with a slow movement which forms an introduction to the Symphony and leads up to the first Allegro. This was a more common practice with Haydn than with Mozart, and has been followed by later composers of symphonies, among whom were Beethoven in his second, fourth, and seventh Symphonies and Brahms in his first.

Very often it seems to be merely a survival of the idea of the French overture (see Lully, p. 65), which was adopted very freely by composers of all nations, the idea that an important work ought to have an imposing opening to arrest attention, but the great men often used it to much better purpose. The slow introduction to the Prague Symphony does open in a rather formal way; its first bars reiterating the keynote D with triplet figures running up to it from the dominant A is one of Mozart's common figures of speech (compare the beginning of the Jupiter Symphony), but common figures of speech, or 'pet phrases', as they are called, do not much matter either in language or in music when the man who uses them has really got something to say. They are irritatingly offensive when he has not, and is only writing or talking for effect. Mozart has something to say, as you realize when, after this opening phrase, he marches up the notes of the key chord and reaches a chord of F sharp major resolving on to B minor. This striking harmonic idea gives him his chief text for the introduction. Notice it repeated softly on another pair of chords and yet again by the woodwind (flutes, oboes, and bassoons) passing into E minor, from which point the violins begin a new melody. Bold modulations of key occur in the introduction (D minor, B flat, G minor) as though the composer wished to range widely before he settles down to the main business of his scheme. There are also strong contrasts of tone; at one moment the whole orchestra is massed upon a big chord; at another, delicate figures for the violins or separate wind instruments are heard individually.

The variety of Mozart's orchestration can be well studied here and in the Allegro which follows. See, for instance, how many details go to make up the interest of the chief Allegro theme; there are the violins playing a throbbing syncopated figure, the basses pressing up beneath them, also syncopated, though in a broader style, then the flutes and oboes in octaves rippling down the scale followed by a plaintive melody for the oboe alone. The development, too, is quite entrancing in the way the separate instruments dovetail into one another and especially the game they make with that downward scale passage which the flutes and oboes first introduced.

The slow movement gives a good example of Mozart's fondness for chromatic decoration of his melody, for after two bars of very simple outline the violins begin the process, and when the flutes take up the tune they carry the chromatic variation still farther. It is altogether a most tenderly thought-out movement beautifully coloured by the instruments. Again, there is no minuet. In the Finale the violins begin a race which is taken up by all the members of the orchestra in turn. Though it has none of the more serious elements of a fugue, such as we found in the Finale of the Quartet in G, the chasing of one instrument by another, the imitations and suggestions of 'stretto', show how thoroughly at home Mozart was in a contrapuntal style. The whole symphony strikes one as intensely happy, so that it stands as a truly fitting record of one of the brightest moments in Mozart's career, which contained too few bright moments, when for the time he felt all the flush of success and the joy of a friendly enthusiasm around him.

The reason why the world has agreed to place the three masterpieces of 1788 in a place apart by themselves seems to be that each is so unlike the others and unlike those which had gone before. We may agree that nothing more brilliant in its own way could be conceived than the Prague Symphony, but we have seen him working in its direction in the Paris and Haffner Symphonies and elsewhere. Each one of these three sheds an entirely new light on Mozart's character. We may establish certain comparisons usefully, find likenesses of style between the first movement of the Symphony in G minor and that of the string Quintet in the same key, or the still more striking one between the Finale of the Jupiter and that of the Quartet in G, but the essential character of each is all its own.

The Symphony in E flat has a breadth and graciousness of outline which it would be difficult to match in any work before Beethoven. Mozart uses a larger orchestra than in most of his symphonies, and clarinets take the place of oboes. The score contains one flute, two clarinets, two bassoons, two horns, two trumpets, drums, and strings; that is, the same instruments as in the Jupiter with the exception that the Jupiter has oboes instead of clarinets.

The Symphony in E flat begins with an adagio introduction, as the Prague Symphony does, but instead of a unison rhythm we have a majestic one in full harmony. Moreover, this rhythm is the basis of the whole introduction. When the strings vary it with rapid downward scales it is reiterated softly on the wood-wind; when the flute adds a new interest in a passage of broken quavers the same rhythm is heard throbbing on a single note played low down by violas, violoncellos, and basses. It is partly veiled by a long roll on the drums, but asserts itself again strongly when the violins, horns, trumpets, and drum, in fact all the stronger members of the orchestra, combine to lead towards a climax of tone. The whole orchestra breaks off upon a strong discord, after which a soft phrase of melody, curiously scored for flute, violin, and bassoon playing in three octaves, leads to the Allegro. The introduction shows well how far Mozart's orchestration had proceeded. He is just a little tentative in his use of the clarinets; the brass instruments are chiefly rhythmic, but this last phrase shows his appreciation of wood-wind and strings not only as elements of contrast but in combination forming together new tints.

There is, too, a new feeling in the Allegro. He has passed beyond the stage at which a quick movement is necessarily one of lively feeling. The gently swaying tune from which it grows is as different as possible from the crisply pointed rhythm of most of his earlier allegro themes. Its orchestration, too, is so delicately wrought that he must, one feels certain, have thought of the tune and the instruments playing it together. The violins begin and are immediately echoed by the horns; they add a second phrase, to which bassoons respond. Then we have the tune more richly sounded by violoncellos and basses, and against that clarinets and flutes echoing its ideas while the higher strings decorate it with new harmony. It is exceedingly simple, yet this one page is sufficient to show why we speak of Mozart as a great master of orchestration. It is because every note adds an indispensable touch to the colour, and if you can read this page of the score and really hear mentally the instruments you have gone some way towards mastering one of the problems which it becomes more difficult to explain as we come nearer to the music of our own time, the problem of orchestral sound.

We must not attempt to analyse the E flat Symphony, though it would be interesting to trace through all its phases of melody and colour that peculiar graciousness which is the chief factor in its individuality. The fascinating slow movement in A flat, though trumpets and drums are omitted, is as full of variety of colour as the first movement. The full orchestra reasserts itself in the vigorous minuet, and one cannot pass by this movement without specially pointing to the trio. For here more than anywhere else we see what new resource the clarinet brought to the orchestra. The melody of the trio is played by the first clarinet accompanied by the second one in an *arpeggio* figure. Two oboes playing this would have a very buzzy effect; the more liquid tones of the clarinets ripple instead of buzzing.

As regards the Finale we must only glance at the first and last bars in order to realize the originality of the ending. In many symphonies of the eighteenth century the ending seems to us now a little laboured. Composers seemed to find it necessary to go on repeating perfect cadences and striking big chords, and Mozart did so as constantly as anybody. But here the first phrase of his principal tune is the last phrase of the symphony. He seems to have caught a gleam from Haydn's humour in ending with delightful abruptness, and, though not quite so daring, this ending is to some extent in the same spirit as that of J. S. Bach's second Brandenburg Concerto (see p. 158).

The G minor Symphony is framed on a smaller scale; the orchestra of the original version is the usual small one without trumpets, drums, or clarinets, and with oboes; in a later version Mozart added clarinets, and each has its special merits. There is no attempt to make a stately impression at the outset; the first melody of the Allegro slips shyly into existence, its little pairs of quavers gathering confidence for a wider sweep as a young bird flutters its wings before flying. As in the Quintet in the same key, the tune gives rise to all sorts of developments later, yet though many things happen the first fresh beauty is never brushed off. The whole is extraordinarily supple and buoyant, with a tragic undercurrent, from the first tune onward to the soaring *arpeggio* which gives the motive power to the Finale. The G minor Symphony is lyrical while the 'Jupiter' is dramatic, and that is why it is so intensely lovable.

We will make no analysis of it here. If the examples and comparisons of these two chapters have been understood they will suggest general lines which may act as guides in the study of this and other symphonies by Mozart and Haydn. There is no more delightful musical adventure than taking a symphony which one has heard once or twice and exploring over the whole ground, finding what is unexpected in the developments of rhythm and harmony, the changes of key, and the new colours given by the different uses of the instruments. To map out the ground, set up signposts, and provide a chart would be to spoil the sport of the true adventurer. Try your own luck with Mozart's G minor Symphony.

We have already described some of the characteristics of the first movement of the 'Jupiter' for purposes of illustration (see p. 162), and have suggested a comparison of its Finale with that of the Quartet in G major. Here the trumpets and drums are again in the score, and although there is no slow introduction we feel at once that the whole is in the grand manner. The slow movement with its impassioned outbursts of tone striking across its smooth aria-like melodies, the very full treatment of the minuet, and the Finale with its many themes combined in the closest counterpoint, all help to carry out the largeness of design which makes it deserve the name of the greatest of the gods.

MOZART'S PIANO CONCERTOS

We have passed untouched whole tracts of Mozart's kingdom. The chamber music for piano and strings, the music for wind instruments and concertos of various kinds. But we cannot leave the last without a general word as to the piano concertos. His upbringing as a solo performer and his need, even in his latest years, of following that line of art as a profession, combined with his great capacity for dealing with the orchestra, naturally led him to bring the two things together. We know that he would often improvise upon the piano as part of the programme of an orchestral concert. Moreover, by the time that he settled in Vienna, the piano, with its power of producing a singing quality of varied tone, was fairly ousting the harpsichord from its old-established position. The piano was fit to hold its own against orchestral instruments, and in his concertos Mozart set himself to find a balance between them, to make the piano part carry on ideas begun by the orchestra and turn them to more subtle uses, or again to make the orchestra proclaim aloud what the pianist had hinted more gently.

The dramatic interest of a piano concerto is often like that of the speeches of Brutus and Mark Antony on the death of Julius Caesar in Shakespeare's tragedy. The solo instrument is the speaker; the orchestra is the crowd of citizens. In the forum scene (Act III, sc. ii) the citizens cry for satisfaction, Brutus seizes upon their mood and sways it into harmony with his view. When the cries of the people burst out again it is to applaud him and to 'bring him in triumph home into his house'. So moved are they that they will scarcely bear to hear another view, but Mark Antony knows that he equally can move them in an opposite direction. The comments in the course of his speech begin to chime with his defence.

1st Citizen. Methinks there is much reason in his sayings.
2nd Citizen. If thou consider rightly of the matter,
Caesar has had great wrong.

Till at last the anger of the crowd waxes hotter than his own, and their actions are carried beyond his control. Here we have practically the elements of concerto form as viewed by Mozart. He began his principal theme upon the orchestra, giving it in a more or less elementary way, the piano developing it more fully later on. Then a second passage for the orchestra, called a *ritornello*, would burst in, echoing the piano's statement, and eventually giving way before its second theme. The accompaniments were like the commentaries of the crowd, growing in force until another *ritornello* led to the development.

We must not, of course, press the simile too far, and it would be quite wrong to suggest that tragedy and violence were the underlying currents of Mozart's thought. Far from that, his piano concertos overflow with grace and happiness. It is only in the idea of one mind leading and moulding the mass of lower intelligence that we find a true parallel between the concerto form and the scene in Shakespeare. More modern composers have struck the note of tragedy with it, Brahms, for example, in his Concerto in D minor, Op. 15, but Mozart was in the flowering time of music, when pure beauty was the sole end in view, and dialogue of this kind was one means of gaining it.

Apart from these peculiarities the general form of his concertos is that of a sonata in three movements, an Allegro, a slow movement, generally rather compressed, and a lighter Finale usually of the rondo type—that is to say, a movement in which one tune alternates with a number of contrasting episodes. His writing for the piano has those elements of flowing melody heightened by decoration which he transported from the operatic aria to his piano sonatas (see p. 231), and generally before the end of his chief movements he allowed himself an opportunity for improvisation in a *cadenza*. The orchestra ceases altogether for a time that the pianist may have a free hand. Very often he did not even write what should be played, but left it to his own or his successor's imagination at the moment of performance. The *cadenza* is a magnificent opportunity for a great pianist who is also a great musician to show his mettle. But, alas, it too often shows us that many a clever pianist is made of more perishable material.

LATER WORKS OF HAYDN

It would be a very great mistake to ascribe to the influence of Mozart's example all the added richness of harmony and colour which we find in the later quartets and symphonies of Haydn. The early quartets which we have studied show Haydn to be a man of such strong vitality and power of expansion that one must suppose that the latter half of his work would have shown an increase of interest even without the stimulus of Mozart's genius. It would be equally wrong to suggest that the stimulus had the effect of making Haydn write like Mozart. To the very end of his life his style remained so entirely expressive of his own feeling that anyone who really knows the work of both men could scarcely ever be deceived into mistaking the one for the other.

The later quartets of Haydn fall naturally into two divisions, those which he wrote in the years of his service to Prince Nicholas, that is to say while Mozart was still living, and those of his old age, when, no longer the servant of a noble patron, he was regarded as a master by the whole of Europe. The first group contains the six quartets of Op. 50, Opp. 54 and 55 with three quartets in each, and the set of six which make up Op. 64 and are probably the best known of all. The last group contains Opp. 71 and 74 (three quartets each), Op. 76 of six quartets, Opp. 77 and 103.

The fine series of Op. 76 is particularly rich in its slow movements, and it is only in Haydn's increased power of writing broad and deeply-felt melody that one finds a sign of his increasing age. Op. 76, No. 3, has for the subject of its slow movement the magnificent 'Emperor's Hymn' which Haydn was impelled to compose in order that Austria might have a national anthem worthy to stand beside the one which he had heard in England. This tune is none the less Haydn's because it springs out of Croatian folk-song. To compare it as it appears in the quartet with the various versions of the popular song is to realize that all its splendour in the balance of its rhythm and the sweep of its melodic curves is the gift of Haydn.[1] In the quartet Haydn has first given the tune, then four so-called

[1] The tune is known to English people as set to the hymn 'Praise the Lord, ye heavens adore Him' (*Hymns A. & M.* 292).

variations upon it; they are not real variations, because the tune is always present in its original shape. In the first, the second violin plays it with no other accompaniment than a running counterpoint of the first violin; in the second, the violoncello plays it surrounded by the other three instruments; and in the third, the viola takes it up with more chromatic harmonies wreathed round it. Finally, the tune returns in the fourth variation to the first violin with again fresh harmonies and figures supporting it. This treatment of his own greatest tune, giving each of the four instruments equal rights in it, seems like a profession of Haydn's artistic faith in the capacity of the string quartet.

Other slow movements in the same series which may be taken as typical examples of Haydn's mature melody are the Largo in F sharp major (Op. 76, No. 5) and the Fantasia in B major (Op. 76, No. 6). Both these movements are in keys remote from the main key of the quartet, the former occurs in a Quartet in D major, the latter in one in E flat major. The freedom of Haydn's modulation from key to key in the latter is a peculiarly strong example of the lesson he had learnt from Mozart and of his way of applying it to his own purpose.

But we must end our view of Haydn with a few examples taken from the symphonies which he wrote for Paris and London. In these he used generally the same orchestra that Mozart had used in his 'Jupiter' Symphony; a woodwind group consisting of one flute, two oboes, and two bassoons, with two horns and two trumpets and drums for brass and percussion, and strings. One frequently finds the violoncellos and double basses playing independently of one another. He sometimes would make excursions into special effects of orchestration, as for example in the Allegretto of the 'Military' Symphony (No. 8 of the Salomon set), where he added clarinets to the woodwind, and triangle, cymbals, and a tambourine to the percussion, in order to get all the brilliancy and glitter possible. In the Finale of this Symphony the percussion instruments reappear, but the clarinet is dropped out.

The score of No. 92 (*c.* 1788), however, which is often called the 'Oxford' Symphony, because it was the one performed at the Sheldonian Theatre when the University gave him an honorary degree, represents his normal combination of instruments. It begins with a slow introduction, as do the Prague and E flat Symphonies of Mozart, but the introduction is not an emphatic call to attention. On the contrary, a very quiet theme on the strings, like a slow minuet, leads the way. It is the writing of a man who is perfectly confident that he will be listened to; just a quiet reflexion upon an idea to which he does not want to attach too great an importance though it has charmed him for the moment. This use of the slow introduction is very prevalent in Haydn's later symphonies. The opening of the famous 'Surprise' Symphony in G (No. 2 of the Salomon set) is a close parallel to that of the Oxford Symphony. Sometimes he would carry the idea farther, producing an effect of mystery and holding his audience in suspense until the simple theme of the Allegro breaks in like a ray of sunshine dispersing the clouds, and sometimes he would give a hint of what that theme would be though for the moment it is disguised by the slow time and the brooding harmony. The Symphony in D (Salomon No. 9), often called the 'Clock', because of the ticking effect of *pizzicato* strings and bassoons in the accompaniment to the slow movement, has an introduction which vaguely hints at the scale passage from which the Allegro starts. A still more striking instance of such a preparation is found in the Symphony in B flat (Salomon No. 6) which actually begins with the first subject played by the strings in unison with formal sedateness, but changed into the minor key. When that theme arrives in its allegro and major form it seems infinitely fresh and full of merriment. The contrast is all the stronger for the likeness.

It is well worth while to go through a dozen or so of Haydn's later symphonies comparing the different means by which he introduces them. One can often tell the experience of an artist, whether musician, actor, or public speaker, by his manner when he first faces his audience. Haydn's manner is one of complete assurance.

But to return to the Oxford Symphony, the first Allegro itself is the least distinctive movement of the four, though its principal theme, swaying to and fro upon the notes of the dominant seventh, sets in motion a strong rhythmic impulse which is maintained throughout. The Adagio, written in a kind of ternary form of which Haydn was fond (a principal theme in a major key with a contrasting section in the minor and a return), has one of his most perfectly organized melodies, which should be analysed in detail. By the organization of a melody is meant the way in which one phrase gives rise to another so that while there is great variety all the parts seem relevant and each contributes something to a big scheme. Here the scheme covers no less than twenty-eight bars, and every detail is rhythmically connected with one or other of three phrases (Ex. 51), namely, (*a*) the initial phrase of two bars which is extended into a number of different forms, (*b*) a small chromatic passage in bar 7 which first appears incidentally as the approach to the cadence, but afterwards gives rise to the middle section of the tune, bars 17 to 22, and (*c*) a little triplet figure ornamenting the cadence in bar 8 and made more important in the same middle section.

Ex. 51

The movement is delicately orchestrated. There are little touches on the horns which rival those of Mozart's E flat Symphony, and towards the end of the tune the oboe soars away above the strings with intensely poignant effect. The altered orchestration, too, when the theme comes back after the minor section, must not pass unnoticed; the bassoons playing the triplet figure (*c*) against the chromatic one (*b*) of the strings, the oboes, bassoons, and horns echoing the cadence, the violas, violoncellos, and double basses playing the tune below a counterpoint for the violins (compare Mozart's E flat Symphony), and finally the coda begun by the woodwind alone and recalling a passage in the minor section, are all eloquent. It should be added that here Haydn keeps the trumpets and drums in the score instead of dropping them out, as was often done for the slow movement, but he uses them only to emphasize the loud rhythms of the minor section. He considers them to be too noisy to be really expressive.

The minuet should be noticed for its irregular rhythms of six bars, in which Haydn revelled, its surprises in abrupt modulations and sudden pauses in the middle, and the orchestration of the trio in which horns and bassoons are brought together and stand out against the *pizzicato* of the strings. The Finale is built upon one of Haydn's most vigorous tunes, and it illustrates as well as anything could what his knowledge of Mozart had added to his technique, while the addition never intrudes for a moment upon his own individuality. The chromatic harmonies which he places against his tune and the contrapuntal treatment which he gives it may be signs of Mozart's influence, but Mozart could no more have written this Finale than Haydn could have written his G minor Symphony. Haydn's frank jollity is expressed in it all, and he uses these means not to suggest any intellectual subtlety, but in order to heighten its vigour.

The well-known Symphony in D (Salomon No. 12), the last one written for England (1795), may very fitly be compared with the Oxford Symphony. Here, as in a number of the English symphonies, he uses the full force of woodwind instruments, two flutes and two clarinets as well as oboes and bassoons, but it is also noticeable that he writes very little music of real distinction for the clarinets. He still seems to regard them, like the trumpets, as something with which to make a big noise. The Adagio gives the emphatic call to attention in its first two bars, but in the tender passages which follow the clarinets are discarded. On the other hand, it is interesting to see how many delightful opportunities he gives to the bassoon, and in the minuet he shows his appreciation of the wonderful effect to be got from a soft roll on the drum. Another of his symphonies of the same year (Salomon No. 11) has gained the name of the 'Drum Roll' Symphony because it begins with a whole bar devoted to a muffled roll on the drum. We are so used to this effect now, since Beethoven has got such wonders from it (see p. 332), that we are apt to forget that once the drum was looked upon as a sort of menial of the orchestra, who could never have anything of his own to say, but must just reinforce the rhythm when he was wanted.

To revert to the Symphony in D, its first movement is richer in colour and more striking in melody than the first movement of the Oxford Symphony, but the slow movement, though written on the same plan, hardly comes up to the earlier one in depth of feeling or beauty of design. To compare the two slow movements is the surest way of realizing what an inspiration the one in the Oxford Symphony is. One loves the great moments all the more for distinguishing them above the rest and to do so need not spoil our enjoyment of what does not reach so high. But the Finale of the Symphony in D is one of the most exciting that Haydn ever wrote, and, like so many of Haydn's best movements, it is based upon a Croatian ballad. The ballad tune is given out at once by the first violin over a drone bass (horns and double basses), its second stanza being taken up by all the orchestra.

Having suggested some of the features of Haydn's later symphonies, particularly those of orchestration, we may now step aside and, as in the case of Mozart, invite those who are keen enough to go on by themselves. There can be no difficulty in getting a very fair practical knowledge of the later symphonies of Haydn from broadcasts and recordings. Unfortunately, however, many editions of scores or transcriptions number the symphonies differently, and so, to make the course of development quite clear, we will end this chapter with a list of twenty-four representative symphonies placed as far as possible in chronological order. The numbers on the right are those of the collected edition.

1772	Symphony in F sharp minor (Farewell)	45
	,, in C major (Maria Theresa)	48
1774	,, in E flat major (Schoolmaster)	55
1781	,, in D major (Hunt)	73
1785–6	Paris Symphony No. 1, C major (L'Ours)	82
	,, ,, No. 2, G minor (La Poule)	83
	,, ,, No. 4, B flat major (La Reine)	85
	,, ,, No. 5, D major	86
1787	Symphony in G major	88
1788	,, in C major	90
	,, in E flat major	91
	,, in G major (Oxford)	92
1791–2	Salomon Symphony No. 1, C major	93
	,, ,, No. 2, G major (Surprise)	94
	,, ,, No. 3, C minor	95
	,, ,, No. 4, D major (Miracle)	96
	,, ,, No. 5, C major	97
	,, ,, No. 6, B flat major	98
1793–5	,, ,, No. 7, E flat major	99
	,, ,, No. 8, G major (Military)	100
	,, ,, No. 9, D major (Clock)	101
	,, ,, No. 10, B flat major	102
	,, ,, No. 11, E flat major (Drum Roll)	103
	,, ,, No. 12, D major (London)	104

Suggestions for Further Reading and Listening

THIS is a long chapter, inevitably so, for, if its time span is limited, the music it surveys is of almost incomparable richness. Some books on Haydn and Mozart have already been referred to at the end of Chapter 9, cited for their biographical content. They will, however, continue to be useful, here and later on. At this stage they should be supplemented by other studies. Pride of place is taken by H. C. Robbins Landon's monumental *The Symphonies of Joseph Haydn*.

Though too specialized for apprentice music-lovers, it counts as the ultimate authority on its subject. As a first port of call, the same author's concise *Haydn Symphonies* in the 'BBC Music Guides' series is recommended.

In that same series may be found A. Hyatt King's *Mozart Chamber Music*. But for Mozart's chamber music, and his symphonies, consult both Einstein's book on Mozart and also *The Mozart Companion*, edited by Robbins Landon and Donald Mitchell. Mozart's piano concertos are of course discussed in both of these volumes, but for a close-up view of this very important side of Mozart's output look out for Arthur Hutchings's *A Companion to Mozart's Piano Concertos*, in which each work is examined separately. Tovey's writings on Haydn and Mozart, whether in his *Essays in Musical Analysis* or his *Essays and Lectures in Music* (which contains a whole chapter on Haydn's chamber music), are classics of their kind. But a word of warning: stimulating though he is to read on almost any topic, the pith and potency of his insights can be savoured more fully by relatively experienced students of the period. That general observation applies even more strongly to Charles Rosen's *The Classical Style: Haydn, Mozart and Beethoven*, an analytical study of the music of the three composers, brilliant but aimed at a fairly sophisticated public.

Colles brings Boccherini and Dittersdorf into the picture, and, if the latter is still relatively ill represented on record, Boccherini is adequately served. The more important symphonies of C. P. E. Bach are available and one or two by Johann Stamitz. The text does not mention Sammartini, but, since he is generally ranked among the founding fathers of the symphony, readers should take note that some of his symphonies are on disc.

The individual works by Haydn and Mozart present no problem. They are available on record, and recur often enough on the radio or in the concert hall.

CHAPTER 12

Music, Words, and Drama

If there is one thing more than another which is characteristic of eighteenth-century music, and particularly of that very large part of it which came from or through Vienna, it is the delight in what is beautiful for its own sake. The growth of musical art seems to pass away from its association with other things, the arts of poetry and dancing and even the deeper feelings of mankind expressed in religion, in order to become thoroughly itself, to get all its means of expression under control and to speak with its own voice. The shaping of the orchestra and of the symphony at the same time is the strongest evidence of this, and when we look at music actually associated with words conveying poetic or religious ideas we still often feel that the music asserts its independence, that we enjoy it more for its own sake than because it intensifies those ideas.

CHORAL MUSIC OF HAYDN AND MOZART

The Masses and other church music of Haydn and Mozart, particularly the former, give innumerable instances of this. Haydn's remark that he did not think God could be angry with him for praising Him with a merry heart means just this, that all beautiful things seemed to him fit for religious service, because his music did not grow out of religious thought but religion was a part of his musical inspiration. His meditations upon 'The Seven Words from the Cross', written for the cathedral at Cadiz, is the work where his music seems to be brought into the closest touch with the thought of the words, yet we have seen (p. 208) that it was originally composed for orchestra alone. The choral arrangement of about 1796 is developed upon symphonic lines and the orchestral writing still often maintains interest which is distinct from the text.

He felt the composition of his great oratorio *The Creation* to be actuated by religious purpose, but it is the exuberance of the music itself which has made it live. It makes very little appeal to the religious sense; the words contribute material for Haydn to treat with a wealth of simple, perhaps naïve, musical description. All the different parts of nature coming into existence, the light, the elements of land and water, plants, fishes, animals, and mankind, each in turn gives character to the outer features of his music, but in each case we admire his power of indulging his fancy in these ways without interfering with the clear beauty of his own melody, which rises above the suggestions of the words. The big choruses which close each part, 'The heavens are telling', 'Achieved is the glorious work', and 'Sing the Lord, ye voices all', show the genuineness of Haydn's religious feeling, but flow too easily to make us feel that they really sum up the oratorio as a thing of deep religious significance.

Mozart's choral church music goes farther than Haydn's, because, as we have seen, his intellectual grasp was firmer, but, since most of it was composed as a part of his humiliating service to the Archbishop of Salzburg, there were other reasons besides his preoccupation with purely musical questions to keep him from striving consistently after the expression of religious feeling in his art. The one work where such feeling is conspicuously, indeed overpoweringly, strong is the Requiem

Ex. 52

Mass, which he was actually composing on his death-bed. The last phrase he wrote (the first bars of the 'Lacrymosa', Ex. 52) is as completely the outcome of the sense of the words as anything in J. S. Bach's Passion music or cantatas.

The cry of the rising minor sixth ('That day of tears') and the breathless detached notes gathering confidence and rising chromatically to a terrible climax ('When shall rise from ashes man arraigned for judgment') are the things which stamp the music; one is impressed not so much with its beauty as with its truthfulness of expression. It is a reversal of the more ordinary position of these two aspects of art, beauty and truth, as found in the eighteenth century, and the fact that it is constantly so in Mozart's Requiem is the most important sign that the whole work is the product of a time of stress, when life was closing in upon him, and he summoned all his powers to battle with the illness which eventually prevented his finishing it. The Requiem as it exists in modern editions is practically Mozart's work down to the end of the 'Hostias'. The 'Requiem aeternam' and 'Kyrie' were fully scored by him; the other numbers up to this point were all at least sketched out so far as their ideas were concerned. His friend and pupil Süssmayr finished them and added the remaining numbers, 'Sanctus', 'Benedictus', and 'Agnus Dei', probably working upon some ideas communicated to him by Mozart or sketches he may have destroyed.

All the circumstances, then, of the composition of the Requiem were exceptional. It is separated by a large space of time from the body of Mozart's church choral music composed at Salzburg; unlike the earlier music, it was the result of strong personal feeling working under extreme difficulty. That earlier music can be for the most part divided into two classes, that which, like Haydn's, delights in the process of making music for its own sake, and is therefore essentially secular in feeling, and certain essays in contrapuntal style to be found among his motets, which seem to recall some of his experiences in Rome and his studies under Martini (see p. 199).

This general attitude towards music, though caught, fixed,

and carried on to bigger ends by the Viennese composers, was really the product of Italy. It overran church music and the opera alike, and the difference between Mozart and Haydn and their Italian contemporaries was that these two great men carried the impulse to its logical conclusion, found the forms in which it could be appropriately expressed without incongruity or conflict of ideas—that is to say, pure instrumental music.

We are not going to make any survey of the Italian music of the time nor mention names of men and works which have no practical meaning for music-lovers of the present day. We may find one example, however, in the works of Pergolesi (1710–36), a short-lived composer born in the neighbourhood of Ancona, two small specimens of whose music are occasionally to be heard nowadays and had considerable importance in the history of the art. One is his setting of the hymn *Stabat Mater* for women's voices and stringed orchestra; the other is a comic opera in one act called *La serva padrona* ('The Servant as Mistress'), in which are two singing characters, a young maid-servant and her master, whom she bullies unmercifully, and a silent man-servant, of whom the girl makes a confederate. In point of subject we could not find two musical works farther separated from one another than these, the former treating one of the most solemn themes of the Christian religion, the other devoted to an entirely trivial but laughable comedy. The two should have nothing in common, yet we find the style of the opera bursting in among numbers of great beauty and dignity in the *Stabat Mater*, and the intrusion necessarily offends when the mind is concentrated upon the meaning of the sacred hymn.

To hear these works of Pergolesi is to get some notion of the directions in which Italian music was tending before the time of Haydn and Mozart. It has an exuberance of vocal melody quite distinct from the subject to which it is applied. At its worst it would become wholly irrelevant to the subject, at its best it preserved its connexion with some difficulty according to the demands made by the subject. In the *Stabat Mater* these demands are of the highest; in *La serva padrona* they are as slight as possible, and so Pergolesi could meet them in the opera with much greater consistency than in the sacred work, and the spirit of light-hearted fun and good humour in the little drama agrees easily with the happy flow of his melody.

SOME PRINCIPLES OF OPERA

We shall allude to *La serva padrona* again later, but before we begin to trace some of the special movements which marked the history of opera during the eighteenth century it will be helpful if we turn aside to try to discover a little more accurately what is the object of opera.

It is clear from what has been said that opera is an even more complicated art than choral or other sung music. The latter sets certain limits and responsibilities upon the musician, for if he joins his music with words at all he must bring it into sympathy with the words and control his music so that it expresses the same feeling and respects the form of the sentence, and in the case of poetry that of the verse as well. But the operatic composer has a third quantity to consider, over and above the feeling of words and music. There are all those different elements which are known as the 'action' of the play; the characters of people represented, the events which take place, everything which the audience sees while listening to words and music, from the scene in which the play is acted to the attitudes and gestures of the players, all of which in good drama well acted mean something. As sung music deals with two of these things (words and music), so a spoken play deals with two others (words and action), and the ballet completes the circle by taking as its material the only remaining pair, action and music.

But the opera uses all three together, and the difficulty lies in making all three really do their part in presenting ideas to the audience. We do not want a lot of useless sights and sounds which cumber the senses without helping us to understand better and feel more deeply the ideas underlying the drama. It is quite open to a lover of the theatre to say, 'When I go to the theatre I want to follow every word and see what happens, and not have the people on the stage singing when in real life they would be speaking, and not have the whole play kept waiting while a lot of orchestral music is dinned into my ears'. And it is equally open to people who care for music to say, 'When I listen I want to be able to sit still and shut my eyes and let my ears do all the work. I want not to be bothered by having to look at tableaux represented on the stage or by having to follow a story which is nothing to me in comparison with the power of music.'

We can admit at once that drama and music alike have a power when they are free from each other which is lost when they are brought together and have to conform to one another. There must be a certain amount of compromise between them, and the question is whether the compromise is made worth while by giving us something which we do not get in pure drama or pure music. The fact that ever since the time of Monteverdi, well over three hundred years ago, and indeed earlier, musicians and poets have kept on persistently trying to express themselves in opera, in spite of every difficulty and in spite of constant misdirection of their efforts, is strong evidence that there is something to be done with it which cannot be done by any simpler means. They are always beginning again upon opera, readjusting the balance between the parts (music, words, and action), discarding what has become meaningless in the older work, reforming the compromise upon a fresh footing, and so striving to get nearer to the heart of what they want to say.

The justification is that music is an expression of human feeling which cannot be translated into words. When we describe music, as we have often tried to do in this book for example, our words do not really tell the effect the music produces upon us, they only give a rough suggestion by analogy of that effect. That is why it has been so constantly necessary to urge you to go to the music itself and hear it if you really want to understand what it says.

So a musician constantly feels that the addition of his art to the drama can open up a fresh range of ideas which words and action could never convey, and he is right so long as he realizes that no one of these three means of expression must absorb the whole attention or go on as though it were alone. That is very important. In order to make them combine, each one must be different in character from what it would be if it were left to stand by itself; it must be incomplete without the other two.

Take a very simple illustration. Suppose you are walking with a friend in the street and you see a rainbow in the sky. You exclaim 'Look there!' and you point while you gaze at it. With two words and a simple action you have explained all about it and your friend has seen it too. But if you are alone in your room and see the rainbow from the window and want your friend who lives a few doors away to see it, you ring him up on the telephone and say, 'Look out in a north-westerly direction and you will see a rainbow'. You required a dozen words to convey the idea which you could have got more precisely in two words with action to help you.

It is the same to a greater degree in opera, where there are three means of expression at hand to help; they economize one another. We saw an instance of how action economizes words and music in opera (p. 50) when we compared Mendelssohn's scene of Elijah being taken by a whirlwind into Heaven with Wagner's scene of Brünnhilde riding into the flames near the end of *Götterdämmerung*. We might take the same passage in the opera to show how music in turn economizes words, for in those few bars Wagner brings to our minds the chief features of his heroine's life, how she had ridden as the messenger of Wotan, and afterwards, when she had displeased him, been placed upon the rock encircled with fire. A mere phrase played by the orchestra recalls these things though it would take many words to picture them.

But perhaps it will be suggested that it is rash to cite Wagner as a composer who used words, music, and action to economize one another, for in order to hear an opera by Wagner we frequently have to set out to the opera house after an early tea and remain there until far into the night. It is true that the economy we speak of has not generally resulted in making opera a shorter form of art than an ordinary play or a piece of concert music. The reverse is the case, and a number of reasons outside the artistic principle in question are sufficient to account for it. It is not a question of the time a work takes to perform but of the strength of the impression which can be produced at any one moment. A composer of almost unlimited resource like Wagner may choose to go on piling one impression upon another trusting to the variety of his means to keep the interest alive, or he may, and Wagner sometimes does, fall into the mistake of redundancy, repeating in words what the music could sufficiently suggest more rapidly, or elaborating the music beyond the point necessary to convey the spirit of the drama.

We will not digress into a study of Wagner's special treatment of the problems of opera; that must come in its own place in a later volume. We merely use him here as the most salient illustration of the fact that opera, with its peculiar combination of means, can bring to our minds certain types of thought and feeling more directly than can be done by any less complicated form of art.

What are those types? Clearly those which have least to do with matters of fact and most to do with the inward emotions; what Wagner himself called 'states of the soul' of individual human beings. Since the genuinely musical expression is something outside the ordinary expression of everyday conversation, it becomes most eloquent just at the moment where words and actions fail. In Gluck's *Orfeo*, for example, when Orpheus has braved the terrors of Hades to recover his lost wife, has brought her back to life, and just at the moment of his triumph has lost her again by yielding to her entreaty to look at her, his grief finds expression in the wonderful aria 'Che farò senza Euridice' (How shall I live without Eurydice?). The words in themselves are impotent; the music is all-illuminating. It is the highest point of feeling in the whole opera. Or again, to take a very different case, the aria 'Porgi amor' in Mozart's *Figaro*, in which the neglected wife of the worthless count pours out the fears which beset her, carries us beyond the heartless gaiety of the comedy straight into the region of human sympathy. Again, the music puts us immediately into touch with Hans Sachs musing in his chair when the curtain rises upon him in the third act of *Die Meistersinger*, much as Mozart's aria puts us into touch with the countess, save that here it is done without any words at all. And just to name one instance in a more recent opera where the music surpasses the capacity of words, there is the extraordinarily intense moment in Richard Strauss's *Elektra* where the heroine of the drama recognizes her brother, Orestes, on whom all her hopes had been fixed and whom she had thought to be dead.

These are a few of the conspicuous scenes by which the operatic drama justifies itself, and apart from them and similar ones there are many places where the music fitly takes a secondary place, accentuating the meaning of the words and action and commenting upon it. But below this again in every drama there are necessarily prosaic moments, details of conversation between the characters, mere explanations of events, where the music must retire farther into the background to avoid absurdity.

Should it stop altogether, leaving the actor to speak what must be spoken and so not risk its dignity by being linked with ideas to which it cannot contribute? That is a question which has caused a great deal of discussion. Beethoven in the only opera he wrote, *Fidelio*, adopted the plan of mixed speech and song; it is reported of Brahms when he contemplated an opera, which however he never carried out, that he was determined to have spoken dialogue between the musical numbers. This was the plan generally adopted in German and French comic operas, and we English people know it well in the delightful comic operas of Gilbert and Sullivan. In such things as these last, which are all fun and frolic, the change of voice is no drawback and indeed often adds a touch of piquancy, but where there is any serious matter on hand it is apt to sound so incongruous that all the greatest operatic composers have decided against it.

RECITATIVE

The Italian invention of *recitativo secco* ('dry recitative', see p. 19), in which the words were sung on notes which passed as rapidly as speech, accompanied only by detached chords on the harpsichord, had the merit of keeping the musical thread intact and avoiding a wrench between the dialogue and those parts where the music became of more material importance. It opened the door of course to a great deal of slipshod work; whenever a composer had nothing to say he could run on in pages of 'dry recitative' until he thought it was time to vary the process with an aria, but when it was well used, as by Mozart for example, it could be an admirable means for carrying on the dialogue vivaciously. You may get a notion of the general effect of this sort of recitative by hearing Rossini's *Barber of Seville*, which at the present day is usually performed with the recitative accompanied on a piano.

The French adapted the principle to suit their own language and their own ideas of art. With them recitative remained more declamatory than with the Italians, and from the time of Lully onward a less strict line was drawn between those parts of the French opera where the music was merely an accessory and those where it was a vital interest. That no doubt was due to the long-standing tradition of the 'chanson', which regarded music as a means of expressing poetry rather than as an end in itself.

When the Germans came to make serious opera of their own they had to face the problem and to find a way of dealing with it suitable to their own language and the things they had to say, but that was at a later date and we need not at the moment take it into consideration. Even at the end of the eighteenth century German opera was still in its infancy, and its only important productions were light comedies called 'Singspiele' (song-plays) with spoken dialogue. Dittersdorf wrote about twenty of these; his *Doktor und Apotheker* ('Doctor and Apothecary') was the most famous, and in Vienna it was so successful as to eclipse for a time Mozart's Italian opera *Figaro*. Mozart himself contributed several works to the German 'Singspiel', of which *Bastien und Bastienne*, written when he was a boy of twelve and performed at a private theatre in Vienna, was the first, and *Die Entführung aus dem Serail* ('The Elopement from the Harem'), produced by the Emperor's command at the 'National-Singspiel' founded in 1778, the most brilliant. This work shows that Mozart understood the *recitativo secco* to be the special property of the Italian language and one which could not be transferred to the German language. But he made no attempt either here or elsewhere to find a way of setting German words in continuous opera. His last and biggest German opera, *The Magic Flute*, retained a large quantity of spoken dialogue.

ITALIAN AND FRENCH OPERA

At the beginning of the eighteenth century, therefore, we have only two styles of complete opera to take into serious account, the Italian and the French, and of these the former was the one generally recognized by the whole of Europe as representing an authoritative standard. Operas and opera singers were poured out from Italy into every other important centre from Vienna to London, and only a small group of people in Paris maintained that any kind of opera other than that which Italy provided was possible. They, however, maintained it so doggedly that, as we saw in the first chapter of this volume, Paris became a hotbed of controversy from which came results second in importance only to the growth of instrumental music in and around Vienna.

The music which came from the South at its best fostered the love of musical beauty for its own sake. There may have been hundreds of Italian operas which added nothing to the stock of beautiful things, but the justification for the form was that the musical beauty should be concentrated upon the succession of arias strung together upon a thread of 'dry recitative'. But though this could result in great art in the hands of such masters as Alessandro Scarlatti and Handel, it cannot, as we have seen, be the only aim of opera, which is essentially a many-sided art; and the French opera kept the path open for the fuller realization of the dramatic expression necessary to complete the scheme, until one man who had been trained in the Italian school was strong enough to follow up that path. That was Christoph Gluck.

Suggestions for Further Reading and Listening

CHAPTER 12 is concerned with the relationship between words and music, initially at least in terms of eighteenth-century church music. Haydn and Mozart therefore loom large, and here again the various books on these two composers specified earlier should be consulted. Readers are also recommended to turn to the appropriate sections of H. C. Robbins Landon's *Essays on the Viennese Classical Style.* He is illuminating on the nature of late eighteenth-century sacred music in central Europe. There is also a deeply considered essay on the principle of church music of the period in Charles Rosen's *The Classical Style.* Less intense is the chapter 'The Period of Haydn and Mozart' in Percy Young's *The Choral Tradition,* which includes a commentary on the indigenous Italian tradition. For a detailed examination of Haydn's *The Creation* and *The Seasons,* see Volume V of Tovey's *Essays in Musical Analysis.*

The various works mentioned in the first part of the text are all easily available, both in score and on record, though Haydn's *Seven Last Words* is at the moment only to be had in its chamber-orchestra form (Supraphon). There is no problem over Pergolesi's *Stabat Mater* or his opera buffa *La serva padrona,* and indeed the latter is a favourite with small-scale touring operatic companies. Colles quotes examples from Gluck, Mozart, Wagner, and Richard Strauss which illustrate the extra-expressive dimension which music can bring to a situation. These are all quite simple to track down in vocal scores and to pin-point on recordings. The different kinds of recitative in vogue in the eighteenth century can be demonstrated perfectly well from recordings of *La serva padrona* and *The Marriage of Figaro.*

Supplementary reading on opera could well start with E. J. Dent's *Opera,* a witty classic of compressed erudition, and go on from there to Donald Grout's invaluable *A Short History of Opera*. Readers who want to go deeper into the subject will find Michael Robinson's *Opera before Mozart* extremely useful: combining detail with general principle, its scope ranges from the turn of the seventeenth century until about 1780. For general information on opera consult the *Concise Oxford Dictionary of Opera*.

CHAPTER 13

Opera in Paris and Vienna

THE man who did most to keep the French standard of opera alive was JEAN PHILIPPE RAMEAU who, unlike its founder, Lully, was actually a Frenchman. He was born at Dijon in 1683, so that he was only a child when Lully died (see p. 71), and his father was organist of the cathedral in that town. The early part of his life did not bring him into contact with the stage at all, except that when he was about seventeen years of age he travelled a little and visited Milan, where he must have become acquainted with Italian opera, and afterwards played the violin in a theatre orchestra. But the harpsichord and the organ were his instruments, and for some time it seemed that he might settle down to the career of a cathedral organist as his father had before him.

He held various church appointments and succeeded his brother as organist of the cathedral at Clermont in Auvergne, and while he was there he occupied himself in the study of the theory of harmony. This aspect of music became for a time so engrossing that when he had completed his *Traité de l'harmonie* ('Treatise on Harmony') he threw up his organist's post in order to go to Paris and superintend its publication. He was already close on forty years of age, and for the next ten years he went on writing voluminously on musical theory, supporting himself by playing and teaching and composing pieces for the harpsichord, and it was not until 1733 that his first grand opera, *Hippolyte et Aricie*, was produced. He was then fifty years old, so that he presents what is probably a unique instance of a man able to begin an operatic career when he had passed middle age and continue it with honour for nearly thirty years. He died at the age of eighty-one (1764), and his last opera to be performed, *Les Paladins*, was produced in 1760.

RAMEAU'S *CASTOR ET POLLUX*

But his most famous work was *Castor et Pollux*, written fairly early in his operatic career, some of the ballet tunes from which are still to be heard at orchestral concerts. We may get some practical notion of his aim by making a short study of this score. The general scheme of the drama reminds us very strongly of the plan of Lully and Quinault (see pp. 69 ff.). The classical story of the brothers Castor and Pollux is developed in five acts preceded by an overture and a dramatic prologue. The orchestral overture is in the ordinary form of a slow movement followed by a quick fugal one, and has no special connexion with the story which follows. It represents a convention which Rameau apparently inherited unthinkingly, but from which he departed in some of his later works.

The prologue is a prayer to Venus to bring peace and happiness upon the world. Minerva calls upon Cupid to invoke the aid of his mother, and Venus and Mars descend to earth. The remarkable thing here and in the opera itself is the masterly use made of the chorus and the ingenious way in which the characters are woven into an *ensemble*. It marks one of the chief points of contrast with the prevalent Italian style, for whereas the effect of the Italian aria was to concentrate attention solely upon one individual at a time, Rameau's opera merges the individuals in a common interest. An admirable case in point occurs where Cupid pleads 'Plaisir ramenez-nous, Vénus, descends des cieux' ('Pray return, Venus, descend from heaven'), the musical phrase of which is immediately taken up by each voice of the chorus in turn.

The orchestral music accompanying the descent of Venus and Mars is an interesting attempt to describe musically what is seen upon the stage. The violins have wreathed passages in descending triplet quavers. The happiness which the gods bring is of course displayed in a series of dances, gavottes, minuets, and a 'tambourin'; the last delicately scored for 'little flutes', violins, bassoons, and bass strings. It is worth notice that the bassoon part here is independent of the stringed basses.

The drama itself opens in the funeral place of the kings of Sparta, where a pyre is prepared and the people, again in striking choruses, mourn the death of Castor. Moreover, the music actually suggests the different groups of people who take part in the scene. That of the athletes is quite different in style from the first chorus of mourners; it is broader, one might almost say more muscular. Amongst these groups the principal characters take a comparatively insignificant part. Their airs are all very short, breaking off into declamatory passages. Talaire, the lover of Pollux, urges him to seek the help of the gods to restore his brother Castor to life, which is accomplished in the second act in the temple of Jupiter. It is decreed, according to the legend, that Castor may share the immortality possessed by Pollux; that is to say, that he can only return to life while Pollux takes his place among the dead. There is a scene of genuinely fine emotion here, in which Pollux is torn between the claims of duty to his brother and his love for Talaire. His air, 'Nature, amour, qui partagez mon cœur, qui de vous sera le vainqueur?' ('Nature, love, who divide my heart, which of you will be the victor?'), is particularly interesting, because it is one of the rare cases where Rameau adopted the ternary form so persistently used by the Italians. He evidently did it for a definite dramatic purpose. Pollux is in a state of indecision, and hence it is natural that he should come back to the question from which he started.

The subject of the next two acts is very similar to that of the story of Orpheus and Eurydice. Pollux descends to the infernal regions in order that his brother may be liberated. One cannot escape the feeling that Rameau's treatment of the idea offered some suggestions to Gluck when later he wrote his famous *Orfeo*. It was natural for practical reasons that both composers should divide the episode into two acts; one in which the hero, in this case Pollux, encounters the infernal spirits, the other in which having passed through their region he arrives at the home of happy spirits. The contrast gave excellent opportunity to the musician for music of different character. In Rameau's third act the *ensemble* is very elaborate. There is a scene between Pollux, Talaire, and her sister Phoebe, culminating in a trio for the three voices, upon which follows the chorus of spirits mingling with the three solo voices. In both scenes the ballet is important. Vigorous and uncouth music is supplied for the dances of the infernal spirits, smoother and more gracious melodies for those of the happy spirits.

Rameau's dramatic scheme is not far behind Gluck's; where the latter goes farther is in his power of combining dramatic appropriateness with distinctively musical beauty. In Rameau's fourth act Mercury appears to take the place which Cupid fills in *Orfeo*; that is to say, he brings about the happy ending. The fifth act of *Castor et Pollux* represents the deification of the brothers among the stars, a scene which gave obvious occasion for all the display of pageantry of which the opera was capable. Again the ballet and the chorus are of first importance; both include symbolical figures representing planets and stars joining in song and dance culminating in a 'chaconne' and effective choral finale. In the use of the 'chaconne' (or 'passacaglia') as the most elaborate dance Rameau is following the example of Lully (see p. 70).

One feels that the whole opera is planned to deal ably with certain kinds of stage effect rather than to reveal the feelings of the principal characters, though, as we saw in the song of Act II, Rameau could respond to a call for definite feeling when it came. His response, however, is momentary, and might easily pass unnoticed among the more prominent attractions of the scenes and actions of the stage figures. We know in fact from his own statement that he personally did not attach the highest importance to the character of the words which he set. It is told of him that he said that a musician should be able to set anything to music, and many of the plots of his operas suggest that he was ready to act upon the principle. His characters remain remote, classical figures, not, like Gluck's, living human beings. But against this fault of neglecting the individual must be set the virtue of picturing masses of people in his vivid writing for the chorus. The Italians neglected this almost entirely. Lully's chorus was comparatively formal, so that one might often transpose a choral number from one situation to another without producing any incongruous result. One could not do this with a single chorus in *Castor et Pollux*.

We must leave the Parisian opera for the moment and return to Vienna to trace some of the influences which led to Gluck's contribution to these questions.

GLUCK'S REFORM OF OPERA

CHRISTOPH WILLIBALD GLUCK was born in 1714, the same year in which C. P. E. Bach was born, and after some preliminary musical education at Prague he visited Vienna, where he found a patron who took him to Milan to study under Giovanni Battista Sammartini, a famous composer who cultivated instrumental music far more assiduously than most Italians did at that time. Gluck began to compose strictly on the lines of Sammartini's instruction, yet was so clearly cut out as a dramatic composer that he turned out one opera after another. But he gave no particular evidence that he was likely to make any stronger mark than the other men of his day whose operas were performed, applauded, or condemned according to circumstance and then cast on one side.

His hasty visit to England in 1745 has already been mentioned; it was then that he met Handel who, when his operas failed to please the public, told him that he had taken too much trouble, though at the same time Handel complained of Gluck's lack of counterpoint (see p. 20).

On the same journey Gluck stayed in Paris, an event of more importance to his career than his visit to London, for in Paris he heard some of the operas of Rameau and was struck by Rameau's use of recitative and of the chorus. Hearing opera of such different design from that of his Italian masters must have set Gluck thinking, but he was slow to move; he went back to

Vienna and produced quantities more of the work which he understood from experience. His operas were accepted not only in Vienna but in the cities of Italy, Rome, and Naples. He was guided as to the design of these works by Metastasio (see p. 192), many of whose librettos he actually set, and whose fame as a dramatic poet was great enough to bring popular success to any work in which he had a share. Gluck might well hesitate before parting with so powerful an ally, the more so since he was anything but indifferent to public applause.

It was not until the year 1762, when he was forty-eight years of age, that he produced in Vienna the opera *Orfeo ed Euridice*, which was the great turning-point of his career. Though he was then very nearly of the same age as Rameau when he brought out his first opera, and *Orfeo* is the first of Gluck's operas to be important to the world at large, the circumstances of the two were very different. Gluck had not only a long stage experience behind him, but he had all the experience of men and life gained from his travel in several countries. Above all, he knew what are the things that appeal straight to the hearts of an audience, and so no matter what theories he might form and follow in the construction of his operas he was in no danger of losing sight of the human appeal.

It was not so much Gluck's own conviction that Italian opera needed thorough reformation as his meeting with Ranieri de Calzabigi which determined him to set the story of Orpheus and Eurydice, which had been set and reset in a conventional way by many hands, and to treat it according to its own requirements. With Calzabigi as librettist, and largely under his influence, Gluck decided that the story should not be forgotten while a singer took the middle of the stage and showed off the agility of his vocal technique. He rebelled especially against the crude alternation of arias with recitatives: one number in whatever form must lead logically to the next.

It is hardly necessary to say that he had all sorts of difficulties in the practical preparation of his opera for performance. To the singers and players in the Viennese Opera it seemed like a wilful reversal of every tradition to which they were accustomed. But Gluck met all objections stubbornly and insisted upon his ideas being carried out most strictly. He was fortunate in securing a man for the principal part of Orpheus who thought more of his art than of himself, a quality which was rare among opera singers of that day. But with the rest of the company his work was not so smooth. Some remonstrated and threatened to rebel, and at one time the Emperor had to interfere in order to secure the rehearsal and production of the opera. When it actually was seen the public was frankly puzzled, the more so since opera-goers then were not used to being puzzled. Nowadays a composer of opera who does not startle our sensibilities in one way or another is likely to be voted tame, but the Viennese public expected a certain code of procedure in every opera whether the music was new or old. The idea that the whole form should be remodelled according to the conditions of the story which the opera tells was incomprehensible at first.

Even Gluck himself seems to have had some doubts, at any rate about the practical expediency of the reforms, for after *Orfeo* he returned to librettos of the Metastasian type and for the next five years brought out nothing original. While he matured his plans he was content to give the public what it wanted, but in 1767 came *Alceste*, an opera in which his principles appear as strongly as in *Orfeo*, and are more mature in their application to a great tragedy. Not only did he reassert them practically, but he wrote a preface to the score which was a bold declaration of his faith and condemnation of the conventionalized opera in which up till then he had been content to trade.[1]

The preface condemned all musical elaboration made for the satisfaction of the singers or the composer; that is to say, the florid passages inserted to show the singer's voice, and orchestral passages put there to complete the numbers apart from the

[1] For the text of the preface see Alfred Einstein's *Gluck* ('Master Musicians' series), and for a complete critical study of the whole question of Gluck's attitude see that work and Ernest Newman's *Gluck and the Reform of the Opera*.

dramatic needs of the opera. The overture, Gluck said, should prepare the listeners for the action, and consequently should not conform to one type as both the French and Italian overtures had usually done. The instrumental accompaniments should employ instruments according as they could contribute to the feeling of the moment, and above all simplicity, he declared, should be the composer's aim in all parts of his work.

Both *Orfeo* and *Alceste* as well as the later works of Gluck were true to these principles, but there is one passage in this preface in which he asserts a theory which he certainly never carried into practice; that is the passage in which he declares that the proper function of music is to support the poetry and strengthen its expression, in fact that the music is of secondary importance. He was led to this statement and to others like it, such as the remark attributed to him that when he began to compose an opera he tried to forget that he was a musician, simply by the natural tendency of a man who is attacking an evil to be carried over to the extreme of defending an opposite evil.

We saw in the last chapter that the one rational defence of opera at all is the fact that the music has something of its own to say which cannot be said by the words. An opera in which the music was really only a tributary to the words would indeed be a futile expenditure of effort. If Gluck forgot that he was a musician that did not make him less of one, and no one who hears his operas forgets it. They live by their musical beauty, but the music framed on the principles which he worked out in the preface to *Alceste* allows the interests of the drama, words and action, to have free play.

Alceste had a more immediate success than *Orfeo*, but Gluck, with his eye always on the practical issue as well as on the artistic, wished for a clearer field of action than Vienna could be, overrun as it was by Italian music and musicians. He began to think of Paris as a possible centre from which to issue his operatic reforms. Various circumstances had kept hot the Parisians' interest in opera since the time of Rameau's chief productions.

Some years before (1752) an Italian company visiting Paris had given light opera there, and in their repertory was Pergolesi's *La serva padrona*. Its brilliant humour, sparkling melody, and the ease with which the dialogue flowed in recitative had caught the Parisian imagination, and it had been accepted by a public not very well informed as typical of Italian opera much in the same way as the English public early in this century accepted Tchaikovsky's symphonies as typical of Russian music. Critics declared that Italian was the language of music because it was evident that the Italians had found out how to treat their language in music. Their own nation, they said, had not done this, and therefore the French language was incapable of musical treatment. Rousseau went so far as to declare that the French had no music of their own, and that if they ever had it would be so much the worse for them.

The arguments produced against French opera were all those which were until recently produced against English opera when that subject periodically came up for discussion. The anti-French party disposed of their composers, their singers, and their language in one sweeping condemnation. But the difference between the 'Guerre des Bouffons' ('War of Comedians'), as it was called, and the English controversy was that while the latter was merely the subject of desultory discussion, which always left matters just where they were before, the former was carried on with the greatest heat and determination to gain proof on both sides. The Parisian opera-goers, whether for or against their own music, at least showed that a purely artistic question was to them a vital one.

The national party did not mind securing a foreign ally. Their main point was not so much to prove the worth of their own composers as to prove the capacity of their own language and their own style of treating it in the opera. Lully was an Italian by birth, but he had made French music; Gluck was an Austrian by residence, but he might uphold it. So after his variable fortune with *Orfeo* and *Alceste* in Vienna Gluck was ready to take up the cause of the Parisian party which opposed itself to conventional Italian opera, and that party was ready to accept him as champion. With this in view, before he left Vienna he had composed a tragedy, *Iphigénie en Aulide*, to a French libretto adapted from Racine's drama, and thus armed he at length accepted an invitation to go to Paris in 1774 and produce it at the Opéra. In this venture he was able to gain the support of the Queen, Marie Antoinette, whom he had known years ago when she was an Austrian princess, and so he was sure of securing all the interest which friends and opponents could arouse, and of escaping the artist's one serious enemy, which is apathy. His work flourished in Paris; the new opera was followed by adaptations of *Orfeo* and *Alceste*, the texts being translated and the music considerably modified, and the nationalists began to feel that their language at any rate was vindicated.

The opposite party, however, was not routed. The advocates of Italian opera could play the same game with better logic and, they hoped, with equal success. They could reasonably find out the strongest Italian composer and bring him to Paris to assert his superiority over the Teutonic Gluck, who was thus championing the French language and style. But whom could they get? Had the crisis occurred only a few years later they might have found out the young Mozart who, although an Austrian, was steeped in the traditions of Italy, and who would have shown them the best that those traditions could produce. We have seen (p. 202) that so nearly did the dates fit that while the controversy was still in progress in 1778 Mozart was actually in Paris and eating his heart out for a chance of proving his powers as a composer of opera. He, however, was there too late, and even had the Italian supporters not already found their man they could scarcely have been expected to choose a young fellow just turned twenty-two, whose one grand opera (*Mitridate*), written for Milan when he was fourteen, had been considered successful only because it was the work of a mere child.

The Italian party wanted a real master to set against the towering strength of Gluck. They naturally turned to the man who had made the whole of Europe applaud his one brilliantly successful opera some years previously, and so seemed to them to be the very embodiment of the cause they wanted to advance. Just as earlier in this century an advocate for contemporary Italian opera would have first pointed to Puccini, the composer of *La Bohème* and *Madam Butterfly*, so they naturally thought of a man (whose name, by the way, is rather similar) who had made a great hit with one opera, *La Cecchina*, or *La buona figliuola* (The Good Girl: it was based on Richardson's *Pamela*), some years before, and who had poured out some two dozen others since. His name was Niccola Piccinni.

It is a curious reflection upon the different standards which time brings that it would not have been necessary for us to mention his name here at all on account of *La Cecchina*, though in its day it was performed in every opera-house in Europe. Its popularity was merely the fashion of the moment, and neither it nor any other work by Piccinni made any permanent mark on the history of the art, or left us anything we value for its own sake now. It is just as well to remember this, since we are so constantly reminded of the great works which were scorned and derided when they first appeared. In our desire to avoid that error at the present day we are liable to fall into the opposite one of fervently embracing what is wholly a passing fashion.

Piccinni, then, only claims to be remembered because he was brought to Paris to oppose Gluck in 1776. He was the younger of the two, but he seems to have known that his transitory success was over, and to have had no personal desire to set himself up as a prophet. He came, however, tempted by the lucrative offer. The two composers were to be set to work to compose on one theme; Gluck had already been given versions of two romances by Quinault (see p. 64) previously set by Lully, *Armide* and *Roland*, and it was proposed that Piccinni should also set *Roland*. This direct competition Gluck very rightly refused as unworthy of both of them. His *Armide* was written and might be produced under proper conditions, but he destroyed what was written of *Roland* and left that field open to his opponent. The two subjects, however, were sufficiently comparable to make good grounds of discussion for the partisans.

Gluck's *Armide* came out first in September 1777, and was established as a masterpiece before Piccinni's *Roland* was ready. He was destined to write one more great work for the Parisian stage, with which he secured his final triumph in May 1779, *Iphigénie en Tauride*, a companion to his earlier *Iphigénie en Aulide*. A last French opera of his, *Écho et Narcisse*, of the same year, has not maintained itself.

Again Piccinni was brought forward and also given a libretto on Iphigenia in Tauris. If he knew how Gluck had behaved in the matter of *Roland* it was scarcely to his credit that he accepted the commission. But his acceptance made no difference to the event. Gluck's position was unassailable, especially since his work came out first and was acknowledged at something like its true worth before Piccinni got a hearing. Gluck's was a serious musical treatment of the classical drama; Piccinni's was merely an opera on a poor libretto, having the same story as its basis.

The production of Gluck's *Iphigénie en Tauride* took place on 18 May 1779, too late to be heard by Mozart on his visit to Paris, which had come to an end the previous September. But Mozart could have heard a repeat performance of *Armide*, and he was certainly aware of the stir which Gluck's work was just then making in the French capital. In any case the end of Gluck's career was the beginning of Mozart's as one of the operatic composers who really count. The next time that Mozart had an opportunity of producing an opera at the carnival season in Munich, in 1781 (see p. 202), he chose in *Idomeneo* a classical theme which gave scope for some of that kind of treatment which Gluck had followed in *Iphigénie*.

In this work the style of Gluck and, indirectly, that of Rameau in the use of the chorus are found contending with what is specially characteristic of Mozart. But Mozart was to leave his mark more distinctly upon quite another type of opera, and the things by which he chiefly lives in the theatre are the later Italian comedies, *Figaro*, *Don Giovanni*, and *Così fan tutte*.

The first thing which will probably strike you in Gluck's operas is that after all that has been said of his reforms and his determination to return to natural and simple expression, the whole thing is still extraordinarily formal. That is partly because we cannot help coming to him with some ready-made notions, based on Verdi or Puccini, of what an opera should be like, and partly because, as we have already suggested, Gluck was sometimes better and sometimes worse than his creed. He was better in the fact that when the music took real hold upon him he did not curb it to suit the smaller needs of dramatic propriety, and so we get those wonderful lyrical moments of which 'Che farò' is a typical instance. He was worse because one may point to things which are purely a makeweight in the scheme like the bustling overture to *Orfeo*, which seems written chiefly to hide the sound of rustling dresses and preliminary conversation with which every audience at an opera settled into its seats in the eighteenth century.

But sometimes, too, that simplicity of aim may deceive us, if we are careless listeners, into thinking that he was writing by rule when really he was feeling every note deeply. Take the first chorus of *Orfeo*, and when you have played it or sung in it often enough you will not think its stateliness is a mere matter of form, but realize that it is part of its very being. Orpheus and his companions are grieving for the death of Eurydice, but Gluck knows better than to begin by tearing passion to tatters. In the steady march of the bass there is a throbbing persistence which suggests the sense of an irresistible fate, nor can it be a mere coincidence that the melody bears a clear likeness to that of 'Che farò', the air in which later Orpheus mourns his second loss.

To suggest the same idea by the use of the same phrase of music was quite unusual in the opera of Gluck's day. Audiences were not sufficiently thoughtful to make it worth while for composers to think so closely. Gluck himself made no general habit of doing so. We find it in music that was not operatic before his time; in Bach for example. In modern music following Wagner it has become so general as to be a commonplace. In the course of the chorus, and without interrupting it, Orpheus three times sings the name of Eurydice and nothing more, each time dropping to a low note on the last syllable, and the last time beginning upon a higher note than before and so expressing a more intense feeling.

All through *Orfeo* Gluck uses orchestral accompaniment, even in the recitatives, indeed he uses two orchestras, the second echoing the first behind the stage. A wonderful effect is produced by this means in the recitatives and airs of Orpheus's soliloquy, when he has asked his companions to leave him and he stands alone by the tomb.

Ex. 53

The end of each vocal phrase is repeated by the second orchestra, as though to picture his loneliness; the tones of his own voice are thrown back to him in an echo. One can see the difference between Gluck's deeper feeling in this part, which has to do with a human tragedy, and his more superficial style when the story is carried on by the appearance of Cupid to Orpheus, by comparing Orpheus's songs with that with which Cupid greets him.

In the second act Gluck concentrates more upon the pictorial side of opera, and here one has to remember that its pictures were not the realistic ones to which the modern stage has accustomed us, but rather symbolic. The opening dance of the Furies interrupted by the sounds of Orpheus's lute (the harp of the second orchestra behind the stage) may seem trite by comparison with the effects of a modern orchestra, but Gluck was not aiming at such effects and failing to get them; he was using the effects which would be appropriate to the scene as it then appeared. The chorus of spirits and the appeal to them in song by Orpheus, an appeal constantly interrupted by their cries of 'No, no', is an intensely dramatic scene, all the more so for the fact that the means used are far simpler than those of Rameau, for example, in a similar scene in *Castor et Pollux*.

We need not dwell upon the obvious contrast between this act and the next, in which Orpheus at length meets the spirit of Eurydice in the Elysian fields, but the exquisite tenderness of the ballet music in the latter scene, particularly the slow air in D minor for flute, with the rippling accompaniment in semiquavers below it, ought to be known. Fortunately it is sometimes to be heard at concerts.

One of the finest instances of Gluck's use of dramatic recitative is the conversation between Orpheus and Eurydice, as he leads her back to the upper world. The condition of her rescue is that he shall not look back at her as she follows him, and she, mistaking his face turned from her for indifference, implores him to turn. But the series of recitatives, arias, and duets in which their feelings are expressed, and the skill with which the numbers are linked together cannot be described here. It becomes perfectly clear and convincing when seen and heard on the stage. One further word about 'Che farò' may be given to show how the development of this aria grows out of the emotion of the moment. After the middle section, where the music modulates, a return is made to the first theme according to the usual principle of ternary form. But it is not a repetition of the air in a formal way. The upward *arpeggio* figure, which was a prominent feature from the first, is pressed further and emphasized till a high note never used before is reached, so that the climax of feeling comes at the very end.

The restoration of Eurydice by Cupid's intervention one cannot help feeling to be perfunctory. Gluck must have felt in his heart even if he did not realize with his brain that the happy ending made an anticlimax. At any rate you have only to compare the recitative by which the business is settled with those of Orpheus in the first act, or with the dialogue between Orpheus and Eurydice just preceding to see the difference between commonplace recitative and inspired declamation.

With the limits of our space and the little hope of adequate illustration it would be futile to try to trace Gluck's gradual growth to consistency and sureness of handling through the chain of his big works culminating in *Iphigénie en Tauride*. Anyone who has realized the spirit which moved him to the first, *Orfeo*, and who knows the music well enough to be able to distinguish the great moments from those which do not reach so high, has made fairly good preparation for the enjoyment of any of the operas when occasion offers. In the later operas it will be possible to realize how he advances in two ways: (1) in making the overture appropriate to the opera which follows it, and (2) in distinguishing the characters of the people and their different sentiments by the kinds of melody they sing. The overture to *Iphigénie en Tauride* is a triumphant example of the first. It pictures the tempest in which the play opens, and at its height the curtain rises and without any break the voice of Iphigenia is heard above the storm calling upon the gods. It is a parallel opening to that of Wagner's *Die Walküre*. The first scene of *Iphigénie en Aulide* gives at once an instance of the second in the prayer of Agamemnon to Diana and the contrast it makes with the declamation in which he rebels against the idea of sacrificing his daughter.

In only one important instance did Gluck leave classical drama for a romantic subject, and that was in *Armide*, a story which was a time-honoured one for operatic treatment. The general outline of Gluck's *Armide*, since it was based on Quinault's libretto, is so similar to Lully's (see pp. 69 ff.) as to need no further description; it is the richness of his treatment in every detail, the beauty of the airs, the elaborate *ensembles* between principal characters and the chorus, the great variety of the ballet music which make of it a new and far more vivid thing.

GLUCK'S SUCCESSORS

Gluck's work was too much the outcome of his own personal conviction and individuality to produce direct successors or found a 'school' of composition. His influence upon others was indirect. Méhul, a young French composer, who heard the first performance of *Iphigénie en Tauride*, was deeply impressed and, to some extent, influenced by him in his later work; Grétry, who was rather older, was more influenced by Italian melody, but turned the current of French opera towards a lighter style than that which was the outcome of Gluck's deep thought and long struggle.

LUIGI CHERUBINI, an Italian by birth, who, however, had been trained not so much in the contemporary mannerisms of Italian opera as in the older and finer styles of contrapuntal music, settled in Paris in 1788 and produced a number of operas of which *Médée* was the most important. A 'rescue' opera[1] '*Les Deux Journées* (known in England as 'The Water Carrier') is occasionally revived. Though Gluck's influence may be found in some of his work it is only one among many. Cherubini was indeed a cosmopolitan musician of wide experience and profound scholarship, who had all the possibilities of technique and style so thoroughly at his disposal that no one personality, not even his own, is very strongly felt in his work. He made for himself a great position, was head of the Paris Conservatoire founded in 1795, and in that capacity he naturally exerted a wide influence upon French music. His operas were

[1] A special type of *opéra-comique* (not comic in subject) which flourished about the time of the French Revolution, on a story which involves the characters in mortal danger but ends happily with their 'rescue'. The greatest example is Beethoven's *Fidelio*, which conformed to this French type by its origin in a German translation of a libretto first used by Pierre Gaveaux in *Léonore* (1798).

performed in Vienna and largely in Germany; his orchestral works became famous in England, and his overtures are sometimes to be heard at concerts even at the present day.

MOZART'S OPERAS

Mozart, on reaching maturity as an opera composer, was, as we have seen, considerably affected by Gluck at first, and this experience stimulated him to search out the essential characteristics in the subjects which he touched. But the cast of his mind was wholly different. Instead of rebelling against the conventions of the kind of opera on which he had been brought up, he set himself to make the best possible thing of it within its limits. In doing so he succeeded in showing that the mould was not worn out and worthless for a man who had the right stuff to pour into it. His most famous Italian works, *Figaro*, *Don Giovanni* and *Così fan tutte*, may be considered to be descendants, though very remote ones, of that type of Italian light opera of which we have mentioned *La serva padrona* as an example. In them nothing is to be taken too seriously. Plot and counterplot, producing absurdly extravagant situations, calling for quick interplay of character on the dramatic side, balanced by pure beauty and shapeliness on the musical side, were the things with which he dealt to the best advantage. They are, in fact, the same qualities turned to different account which we found in his symphonic works. The operatic tunes are not always so sharply cut or distinct from one another as are those of the symphonies, and that illustrates the principle touched upon in the last chapter, where it was pointed out that opera using several means of expression at once does not require so much for any one of them as the separated arts do.

To see Mozart's symphonic treatment of an operatic situation at its best we may look at the finale to the second act of *Figaro*. A great deal has happened in the course of the act. It began with the countess's sorrowful reflections in the aria 'Porgi amor'; then came Susanna her maid and Figaro the count's man, with their plot to pay the count out with a practical joke by dressing up the page, Cherubino, as a girl. While they were preparing him the count, scenting mischief, had appeared on the scene, demanding to be let into the inner room where Cherubino was hidden. That young scapegrace, unknown to the countess, had solved the difficulty by jumping out of the window while she tried to make up stories to avert the count's anger. At last the count, forcing an entrance, had found no one but Susanna. So both the count and countess had been fooled, the former because he had not got to the bottom of the mystery, the latter because she had given herself away unnecessarily.

The finale begins with an agitated duet between the count and countess, followed by a trio, in which Susanna takes part. The object is to heighten the interest progressively by further complications of the plot, and to make at the same time a musical climax. We have the gardener complaining that his flowers have been destroyed by a man jumping out of the window, which naturally gives the count a considerable clue to the mystery, and Figaro declaring himself the culprit, but unable to establish the fact very satisfactorily, and the other minor characters coming in to make the confusion greater. So gradually the plot and, at the same time, the musical score thicken, till at last seven voices join in the climax. It is useless to analyse the detail; one can only appreciate the scene when it is heard and seen on the stage. The one thing to realize is the brilliancy with which the play is carried on and timed while the music develops on its own lines, each character darting in to add fresh point to the whole. Its extent and command of climax, its unfailing match between dramatic propriety and musical beauty, make this perhaps the most perfect dramatic scene ever written by a composer.

In his mature works Mozart was just as opposed to giving way to the desire of singers to show off their skill as Gluck had been. His arias are designed to express the feelings uppermost at the moment, from the pathetic charm of 'Porgi amor' and 'Dove sono' to the martial vigour of 'Non più andrai' or the exquisite charm of Cherubino's canzonet 'Voi che sapete'. It is true that there is much greater abundance of ornament in the arias of *Don Giovanni*, and there are the famous Queen of Night's songs in *The Magic Flute* in which *coloratura* is pushed to its farthest limits. But all these things are used to give special character to the music, just as the passages of a violin concerto arising out of the capacities of the instrument give a special type of interest which nothing else could give. Their presence is not a concession to the demand for display, but the use of technical ability to serve the ends of the artist.

The most marvellous thing about Mozart's operas is the way their music defies analysis in words. Over and over again we may be at a loss to account by the light of reason for the music taking the particular course it does take, and, on the other hand, to name this or that point where one notes some feature of peculiar appropriateness does not really advance the understanding or enjoyment of his work to any great extent. It may even interfere with it by suggesting that Mozart took particular thought to secure such a point, when really he merely passed it in his stride.

When we come to see the operas actually performed, however, the details, accountable and unaccountable alike, fall into place. Mozart seems to be the most unconscious writer who ever lived. It all comes from him apparently without his taking thought as Gluck and Wagner did, yet it is never thoughtless as so much Italian opera written by Italians has been, for, taken, as a whole, it justifies itself to artistic perception independently of intellectual reasoning.

To give sketches of the stories of the operas would take a great many more words than the result would be worth, for they are often so involved that a description in words is apt to give the impression of a confused rigmarole. While Gluck's choice of subjects kept mainly to the clear lines of classical Greek drama, Mozart plunged boldly into subjects of innumerable different kinds. Indeed, his great facility in writing and his constant need of accepting any offer which was made to him prevented him often from exercising a scrupulous choice of subject, though that of *Figaro* at least is in the highest class of pure comedy. For the sake of clearness we may end this rapid glance at his work by recounting the principal operas with which the opera-goer in England comes in contact at the present day, recalling again a few circumstances connected with each.

Out of a number of youthful efforts the only one which may be met with is the little German 'Singspiel' *Bastien und Bastienne*, and the first important opera in the grand style is *Idomeneo* (1781), which followed soon after Mozart had witnessed Gluck's triumph in Paris (see pp. 202 and 288). *Die Entführung* in the next year was his contribution to the Emperor's attempt to further German opera in Vienna. Then at the time of his own success at Prague come two of his great comedies, *Figaro* (1786) and *Don Giovanni* (1787), both welcomed in that town, and the latter written specially for performance there. The third, for which the libretto was supplied by the same man, Da Ponte, who had compiled the two preceding ones, was *Così fan tutte* (1790), after which comes a change again to the serious style of *La clemenza di Tito*. This, written in a hurry for the coronation of the new Emperor, made use of an adaptation from an old libretto by Metastasio, a story of imperial Rome in the grandiloquent manner which opera, thanks to Gluck and Mozart himself, had outgrown.

Last of all comes that most extraordinary work *Die Zauberflöte* ('The Magic Flute'), written to a German libretto by Schikaneder, an actor-manager, who asked Mozart for music to a fairy play, by which he meant a work with no more consistency of design than one expects to find in a modern English pantomime. The story used to be set down as sheer nonsense, but modern criticism has done something to unravel its tangled threads in which Eastern fairy tales with a maze of magical occurrences and the mysteries of freemasonry seemed inextricably mixed.[1] It is sufficient evidence of Mozart's astounding

[1] See E. J. Dent's *Mozart's Operas—a Critical Study*.

genius that in the last few months of his life, when his health was shattered, he was able to produce from such material an opera which, more than a hundred and fifty years afterwards, is still regarded as one of the great things of the art by the sheer force of its musical beauty.

Suggestions for Further Reading and Listening

FURTHER discussion of the subjects covered in this chapter will be found in the various general histories of music already mentioned, and in the books on opera named at the end of the last chapter. Readers are also reminded of the relevant chapters in *The New Oxford History of Music*, Volume VII.

With regard to individual composers, the standard critical biography of *Jean-Philippe Rameau* is by Cuthbert Girdlestone. The best introduction to Gluck is provided by Alfred Einstein in the 'Master Musicians' series, though Martin Cooper's biography, of much the same, mid 1930s, vintage, is well worth consulting. There is little literature on Piccini, but Eric Blom devoted a chapter to him in his *Stepchildren of Music*.

The material on Gluck's successors (pp. 134–5) is fully amplified in *The Rise of Romantic Opera*, a series of lectures by E. J. Dent which have recently been prepared for publication by Winton Dean. Post-Gluckian and Revolutionary Opera are, in fact, topics that have much attracted attention during the last decade or two. Note for instance, Basil Deane's biography of Cherubini, in O.U.P.'s 'Studies of Composers' series. Mozart's operas have inspired an enormous amount of literature in every language. For years, the chief work in English on the subject has been E. J. Dent's *Mozart's Operas*; but now there is also William Mann's comprehensive *The Operas of Mozart*.

Colles's study of Rameau's *Castor et Pollux* needs backing up with a vocal score, and with the excellent and stylistically authoritative Harnoncourt recording. Apart from the quality of the music and of its performance, these records can serve to demonstrate the French tradition of recitative, so different from that of the Italians.

Gluck's operas are much more strongly represented in the gramophone catalogue than they were. Not only are there three versions of *Orfeo*, in its original Italian form, but also *Alceste* and *Iphigénie en Aulide*, not to mention excerpts from others of his operas. By contrast, there is little to be heard of Piccini, whereas Cherubini's *Médée*, recorded in 1959 with Callas in the title role, is still available. Of the recording of Mozart operas there is no end, and it is impossible to particularize; but watch the gramophone magazines, and make good use of those public libraries equipped with a record section.

CHAPTER 14

Beethoven

In one of the back streets of Bonn, between Cologne and Coblenz on the Rhine, there is a small house containing at the top a tiny garret with a sloping roof. In this room Ludwig van Beethoven was born on 16 December 1770. Like Mozart, he was the son of a musician engaged in the service of a local court, but anyone who visits both the house of Mozart's birth in Salzburg and that of Beethoven's in Bonn can see that the circumstances of their childhood were widely different (see p. 195). Beethoven's father was a tenor singer in the chapel of the Elector of Cologne, a post which brought him in only a poor income. He was not, like Leopold Mozart, a man of any distinction in his profession, and though he gave his son his first music lessons he was very soon glad to hand over to others such education as Ludwig received. There were no triumphant tours over Europe for him; not that that was an evil in itself, but then there was not for him that systematic training for a musical career which Mozart received.

Beethoven, like Haydn, got his education largely through the need for acting upon his own initiative. When he was twelve years old he got the post of accompanist (on the piano or harpsichord) in the electoral theatre, which was practically the post of conductor, for at that time the practice still survived, at any rate in the smaller theatres, of making the man who accompanied the recitative also responsible for keeping the band together. We must not suppose that the fact of Beethoven being given this work at the age of twelve shows that he was recognized as a genius. He was of course seen to be a clever boy beyond his years in musicianship, but it rather goes to show how very little conducting was realized as an art. Nowadays the conductor controls the whole musical interpretation of an opera, or at any rate he is supposed to do so; then the conductor was expected merely to give the tempo to the band in the accompaniment of the singers. So little was this young conductor considered that it was thought unnecessary to pay him for his services. His only payment was that of experience until, in 1784, a new Elector succeeded upon the death of the old one, and in the course of reorganizing the arrangements of the chapel Beethoven was made second organist with a small salary.

During these years he composed regularly, not with the superabundant confidence of Mozart at the same age, but with a steady persistence which showed that he meant to learn how to do it. He never at any time in his life had that facility which we find in most of the great earlier composers; there are many stories told of their speed in writing this or that work, and they showed by the quantities they left behind them that composition was to them a comparatively easy matter. Slowness is the first quality in Beethoven's character, marking him as typical of the change of attitude of musicians towards their art which came almost precisely at the turn of the century. We shall see that almost all Beethoven's great works (they began to appear at about the year 1800) were the result of long thought and mental struggle, during which he gradually shaped them out by a process of writing and rewriting, and that sometimes he took up a work after it had been finished and performed to remodel it more in accordance with his mature reflections.

It is uncertain how it came about that in 1787 he was able to make the long journey to Vienna, where he visited Mozart and succeeded in impressing him by his extemporized playing on the piano. Probably some friend interested in his progress sent him. Though the visit was a short one it was of immense importance to Beethoven. It gave him his first sight of the big musical world where great things happened, and it introduced him personally to the man who was making those things happen. This was the year after the success of *Figaro* and the Symphony in D at Prague. Mozart was in the act of preparing *Don Giovanni* for his second visit to Prague. He was for the moment on the crest of the wave.

Beethoven's compositions in the next few years after his return to Bonn are either more numerous or have been more carefully recorded as of greater importance. The year 1792 is the next landmark in his career. As far as outward circumstances are concerned it might be called the only landmark, for it saw the one important change in his life, his permanent removal from Bonn to Vienna. In this year he met Haydn travelling to and from England (see p. 209), showed him some of his work and was encouraged to go forward with it, and later in the year the opportunity was given him by his master, the Elector, to go again to Vienna, this time for definite study under Haydn. There seems to have been no precise understanding about his return, but, from the affectionate leave-taking of his friends in Bonn, who were many, it is evident that they realized the parting to be a long one. It was in fact a parting for good, for once caught in the busy life of the world's greatest musical centre no other sphere of action was large enough for Beethoven.

Like Mozart before him Beethoven made his reputation in Vienna as a performer. He played the piano at the musical gatherings of the Viennese nobility, and the wonders of his improvisation soon raised his reputation high. But from the first the reader of his life or his letters must realize the difference in their relationship. Beethoven did not ask for favours, he gave them; and his best friends, both men and women, people who ordinarily might have treated a musician to that mixture of patronage and flattery which is still common amongst amateurs, accepted his attitude unhesitatingly as a just one. They not only admired but loved him, and that in spite of all the outward features of his manners and habits which might offend a fastidious taste. We are not going to tell again the many stories of Beethoven's rudeness and arrogance, and of the ill-treatment and cruel suspicions of the actions of people who were devoted to him. The appearance of such things in a big nature is altogether different from their appearance in a small one, as refuse thrown up by the sea differs from that covering the surface of a stagnant pool. In Beethoven they were counteracted by the massive strength of his character, his overwhelming devotion to his art, and the capacity for tenderness which underlay the stormy exterior. Moreover, they were aggravated by physical causes, the chief among them being the deafness from which he began to suffer a few years after he reached Vienna. Morose irritability and particularly suspicion of others are well known as frequent accompaniments to disease of this kind; but when the disease attacks a man whose whole life and soul is expressed through the ears in music the affliction must prey upon him as the most terrible of evils.

At first the business of establishing himself as a performer and of studying composition, and more particularly of counterpoint with Haydn, occupied Beethoven fully. But his relations with his teacher were not altogether happy. Their contradictory natures jarred upon one another. Haydn probably could not understand Beethoven's incapacity to take life with the same easy stride which had carried him so well along its path. He missed the facile progress which he himself had made apparently against greater odds than Beethoven had to encounter. Beethoven, on the other hand, complained that Haydn did not enter with sufficient seriousness into his work. Their whole casts of mind were opposed. Even their racial difference would be sufficient to place them poles apart. Haydn, a southerner with possibly a Slavonic strain in him, who took in music and gave it out almost as unconsciously as he breathed, Beethoven a northern German of Dutch extraction, who instinctively submitted every impulse to be judged by a process of reasoning, naturally approached every subject from opposite points of view. To Haydn, no doubt, many matters of custom seemed to be unchangeable laws, and when Beethoven met his statement of the fact, 'It is so,' with the questions, 'But why is it so?' and 'Need it always be so?' he found he had a tiresome pupil and Beethoven found he had an unsatisfactory master. Yet each was too great not to realize the greatness of the other, though when

Haydn went away again to England Beethoven was glad to get other teaching.

EARLY COMPOSITIONS

It was while he was studying counterpoint with Albrechtsberger (1795), a teacher who probably suited Beethoven all the better for the fact that though he had profound knowledge he was not a great creative artist like Haydn, that Beethoven's own important compositions began to make their appearance. In this year he wrote his Trios for pianoforte, violin, and violoncello (Op. 1), and his three piano Sonatas (Op. 2) in F minor, A major, and C major, which, by the way, he dedicated to Haydn, showing his admiration for the artist whom he disliked as a teacher. At about this time or a little earlier he had composed the Trio for two oboes and cor anglais (Op. 87),[1] the latter instrument a larger kind of oboe with a lower compass much used in the modern orchestra, the piano Concerto in B flat (Op. 19), and that in C major (Op. 15).

These are the things which show him definitely starting upon the career of composition which was ultimately to change the whole face of musical art, not only enriching it with works of imperishable beauty in almost every branch, but leading the way towards all the fresh infusion of power which music has drawn from so many sources during the last century. Add to them the productions of the next few years, including the two Sonatas for piano and violoncello (Op. 5), the Trios for strings (violin, viola, and violoncello, Op. 9), further piano Sonatas (Op. 10) and the famous 'Sonate pathétique' (Op. 13), that in B flat (Op. 22), and others, the first six string Quartets (Op. 18), the Septet (Op. 20) for clarinet, bassoon, horn, and strings, and the first Symphony in C major (Op. 21), which brings the list up to the year 1800, and you see Beethoven at last taking a firm hold upon all the forms of solo, chamber, and orchestral music which he was to carry on to hitherto unsuspected developments.

[1] The late opus number of this trio, as of certain other early works, is due to the fact that it was not published at the time it was composed.

We may well say 'at last' when we remember that by the age of thirty, which Beethoven reached in the year 1800, Haydn had carved out for himself the main principles of the quartet and the symphony; Mozart had produced the great bulk of his work except his greatest operas and symphonies. Haydn may well be forgiven if he felt some disappointment at the slowness with which his pupil got to work. It may seem more extraordinary that others among his friends, amateurs such as Count Waldstein who helped him in his life at Bonn, the Princes Lichnowsky and Lobkowitz who were among his staunch adherents from his first coming to Vienna, never doubted his supremacy among artists. That, however, is accounted for by Beethoven himself. It was the man, not his immediate achievements, upon whom his friends based their faith. He had that absolute confidence in himself which only giants among men can afford to keep. No matter how little his output might correspond for the moment to what was expected of him, he knew that his big powers would somehow or other result in big work. For him to take command of the society about him, to claim their compliance, even to trample unmercifully upon people who displeased him, before he had proved in actual works his right to such a position, was not to play a gambling game, whatever else it might be, because he knew that he only needed time to justify himself completely.

Not only was he without Mozart's astounding facility, except indeed when he improvised at the piano, but he had nothing like the early originality of Haydn. He did not in these first compositions immediately begin to strike out a new path for himself. In some of them it is quite difficult to perceive the mind of Beethoven at work. The common shapes of sonata form he accepted just where Mozart left them. In the early sonatas for piano and other instruments there are a number of turns of expression which come straight from Mozart's vocabulary. You have only to play over the Adagio of his first piano Sonata (Op. 2) side by side with the Andante of Mozart's C major piano Sonata (K. 309; both are in the key of F major) to realize this. The main melodies are Beethoven's own, though they might have been thought of by almost any composer of the period, but his ways of ornamenting them, breaking them up with rapid scale passages, and particularly the additions of chromatic harmony here and there, are entirely Mozart's. Or, again, to go back for a moment to that little Trio for oboes and cor anglais, even a fairly experienced listener might easily put it down to Haydn, and in doing so he would not think it one of Haydn's best works. It has caught something of his easy and genial spirit without being peculiarly interesting. We may say, speaking roughly, that the manners of both Haydn and Mozart are so obviously adopted in certain of these early works of Beethoven that if we had not got the things which followed them by which to test his musical character we might have a good deal of difficulty in tracing his personality in them. Nevertheless some things, particularly in the piano sonatas, would stand out clearly as his own. No one could miss the profound beauty of the melody of the Largo appassionato which forms the slow movement of the Sonata in A (Op. 2, No. 2), or think that the majesty of its climax where it rises through the keys of D minor and B flat major was the thought of any brain but Beethoven's; but elsewhere, especially when he is writing for instruments with which he was less intimately acquainted than the piano, the general tone and colour bear a family resemblance to his predecessors. This is not surprising: influences are always less remarkable in a young composer than new departures.

One cannot emphasize this too strongly, because people, and especially young people, who make their first acquaintance with Beethoven through some of his very early works, often rebel against the demand to regard them and him with special awe and reverence. A great deal of his music seems very much like a great deal of other music, only not so attractive. It neither sparkles like Mozart's nor glows like Haydn's.

We will presently try to realize some of the ways in which Beethoven put his hallmark upon his own music, so that one can recognize him in it even where its outward shape is to a certain extent the result of circumstances from which he could not shake himself free for some time. It is comforting to know that when he had succeeded in doing so he was as inclined to be impatient of his first efforts as anybody else could possibly be. It is well known that when he heard somebody playing his thirty-two Variations upon a theme in C minor, a work from which many of us have suffered in our school-days, he exclaimed 'Oh, Beethoven, what an ass you were in those days!' and that is only one instance among many. He was ruthless in condemning whatever in his music he felt had been thoughtless, though such music was in fact the stepping-stone by which he had learnt to express himself more truly.

METHOD AND STYLE

Before we begin to turn to detail, however, we must follow his life a little farther, not so much to record its events as to get some idea of how he worked and developed. Events, indeed, matter less in the study of Beethoven's music than in that of almost any other composer. He never moved from Vienna except for the summer holidays in the country, which were only holidays in the sense that then he could give himself to the work of his life more entirely without interruption, or for the visits to Baden and elsewhere which he took for the sake of his general health or to try some fresh but always futile treatment to cure his deafness. In Vienna itself his story is mainly that of the successive appearances of his works at the houses of his friends or at public concerts. There were times when success favoured him, or when happiness both artistic and personal seemed nearly within his grasp. Such a time occurred in the year 1806 when he was writing both the fourth and fifth symphonies, almost the most crowded period of his creative life, during which he became engaged to be married to his pupil the Countess Therese von Brunsvick. But the engagement was never fulfilled. This, like all other prospects of happiness, eluded Beethoven. He was not always in poverty, but he never became rich, and he died poor. Almost the whole of the rest of his story is the series of difficulties over money matters (he was even more incapable of managing business than Mozart had been); his troubles with relatives who sponged upon him, especially his nephew and ward, Carl, to whom he ultimately left what little property he possessed; the opposition towards his works shown chiefly by professional musicians, and the faithful admiration extended to them and him chiefly by amateurs. We need not attempt here to describe it all in detail, only the general stress and unhappiness of his life, which his growing fame seemed powerless to relieve, must be borne in mind if his music is to be understood.

Outside the purely personal considerations we must not forget the drastic changes which passed over the whole of European society just when the new century was beginning, changes which affected artistic and intellectual life as radically, if not quite as rapidly, as they affected political life. The great revolution in France was the first strong outward sign that the older civilization of the eighteenth century was breaking up, and in the first years of the nineteenth century the whole of Europe was in a ferment. It may seem that wars and material catastrophes, as we pointed out on p. 87, do not check artistic progress effectually, but the intellectual ideas of which wars are a symptom must affect the course of an art very powerfully. Twice during the most productive part of Beethoven's career Vienna was occupied by the armies of Napoleon, but his work went steadily forward. Nevertheless, the idea which brought those armies into existence, since it permeated the whole of European life, was at the very root of Beethoven's music. That idea which dethroned kings, swept away the landmarks of the older social régime, and changed the whole attitude of individuals towards religion and the state, was simply this, that nothing was any longer to be taken on trust. Life could be made what men chose to make of it if only they were strong enough. The French revolutionists' cry of 'Liberty, Equality, and Fraternity' was the party cry of the moment, and as we know brought anything but a literal fulfilment. What it really meant was the assertion of independent thought and action, and this spirit was stirring in the English and German nations, who were vigorously opposed to its most violent political developments in France. It was the spirit which gave birth to the inventive genius of the nineteenth century, which ultimately brought railways and electricity, Reform Bills and Trades Unions; it animated the poetic thought of Goethe and Schiller, and infused itself into the music of Beethoven from the 'Sonata appassionata' to the ninth Symphony.

Here we may find the strongest reason for Beethoven's slow working and his comparatively small output. Haydn and Mozart could turn out symphonies and quartets by the dozen because they accepted certain principles of order without question. Everything that was beautiful was worth expressing and could be expressed by certain means which they and their contemporaries had learnt to use readily. With Beethoven every work must be a matter of strong personal conviction; it must be thought out afresh from the beginning, since nothing was fixed once and for all; there were no rules to be taken for granted. When he looked back to his early works and found how much he had taken for granted, the discovery disgusted him and caused such outbursts of anger against himself as his remark about the thirty-two Variations. His was not a nature to indulge in a violent revolution like Monteverdi; to issue manifestoes about what art ought to be and what it was not, like Gluck and Wagner. That would have been to set up a new set of rules in place of the old ones. He was too entirely a musical artist to make words first and music afterwards, but with everything he produced the conviction that he must solve each problem in its own way forced itself more strongly upon him. Something which before he had accepted unhesitatingly had to give way before his clearer vision. First it was the mannerisms of melody and ornament which he had inherited from Haydn and Mozart. Then he felt that his own ideas as he first put them on paper did not represent his feeling truly and accurately. He adopted the plan of putting them down just as they came, merely catching a glimpse of his thought as it passed; then he sifted them, discovering what part really represented that thought, what was the chance of the moment or due to mere convention of style; and so, rejecting the latter and perfecting what he felt to be genuine, he gradually formed his melodies, extended them, and moulded them into complete shape.

These things fill his sketch-books, large volumes of rough music paper which he constantly carried with him, and many of which have been preserved.[1] In them we can see many of his greatest works gradually taking form. People have been surprised to learn that he worked in this way, and have wondered how the finished melody could appear to be so spontaneous when it was arrived at by such labour. They have even talked nonsense about inspiration, and imagined that a great composer ought to write down everything on the spur of the moment, conceive a symphony in a flash, and never rest till the score was completed. True, there have been men who could work like that; Mozart must often have done so, and Schubert certainly did. But inspiration is not in the least affected by the process of composition. Beethoven's inspiration came before he put anything on the paper at all, and he caught it fixing it in his mind by the few rough scrawls of melody which he jotted in his sketch-book. They would be enough to recall the sense of it to him. Everything he did afterwards was merely clearing away the rubbish which he knew obscured his thought, and whether there was much or little of this process to be done made no difference to the beauty of the inspiration when once it appeared cleared of every contamination. Sometimes the sketch-books[2] show that for the moment he cleared away an essential feature, mistaking it for rubbish, and had to put it back again afterwards.

Here is an example in the growth of the tune which forms the

[1] Some of these sketch-books may be seen displayed in the British Museum.

[2] For these and other sketches of Beethoven see Nottebohm, *Zweite Beethoveniana*, and Mies, *Beethoven's Sketches*.

splendid central movement of the piano Concerto in E flat. The following (Ex. 54 *a*) is the first rough sketch:

Beethoven evidently felt the commonplace fussiness of the first bar (A) to be an interference with his thought, for next time he tried to give it more dignity by expanding it into two bars (Ex. 54 *b*). This deprived him of the beautiful rise of the fourth

in bar 2 and made him also abandon the corresponding drop of a sixth (B) in order to make his fourth bar balance the rhythm of bars 1 and 2. But both these things were essential parts of his thought which he could not do without. They had to come back. Next, therefore, he gave up the rhythm (C) and adopted a calmer beginning which secured once more the rising fourth (Ex. 54 *c*); and in this only one note, the first, had to be altered

eventually to D sharp in order to secure the perfect poise he wanted. The endings had to be sought with equal care. Here are three (Ex. 55). The first sprawls loosely over a wide range of notes; the second contracts, but is still too wide; the third is the restrained final one, all the more expressive for its restraint.

Ex. 55

Beethoven's whole attitude towards the subject of musical form can be understood in the light of this new spirit, which made him bring everything to the test of experience. The great majority of his works were composed within the short period of twelve years; that is to say, from the year 1800 when the first Symphony appeared to the year 1812 when he produced the seventh in A major and the eighth in F major; and they follow the broad lines of existing forms. They are a logical development out of the sonata form which Haydn and Mozart had evolved and applied with various modifications to solo sonatas, the string quartet, and the orchestral symphony. They are in direct succession; there is no break, no throwing aside of the prizes won by his predecessors. But that does not imply that Beethoven took the form for granted all this time, even though he did so at first. On the contrary, the better one knows his work the more one realizes that he constantly considered it afresh to see whether it was fit to bear the weight of what he wanted to express, and only accepted it because he found it fit. Where he was not satisfied with it he altered his design, but as we have seen sonata form was never a matter of hard and fast rules. Haydn had expanded it from the pattern of his Weinzierl Quartets to those of his Salomon Symphonies. It was no less adaptable to Beethoven's growing nature than it had been to Haydn's, and it endured the strain put upon it from the Sonatas of Op. 2 up to the magnificent Symphony in A major.

In his last years Beethoven had something yet to say for which the principles of sonata form would not altogether suffice, and so we find him boldly dispensing with it, launching out alone 'toward the unknown region', to give his last utterances in newer and more purely individual shapes. For that reason we shall not speak particularly of Beethoven's last works, of the Mass in D, the ninth Symphony, the last sonatas and string quartets in this volume. They will form our point of departure when we study a few out of the many aspects of modern music in the third of this series. Nor in dealing with the larger mass of his music will we make an attempt to review the whole ground superficially. We will pursue our plan of looking closely at a few salient examples in various styles and try to get an insight into his nature from them, which may be expanded and deepened as you come into closer contact with his music.

SUMMARY OF PRINCIPAL COMPOSITIONS

But first a few words will be practically useful as to the general order in which his best-known masterpieces appeared. We have mentioned some of those which are grouped round the first Symphony. In 1801 came the fine Quintet for strings (Op. 29), together with his only oratorio, 'The Mount of Olives', which does not altogether deserve the same epithet. Beethoven's sense of the real relation between words and music, and how the feeling of words is best expressed in music, was extraordinarily slow to develop, and indeed was never developed with that certainty which he had in handling purely musical thought. The year was rich in piano sonatas. To it belong the one in A flat (Op. 26), containing the noble funeral march; that in D (Op. 28) often called the 'Pastoral' Sonata because of the gracious flow of its themes and the bucolic humour of its last movement; and the two in E flat major and C sharp minor, both described by Beethoven as 'in the manner of a fantasia'. The last has gained the name of the 'Moonlight' Sonata, which is unfortunate because the name gives people the excuse to think of something else instead of the music when they listen to it. If you can hear the first movement without thinking of moonlight you are much more likely to understand and enjoy Beethoven than if you indulge in fancies which have nothing to do with his meaning.

In 1802 he was at work upon his second Symphony, and the Sonatas of Op. 31, of which the one in D minor is the most striking, also occupied him. That Sonata has been called the 'Dramatic' chiefly because of the recitative passages in its first movement (see p. 216). Two sets of variations for piano (Opp. 34 and 35) are also important for they show him treating the form less as an exercise in technique and more for the expression of definite musical ideas. Op. 34, on a theme in F major, makes each variation a complete piece having some character entirely its own as well as being in a key of its own, so that the whole effect is rather of a suite upon a single theme than of a set of formal variations. The variations of Op. 35 are on the theme[1] which he afterwards used in the last movement of the third Symphony, so that they may be considered to be a sketch for the Symphony.

The violin and piano Sonatas (Op. 30) were written in this year, and in the following one (1803) came the famous 'Kreutzer' Sonata (violin and piano), which was written for a violinist named Bridgetower and first played by him and Beethoven. A quarrel, however, made Beethoven afterwards change the dedication to Kreutzer, a much more eminent violinist and a composer. During this year too Beethoven was at work upon his third Symphony, which was to be dedicated to Napoleon Bonaparte, whom as Consul of the French Republic he admired enthusiastically as a soldier, a statesman, and the champion of liberty. His symphony must be a heroic one to be worthy of such a hero. Strength and daring must be combined in it; the former expressed in its splendid proportions and its obedience to law, the latter in any flight of imaginative melody and harmony which might be suggested to his thought. In the spring of 1804 the score was finished and the title-page bore the name

[1] He had already used this theme in his ballet *Prometheus*.

of the hero when the news that Napoleon had accepted the title of Emperor reached him. The idol had fallen; this great man of the people was then only a tyrant ambitious of personal power. Beethoven would have none of him, and he tore off the title-page. But the Symphony remained heroic whatever Beethoven might think of the man whom he had idolized, and it has been rightly known as 'Sinfonia eroica', or more colloquially 'the Eroica', ever since.

In 1804 appeared the famous Sonata for piano in C which Beethoven dedicated to his old friend Count Waldstein, and which is always known by his name; and in 1805 he turned his attention to opera and wrote his only work of that kind, *Fidelio.* The visit of Cherubini to Vienna influenced him considerably here. He greatly admired Cherubini's polished style of workmanship, and not being himself a born operatic composer he did not realize the defect of Cherubini's qualities. We have seen that the one excuse for opera is that it expresses something which only opera can express. The best things in *Fidelio* are expressed by music alone or music in song. Its beauties are not those which are inevitably connected with a drama acted on the stage. It was not a success when it was first produced in November 1805, but that was largely owing to the troubled state of the time. Vienna was in the hands of the French, and all the Viennese aristocracy who could do so had decamped before the face of the invaders. Subsequently Beethoven revised *Fidelio*, reducing it from three acts to two. The original overture was the one known as 'Leonora No. 2'.[1] This Beethoven afterwards rewrote, using the same ideas but improving the structure greatly in the overture called Leonora No. 3. At a later time he wrote two other overtures to his opera, quite distinct from the first and called Leonora No. 1 and 'Fidelio', the latter being the one used for its revival in 1814 and permanently associated with the opera.

[1] The occurrence of the numbers 2, 3, and 1 in their wrong order is simply the result of a publisher's mistake, but as they have become known all over the world as the titles of the overtures, it is hopeless to correct the mistake. Leonora is the name of the heroïne of the opera.

Beethoven's *Fidelio* is a romantic story set in Spain. The original French libretto for Gaveaux's *Léonore* (see p. 293) claimed to be based on a true story occurring during the French Revolution at Tours, where the librettist, J. N. Bouilly, held an official post. Florestan has been wrongfully imprisoned by Pizarro, the governor of a state prison near Seville, and Pizarro is determined to secure the death of his prisoner and to conceal the crime. Leonora, the wife of Florestan, risks her own life in order to save her husband, by coming to the prison disguised as a boy and calling herself Fidelio. She secures admission by engaging to help the jailer Rocco in his work, and is made to enter the cell of Florestan and take part in the gruesome work of digging the grave of Florestan beneath the floor of the cell. She finds her husband, who does not recognize her, in the last stage of despair and fainting from starvation. Pizarro enters to hurry the work. Don Fernando, the minister of prisons, is expected, and Pizarro must carry out the plot before his arrival or run the risk of exposure. Leonora's one hope then is in delay, and in order to cause it she at last declares herself to be the wife of Florestan and throws herself between the men. At the critical moment a trumpet fanfare is heard proclaiming the arrival of the minister; Florestan and Leonora are saved, Pizarro is accused before Don Fernando and condemned, and so with the punishment of the villain and the restoration of Florestan and Leonora to life and happiness the opera ends.

We have described the main outline of the story chiefly because it serves as a commentary upon the series of overtures, all of which are frequently heard in the concert room. In those called Leonora No. 2 and Leonora No. 3 Beethoven evidently had the main plot of the opera strongly in mind. In the later pair, Leonora No. 1 and 'Fidelio', he aimed not so much at giving an epitome of the drama as providing a prelude which would prepare the way for the general feeling of the opera with less regard to its incidents. Leonora No. 1, indeed, is comparatively slight, and its bright spirit seems to be suggested more by the subsidiary comedy of the first act, the scenes in which the jailer's daughter fancies herself in love with the supposed boy Fidelio, than by the main theme of the opera developed in the second act, although there are some phrases which are contained in the subsequent music of Florestan.

Beethoven was evidently in great doubt as to what would make the best prelude to his opera, and from that point of view his final effort, now known as the *Fidelio* overture, is the most satisfactory. But in themselves the earlier ones are the finest music, and Leonora No. 3, containing the essential features of Leonora No. 2 placed together in better proportion, stands at the head of them all.

The slow introduction to Leonora No. 3 opens with a long descending passage which gives the suggestion of passing from daylight into gloom, and seems to carry us down into the dismal cell where Florestan lies chained. Almost immediately there follows a hint of his song from Act II, 'In des Lebens Frühlingstagen ist das Glück von mir gefloh'n' ('In the springtide of life happiness has fled from me'), so that the contrast between his hopeless state and the strong pulsing life of the allegro movement seems directly pictured. That wonderful movement, welling up out of a syncopated melody begun softly by violins and violoncellos, is indescribable, but its wealth of romantic beauty appeals instantly to the hearer. At the height of its development it is arrested by the distant sound of the trumpet upon the prison tower. There is a dramatic pause, after which a new melody charged with a mysterious sense of expectancy steals in. The trumpet call is also introduced in Leonora No. 2, but this melody which fills the same place in the opera was not made use of in the earlier overture. The sense of agitation is also heightened by a curious ascending chromatic passage between violins and basses, which would be in octaves were it not that the bass lags behind, so that we get a series of discordant minor ninths finally resolved into the joyful return of the first subject. Again, before the last presentment of that subject there is a hurrying passage for the violins in which the accent is continually thrown across the bar, producing a feeling of the intensest excitement.

The result of the whole is that we feel we have got the essence of the drama distilled in music before the curtain rises on the opera. Beethoven must have felt this too, and to avoid anticipating the climax he deposed the overture Leonora No. 3 from its place and substituted his later overtures.

The year 1806 was crowded with instrumental composition. Beethoven was working at the great Symphony in C minor, and in the full tide of work he put it on one side to compose the smaller but intensely beautiful one in B flat, which thus became his fourth Symphony. Moreover in this year he had on hand the Concerto in G for piano and small orchestra; the three string Quartets (Op. 59) dedicated to the Russian ambassador, Count Rasumovsky; the piano 'Sonata appassionata' in F minor, composed in the summer (at the house of Count Brunsvick, to whose sister Beethoven became engaged); and at the end of the year the violin Concerto was played for the first time. It is an overwhelming output when we remember that each of these things is a masterpiece in which there is no overlapping of thought, no single idea which might as well belong elsewhere. Yet his energy in the next few years scarcely slackened. In the spring of 1807 a remarkable concert was given in Vienna, at which all the four completed symphonies (C major, D major, E flat major—'Eroica'—and B flat major) were performed, and in this year the 'Coriolan' Overture and the Mass in C were written while he made progress with the C minor Symphony (No. 5). This was completed in 1808, with the sixth called the 'Pastoral' Symphony. The last stands apart from the others of the series. It is the frank expression of, or musical commentary upon, scenes of country life and Beethoven's feeling of love for the country. In the slow movement he goes so far as playfully to imitate the calls of birds, the nightingale, the quail, and the cuckoo; the running brooks, a thunderstorm, and peasant merry-making are all pictured in it. Beethoven was giving himself a holiday from serious thoughts and deep feelings. Certainly, no one ever deserved a holiday more. In this year Beethoven secured the friendship of the Archduke Rudolph, to whom he dedicated the piano Concerto in G, and whose title is famous in the beautiful Trio in B flat (Op. 97) composed at a later date (1811), and often spoken of as 'the Archduke' from its dedication. This man was a good friend to Beethoven and with several others subscribed to give him a regular income to secure him from want. The piano Sonata (Op. 81 *a*), whose three movements are called 'Les adieux, l'absence, et le retour', was written in the following year to tell something of what Beethoven felt on losing him for a time and to celebrate his return.

In 1809 also (the year of Haydn's death, though that was not publicly noticed by Beethoven) were written the last and noblest of his piano concertos, the one in E flat, known in England as 'the Emperor' simply because of its grandeur, and also a string Quartet in the same key called the 'harp' Quartet because of the form of some arpeggio passages it contains.

In 1810 and 1811 there is a certain slackening in the amount of big work produced, but Beethoven was preparing for another outburst of symphonies. Still, 1810 contains the music to 'Egmont', the string Quartet in F minor (Op. 95), and 1811 the Trio already named, the overtures 'King Stephen' and 'The Ruins of Athens'. But in 1812 came the Symphony in A (No. 7) and its smaller companion in F (No. 8), and at a concert given to celebrate the defeat of the French by Wellington in the battle of Victoria and by the Russians, with climate and starvation to help them, at Moscow, the Symphony in A was publicly performed on 8 December 1813. With it was given another work by Beethoven which it is agreed was unworthy of him, a battle-piece called 'Wellington's Victory', which, except for its historical interest, need not be remembered.

After this Beethoven's creative work became continually slower and more difficult to him, partly because he was involved in every kind of personal difficulty, including lawsuits and quarrels, partly because his deafness drove him to a more and more introspective habit of mind which made it increasingly difficult for him to find the right expression of his inmost thoughts. In 1814, when *Fidelio* was revived at the Opera, we find the beautiful piano Sonata in E minor (Op. 90) and the overture 'Namensfeier'.

In 1815 there was little new work beyond a cantata on Goethe's twin poems 'Meeresstille und glückliche Fahrt', and after that composition almost ceased. But there was renewed energy from 1818 onward when the Mass in D and the ninth Symphony occupied him in turn. With Beethoven it always seems that one effort generated another, for in these years came the last set of piano sonatas (from Op. 106 to Op. 111). Parts of the Mass and the whole of the Symphony with a new overture, 'Die Weihe des Hauses' ('The Dedication of the House'), were at last produced at a concert given in the theatre 'An der Wien', where so many of Beethoven's works had been produced, on 7 May 1823. He continued full of plans and ideas for future works in the few years which were left him, but all he could actually complete were the series of six string quartets including the 'Grand Fugue', great rhapsodies in which he strove to make permanent the visions which crowded in upon him. In the course of 1826, however, illness seized him and he could not go on. His body was exhausted though his brain was as fertile as ever, and he died on 26 March 1827.

THE PIANO SONATAS

We can get a view of Beethoven's music most readily through the piano sonatas, and as we have seen that practically every phase of his career is reflected in what he wrote for the piano, and almost every big effort in other directions is accompanied by the composition of these works for the piano, we may take the series of thirty-two piano sonatas as fairly representative of the whole man, a sort of private diary for himself and his friends. We must necessarily choose out certain specimens, neglecting others, and as our main object is to get at the elements which formed his musical character it will be well to pay the closest attention to what appeared while that character was in the making. We can then afford to pass the later works with slighter reference, leaving those who really want to know to make their own discoveries as we did in the cases of Haydn and Mozart.

The first three sonatas, in spite of all the suggestions of other minds contained in them, give us plenty to think about. The first in F minor is the least mature. An arpeggio figure over the notes of the key chord was so common an opening with the composers of the eighteenth century that it may almost be compared to the conventional 'Ladies and Gentlemen' with which a public speaker begins his speech (cf. Ex. 45, p. 229). But although Beethoven uses it here in almost exactly the same form as Mozart did in the Finale of his G minor Symphony (K. 550),[1] it is no figure of speech to be got over and forgotten. Notice the way he ends it crisply with a sharply turned triplet figure, and then how he urges the importance of both the arpeggio and the triplet by repetition and reinforcement upon other degrees of the scale.

The second theme, when it arrives in the twenty-first bar, proves to be a free inversion of this arpeggio theme in the same rhythm, but speaking in a softer and more persuasive tone of voice. In this movement, then, we get two of Beethoven's salient characteristics: his abruptness of speech, and his way of becoming immediately absorbed in the subject which he has begun upon. We may find a third by comparing the codetta before the double bar with the coda at the end of the movement. In the former a perfect cadence is reiterated, culminating in the emphatic dominant chord, which sinks to the quieter tonic chord of the new key (A flat). In the latter the same point, instead of being a dominant chord, is one which modulates out of the key. The phrase is repeated a tone lower, still further suggesting a foreign key, and then a series of chords leads grandly back to F minor.

[1] The late Sir Hubert Parry compared the structure of this passage with the similar one in Mozart. His analysis deserves study, but the comparison is rather for the teacher than the pupil, for to the latter it might suggest that Mozart could not use the art of immediate and consistent development, and the whole point of the chapter on his symphonies in this book has been to show that he was consummate master in that art.

THE CODA

It was a favourite device of Beethoven suddenly, when one expected familiar things, to open up a new vista of harmony and shake off the fetters of convention. Since the coda is the place where one begins to foresee the end, he particularly loved to give something unforeseen there. Sometimes these surprises were humorous, as Haydn's generally were, for example in the finale of the Sonata in C minor (Op. 10, No. 1), a movement which has something of Haydn's rollicking spirit, and where just before the end he checks the flow to give the second subject, getting slower and slower in the remote key of D flat major. He gradually lulls his hearers to rest, and then, with a sweeping arpeggio, picks up the thread of his discourse and makes a rapid end. Yet in the humour there is something reflective and regretful: it is not like the boyish practical joking of Haydn.

A similar case is the coda to the last movement of the Sonata in C (Op. 2, No. 3), where it is impossible to draw the line between humour and sorrow. We only feel that both are there. Sometimes these adventurous codas are wholly tender in feeling, such as the one to the rondo of the Sonata in E flat (Op. 7). Here Beethoven leads up strongly to the dominant (B flat) from which the commonplace mind expects him to return by the ordinary road. He changes it to B natural, dwells softly on the new note, and then introduces the chief theme in the key of E major with a sigh, as though it longed for greater freedom, but it is caught back again by a fate which compels it into the key of E flat.

So rich and varied are the sudden transitions of Beethoven's codas that we might fill a volume of the size of this one in examining them. The fact that there is nothing of the kind which is very distinctive in the last movement of the first sonata is one of its chief signs of immaturity, and that movement should be played in order to point out the difference between what is really Beethoven's self and what is more or less conventional work.

The second sonata contains a much greater variety of material in its first movement than the one before it does, but what marks it most is the wonderful slow movement.

SLOW MOVEMENTS

Here we get the first of the long series of Beethoven's slow movements, which are one of the greatest evidences of his genius. Speaking generally, we may say that Mozart was most spontaneous in his first allegro movements, Haydn in his minuets and finales, Beethoven in his slow movements. That, of course, is the very roughest generalization, liable to be upset by many special instances, but on the whole it is supported by the characters of the men. Mozart's keen intellectual energy, Haydn's frank joy in living, Beethoven's profound feeling found their most natural expressions in these various types. One need not analyse closely the Largo of the Sonata in A to perceive its depth. That stately melody moving over the staccato bass tells at once that we are meeting Beethoven in his most serious mood. Here nothing is added merely for decoration to keep an interest alive which might otherwise flag; Beethoven marches serenely through the whole of its development without one misgiving or one afterthought.

The majority of the early sonatas have long and intensely beautiful slow movements, with melodies ranging over a wide expanse, but always proceeding straight from the first thought, with nothing diffuse or superficial. That of the Sonata in E flat (Op. 7) is, except for its contrasting section in A flat, almost entirely evolved from the melodic germ of the first two bars.

Ex. 56

Beethoven uses the greatest freedom of form and modulation, trusting implicitly to his thought to develop itself logically.

Others among the greatest of these are the elegiac Largo in

the Sonata in D major (Op. 10, No. 3) and the less passionate but equally majestic Adagio to the Sonata in B flat (Op. 22), which, by the way, is developed in complete first-movement form. Those which do not reach to the same heights often have a pure lyrical beauty of their own. Such are the adagio movements of the Sonata in C minor (Op. 10, No. 1) and of the 'Sonate pathétique' (Op. 13), in both of which the great charm lies in the initial melody presented as a whole in the first eight bars and set off against contrasting ideas of less importance.

The third Sonata of Op. 2, in C major, is on a bigger scale than its predecessors. One sees again Beethoven's abruptness in the muttered phrase with which it opens, and his consistency in his treatment of the little group of semiquavers. Presently he breaks away from them in freer movement, soaring up in a clamorous passage. The opening of this movement ought to be carefully compared with the opening of the Sonata in B flat, Op. 22, which is similar in idea. In the later work, however, the idea seems to be better carried out in the semiquaver passage, rising in a wave which bursts into a radiant melody at its height. Even if we find a few passages in his first movement in C major which seem a little less significant than others, one feels that Beethoven has launched out upon a bigger scheme than he attempted to deal with in either of the first two sonatas of this set. He is working on the lines which he afterwards followed up in the 'Sonate pathétique' (Op. 13) and the 'Appassionata' in F minor. Strongly opposed ideas, passionate moments of feeling succeeded by gentler reflections and violent contrasts of tone follow one another through the long development. Look at the sweeping arpeggios passing through various keys till they come quietly to rest upon a reminiscence of the first subject in D major; then see the turbulent sequences in octaves involving strong discords which obliterate for a time that subject, and finally, when the course of the movement seems to be nearly run, Beethoven takes a great plunge on to a chord of A flat (bar 220) followed by mountainous waves of arpeggios which ultimately scatter themselves in a cadenza. Here, indeed, the stormy spirit expresses itself unflinchingly. You must not miss the sudden outburst in the middle of the gentler slow movement, where the theme, which before (in E major) had been contemplative rather than vigorous, is suddenly asserted *fortissimo* in the key of C as if in rebellion against its original calm character.

THE SCHERZO

The Scherzo of this sonata sufficiently forecasts Beethoven's subsequent use of that form to be taken as typical. Haydn in his later years had tended to turn the minuet into a scherzo, an Italian word which means a joke or plaything. He had abandoned the dance measure but generally kept the name of minuet. Beethoven adopted the name scherzo, and his treatment of it here is very like Haydn's treatment of his later minuets. He begins in the manner of a trio for strings, each part entering in turn with the tripping figure which is the principal theme. It is thoroughly jocular in spirit, though again it has not the unclouded good humour of Haydn. Those strong chords and *sforzandi* in the middle make one feel that Beethoven's humour could cut deeply, and the coda in which the theme gradually disappears with a growl in the bass shows that it is not a humour to be trifled with. As Beethoven progressed his scherzi became more complex, not so much technically as emotionally, until we come to examples like that in the fifth Symphony, which cannot be considered as humorous or lightsome in the least; in it the sense of brooding tragedy is all the more felt for the fact that it is veiled by the delicacy of the form There are jokes which make one want to cry, but only a grown-up person can understand that.

Generally we have to go outside the piano sonatas and look among the chamber music and the symphonies for Beethoven's most characteristic treatment of the scherzo. Each of the six Quartets of Op. 18 contains a scherzo (though the one in No. 5, A major, is called a minuet), but in the piano sonatas its appearance is infrequent. Sometimes its place is taken by an allegretto which has not the scherzo character, as in the F major Sonata (Op. 10, No. 2), where the allegretto takes the place of both slow movement and scherzo, combining some of the feeling of each; sometimes by a genuine minuet as in Op. 10, No. 3, and in Op. 22. Very often the scherzo or its equivalent is passed over altogether and the sonata adopts the old three-movement form which C. P. E. Bach always used. That is the case in the first two out of the three which are grouped as Op. 31. In Op. 31, No. 3, however, Beethoven adopts the unusual plan of writing both a scherzo and a minuet without a slow movement. To hear them played together is to realize at once the essential difference between the character of the two. The scherzo is not even in triple time, which was generally the one feature to survive and remind us of its evolution out of the old dance. Its staccato bass and the persistent rhythm:

Ex. 57

are the things on which Beethoven relies to give it the crisp character of a scherzo. With this the suave measure of the true minuet following contrasts effectively, and his bringing them together is a definite acknowledgement that henceforward the two represent to him distinct types, and the names can no longer be vaguely interchanged as had often been the case before.

CHANGES IN SONATA FORM

Other changes in design had already been made by him to suit the needs of the moment. The transposition of the order of the several movements, particularly the placing of the slow movement first, which Haydn had tried in his early quartets but generally abandoned (see p. 223), seemed to Beethoven desirable in the two sonatas 'like fantasias' (Op. 27). The first one (in E flat) begins with a curiously formal and rather tentative movement broken in upon by an impulsive allegro. The formality and hesitancy are, of course, intentional features that the allegro may come with the greater force, which is even exceeded by the rush of the scherzo later. The whole of this sonata shows Beethoven determined to link the several movements together in one great scheme. At the end of each there is a direction to the player to go straight on to the next one, so that there should never be a pause for applause when it is played in public. Not only this, but the movements are less self-sufficing than in the earlier sonatas; they depend intimately upon one another. There is the andante, of which we have spoken, with the allegro in the middle of it; then the scherzo with its trio, for the second time sweeping away the formal atmosphere of the andante; then a brooding adagio, though Beethoven is too restless to dwell upon it for long, for he brushes it aside with a cadenza leading straight into a vigorous rondo, the last and most fully developed movement in the sonata. Still, however, he cannot be content to end in an exuberant spirit without one look back to the adagio which he had cut short before. And just before the coda he recalls it.

This tendency to join his ideas more closely grew upon Beethoven with years. Not that he ever adopted it as a fixed principle, for sometimes he chose to separate his movements distinctly from one another, and indeed the last of his piano sonatas (Op. 111) is so divided. But often he could not bear to pause between one idea and the next, and he would take a last look in the course of a finale at some feature in an earlier movement which meant much to him. The fifth Symphony gives us a striking example, for there, as everyone will remember, the Scherzo wells up to a climax culminating in the triumph of the Finale. Yet Beethoven is not content with his triumph, for before the end he lets us know that the tapping rhythm of the Scherzo still haunts him.

The second of the 'Fantasia' Sonatas, in C sharp minor, probably the most popular of all, is much simpler in design than the first. It contains only a slow movement, a delicate Allegretto, and a rushing, tearing Presto. The real objection to the name of 'Moonlight' is that it is apt to make people think only of the slow movement and separate it from its context. The slow movement is certainly one of the most lyrically beautiful things ever written; its pure melody appeals to the heart of every one at once, and we need not make words about it. But Beethoven does not stop there. In the Allegretto he rouses himself from his reverie, half regretfully, for he still dwells upon harmonies which melt into one another, but in the Presto he casts it off altogether and braces himself for action. He does it with difficulty, for the yearning sense comes back upon him in all the three themes grouped together as the second subject. Notice the persistence of downward phrases in these counteracting the virile upward ones of the first subject. The strife between the two goes on to the end, but the sonata taken as a whole is a continual *crescendo* of energy, no vague moonlit dream.

LATER SONATAS

In the later sonatas (not the latest), of which the 'Waldstein' and the 'Appassionata' are the outstanding examples, we see Beethoven working upon a still larger canvas. Here he unifies his ideas not so much by linking the movements together, though the slow movement of the Appassionata passes straight into the big Finale, as by putting many ideas into one movement. So big are his first and last movements that the middle ones are reduced, and in fact he cut out the slow movement[1] which he originally wrote for the Waldstein.

Many of the sonatas of this period have only two movements, from the beautiful little one in F (Op. 54) which stands between these two giants, to the larger Op. 90 in E minor. Beethoven's style was altering all through this time. In many of them we miss the sustained purity of melody which made the earlier ones, and especially their long slow movements, so appealing. Instead we have greater force of phrase, more nervous energy, and strength in development. It is the work of a man who is becoming daily more cut off from the rest of human life and is

[1] This is published separately as the 'Andante favori' in F.

forced to live in the region of his own thought. Most of these works cannot be so fascinating to one when one is young, and perhaps they are best left alone then. One grows up to them gradually.

But we get a glimpse of Beethoven's more simple style again in the E minor Sonata (Op. 90). Its melodies in themselves are enough to assure us that he was not outgrowing the love of beauty for its own sake, though other considerations often pressed in upon him and clamoured for expression.

If you have followed some of the examples mentioned and heard them in the actual music played upon the piano (not unless), you must have got some notion of Beethoven's character, of how he stepped out far beyond his predecessors in the boldness and variety of what he had to say, and of why his position is unique. If so, we may safely leave individual works to explain themselves as you have opportunity for getting to know them.

THE ORCHESTRA

But though we have to pass over whole classes of works including the string quartets, the greatest masterpieces in that form ever written, we cannot close without a glance at what Beethoven did with the orchestra, particularly in the first seven of his nine symphonies.[1]

In the matter of orchestration Beethoven was able at once to take a bolder line than had been possible to those who went before him. They had helped to form the instrument, to settle the balance of its component parts. Beethoven inherited their technique, and in the first Symphony he makes use of what to Haydn and Mozart was a very full orchestra. The woodwind consists of flutes, oboes, clarinets, and bassoons (two each), two horns, two trumpets, drums, and strings, and it is worth while to notice that the brass and drums are used in every movement, which means that Beethoven never thought of them

[1] For detailed analysis of the symphonies and a careful description of all the circumstances of Beethoven's life with which they were connected, the best English book is still Sir George Grove's *Beethoven and his Nine Symphonies*.

as mere makeweights for noisy moments. It is true that some of the limitations of older times seemed to cling round him. He is rather fearful of letting the clarinets speak by themselves, and sometimes he makes the woodwind double each other and the strings clumsily. These things serve to show his starting-point. On the other hand, we find the trumpets and drums asserting their individuality; the former in the coda to the first movement, where they imitate the rest of the orchestra in a passage from the principal theme, the latter in the Andante, where twice the drum sustains a rhythm (Ex. 58) alone through a number of bars.

Ex. 58

The Symphony contains four movements. A short slow introduction of striking harmony (the first chord heard is a flat seventh on the key-note) leads to an Allegro. Then there is a delicate andante, the theme of which recalls the slow movement of Mozart's G minor Symphony, a so-called minuet which is really an unmistakable scherzo, which no one but Beethoven could have written, and a Finale. One wonders, on the other hand, that Haydn did not write the tune of the Finale. It is so much more like him than like Beethoven. This is enough to show that there is the same uncertainty in the first Symphony that we found in the first piano sonata, and may be also seen in the first two piano concertos. Beethoven does not quite know what is his true self.

By the time he reached the second Symphony in D his knowledge had cleared considerably. Here he used the same orchestra (omitting trumpets and drums in the slow movement, however), but he handles all more firmly (notice the lovely tone of the clarinets playing the tune of the Larghetto an octave above the bassoons), and his ideas are almost all of the kind which are most characteristic of him. In the long introduction with which it begins we may perhaps find a few mannerisms to remind us of

Mozart's Prague Symphony, but the big chords which punctuate it, the dignified oboe melody (the first one heard), the sudden leap away to the key of B flat, and the groping modulations which follow that impulsive moment, are all like nobody but Beethoven.

The Allegro of the Symphony in D is more exuberant than that of the first Symphony. The insistent use made of the semiquaver figure in the chief subject ought to be compared with the piano Sonatas in C and B flat (p. 324). The Larghetto, though without any of the tragic feeling of the greater slow movements in the early sonatas, is filled with deep melodic expression. The Scherzo has no trace of suave minuet rhythm; it is all clearly cut, a piece of Beethoven's most pointed humour. The theme of the trio (oboes and bassoons) suggests the similarly placed theme in his ninth Symphony, and the explosions of energy which begin the Finale and are constantly striking across its course bring us face to face with a more imperious spirit than any which music had known before.

That spirit breathes still more freely in the 'Eroica' Symphony. The will to command is over it all in spite of his anger at Napoleon's imperialism. It is this will in Beethoven himself which makes it heroic. We must not be led away by the attempt which has been made to treat it as programme music, to connect it with a series of events as Strauss's 'Ein Heldenleben' is connected. You will find that attempt in practically every annotated programme written for concert performances. People have wondered what the Scherzo and Finale could have to do with the hero since the slow movement before them is a funeral march, and Berlioz went so far as to make the quite silly suggestion that the Scherzo represented funeral games such as those with which the Greeks celebrated their great men. Beethoven has nothing to do with any chronological statement of events. He is thinking as entirely in purely musical terms here as in the second Symphony; the spirit of stern self-command may be just as forcibly expressed in the busy activity of a Scherzo as in the stately tread of a march. You cannot get at the heart of it by explanations or making up stories about it, but by listening constantly you can gradually realize that it all expresses some aspect of heroic character, from the strongly swaying arpeggio of the first movement to the solidly built-up variations of the Finale.

People have been at great pains to explain these variations, but most of the difficulty has come by separating them from one another. Once realize their continuous progress from the dim fragmentary statement of the bass of the theme to its full presentment, and again through its many developments to its triumphant and coda, you see that the whole is perfectly conclusive. Beethoven for once gives us his whole way of working in the finished product, his idea gradually coming from the rudimentary suggestions of the sketch-books into the full light. It is the growth of a soul.

The fourth Symphony in B flat is on smaller lines than the two between which it stands. Both the 'Eroica' and the C minor Symphonies plunge straight into the compelling ideas of the allegro. The fourth muses upon faint half-expressed ideas in a slow introduction before it gathers sufficient force to make the plunge. When the allegro does come it is radiant with happiness. The staccato quavers which are so strangely tentative in the introduction become crisp and energetic in the principal theme of the allegro. There are moments when the shadows return. One most striking one is the passage at the end of the development where a chord of F sharp major is answered by a soft roll of the drum on B flat, but joy is the dominant spirit. The slow movement is as fresh in melody as that of the second Symphony, but more stately. As a point of orchestration the places where the drum maintains the rhythm

Ex. 59

alone must be noticed and compared with the similar point in the first Symphony (Ex. 58).

It is curious that Beethoven in his happiest moment recalls a breath of Haydn's style in the tune of the Scherzo, and again, though less distinctly, in that of the Finale. This symphony was violently attacked when it appeared for having every fault conceivable, yet now it is seen to be the most transparently clear of any, except perhaps the 'Pastoral', and the most free from that wrestling strenuousness which is found in the greater symphonies.

The fifth, however, remains the most popular, and it is the one with which most people begin their experiences of Beethoven's symphonies. The very strenuousness of its first movement gives something which everyone can feel at once. Never have four notes been so pregnant with power as those of its principal theme. Their rhythm is scarcely ever absent; they invade the field of the more reflective second subject, they are the motive power of the whole movement. The theme of the slow movement was the subject of as much careful sifting as was that of the Concerto in E flat, but once found it appears equally inevitable. It gives the perfect repose between the strife of the first movement and the painful questioning of the Scherzo. Beethoven had to seek peace, storm came to him unsought; but the search was rewarded in the sublime calm of these melodies.

As we have seen (p. 327), the Finale comes as the solution of all the doubts and forebodings of the Scherzo. In it Beethoven uses a larger orchestra than ever before. Three trombones appear for the first time in his symphonies, a piccolo (small flute) and double bassoon add a wider range to the woodwind. Thus in a moment of triumph he comes into his full orchestral heritage.

It is rather a shock to turn from the blaze of this Finale to the quiet, pictorial attitude of the 'Pastoral Symphony' (see p. 318), in which the themes are almost naïve in their childlike simplicity.

In the storm movement he again uses the trombones and the piccolo, though merely for thunder and lightning effects; generally his orchestration is as simple as the themes. The storm, then, is a theatrical one, not the storm of a big character trying to express itself, and similarly in the other movements Beethoven is going outside himself in a way he seldom does elsewhere. But one need not accept the sequence of events in order to enjoy the music, nor take up just the opposite attitude of mind to that which is necessary for the appreciation of the 'Eroica' although he tells us in so many words what it is all about. The Allegro represents feelings of pleasure on arriving in the country; the Andante is a scene by a brook with the birds singing overhead; the Scherzo is a merry-making of country folk, then comes the storm, and lastly a shepherd's song of thanksgiving for safety after the storm.

The pastoral feeling, though not the pastoral description, lives on into the great seventh Symphony in A, in fact, elements from all the earlier symphonies (except perhaps the fifth), though not actual themes, seem to play a part and help it to sum up the work of Beethoven's maturity. Its introduction, though much more defined, recalls that of the fourth Symphony, the dance-tune on which the first allegro is formed has the open-air feeling of the 'Pastoral', though it is turned to busier uses than anything in the earlier work, the solemn march of the slow movement bears recognizable likeness to the spirit of the funeral march in the 'Eroica', and the Scherzo has points of connexion with the fourth and even the second. In spite of the big plan it is noticeable that Beethoven does not use his big orchestra. He leaves out the extra instruments, and the extraordinarily powerful climaxes are not sonorous like that of the Finale in the fifth Symphony so much as rhythmic.

The seventh Symphony has been called the dance symphony, but the description cannot convey much to us who are used to thinking of dance music as something particularly stiff and undeveloped in rhythm. Real dance music is that in which the rhythm throbs and grows more hypnotic every moment, till, like the tune of the Pied Piper, it compels every soul who hears it to dance to its measure. In that sense the Finale of Beethoven's seventh Symphony is the greatest dance ever written.

With these few hints upon the characters of the symphonies

we must leave Beethoven and our sketch of the growth of music for the moment. It has been a long march from Haydn's experiments with a country orchestra at Weinzierl to the seventh Symphony of Beethoven, and, without a Pied Piper to lead the way, it is likely that a good many who have tried to make it have fallen out on the roadside. But those who have come through to this stage must have noticed that as we get on in the development of the art purely technical matters fall into the background, till in Beethoven they seem to be swallowed up in his direct thought and the absorbing interest of his own mind. Perhaps the consideration will encourage some to take a long breath and get ready for another long journey.

Suggestions for Further Reading and Listening

So abundant is the literature on Beethoven that the problem is one of selectivity. Inevitably he occupies a place of honour in all general histories of music. Readers will find, for instance, that Chapter XV, 'Ludwig van Beethoven', of Grout's *A History of Western Music* neatly complements Colles's text, and also discusses those final works of Beethoven that are dealt with in a later section of *The Growth of Music*.

The most detailed study of Beethoven, the man, is Thayer's monumental and even historic *The Life of Ludwig van Beethoven*. This magnum opus should be consulted in its most recent Elliott Forbes version, in two volumes. There is also a documentary biography by H. C. Robbins Landon. For vivid and readable sidelights on the great man, see *Beethoven: Impressions by his Contemporaries*, edited (which really means stitched together) by Sonneck. This includes a number of portraits of Beethoven. *Beethoven, a Pictorial Biography* by Erich Valentin has no less than a hundred and fifty contemporary pictures scattered about its very respectable text. For general purposes, however, Marion Scott's admirable *Beethoven* in the 'Master Musicians' series—a book concerned with his music as well as his life—could hardly be bettered. Analytical guides are plentiful. Apart from Marion Scott's book, there is the compendious *Beethoven*

Companion, edited by Denis Arnold and Nigel Fortune. This is written by a team of specialists, Winton Dean, for example, contributing a chapter on Beethoven and opera. Charles Rosen's *The Classical Style* is once again necessary reading for the serious student, as are Tovey's *Beethoven* and *Essays in Musical Analysis*.

In the 'BBC Music Guides' series, Beethoven's concertos and overtures are discussed by Roger Fiske, the symphonies by Robert Simpson, the piano sonatas by Denis Matthews, and the string quartets by Basil Lam. Though these do not make 'light' reading, they are fairly short, usually running to about sixty pages, and can be supplemented by Tovey's drier *Companion to Beethoven's Piano Sonatas* and also Eric Blom's *Beethoven's Pianoforte Sonatas Discussed*. One of the best, and most accessible, surveys of Beethoven's string quartets is by Philip Radcliffe. Those who wish for a still more close-up, specialized view should turn to Daniel Gregory Mason's *The Quartets of Beethoven*, and *The Beethoven Quartets* by Joseph Kerman.

Recordings of music by Beethoven are so numerous that it is pointless to pick anything out for special mention—with one exception. In association with Colles's commentary on the sketch books, Denis Matthews's three-disc set of illustrated lectures, *Beethoven's Sketchbooks*, are valuable aids to study.

CHAPTER 15

New Paths

To make a list of the ten greatest musical geniuses of the nineteenth century might not be quite easy. A committee of musicians who sat down to compile one would probably agree perfectly in voting for seven or eight, and quarrel desperately over the remaining two or three names. If they were asked to put their list in an order of precedence, the greatest man at the top, the second greatest next to him, and so on, the quarrel would begin much earlier; probably the first place would be hotly disputed, and terrible things would happen when the delicate question of placing the tail members of the team came up for decision.

For the fact is that genius, being distinguished by an extraordinarily large number of different qualities, is immeasurable and incomparable. A tiny prelude of a few bars long may be worth more to the world than a symphony in four movements for full orchestra; while, on the other hand, a song which is flawless in its expression of a lyric verse may yet be classed below an opera weighted down with passages of uninspired music which rises to supreme moments of splendour at the great crises of the drama. Ben Jonson said, 'In short measures life may perfect be'. Art too may be perfect in the shortest of measures, and, since there are no degrees of perfection, once we have said that a thing is perfect there is no comparing it with anything else. But short of perfection, and of course there are bound to be very few works of art of which the term can be rightly used, the measurement of effort is confusing in the extreme. The man who has a big thing to say and fails to get it said with absolute precision may yet have done far more than the man who left us some small thoughts expressed in forms of transparent clearness. We cannot measure these things against one another with any accuracy, and fortunately we are not called upon to try.

Our main business here is to understand some of the chief ways in which the great geniuses of the nineteenth century used their inheritance from the past, and carried on and amplified musical expression so as to leave a richer inheritance to us of the twentieth century. With this in view we must draw distinctions. We shall see Mendelssohn ranging brilliantly over every conceivable type of composition for instruments and voices, while Chopin sits at his piano and scarcely thinks apart from its keyboard. We shall see too that one man's meat is another's poison; that Brahms could no more compose an opera than Wagner could finish an attempted string quartet. We shall come upon instances where even great men mistook their vocation, attempted what for them was impossible, or were for the moment misled into accepting the second-best from themselves. And to draw such distinctions will help our understanding if we always remember that we are studying them as great men and not as little men, and never fall into the fatal mistake of measuring their works by their faults.

We will not begin, then, with a list of the ten greatest geniuses of the nineteenth century, but we will begin by trying to make a list of ten men who have had the greatest influence upon the art of music as a whole in the nineteenth century. That is a different thing. The list will necessarily be made up of geniuses, but not necessarily in every case of the greatest. For there have been some whose circumstances in life prevented them from reaching any position of commanding influence in the world of art, or whose art was of so personal a kind that for the time being at any rate it was passed over by their contemporaries, and whose supreme importance has scarcely yet been realized.

We will put our list in the form of a table, and name the ten men according to the dates of their birth. Also, for a reason which will appear later on, we will give not only the birthplace of each but the 'life-place', that is, the place in which each lived for the greater part of his life, or which for one reason or another became the chief centre of his influence.

Name	*Dates*	*Birthplace*	*Life-place*
Franz Schubert	1797–1828	Vienna	Vienna
Hector Berlioz	1803–69	Grenoble (France)	Paris
Felix Mendelssohn	1809–47	Hamburg	Leipzig
Frédéric Chopin	1810–49	Zelazowa Wola (Poland)	Paris
Robert Schumann	1810–56	Zwickau (Saxony)	Leipzig
Ferencz Liszt	1811–86	Raiding (Hungary)	Weimar
Richard Wagner	1813–83	Leipzig	Bayreuth
César Franck	1822–90	Liège (Belgium)	Paris
Johannes Brahms	1833–97	Hamburg	Vienna
Peter Ilyich Tchaikovsky	1840–93	Kamsko-Votinsk (Russia)	Moscow

This list includes, broadly speaking, representatives of all the biggest movements which have taken place in the art of music during the century. It might be extended a little but not very far without leading us from the highways into the byways, and as we shall have our work cut out to explore even the main roads of music we will not be tempted by even the most fascinating of side-tracks at the outset. Learn this table, then, by heart, but learn it not parrot-wise but with intelligence.

Every one of these ten men, save Schubert, was born and died in the course of the nineteenth century. Schubert, born just before the turn of the century, was a younger contemporary of Beethoven in Vienna and only survived him by one year. But note that again the geographical centres of action change (see p. 189). After the death of Schubert, Vienna, the home of the symphony, only once reappears much later, and then as the adopted city of Brahms. Paris still is the stage of great actions as she was in the time of Gluck, but she is not the birthplace of the great composers. Berlioz is the only French-born member of the group; Chopin, a Pole, of French extraction, it is true, and Franck, a Belgian, however, were both drawn to Paris, and we shall find that the many-sided life of Paris had the strongest influence upon several others.

The preponderance of Germans among the big musical

figures of the nineteenth century is of course obvious. Of the two who hailed from Hamburg—Mendelssohn and Brahms—one was a Jew by race though not by religion, the other a Teuton. The likeness of Brahms's name to 'Abrahams' often made people imagine him to be Jewish, much to his annoyance. The two other Germans, Schumann and Wagner, were natives of Saxony, and it is worth observing that Prussia, and its capital Berlin, contributed nothing whatever of importance to the development of the art of nineteenth-century music.

Indeed, from the time of Frederick the Great, Prussian attempts to organize music were steadily resisted by the great men. J. S. Bach could scarcely be persuaded to visit Potsdam, and the one visit of his old age, the merest visit of ceremony, is memorable because it is exceptional (see p. 97). Mozart was tempted to settle in Berlin by the most generous offers of royal support at a time when he sorely needed material comfort, but he turned his back upon the offer (see p. 207). Mendelssohn was actually lured into accepting an appointment there; he hated Berlin as an artistic centre though his family's home was there (see p. 414), and its worries shortened his life.

The riches which Germany has brought to the world of music are the products of Saxony, Thuringia, Hanover, and the Rhine provinces, and amongst these Leipzig was for a time the richest treasure-house, as it had been in the days of Bach. Wagner created another home among the Bavarian woods at Bayreuth.

Liszt and Tchaikovsky stand apart from the others of our group of ten names. The former was Hungarian by birth, but his early career as one of the greatest pianists, possibly the greatest who ever lived, made him more truly a citizen of the world than any of the others, and while he is the only one amongst them whose greatness as a composer may be questioned, his influence as a foster-parent of music was one of the strongest during the century. He must take a high place in a list of music's strong men, though he might not appear at all in one of the greatest composers. Weimar may be named as his 'life-place', for it was there that as musical director he exerted himself most actively in furthering every young musical enterprise, and in particular performed the works of Wagner.

Tchaikovsky, on the other hand, brings in an entirely new point of view. Russia was outside the pale of European music until almost the middle of the century. Musicians might travel to it; they hardly expected music to come from it. St. Petersburg and London were expected to supply applause, nothing more. Both are showing now that they have a more solid contribution to offer; but while in England this is only a revival of former glories, in Russia it was a new departure. Tchaikovsky was far from being the first among Russian composers, but he was the first to impress the world with the sense that Russia had really 'grown up', and that was one of the biggest events in the musical history of the nineteenth century.

A CHANGED OUTLOOK

The growing up to a sense of national independence does not appear in Russia alone; it is one of the strongest and most widespread contrasts which the music of the nineteenth century presents to that of the eighteenth. The famous 'Guerre des Bouffons' in Paris (see p. 285) was primarily a question of the French language *versus* the Italian language, and the greatest champion of the national party was Gluck, a foreigner. Haydn, though his mind was much occupied with the peasant songs of Croatia (see p. 190), had never a thought of creating a national school of musical composition.

But in the nineteenth century the musical minds, especially those who sprang from the smaller nations, were not content merely to become tributaries to the broad stream of the world's music. Chopin, though he lived in Paris, founded his most exquisite art upon the dance rhythms of his own Poland; Smetana headed a movement in Prague for the establishment of Bohemian music, a movement which owed much also to the music of Dvořák; Grieg turned to the folk-songs of Norway, and their scales, intervals, and rhythms give a distinguishing character to his music. 'All the rivers run into the sea, yet the sea is not full'; all these and other separate national types of music become in time the possessions of the whole world; the composers do not write for their own countrymen alone, but they gather strength and beauty from the life immediately around them, to which they belong and which they love. And the conscious effort to do this on the part of so many different composers has been chiefly the result of a changed attitude of mind towards music. The older composers were children of nature; they followed an instinct which compelled them to make beautiful things in sound. They did not inquire deeply why they followed it; they did not argue about it or try to say in words what they meant by it, but it was the thing they lived for, and since they gave their lives for it they expected it to bring them a living. Gluck alone amongst them expounded critical theories (see p. 283), and they were with regard to opera more than pure music. But in the new century we find one man after another expounding his views. Music and music only is sufficient for very few of them. Berlioz gives a literary interpretation of one big work after another; Schumann starts a newspaper for the discussion of musical questions; Wagner pours out pamphlet after pamphlet to explain himself and 'the music of the future'. Certainly a big change has come. What is it?

We have already hinted at it (pp. 308–13) in studying the life of Beethoven, and with it we come now to the beginning of our story. That sense of personal responsibility which took complete possession of Beethoven was set deep in the whole social and political life of Europe as it emerged from the turmoil of the Napoleonic Wars. The old life of state and ceremony, even where it was not outwardly destroyed as it had been in France, was visibly shaken. It might suit many nations to preserve its outward features, but there was no longer any faith in the divine right either of kings or of institutions. Men were never so ready to think freely; there have been rarely so many individuals ready to clothe the thoughts of men in literature and poetry. For with the growth of what we described as the 'inventive genius' of the nineteenth century, the genius which linked all the countries of Europe with railways and drew a web of steam routes across the seas, the genius which made men question the truth of every established power, from the church to the principles of science, there sprang up also a great love of the world, its wonders and its beauties, a curiosity as to the past and a desire to rediscover the world of the past and the spirit which animated its people. The romantic literature of France with Victor Hugo at its head, the dramatic and lyric poetry of Germany captained by Goethe and Schiller, our own poets from Wordsworth and Byron to Shelley and Swinburne, are so many expressions of different aspects of this spirit. Was music to stand aside from all this life and remain self-sufficient, at best the symbol of one soul's aspiration, at worst an entertainment for fools? That was the question which the makers of music had to face.

THE TURN OF THE CENTURY

Leaving Beethoven out of count for the moment, let us see who were the commanding figures in music at the turn of the century, and how far they were capable of throwing themselves into this new life. Cherubini (see p. 293) was the leader of music in Paris. He had already reached middle life, a man of profound musical cultivation, trained in a severe school and taking a severe view of his art, the last man to become the discoverer of new paths. His conservatism was no doubt one cause of the disfavour with which Napoleon regarded him.

A group of composers of opera, all bent primarily on providing effective entertainments, surrounded and followed Cherubini in Paris. Scarcely anything of real greatness seemed at the moment likely to come out of Italy, though among the men born at about this time were several whose names it is impossible to forget. There is Spontini (1774–1851), who in 1808 began to overawe Europe with the solemn pretentiousness of his opera *La Vestale*, and who went on impressing Europe and himself by the immensity of his scores for half a century. Another operatic idol, a little younger, was Rossini (1792–1868), a very different kind of man from Spontini. He possessed a sense of humour, rare among musicians, which he could turn against himself as readily as against any one else. Such humour would have seemed profane to Spontini; but it has helped to keep alive some of Rossini's works, *Il barbiere*, for example, though all Spontini's are dead. But another characteristic of Rossini's music, which keeps it alive in the sense of gaining it performances, is its vocal showiness. Spontini was too serious-minded to fill up every air with the florid passages which delight the heart of every *prima donna* in *Il barbiere*. Showing off the voice was really the be-all and end-all of Italian opera at this time. Rossini, Donizetti, and Bellini might do it in different ways, might display humour or skill or grace of melody if they chose, but they had to do it. They were the servants of the singer as completely as though Gluck had never issued his famous protest (see p. 283), and on the whole they were very well content with their servitude.

Among the German-speaking peoples, however, there was a newer and truer influence at work. The man who was to go farther and found a type of opera which was not only German in language but expressive in a large degree of the new artistic aspirations came of a south German family of musicians, though it happened that he was born in the extreme north of Germany.

WEBER AND OPERA

CARL MARIA VON WEBER (1786–1826) was a cousin of Mozart's wife. His father, like Constanze Mozart's and other members of the family, was a minor musician, and for some time during Carl Maria's childhood a theatrical manager. He was as ambitious for his son to become a musician as Mozart's father had been, but he had less understanding of what real greatness in music means. He would have been well content if the boy had shown aptitude for the career of a performing pianist, and was disappointed by his lack of readiness to astonish the multitudes at an early age. He did the best thing possible, however, when he placed his son at the age of twelve years under the tuition of Michael Haydn (see p. 190) at Salzburg. But Weber had other masters, both regular and irregular, worthy members of the musical profession like Heuschkel, who first gave him the foundations of his piano technique, and friends in many grades of life from the court to the theatre, from whom perhaps he learnt more than from his regular teachers. His friendship with the Abbé Vogler was an important episode in his life when as a very young man he was most alive to new impressions. The name of Vogler is now kept alive for English people chiefly by Robert Browning's poem in *Dramatis Personae*. But Browning's picture of the idealist musing over the organ keys is hardly one of the actual man. Vogler was one of those strange mixtures of worldly vanity and piety, of charlatanry and true art, which appear from time to time and of which Liszt may be regarded as a more recent example if one chooses to take an unkind view of him. Mozart, who met Vogler at Mannheim, was repelled by him; Weber was fascinated by him and had thoughts of writing his life. The very mixture of qualities and the variety of tastes, ambitions and abilities, which Mozart was inclined to despise in Vogler, attracted Weber, for to Mozart music was life; to Weber it was a part of life, and life was becoming full of many interests.

If Weber had had only artistic talent and not genius he would probably have dabbled in one kind of artistic activity after another and achieved nothing permanent. He used his pen for other things than music; he attempted a novel, wrote criticism, and even thought of starting a musical paper such as Schumann actually founded later (see p. 409). In all this one sees the symptoms of the new spirit of the age at work. For three years (1807–10) he was engaged as secretary to the brother of the King of Württemberg and lived at Stuttgart, but he got into trouble there as a practical joker and over some transactions of business, and though his character was cleared he was banished from the kingdom. The event, however, had a steadying effect upon him. It was impossible any longer to drift, to be content with the momentary successes of concert-giving. It was necessary, as he himself said of his work, though in another connexion, to make 'every stroke tell'. He had already written much music for the theatre and the orchestra, including two symphonies. But all the strokes which tell come after his years at Stuttgart. The concertos, the piano sonatas, the majority of the songs are among them. For a short time he was *Kapellmeister*, that is, conductor of the Opera, at Prague, and carried out a thorough reorganization of the theatre; then he moved to a similar post at Dresden, a post which he held until his death and in which at a later date Wagner followed him (see p. 435), and here he began to compose *Der Freischütz* (*The Marksman*[1]), which was to be his masterstroke. The fact that when *Der Freischütz* was performed for the first time in Berlin in 1821 it was immediately an overwhelming success shows how thoroughly Weber was a part of the spirit of his time and his people. It was precisely what his audience were ripe for, a simple story based upon an old folk-legend and expressed quite naturally in melody. There is here neither the real classical grandeur of Gluck nor the pseudo-classical pomp of Spontini. There is none of the subtle interweaving of events and characters of Mozart's comedies (see pp. 294–6), but there is also none of the vapid vocal display of contemporary Italian opera. Listen to the scena in which the heroine (Agathe), waiting for the coming of her lover, looks out into the night and dreams and prays in the moonlight. She hears him coming, and the scene ends with their joyful meeting. It is a piece of sentiment, sweet and clean and fresh, and in 1821 even the people of Berlin could appreciate that. No one with any simplicity of heart can fail to love the tune 'Leise, leise', or to appreciate the apt phrases of recitative which contrast with it, and the ecstatic tune 'All' meine Pulse schlagen' which makes the happiest of endings.

[1] An incomplete translation of an untranslatable title: the story is that of an unsuccessful marksman who, in order to win the girl he loves, allows himself to be tempted to cast seven magic bullets, six of which are lucky and the seventh accursed.

Weber's life, however, was cut short. He made a beginning which others were to build upon. Another and a more ambitious opera followed, *Euryanthe*, and then he received the invitation from Charles Kemble, the famous English actor, to produce an opera in English at Covent Garden. The result was his visit here in 1826, the composition of his last opera, *Oberon*, and its enthusiastic welcome by the English audience; but he died from tuberculosis almost immediately afterwards in the house of Sir George Smart.

Much of Weber's music had so direct an appeal to his own generation that it has lost some of its force for later generations. It was a powerful inspiration to some of his immediate successors, especially Wagner and Berlioz, and his ideas about opera, as well as his wonderfully imaginative writing for the orchestra, must be studied in connexion with them. But he survives on surprisingly little of his large output, and when one considers him beside Beethoven, who died in the following year, one sees why Weber's influence was strongest immediately after his death and Beethoven's went on growing until it became most powerful with such different masters of the latter part of the century as Wagner and Brahms.

BEETHOVEN'S LAST WORKS

For Beethoven in the last years of his life was isolated from the outer world about him in spite of the fact that it was he who, catching the first breaths of the new air, opened up fresh possibilities to the musicians of the nineteenth century. If you study or analyse any of the last piano sonatas or the last string quartets you realize that there is pervading them a profound dissatisfaction with every established form and every conventional ornament acceptable in the music of the eighteenth century. He discards the charm of carefully balanced chords and harmonic effects; moods of turbulent energy and serene calm succeed one another abruptly; in the piano music the hands are often spread to the two ends of the keyboard in order to make a gigantic sweep of melody over notes which have the least possible amount of resonance in combination. The following from the last movement of the sonata Op. 111 is typical:

The same sonata, and particularly its first movement, supplies complete examples of all these characteristics of Beethoven's later music which made it uncongenial to his contemporaries. His friends were repelled by it; some who had been his most ardent admirers thought these last sonatas crude, and the string quartets with their many short movements, their impulsive changes of expression and their often thin harmonies, seemed to them vague, disjointed, and unfinished. Some even had the impudence to ask him to compose music in his earlier style, as though he were a tradesman whose business it was to supply goods according to sample. Even musicians like Weber, who fully felt the force of Beethoven's genius, were repelled by these things.

Apart from the actual style of the music there are various signs that the last quartets of Beethoven were closely bound up with the tragic experiences of his life. At the head of the Adagio of the Quartet in A minor he wrote, 'Heiliger Dankgesang eines Genesenen an die Gottheit, in der lydischen Tonart' (Sacred song of thanksgiving to the Deity of one restored to health, in the Lydian mode), and this is succeeded by an Andante above which he wrote, 'Neue Kraft fühlend' (feeling new strength). The two alternate, and a final variation of the Lydian melody is marked in every part 'mit innigster Empfindung' (with the most intimate expression). Sir George Smart visited Beethoven in 1825 and happened to come in for the first private performance of this quartet. He refers to it in his diary. 'Beethoven intended to allude to himself, I suppose, for he was very ill during the early part of this year.' The laconic 'I suppose' well indicates the amount of real sympathy which could be looked for from one who was without doubt a cultivated musician, and who had come to Vienna with the special object of learning Beethoven's wishes with regard to the ninth Symphony, which he had already conducted for the London Philharmonic Society.

Beethoven's association not only of states of feeling but of verbal phrases embodying them with his music is shown in the F major Quartet, Op. 135, where the theme of the last movement is preceded by the following, written neither for instrument nor voice, but as a motto:

Ex. 61

The question and its inexorable answer pervade the whole movement.

But the most famous instance of the link between the melodic idea and a verbal one comes, of course, in the introduction to the Finale of the choral Symphony (see p. 216), where the violoncellos and double basses struggle to drive away the purely instrumental melodies of the earlier movements with their almost vocal recitative, the meaning of which is ultimately made clear by the entrance of the bass voice calling the multitudes to the paean of joy:

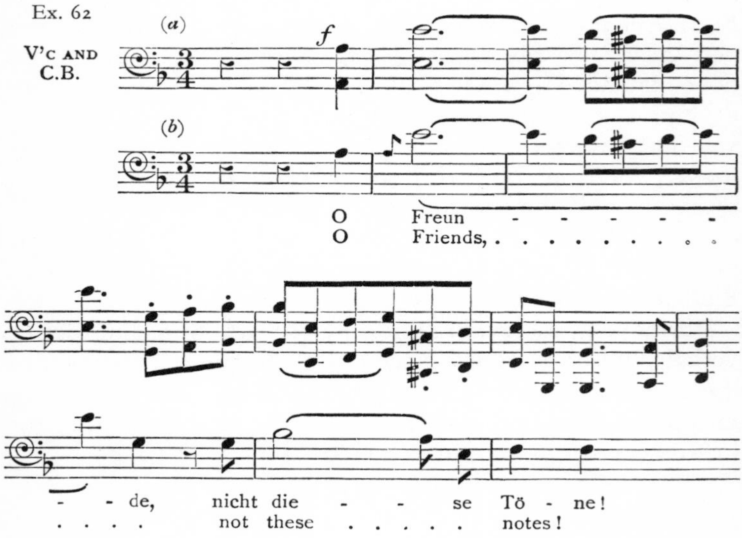

The whole of this passage, and indeed his final adoption of Schiller's ode to complete his colossal symphony, a decision arrived at after many trials of other material, is conclusive evidence of Beethoven's will to throw in his lot with the forces of the new era. 'Seid umschlungen, Millionen! diesen Kuss der ganzen Welt!' It is blazed out in a mighty phrase. Wagner hailed it as the first-fruits of 'the art of the future', always interpreting that expression to mean the fulfilment of his own ideas. But he was right in a larger sense. Sensitive musicians have recoiled and still recoil from the Finale to the choral Symphony. Fanny Hensel, Mendelssohn's favourite sister,[1] spoke of the symphony as 'so grand and in parts so abominable', and of the finale as 'a conclusion meant to be dithyrambic, but falling from its height into the opposite extreme—into burlesque', and there are musicians today who preserve an almost equally implacable attitude towards it. But what we said of Monteverdi may be applied to some extent to this phase of Beethoven (see p. 20). He could not find a new way without beginning by spoiling the old, though in Beethoven's case the old was his own priceless creation.

Suggestions for Further Reading and Listening

THIS chapter starts by nominating ten composers 'who had the greatest influence upon the art of music as a whole in the nineteenth century', continues with a brief discussion of nationalism and cultural context, looks in on Italian opera but lingers with Weber, and concludes with the final works of Beethoven. If its scope is large and generalized, parts of it come into sharper focus in subsequent chapters. Although no one book exactly covers these particular topics, this is the moment to introduce Alfred Einstein's *Music in the Romantic Era*. First published thirty years ago, it remains an extremely useful survey.

In most cases the 'Master Musicians' series can be drawn upon for handy, authoritative studies of the composers listed on page 339. For further reading there are Arthur Hutchings's *Schubert*, the critical biographies by Alfred Einstein and M. J. E. Brown, and Deutsch's *Schubert: a Documentary Biography*.

Philip Radcliffe on *Mendelssohn*, Arthur Hedley on *Chopin*, and Joan Chissell on *Schumann* are all excellent, other recommendations including the *Chopin* symposium, and the *Schumann* symposium, both edited by Alan Walker. To Peter Latham's *Brahms* add Geiringer's *Brahms: his Life and Work* and *Johannes Brahms* by Hans Gal, a little classic of immaculately well-informed and perceptive comment on the composer's personality, compositions, and artistic ambiance. Edward Garden's *Tchaikovsky* can also be recommended.

One of the newest additions to the 'Master Musicians' series is Laurence Davies's *César Franck*, but Léon Vallas's study of the composer, translated by Hubert Foss, should not be disregarded. Walter Beckett's *Liszt* can in its turn be supplemented by Humphrey Searle's *The Music of Liszt* and by Sacheverell Sitwell's *Liszt*, non-technical but the product of an exceptionally cultivated mind. Berlioz and Wagner are rather special cases for, although there are biographies available by J. H. Elliot and Robert L. Jacob respectively in the 'Master Musicians' series, both composers are discussed at some length in later chapters, and reading lists are, therefore, held over until then. Though there is little competition in English, the standard and indeed the outstanding critical biography of Weber is by John Warrack. For amplification of the pages about Beethoven's last compositions, readers are referred back to the Beethoven bibliography in Chapter 14. There is, however, one extra book to be mentioned, since it deals exactly with this period in the composer's career: Martin Cooper's masterly *Beethoven: the Last Decade*.

Anyone who has read 'New Paths' with a little care and then looked ahead to later chapter headings will have noticed that Colles gives short shrift to Rossini, Bellini, and Donizetti. They are mentioned in passing, but are not taken seriously. Such neglect is a symptom of the taste of his time—which was apt to see little virtue in early nineteenth-century Italian opera. The revival of delight in these composers is a relatively recent development, one encouraged by the reappearance of singers who can do justice to their music. Leslie Orrey has written a book in the 'Master Musicians' series about Bellini and there is a growing literature about Donizetti. There is a big, rather heavy, book on Rossini by Herbert Weinstock.

CHAPTER 16

Schubert and Song

WHILE Weber was busied with those innumerable activities, a sketch of which we gave in Chapter 15, and while Beethoven was wrestling with the creation of his latest works, a young man hardly regarded by his contemporaries in Vienna, and unknown to the world beyond it, was pouring out music with feverish haste and laying up a store of melody which was to prove a gold-mine to the coming generation.

FRANZ SCHUBERT, born on 31 January 1797, was the son of a humble schoolmaster, the twelfth child and the last boy of fourteen brothers and sisters, many of whom died in infancy. Consequently, like Haydn, he came to music without any worldly advantages to help him towards the carving out of a career, and without the doubtful advantage of a father's ambition to spur him on, which was an important condition in the early lives of both Mozart and Weber. He was given a good schooling, after which at the early age of seventeen he became an assistant teacher in his father's school, and there he might have remained for the rest of his life but for the fact that he was physically incapable of keeping his pen away from paper ruled in staves. This is no figure of speech. All the evidence shows that to Schubert the art of composition scarcely represented any conscious intellectual effort. He died at the age of thirty-one, yet he left a mass of music in every form the mere writing of which might have occupied an averagely long lifetime had he been checked by the ordinary processes of thought.

There are seven completed symphonies in existence, besides the famous unfinished Symphony and a sketch of one in E major. It is supposed, on uncertain evidence, that another symphony was written at Gastein in 1825 and lost. His chamber music includes the Octet, the piano Quintet in A ('The Trout'), the string Quintet with two cellos in C, several string quartets, two trios for piano and strings. For the piano there are many sonatas, the 'Wanderer-Fantasia', and innumerable shorter works such as the delightful 'Moments musicaux', a profusion of waltzes and other dances, and more music for piano duet than any other composer ever wrote. His choral music contains masses and oratorios with a great number of short pieces; his finished operas number eight, and yet when all this has been said we have not yet mentioned his supreme achievement, the creation of some six hundred songs.

Everything goes to show that his music grew like the lilies of the field. It would be untrue to say that 'he toiled not, neither did he spin', for the actual labour of writing kept him incessantly at work. But when asked about his method of composition he answered that as soon as he had finished one piece he began another, and when well-meaning friends pointed to the great example of Beethoven and suggested that he should improve his music by reconsideration and self-criticism he grew irritable. The instances in which he made any substantial revision of a work—the song 'Der Erlkönig' is one of them—are few. His progress was made not by improving works already finished but by writing more.

It will not be necessary for us to trace in detail a career which was governed by the simple principle of finishing one work and beginning another, varied only by lapses which allowed him to begin the new work before the old was finished. One of these lapses accounts for the fact that the most beautiful of all the symphonies consists only of an Allegro and slow movement and is universally known to this day as the 'Unfinished'.

But there are just a few points about Schubert's life which cannot be ignored, and the first of them is that the seminary in Vienna, which he entered at the age of thirteen, gave him more than a general education. It was for him practically a music school. It boasted an orchestra capable of playing the symphonies of Haydn and Mozart, of Cherubini and Méhul, and even occasionally the early ones, then quite new, of Beethoven. And in this orchestra Schubert played the violin and learnt to know music. It was here that he began to compose, and his boyish works show the force of these examples acting upon his own irrepressible individuality.

But it was in the years immediately after his leaving school that his wonderful outpouring of song began, and in the earliest songs one sees at once the influence of the poets of the day rather than of other musicians, though his earliest efforts are often clearly modelled on such minor song-writers as Reichardt and Zumsteeg. No great master provided him with examples to guide him in the direction of song even if he had wanted guidance. Mozart's ideas of vocal music were inseparably bound up with the elaborated aria forms of the opera; his songs for voice and piano are a mere handful, among which only one or two, such as 'Das Veilchen', and 'Abendempfindung', are masterpieces of simple feeling. Beethoven's excursions into song, beautiful and heartfelt as some of them are, are the offshoots of a genius which expressed itself more naturally by other means. But the true song-writer needs no examples and follows no precedents. His own musical sense becomes fertilized by the poem; the poem gives form to the music; the music gives expression to the poem.

SCHUBERT AND GOETHE

Schubert's earliest songs, such as 'Gretchen am Spinnrade' (Margaret at the spinning-wheel) and 'Der Erlkönig' ('The Erlking', properly 'alder king'), both by Goethe, show how his whole nature was seized by the spirit of poetry at once lyrical and dramatic. The years 1814 and 1815, in which these two songs were written, saw the birth of a whole group of songs to poems by Goethe. 'Heidenröslein' ('The Wild Rose'), 'Rastlose Liebe' ('Restless Love'), and 'Schäfers Klagelied' ('The Shepherd's Lament') are among them, and to place these five side by side is to realize once and for all how completely pliable Schubert's music was to the thought of the poet. In these songs no preconceived ideas of musical form come between the musician and the poet. There is no repetition of words for the purposes of musical balance, there is never a scrap more of melody than the words actually require.

Take 'Heidenröslein' first. It is the simplest of them. A boy sees a wild rose blooming on the heath. It is so lovely that he wants to pick it; but roses have thorns. Still the boy does not care; he wants the rose and will have it. He plucks it and suffers for his rashness. That is all. You may find for yourself the moral or the philosophy underlying the story; neither Goethe nor Schubert will point it out. The poet tells it in a little lyric of three stanzas, each one ending with the refrain:

> Röslein, Röslein, Röslein rot,
> Röslein auf der Heiden;

the musician sets this to a tune of wonderful freshness caught from the phrase 'so jung und morgenschön' (so young and of a morning loveliness) and repeated to each stanza. The accompaniment supplies nothing but the lightest harmony with a tiny tripping interlude between the stanzas. Perhaps it seems rather obvious, and it may be suggested that to make the same phrase of melody stand for 'Freuden' (joy) in the first verse and 'leiden' (to suffer) in the other two is scarcely to give very close expression to the features of the verse.

But here we must consider a broad distinction between two different kinds of song—the strophic song, in which the music repeats itself with each stanza of the poetry, and the continuous song, composed throughout ('durchkomponiert'), in which the music varies with each suggestion from the verse. Practically all folk-songs are of the former kind, and we may notice incidentally that the great majority of English songs until the present generation of composers arose were strophic.

Schubert did more than any one in his time to develop the larger form of songs composed throughout, but his judgement was almost unerring in choosing the right method for each particular instance. To set 'Heidenröslein' to music which distinguished each point and emphasized the boy's pleasure on catching sight of the rose and his disillusionment when the thorn pricked his finger would be to reduce the thing to a bathos which only a modern German of an analytical frame of mind could contemplate with satisfaction. No; Schubert knew what he was about, and it is just his choice of the unemphasized strophic form, the form which ignores details for the sake of the whole, which makes 'Heidenröslein' complete.

All the other four of this group are composed throughout; 'Rastlose Liebe' and 'Schäfers Klagelied' stand next to one another in the collection of Goethe's *Lieder*. There is no hint of allegory in either; each is dominated by a single impulse. The first is summed up in its last two lines:

Glück ohne Ruh,
Liebe, bist du!
(Happiness without rest,
Love, art thou!)

The motto of the second may be found in the line:

Doch alles ist leider ein Traum
(Yet all alas is a dream).

Looked at musically we find that the ruling impulse of 'Rastlose Liebe', its restlessness, is conveyed by the constantly moving arpeggio accompaniment. There is no pictorial suggestion of snow, wind, rain, and the other forces of nature mentioned in the poem, and all the climaxes of the vocal melody fall upon such phrases as 'ohne Rast und Ruh'!', 'Alles vergebens!', and the final 'O Liebe, bist du!'. These are supported by strong harmonic modulations, always a great means of expression with Schubert.

In 'Schäfers Klagelied', on the other hand, the accompaniment as well as the vocal part entirely changes its character with the mention of the flowers, the thunder-storm, and the rainbow. All these things impress themselves and form part of the shepherd's mood of sorrowful reflection. One thing both have in common, and that is the repetition of the last lines, but it is a repetition made not for the sake of a musical coda but in order to impress the poetic idea the more strongly.

A more subtle use of repetition is made at the end of 'Gretchen am Spinnrade'. This is, of course, the well-known song from *Faust* which Margaret sings as she sits alone at her spinning-wheel. The repetitions of the first stanza,

Meine Ruh' ist hin,
Mein Herz ist schwer,
Ich finde sie nimmer
Und nimmermehr

(My peace has fled
My heart is sore,
I find them never,
Nevermore),

are Goethe's own as they occur in the drama, but Schubert has added once more the first two lines at the very end in a way which just makes the song revert to the idea of a dull and brooding grief after the passionate outburst is over. Here the accompaniment has nothing to do either with the prevailing feeling of the poem, as it has in 'Rastlose Liebe', or with its details, as in 'Schäfers Klagelied'. It is outside the poem itself, merely a part of the scene. It represents the monotonous hum of the spinning-wheel maintained incessantly save for one poignant moment where the singer recalls 'his kiss'. Then it ceases until she returns to her work falteringly, then steadily. The perfection with which the melody accentuates each phrase of words and at the same time is built up into a musical whole can scarcely need to be pointed out. That this intimate song was written by a boy of seventeen is one of the miracles of musical art.

'Der Erlkönig' is less miraculous, though in its own way it is a masterpiece. Here we have no deep personal feeling. It is just a most graphic presentment of the legend which Goethe's ballad tells with a relentless swiftness. You may find in the constant triplets of the piano part the ring of the horse's hoofs upon the ground, or the rustle of the wind among the leaves, or the agitation of the father as he clutches the child; it seems to have something to do with each in turn, yet there are practically no pictorial details in the rhythmic figures except the menacing figure of the bass:

Ex. 63

in which one can fancy that one sees the sudden dart forward of the Erlking to snatch the child from his father's arms. The three voices of the father, the child, and the Erlking are wonderfully conveyed both by the *tessitura* (that is, the part of the scale in which the phrases lie) of the voice part and in the modulations of key. The Erlking each time begins to speak in a major key[1] (B flat, C, E flat); he is an inhuman and soulless creature whose voice contrasts almost flippantly with those of warm-blooded human beings. When the boy cries out to his father for the last time the harmony becomes agonized:

Ex. 64

A chord consisting of E flat, F, and G flat was daring in

[1] The original key of the song is G minor and the references are made to the original. It is, however, most frequently sung by baritone voices in E minor.

Schubert's time. His use of it here is easily explicable even by the harmonic system of that day, but still it is a stretch of the system made in order to gain a point of dramatic intensity. It is one of the first of many stretches which that system was to suffer from, or profit by, at the hands of Schubert's successors in the nineteenth century, and the process produced an expansion which in the end completely reshaped all ideas of harmony.

SCHUBERT'S DEVELOPMENT

To return, however, to Schubert's own development, it was in the year 1815 that he began his friendship with Mayrhofer, a poet whose lyrics he set to music,[1] and who was probably constantly helpful to him in widening his knowledge of new poetry.

The circle of his friends began to widen, but it is noticeable that the names are mostly those of men actively concerned in poetry and literature and neither noblemen and leaders of society, as so many of the admirers of Beethoven were, nor musicians. Another whose name will also be found as author at the head of some of Schubert's songs was Franz von Schober,[2] who in the following year was a student at the University of Vienna, and who persuaded Schubert to give up his drudgery of school teaching and to live in his rooms in order to devote himself more freely to musical composition. In this year Schubert's songs took a wide range, but his devotion to Goethe is still shown in the number of that poet's poems which he set and the great variety of the music with which he endowed them. They range from the simple ballad 'Der Fischer' ('The Fisherman') to the titanic 'An Schwager Kronos' ('To Postilion Chronos'), an ode to the time-spirit and the swift though toilsome passage of life, and include the Harper's songs from *Wilhelm Meister* and others. Without pausing to study these songs in detail one quotation from 'An Schwager Kronos' must be given, because it points at once to certain characteristics of Schubert's style when he launched upon a song in 'the grand

[1] See 'Am See', 'Am Strome', 'Der Alpenjäger', &c.

[2] See 'Pax Vobiscum', 'Viola', &c.

manner', and also because it shows him as the forerunner of Wagner's declamatory style (see pp. 446–7):

Ex. 65

Le - ben hin - ein, vom Ge -

- birg zum Ge - birg schwebet der e - wi - ge

Geist, e - wi - gen Le - bens

The abrupt change of key (E flat to E minor, bar 5) in contrast to the modulations by a process of sequential harmonies in the subsequent passage shows a new freedom of style, the sweeping arpeggios of the bass part have an exuberance quite unlike any of the music of the eighteenth-century composers, but often reappearing in the later German masters, particularly in the Wotan music of Wagner, the opening of Brahms's third Symphony, and that of Strauss's *Ein Heldenleben*. Schubert is led in this direction of exuberant freedom solely by the inspiration of a poetic idea; one finds few traces of it in his purely instrumental music. The bold harmonic sequences of Schubert's setting of Schiller's 'Gruppe aus dem Tartarus' ('A Group from Tartarus'), written a year later, should be compared with those of 'An Schwager Kronos'. The song is a second example of the masterful dramatic type.

Another song of this year is the famous setting of 'Der Wanderer' by an obscure poet, G. P. Schmidt of Lübeck, which, compared with 'An Schwager Kronos', is technically comparatively simple. Yet it is one of the most important songs in the whole of the great collection, not only for the truthfulness with which the melody conveys the feeling of the words, but for an historical reason which we will examine presently (see p. 367). The poem gave birth to the song, and the song a little later became the parent of one of Schubert's greatest works for piano, the 'Wanderer-Fantasia'.

Two exquisite songs, subsequently used by Schubert as the basis for purely instrumental works, were written in the following year (1817). These are 'Die Forelle' ('The Trout') and 'Der Tod und das Mädchen' ('Death and the Maiden'). The first became the theme for variations in the Quintet for piano and strings in A major; the second was similarly used in the string Quartet in D minor. The two songs may well be contrasted. The one, a little fable of how the fish could not be caught in clear water but were soon tricked by the angler when he made the water muddy, belongs to the same class of song as 'Heidenröslein', but Schubert set it more fully. The third verse has an appropriate change of melody and key, and the leaping accompaniment, figure (*a*), which pictures the fish in the clear water, gets changed to a more compact one (*b*) with a wonderfully pictorial effect:

The other is no fable; it is a fragment of direct dialogue. The

Maiden struggles to avoid Death, but he takes her hand and stills her cries. The music is equally direct; the only point which needs attention called to it is the subtle way in which the rhythm of Death's song creeps into the piano part four bars before the end of the Maiden's part. That rhythm itself is so like the slow movement of Beethoven's seventh Symphony that one almost wonders whether a reference was intended, but Schubert was not given to quotation.

The year 1818 saw a change in the outward circumstances of Schubert's life; it is also the year of a great change in himself. The outward change was merely the acquisition of a musical appointment, the only regular appointment which he ever held, and that a sufficiently modest one, as music teacher to the daughters of Count Johann Esterházy, a younger member of the family who were Haydn's patrons. This in itself was of small consequence beyond the fact that it provided Schubert with a living and caused him to write a considerable quantity of piano music and duets for the benefit of his pupils. He spent the summer in their country house at Zseliz. The best work by which to remember this time there is the lovely little song called 'Abendrot' ('Sunset') which he wrote there.

INSTRUMENTAL MUSIC

But the change in him showed itself almost immediately in a change in his music which may be described as growing up. This is not so noticeable in his songs, for the composer of such songs as we have been studying could have little or nothing to add to his powers in that direction. Since the composition of 'Gretchen am Spinnrade' he had been fully grown in his capacity for seizing on the inner spirit of any poem which came before him and expressing that spirit in musical sound. But that very art of song-writing is itself dependent upon another mind. It is the gift of sympathy in its fullest form.

The independent power of creating something essentially his own comes to the musician in pure instrumental music, and it was this power which Schubert acquired at this time. Remember that he was only twenty-one years old, and he had before him only ten more years of life. In those ten years he composed practically all the great instrumental works which, apart from his songs, give him his place next to Beethoven among the great composers at the beginning of the nineteenth century. The series begins with the pianoforte Quintet (1819) which has variations on 'Die Forelle' as its slow movement, and which is written for an unusual set of instruments, for the string quartet chosen to go with the piano is not the usual one of two violins, viola, and violoncello, but one violin, viola, violoncello, and double bass. Schubert's fondness for the double bass in chamber music is shown again in the Octet, but there it is added to the ordinary string quartet, and the presence of wind instruments (clarinet, bassoon, and horn) gives the score a greater fullness, so that the deep-toned bass (an octave below the violoncello) produces an effect resembling that of the small orchestra.

In the years immediately following 1819 are several works never completed, which, however, are scarcely less important on that account. First comes a string Quartet in C minor, of which one movement, the first Allegro, was finished and the second, an Andante, was begun. The completed movement is often played and is highly characteristic of his work. Two symphonies followed, one in E and one in B minor, but both were left unfinished.

It is curious to notice, however, that Schubert adopted opposite methods in composing these two symphonies; the one in E he sketched out in full, arranging the four movements, their keys, themes, even the number of bars each was to contain and the instruments to be used. He then began the process of writing the details, and left off in the middle of the first movement. The Symphony in B minor, however, he composed according to his more usual plan, movement by movement. He finished the first Allegro in B minor, went on to the slow movement in E, finished that, and began a scherzo which he abandoned. We may be thankful that the first of these two methods was exceptional. The Symphony in E remains merely an interesting manuscript, but the 'Quartettsatz' and still more the two movements of the Symphony in B minor are priceless musical possessions which rejoice the hearts of music-lovers to this day. The proverb of the bird in the hand gets the fullest consent where such music is concerned.

Nearly contemporary with these works is the great Fantasy in C for piano, in which the 'Wanderer' theme is the principal motive. In 1824 the Octet was written as well as several string quartets, of which the one in A minor is the most famous. The list of great instrumental works then grows steadily. The best of his piano sonatas follow; two more string quartets, D minor and G, the former containing the variations on 'Der Tod und das Mädchen', lead to the two trios for piano and strings, B flat and E flat (the former is so beautiful that it usurps the attention which is due to the latter), and those written in 1827, the last complete year of Schubert's life, are followed in the year of his death by the magnificent Symphony in C major and the Quintet, also in C, for two violins, viola, and two violoncellos.

That is to give the barest outline of the flood of beautiful things which were the outcome of Schubert's ten years of manhood. It is not necessary for us to submit them to close analysis, but it is very necessary to take every opportunity of hearing them and knowing them practically. If we were to analyse them we should find that almost all except the two movements of the 'Unfinished' Symphony contain points at which the actual form is open to some criticism. They are long, there is much repetition, and, when writing in sonata form, Schubert often seems rather bored by the conventional need for a recapitulation to follow the development. He follows out its course rather mechanically and sometimes resorts to the plan of making the whole recapitulation a transposed version of the first statement. But even if one is conscious of these disadvantages, and the listener who does not analyse closely hardly is conscious of them, they still exercise a unique charm. They are all permeated with the song spirit. Often one feels as though Schubert's instrumental melodies must have been written to some poetry which he had in mind.

His development of the 'Wanderer' song in the Fantasy gives an example of his power of expanding into a great instrumental piece a thought which began with a song. This Fantasy is quite different from either his own treatment of song melodies as a basis for regular variations, as in the 'Trout' Quintet and the Quartet in D minor, or from the instrumental paraphrases on songs of which Liszt made many. Liszt's paraphrases on songs by Schubert and others take the whole song and adapt it to the technique of the piano. Schubert's Fantasy on the 'Wanderer' uses very little of the matter of the song. The only actual quotation is of one phrase which is neither the principal theme of the song nor used as a refrain. The passage as it appears in the song is as follows:

Ex. 67

And this appears in the Fantasy as the principal theme, freely developed, of the second movement, Adagio. The whole Fantasy consists of four movements in the manner of a sonata but linked together, and all the other three, that is (1) Allegro con fuoco, (3) Presto (virtually a scherzo), (4) Allegro (written in the manner of a free fugue), are developments out of the following theme:

Ex. 68

This in itself seems to be a kind of extension of the song melody quoted above but so much extended that if it were not for the actual quotation of that melody in the Adagio one could not recognize the reference. Out of the development of this springs yet another melody which has no counterpart at all in the song but is a definite second subject:

Ex. 69

Both these themes are entirely transformed in rhythm to form the subject-matter of the third movement, and the first of them is again altered to be the fugal subject of the Finale.

It is worth while touching on these technical details in order to show two points: first, that a tune which began in Schubert's mind as a song melody could so grow there that it became as different from its origin as the tree is different from the first sprout; secondly, that this Fantasy is virtually a complete *symphonic poem* upon the idea of the 'Wanderer', and we shall have much to do with symphonic poems as we trace the music of the nineteenth century.

THE SONG CYCLES

We need not, however, follow the history of the symphonic poem at the moment. Instead, a few words must be added to complete our survey of Schubert as a song-writer. The years in which his chief instrumental works appeared were no less prolific in songs than the earlier ones.

They include with many single ones the three sets known as *Die schöne Müllerin* ('The Fair Maid of the Mill'), *Winterreise* ('Winter Journey'), and the *Schwanengesang* ('Swan Songs'). The first two, containing twenty and twenty-four songs respectively, are genuine cycles, that is to say, each is a set of poems linked together by a common idea. Both were written by Wilhelm Müller, a minor poet, whose verses Schubert came across by accident, and both were set to music soon after the words were written, the former completed in 1823, the latter in 1827. *Die schöne Müllerin* is the easier to comprehend as a whole because it is an idyllic love-story told in lyric verse. There are three principal characters in the story, the singer who is the lover, the maid of the mill, and the mill-stream which murmurs through all their romance. The story itself is a sad one; the lovers do not 'live happily ever after'. The confidences which the mill-stream has to hear are of many kinds. First the young miller wanders careless and happy by its banks; then it receives his hopes and fears. The full awakening of his love for the master's daughter is told in 'Am Feierabend' ('After Work'); the triumph of success is sung to the stream in 'Mein' ('Mine') with its buoyant refrain 'Die geliebte Müllerin ist mein!' Afterwards there are fresh doubts; the huntsman comes upon the scene, and he is a greater hero than a poor miller. The maiden's favourite colour, the green of leaves and grass, becomes the hateful colour because it is the green of the huntsman's coat, and the miller has to give her up. The song 'Trockne Blumen' ('Withered Flowers') sums up his grief, his only hope the thought that his love may pass his grave when winter is gone and the flowers bloom again. The cycle ends with 'Des Baches Wiegenlied' ('The Stream's Cradle-song'), in which all trouble is stilled by the quiet of nature.

It is not great poetry and it is quite frankly sentimental. But Schubert keeps it on the right side of the line between sentiment and sentimentality because his whole expression of the sentiment is true and simple. His music never wallows or gushes or protests too much, and so he carries his hearers with him at every point.

The songs of the *Winterreise* are less clearly consecutive. They are neither strung together on the thread of a definite story nor unified by one pictorial background such as that which the idea of the mill-stream provides for the 'Müller-lieder'. But from the first, 'Gute Nacht', ('Good-night'), to the last, 'Der Leiermann' ('The Organ-grinder'), they are pervaded by the idea of loneliness, and the very persistence of the idea in spite of the great variety of ways in which it is illustrated makes the cycle rather monotonous for complete performance. Almost every one of its songs, however, is a masterpiece in itself. Among the most typical are 'Die Wetterfahne' ('The Weather-vane'), in which the undulating melody pictures the turning about of the vane in the wind; 'Der Lindenbaum' ('The Lime Tree'), one of Schubert's loveliest melodies with a beautiful rustling accompaniment with which should be compared 'Frühlingstraum' ('A Dream of Spring'); 'Die Post' ('The Post') with its vigorous illustration of the post-boy's horn; and lastly, 'Der Leiermann', in which the old organ-grinder's tune drones wearily through the whole song.

The *Schwanengesang* is not really a cycle. The collective title was given to the songs on their publication after Schubert's early death and is not very appropriate, for the legend of

> The silver swan who living had no note,
> When death approached unlocked her silent throat,

is certainly inapplicable to Schubert, who had poured out song from childhood. The collection, too, includes songs by three authors: seven by Rellstab, which the poet had written in the hope that Beethoven would set them; six by Heine, the only ones by him which Schubert ever set; and one by Seidl, a poet from whom Schubert had often drawn before.

That Heine, the poet who more than any other was to influence German song in the next generation most powerfully, should have dawned upon Schubert's horizon just in time to be greeted with the response of these six musical settings is in itself a remarkable presage of events, and Schubert's music responds to the new poetic impulse. The first song, 'Der Atlas', should be placed beside 'An Schwager Kronos' and 'Gruppe aus dem Tartarus'. Its declamation is akin to theirs, but there is less musical elaboration. All save 'Das Fischermädchen' ('The Fisher-maiden') are touched with tragedy.

The last, 'Der Doppelgänger' ('The Wraith'), is the most tragic of all. A man stands in the silent street before a house where once his beloved lived. He is conscious of another figure standing there. Suddenly the moon lights up the face of the other and, horror-struck, he recognizes—himself. It is his double which haunts the empty scene of his past love and present grief. Schubert's music has the simplicity which only the most inspired things can afford to have. It is inexplicable; one cannot say why these four chords are so relentlessly haunting, though the fact that each contains only two notes contributes to their strangely hollow effect:

Ex. 70

The song has little positive melody, but every note is in place as an expression both of the prevalent feeling and of the particular details of the short poem.

A SUMMARY OF RESULTS

With this wonderful example of concentration upon the essence of the poetry we may leave the detailed study of Schubert's songs. It is time, however, to sum up what he achieved as a writer of songs and to see how his achievement affected his successors.

1. Schubert was the first musician to realize fully that the three qualities of a poem, (*a*) its mood, (*b*) its meaning, (*c*) its form, can find a counterpart in music at the same time. Others before him had laid stress upon one or the other and generally sacrificed one or other of these qualities in order to get close to that which appealed most strongly.

2. The musical impulse was so strong in Schubert that he was in no danger of sacrificing musical beauty to these poetic requirements. His greatest songs, those which reflect the qualities of the poem, can be played as well as sung, as Liszt showed when he made his transcriptions of them, and as Schubert himself indicated by incorporating some examples in purely instrumental works.

3. This triple influence of poetry on music had a threefold influence on his musical technique:

(*a*) The mood of the poem led him to give the piano part of the song an increased significance. (See 'Rastlose Liebe', 'Der Erlkönig', and 'Die Forelle'.)

(*b*) The meaning of particular lines, phrases, and words in the poem made him widen the range of possible harmonies. (See 'Der Erlkönig', 'An Schwager Kronos', 'Der Doppelgänger'.)

(*c*) The form of the poem indicated new musical forms free from the repetitions of aria or sonata, and these new forms were transferred by his successors from vocal music to the instrumental symphonic poem.

GERMAN SONG-WRITERS OF THE NINETEENTH CENTURY

All the great German composers of the nineteenth century were to a certain extent song-writers, and all were indebted to Schubert, some of them far more than they knew, for the freedom and certainty with which they handled their poetic material.

Mendelssohn felt his influence less strongly than any of them. He followed too close upon Schubert's heels to know thoroughly what he had done, for it must be remembered that though a certain number of Schubert's songs had been published in Vienna his fame had not flown far, and he died leaving stacks of unexplored manuscripts which were for some years left in the same oblivion which the masterpieces of J. S. Bach suffered from. Mendelssohn wrote a number of very charming songs, but he never hungered or thirsted for great poetry (see p. 415). His popular setting of Heine's 'Auf Flügeln des Gesanges' ('On the wings of song') is typical; a gracious melody supported by some gently flowing piano arpeggios is sufficient for his delight. Look through Mendelssohn's songs and see how many of them are about spring and flowers and you will get a fairly clear idea of the simple unimpassioned things with which he most naturally linked his easy music. Place Mendelssohn's setting of Uhland's 'Frühlingsglaube' ('Faith in Spring') beside Schubert's setting of the same poem and form your own estimate as to which is the more intimate both as a piece of music and as an expression of the words.

That sort of comparison is very helpful as a means of gaining an insight into the different characters and capacities of composers, but of course one must be careful not to jump to general conclusions as a result of comparing individual songs. In this case the inference is clear, because Mendelssohn's setting is an average example of his style in song, and Schubert's, though a fair example of his way of treating little poems, is by no means one of his greatest songs. But it is easy to find single songs by quite inferior composers which are as good and possibly better than Schubert's.

If one suddenly came upon Edward Loder's 'I heard a brooklet gushing', which is a translation of the second poem in 'Die schöne Müllerin', one might imagine that Loder (1813–65) was an English Schubert, a genius whom his countrymen had wilfully neglected in favour of the foreigner. For it is a lovely little song, in some respects more subtly expressive than Schubert's 'Wohin'; but it is practically alone amongst Loder's songs, and those which are settings of genuine English poems bear no possibility of comparison with Schubert.

Or to take a stronger example, the ballads of Carl Loewe (1796–1869) are famous, and his setting of 'Der Erlkönig', which he composed in 1818 almost at the same time as Schubert wrote his, has often been compared favourably with Schubert's. But Loewe's powers appear at their best almost exclusively in one kind of song, the dramatic ballad, of which 'Der Erlkönig' is a German example and 'Edward' is a Scottish one. He gives one nothing which can be placed beside the numerous lyrical songs of Schubert.

Again, take Berlioz's setting of the 'King of Thule' song as it appears in *La Damnation de Faust*. Its constant brooding over one interval (the augmented fourth) gives it a certain colour which Schubert's plain setting has not got, yet on the whole

Berlioz, in spite of all his love of poetry, had nothing like Schubert's readiness in finding an apt musical expression for it.

When we come to trace the development of song in the work of Schubert's successors, particularly those of German-speaking nations, it is possible to make much broader comparisons, because some of them reset much of the poetry, especially that of Goethe, which Schubert began to set, and one can see in their work the advantages of time and experience. To take the music which Beethoven, Schubert, Schumann, and Hugo Wolf associated with the poems of *Wilhelm Meister* is an extraordinarily telling way of illustrating the advance made through the nineteenth century in adapting musical expression to poetic mood, sense, and form.

The three great German song-writers of the later nineteenth century were Schumann, Brahms, and Wolf. Wagner in his 'Five Poems' and a few other examples left just sufficient to show that he too might have been among the great song-writers if he had not been so completely preoccupied with dramatic music. Indeed, his music-dramas are in a sense the extension of Schubert's song style to the stage. That, however, we may leave on one side for the moment.

Schumann was the man ideally fitted to take up song where Schubert had left it. Temperament, education, and circumstances all marked him out for a great song-writer, for he grew up amongst books and all his earliest ideas of art were closely associated with poetry. But it was some time before the results began to appear in actual settings of poetry to music. Almost all his early works are for piano, and the songs which are most famous now were composed in a rush of enthusiasm in the years immediately following his marriage (see pp. 414, 416). The lyrics of Geibel, Rückert, Eichendorff, and, most of all, those of Heine, fascinated him, and the cycle of sixteen songs called *Dichterliebe* ('Poet's Love') may be taken as typical of Schumann's ideal in song. The thing which most stamps these and other songs as Schumann's own is their human sympathy. One may find something of the same quality in certain songs of Schubert, but it is the constant motive in Schumann. One cannot explain exactly by referring to technical matters how this quality expresses itself, but if you hear either the *Dichterliebe* cycle or the shorter *Frauenliebe und Leben* ('Woman's Love and Life'), poems by Chamisso, you cannot fail to be conscious of it. Schumann seems to be himself living through the experiences of the poet's characters, and this makes his songs peculiarly lovable although his actual range of musical expression is shorter than Schubert's.

Brahms in his songs is more like Schubert in his wide musical range and has not quite the glowing personal sympathy of Schumann. In the case of Brahms musical beauty takes a place above the expression of the poetry, while with Wolf the expression of the poetry is so all-important that he sometimes thrusts the musical qualities aside. Consequently some of Brahms's greatest songs spring from poems which are not very significant and are even rather trivial in themselves; the exquisite music of 'Die Mainacht' ('May Night'), for instance, raises the poem to a power higher than itself.

But rough generalizations such as these are not to be taken for granted. You may find examples in Brahms which suggest the sympathy of Schumann, for instance 'Immer leiser wird mein Schlummer' ('Ever lighter grows my slumber'), and a comparison of Wolf's 'In dem Schatten meiner Locken' ('In the shadow of my tresses') with Brahms's will not show Wolf's to be behind in musical beauty, rather the reverse, in fact. One can only venture upon general conclusions as a result of thorough knowledge of a great number of particular cases, and the weighing of one against another can only begin when we have got a wide knowledge of the works themselves. Since both Brahms and Wolf left well over two hundred songs each, that means an amount of close study which we cannot pretend to undertake in a short course such as this, but the suggestions given can be used as hints for individual study.

WOLF'S CAREER

A more precise word may be added here about Wolf, although to do so at this stage is to upset the chronological progress of our story. But since Wolf was almost entirely a song-writer and nothing else—he wrote besides only a couple of operas, a little choral music, and a few instrumental works—it is most natural to deal with him while we are on the subject of song, whereas both Schumann and Brahms are essential figures in other phases of musical history. There are a good many things in Wolf's short and tragic life which are like Schubert's, but the fact that his life was lived at the end instead of at the beginning of the nineteenth century makes a world of difference.

Hugo Wolf was born in 1860, the fourth son of a fairly well-to-do family living at Windischgraz in Lower Styria. His father was his first music teacher, but, a business man himself, seems to have had some objections to the boy's devoting his life to music. These objections cannot have been pressed very seriously, however, because Hugo was only fifteen when he was sent to study at the Vienna Conservatoire. During his first year as a music student Wagner came to Vienna for performances of *Tannhäuser* and *Lohengrin* at the Opera and Wolf fell down before him in an ecstasy of boyish hero-worship. After two years he got dismissed from the Conservatoire, as Haydn was from St. Stephen's (see p. 191), for an offence which is said to have been really that of another student, and, like Haydn, he then set himself to battle with poverty and win his way in the difficult life of a big city.

No princely patronage came to help him, for that with its benefits and its evils had long since passed away. He tried to teach and lost his temper with his pupils. He soon began to compose songs, and twelve of the early ones later published as *Lieder aus der Jugendzeit* ('Songs of Youth') belong to the years 1877–8. When he was twenty-one he got a post as second conductor at the Salzburg town theatre, where Carl Muck, one of the greatest living conductors of Wagner, was then chief conductor. Wolf was no more successful in this post than as a teacher of private pupils, and he was soon back in Vienna again. A visit to Bayreuth in 1882, the year that *Parsifal* was produced, broke the monotony of the next years, and then in 1884 he took up criticism in a newspaper as a means of earning a living and developing his own character. In that more than anything else, perhaps, you see the difference between him and Schubert. Criticism would have been a waste of time to Schubert; it was necessary to Wolf's development. He needed to clear his own mind by expressing it publicly. Granted that some of his criticism was futile, especially his tilting at his greater contemporary, Brahms, it served his purpose. He began to see what he himself must do to be saved, and all his greatest songs were poured out in the few years following his critical escapades. The fifty-three settings of poems by Möricke, the majority of those by Eichendorff, and about half the fifty-one Goethe songs were written in 1888; the remainder of the Goethe songs, the *Spanisches Liederbuch* (Spanish Song-book, words by Geibel and Paul Heyse), followed in 1889–90, and the *Italienisches Liederbuch* (Italian Song-book, words by Heyse) was the work of the nineties. These represent roughly the sum of Wolf's important contribution to music. And when you come to study them a few facts must be remembered: (1) that Wolf is essentially a disciple of Wagner, not in the sense of copying his work, for Wolf carried what he had learnt from Wagner into an entirely different side of music, but in his attitude towards the combination of music and poetic ideas; (2) that Wolf lived amongst poets and drew his inspiration from them; (3) that by the time that he was growing up the violent partisanship in musical life which was one of the most unhappy products of the strenuous nineteenth century had come to a head.

Wolf died in 1903, and the last few years of illness resulting in madness had made him quite incapable of continuing any musical work. He is therefore, strictly speaking, the last of the great writers of German song in the nineteenth century. The list might be extended with many names beyond those mentioned, but we will not extend it beyond pointing to the fact that the song begun by Schubert had its direct development in other countries. Grieg in Norway and Dvořák in Bohemia strongly reflected their own national folk-songs, but still owed much to the German example. Sterndale Bennett in England, contemporary and friend of Mendelssohn and Schumann, was another descendant of the same family. His songs are much more nearly related to the style of Mendelssohn than they are to the older English songs of such composers as Dibdin, Shield, Bishop, and Balfe. The recovery of its own musical characteristics came later in English song, in the works of a dozen or more fine song-writers headed by Stanford and Parry.

In France and still more definitely in Russia national ideals expressed in national poetry have produced types quite distinct from the lines on which Schubert worked. We shall therefore touch upon them in connexion with other aspects of the musical history of those countries which belong for the most part to later phases of our study. (See Chapter 21).

Suggestions for Further Reading and Listening

AFTER dwelling on Schubert's songs and pausing to consider briefly his instrumental music, this chapter traces the outline of the German art-song, the *lied*, as far as Hugo Wolf. For a more or less parallel survey, it is well worth looking up Philip Radcliffe's contributions, 'Germany and Austria', in *A History of Song*, edited by Denis Stevens. Apart from its intrinsic merits, it sketches in the historical, pre-Schubert background. Schubert's songs have inevitably attracted a great deal of critical attention, and Richard Capell's book on them springs immediately to mind. Maurice Brown's much shorter 'BBC Music Guide' should be consulted, and specialists will find aspects of *Schubert's Song Technique* by Ernest G. Porter stimulating. *The Schubert Song-Cycles with Thoughts on Performance* by Gerald Moore embodies a lifetime's experience of and devotion to its subject. You do not have to be a singer or a pianist to profit from it.

The chapter entitled 'Franz Schubert' in Tovey's *Essays and Lectures on Music* should be read, and reread: it covers a cross-section of the composer's music. For further detail, see Jack Westrup's *Schubert Chamber Music*, Philip Radcliffe's *Schubert Piano Sonatas*, and Maurice Brown's *Schubert Symphonies*, all in the 'BBC Music Guide' series. Under the same imprint is Astra Desmond's *Schumann Songs*, which can be reinforced with Eric Sams's *The Songs of Robert Schumann*. Sams is also responsible for *Brahms's Songs* ('BBC Music Guide'). The definitive biography in English of Hugo Wolf is by Frank Walker, though for a specific commentary on his songs it is once again Eric Sams who has produced the standard study, *The Songs of Hugo Wolf*.

At this stage something should be said about translations. When *The Growth of Music* was written, and throughout the 1920s and 1930s, it was held in some quarters that *lieder* should be sung in English. They were, therefore, often furnished with English words of very varying merit. Nowadays, German songs, or those of any nationality for that matter, are usually performed in their original language. Accordingly, when English texts are made available, they aspire to accuracy as a first priority. The results need not necessarily be prosaic, as is demonstrated in *The Penguin Book of Lieder*, edited and translated by S. S. Prawer.

Recordings of the songs and song cycles mentioned in this chapter are available, including a fair selection of examples by Mendelssohn and Loewe. These should not deter amateur singers and pianists from having a go themselves. There is no better way of discovering how song composers have set about their business.

CHAPTER 17

The Orchestra and Berlioz

THE inventive spirit of the nineteenth century had its direct effect in the mechanical improvement of many musical instruments. We saw (Chapter 8) how the general principles of different classes of instruments were gradually discovered by musicians in the effort to improve their resources. By the year 1800 nearly all the instruments of importance to us now were known and used, but only two classes, the violin family and the trombones, were actually the same as they are now. All the other instruments of the orchestra, as well as the organ, the piano, and the harp, have had in the course of the nineteenth century many scientific inventions applied to them which have (1) made good playing on them an easier matter, (2) made it possible to perform on them music which before was beyond the range of possibility.

Notice the distinction between these two results. The first benefits the performer, the second benefits the composer. Both of course benefit the listener, and as we are studying music chiefly as listeners we must take account of both. But the second kind, the kind which has made it possible for composers to write what before would have been out of the question because no player however clever could have produced the sounds from his instrument, is obviously of greater importance for us.

The mechanical improvements of the organ belong entirely to the first class; by the use of pneumatic tubes and electric currents all sorts of means have been contrived to shorten the distance between the organist and the pipe from which the sound comes. For example, the organist of today instead of having to move a large and cumbersome piece of machinery every time he draws a stop, merely presses a button with his finger or touches a lever with his foot, which acts direct by means of electric or pneumatic contact. He can now even set a whole combination of stops before he begins his performance, and then bring it into play at a single touch. All this saves physical effort and makes possible certain changes of tone which were impossible before, but it does not place any new kind of music within the reach of the organist. The case is very similar with regard to the inventions by which the action of the piano has been improved. The piano today is far more responsive to the player's touch, but it is still to all intents and purposes the same instrument as that for which Beethoven wrote his last sonatas. Nothing as drastic as the change from the harpsichord to the piano (see pp. 173–6) has occurred within the last century, but inventors have gone on finding out how the principle of the piano could be better applied, and composers and pianists have gone on finding that the piano was capable of new effects which were undreamed of by the inventors (see p. 423).

The harp, on the other hand, gives a good example of the second kind of invention. It is, of course, one of the oldest of instruments, but the harp which you hear in the orchestra is practically the invention of the last century.

The harp had, and still has, only seven strings to each octave; in other words, if you run your finger up the strings of the harp, plucking each one, you get, not a chromatic scale of semitones as you do from the strings of the piano, but a major diatonic scale. That shows you at once its limitations; the question for makers of harps was how to make it possible for their instruments to modulate to other keys and to use the semitones not belonging to the major scale in which the strings were tuned, and that question was not satisfactorily solved by any of the makers of the eighteenth century in spite of many attempts.

Of course, for the accompaniment of simple songs, for which the harp was much used by young ladies, the diatonic scale was fairly satisfactory, but for anything like big music the old harp was useless. Most of the improvements, including the one which made the harp capable of taking its place in the orchestra, came from Frenchmen. This was known as the 'double action', which Sébastion Érard perfected in the first years of the new century. It is an arrangement by which the harp is provided with seven pedals, each acting on one of the seven notes of the scale in such a way that when the player lowers the pedal one degree a metal pin 'stops' the string, raising the pitch one semitone; when he lowers the pedal a degree further another pin stops the string higher up, raising its pitch yet another semitone. Thus it becomes possible to play with equal ease in any key simply by arranging the pedals, and it provides for the use of every note in the chromatic scale. It does not, however, give the equality which the notes of the piano have, for two reasons: (1) because a pedal takes an appreciable moment of time to act, so that the rapid succession of chromatic notes is still impossible, and (2) because each pedal acts on all the notes of a given name; all the C flats become C naturals, all the D flats D naturals, &c., by the first action of the pedals applied to them.

We need not go closely into the technique of the harp; all we have to do is to realize how Érard's invention brought a new lease of life to the harp, and at the same time that even this left something to be desired. French artists and manufacturers have gone on experimenting, and a chromatic harp having a string to each note has been brought into existence. French composers such as Debussy and Ravel wrote music for it, but it has not yet replaced Érard's harp in ordinary use.

WIND INSTRUMENTS

All the wind instruments of the orchestra except the trombones have been transformed or at least reformed, but, roughly speaking, we may say that the woodwind instruments have been affected in the first of the two ways indicated and the brass in the second. What is known as the Boehm system of keys and fingering has had perhaps the greatest influence of the many inventions applied to the woodwind instruments. First applied to the flute by Theobald Boehm, it has been used with necessary modifications for the other instruments—oboes, clarinets, and bassoons. But though the wonderfully intricate system of silver keys and rods which you see on the modern instruments of the orchestra has made certain passages possible which were impossible before, its chief value has been to assure efficient playing, true intonation, and certainty of tone and phrasing. The range of the instruments remains practically the same, but players can use it to better advantage.

The case of the brass instruments—horns and trumpets—is a very different one, and more like that of the harp, except that they were in still more dire need of completion, for they had not even the whole diatonic scale at their disposal. We touched upon their difficulties quite early in our study when Bach's second Brandenburg Concerto gave us a lively example of the trumpet's capacities (see p. 157). The plan by which the imperfect scale of horns and trumpets could be transposed into different keys by means of 'crooks', which by increasing or diminishing the length of their tubes transposed the whole downwards or upwards, was there explained.

The condition of horns and trumpets then in the eighteenth century and even in Beethoven's day was this: they could make use of an incomplete scale in *every* key, but they could not produce a complete diatonic scale over their whole range in *any* key. A complete chromatic one was, of course, out of the question. This at a time when composers were writing for orchestra as for everything else with more and more chromatic freedom became a very serious handicap. How could it be met? One way in which composers such as Weber and Spontini got over the difficulty was to use more of these instruments, 'crook' them in different keys, and write for each the notes which the different keys provided. The beautiful horn melody at the beginning of the overture to *Der Freischütz* is arranged for four horns, two in F and two in C, and each pair plays the bit most convenient to its range. The plan is perfectly satisfactory in its artistic result here, but like so many musicians' plans it has a weakness, and the weakness is a commercial one.

Berlioz, the great orchestrator of the next generation,

proceeded to develop it without regard to its weakness. He required a great many instruments in order to be able to write all the things he wanted to write, and this increased the difficulty of getting his works performed. For when you multiply instruments you multiply players, and players have to be paid, and it is not generally the composer who does the paying. Berlioz began the fashion of orchestral luxury which has been continued to the present day. Here is a simple example:

Ex. 71

He wants a horn to reinforce the tune of the trombones. Those notes scattered about the three horn parts which look so queer, sound in unison with the bass trombone. Now one horn in unison with a tenor and a bass trombone (not to mention the ophicleide, an instrument now obsolete) does not have any very material effect, yet Berlioz lavishes three players on the passage and even then does not get it fully reproduced on the horn.

So much for the problem; now for its practical solution. That came quite early in the century by the invention of what is known as the 'valve' system, applied to horns and trumpets alike. It consists of the addition of a mechanism by which three little pistons pressed by the player's fingers open valves bringing an extra length of tube into action. When you lengthen a tube or a string you lower its pitch, and so when you press the first piston all the available notes are producible one semitone lower. The second piston lowers them a whole tone, the third lowers them three semitones, and since two or all three may be used together with cumulative effect it becomes possible to fill in all the blank spaces between the natural notes. So any tune and any chromatic passage at last became possible on the horns and trumpets.

One would think that such a resource would be hailed with joy by composers, but that was very far from being the case. As a matter of fact, the passage quoted above from Berlioz's *Roméo et Juliette* was written many years after the invention of the valve horn, which Berlioz knew all about. For a long time composers turned a cold shoulder on the valve instruments for two reasons: they thought them inferior to the natural ones in tone and intonation, which was true only at first, and they liked exercising their ingenuity, as in this example, to combat the imperfections of the old instruments. Even when they adopted the valved instruments they often went on writing for them more or less as though the valves must not be used except in extreme need; moreover, having adopted the four-horn plan it never occurred to them to return to two, as in many cases they might quite well have done. So far from the inventions producing an economy of players, composers very often wrote for both natural and valve instruments.

The increase of numbers in the orchestra has been one of the most obvious changes in the last century. That is partly due to the conditions. The orchestra is no longer the private possession of an individual kept for the entertainment of himself and his friends, as in the days of Haydn. Public performances in large halls became more general; music was made a democratic enjoyment. It was not all gain—in fact, in some respects the size of orchestras has become a nuisance—but in so far as it meant a greater range of expression and variety of tone as distinct from the mere increase of volume, it has been a real gain.

STRINGED INSTRUMENTS

Though the stringed instruments of the violin family remain exactly what they were a century and a half ago, except that the three-stringed double bass is now obsolete, their greater numbers in the modern orchestra have produced all sorts of ways of writing for them which make their orchestral position very different. We saw that the strings of Haydn's orchestra meant practically a string quartet with the parts doubled. The strings of the modern orchestra are never that for very long at a time. Composers are constantly subdividing the parts and contrasting them with one another. To find the violins, firsts and seconds, divided into six or eight parts and contrasted with a quartet of violas or of violoncellos is now quite common. Berlioz found that even the double basses could be used alone in chords with a very striking effect, and it was he who first fully exploited the separate capabilities of the strings, but especially of the most neglected members of the family, the violas and the double basses.

NEW VARIETIES OF INSTRUMENTS

We said that practically all the orchestral wind instruments were known and used in the eighteenth century, but endless varieties of those instruments have been introduced during the nineteenth. In fact, as soon as the brass instruments became perfected by the use of valves manufacturers began a process very much like the processes of horticulture which produce every year new varieties of rose or narcissus. From the principles of the valved horn and trumpet, brass instruments of all shapes and sizes (consequently of all pitches and qualities), from the popular cornet to the ponderous bass tuba, were evolved; and since every maker who invented a new variety gave some new name to his invention, the instruments of these types became almost as confusing to distinguish as the kinds of roses in a nurseryman's catalogue. We need not trouble ourselves with the varieties but merely notice that the tuba family of instruments, though invented primarily for the military band, became a most valuable addition to the orchestra because it provided tenor and bass parts to the brass groups.

The oboes became associated with the English horn, the bassoons with the double bassoon, and similarly, other instruments were extended into complete families, of which the clarinets are the most varied. They are found in all sizes from the little high treble clarinet in E flat to the bass clarinet which sounds an octave below the ordinary clarinet in B flat. And now there is a double bass clarinet an octave below the bass clarinet. So this multiplication of varieties goes on, but only occasionally something like a real novelty has been reached, again by the method of the horticulturist, that is to say by crossing the species.

Adolphe Sax, one of the most famous of instrument makers, produced a set of instruments made of brass but played with a reed like the clarinet, which he called saxophones, and which are of such mixed origin that they cannot be said to belong to any group but their own. And there have been other hybrids which have been similarly successful, but their existence does not alter the fact that the main instrumental types remain identical with those of the old orchestra, though the technique of playing them and of writing for them has changed.

That will be most easily understood if we turn from the

instruments themselves to the man who in the first half of the last century most thoroughly understood them, and who first sorted the confused mass of the growing orchestra into a definite order.

BERLIOZ AND TONE COLOUR

It was in 1822 that HECTOR BERLIOZ, a young Frenchman, came to Paris ostensibly to study medicine, but really to stimulate his highly gifted imagination by contact with all the intellectual life of literature, poetry, music, and drama which Paris could offer; and no city in the world could offer so much. It was not music as a self-contained art which appealed so strongly to him, but music as the expression of poetic feeling. When he read a poem, a novel or a play, he instantly began to think about it in musical terms, not so much with a view to setting the words to music as in order to translate its feeling into music. His earliest works show this. There are eight scenes from Goethe's *Faust*, distinct from the later *Damnation de Faust*, and overtures for orchestra called *Les Francs-Juges*, *Waverley*, and *Le Roi Lear*.

When he wrote a symphony, which he did almost contemporaneously with these early works, it was not merely a Symphony in C but a *Symphonie fantastique* described as 'an episode in the life of an artist', in which every movement illustrated a story of a young artist's love and longing, ambition and disappointment; a violent business in which the artist saw himself marched to the scaffold and his dreams mocked in a horrible witches' sabbath.

When you come across the *Symphonie fantastique* and read its 'programme' and all that it is meant to imply, the first idea is that Berlioz was a young man of exceedingly disordered mind, if not actually on the verge of insanity. But that idea vanishes if you see the *Symphonie fantastique* in relation to his other work. True, here and elsewhere a love of what is wild and extravagant crops up, but that is only incidental. Look through his works and see the part that great poets, especially Shakespeare and Goethe, played in providing him with high romantic themes, and the morbid excitement of such a thing as the *Symphonie fantastique* is seen to be only one phase of his work and one which he outgrew in later years.

But it was not only that music meant nothing to Berlioz apart from some literary idea; to him musical sounds and especially qualities of sound actually expressed these ideas. In the *Symphonie fantastique* there is a melody which he calls 'l'idée fixe'. It is supposed to represent the ideally beautiful dream of the artist when it is first played smoothly by violin and flute in unison. Later, when he wants to picture the caricature of the artists's dream in the witches' dance this tune is transformed to a jerky rhythm (six-eight time) and played by the sharp-sounding small clarinet in E flat. In his *Treatise on Instrumentation*, a book which has become a standard work on the subject, he mentions this passage and says that he used this particular instrument in order to 'parody, degrade and blackguardize the melody'.[1]

That tone-qualities represented the most definite ideas to Berlioz's mind is shown in many instances. He became entranced and raised to an extraordinary pitch of enthusiasm by such tones. His autobiography as well as his *Treatise* give examples of this, and sometimes his own sense of humour, which was as strong as Rossini's, is turned upon himself in the autobiography. He tells how he was going home dreaming of the wonderful effect of brass instruments in his first big orchestral work, the overture *Les Francs-Juges*, and so rapt was he that he slipped and sprained his ankle. 'For a long time afterwards', he said, 'that passage gave me a pain in my ankle when I heard it; now it gives me a pain in my head.' Of the same work he says, however, and this is important:

> Neither of my masters (Lesueur or Reicha) taught me anything about instrumentation. It was by studying the methods of the three modern masters, Beethoven, Weber and Spontini; by an impartial examination of the regular forms of instrumentation and of unusual

[1] This and other quotations from Berlioz's *Instrumentation* are taken from the English translation by Mary Cowden Clarke, published by Novello & Co.

forms and combinations; partly by listening to artists and getting them to make experiments for me, and partly by instinct that I acquired the knowledge I possess.[1]

Strange though Berlioz's canonization of Beethoven, Weber, and Spontini as 'the three modern masters' may seem to us, it must have seemed even stranger to his contemporaries, but for opposite reasons. While his enthusiasm for Beethoven seems only natural to us and we can well understand Weber finding a second place, the idea of Spontini in that hierarchy seems almost laughable. But the average musician of Paris in 1830 would have accepted Spontini alone of the three, would have kept his laugh for the name of Beethoven, and knew about as much of Weber as the average musician of today knows of Spontini. It was in 1827 that Berlioz insisted upon his master, Lesueur, going with him to hear Beethoven's Symphony in C minor for the first time.

Through the years of his studentship at the Conservatoire and those following, when he was formulating his own ideals in his first overtures and the *Symphonie fantastique*, Berlioz was at war with all the accepted canons of music. Life for him at this time was a struggle both physically, for he was hard put to it to find means of livelihood, and spiritually, for nothing would induce him to abandon those artistic ideals which were vital to him, though his masters and contemporaries could see nothing in them but the wilful eccentricity of an hysterical youth.

BERLIOZ'S CAREER

Berlioz's career falls conveniently into periods from which it is easy to remember a summary of its main facts. The first period came to an end in 1830, when, after several attempts, he gained the Prix de Rome. This prize, won by the composition of a cantata, was and is a travelling scholarship from the Paris Conservatoire to Italy. Its chief usefulness to Berlioz was the respite it gave from the difficulties of his life in Paris, and the

[1] *Autobiography of Hector Berlioz*, English translation, vol. i, p. 58.

experience of Italy to an artist of his intensely pictorial disposition was necessarily a great acquisition. Nevertheless, he was too restless to use the opportunity to the full, and contrary to the rules of the prize he was back in Paris with more compositions and more schemes before the time of his journey was expired.

The next ten years are the time of Berlioz's greatest output in orchestral composition, and also the time in which he ultimately proved his right to be considered a great master of the orchestra. Between 1832 and 1842 he composed three more symphonies, and each one of them was founded, like the *Symphonie fantastique*, on literary ideas.

The *Harold in Italy* symphony is the one most like the *Symphonie fantastique* in general idea and form. Its movements, though written in the sequence of an ordinary symphony, are all given titles to describe their intention. The first, an adagio leading to an allegro, is called 'Harold on the mountains', 'Scenes of sadness, of happiness, and of joy'. A march of pilgrims singing their evening prayer and the serenade of the mountaineer to his mistress take the places of slow movement and scherzo, and the 'orgy of brigands', which is the finale, shows that Berlioz had not even by this date quite outgrown that love of sensationalism which produced the witches' sabbath in the earlier symphony. In the *Harold* Symphony, too, the carrying on of themes from one movement to another is continued, and most of the ideas of the first three movements are at least recalled in the introduction to the last. This may have been due partly to the direct influence of Beethoven's ninth Symphony, but it was also partly the outcome of the fact that Berlioz's association of melodies with ideas outside music made him inclined to use them as though they were actual words.

The *Harold in Italy* Symphony has a solo viola part which was written for no less a person than Paganini, who wished for a concerto for viola. It was not, however, very likely to appeal to a virtuoso, for Berlioz was incapable of writing a work for the display of a solo instrument, and the viola part really takes a very modest place in the middle of a score filled with all kinds of complex instrumental colour. Paganini never played the work.

The other two symphonies are very different. The *Symphonie funèbre et triomphale* was written in 1840 for the burial of the heroes of the revolution, and is a tremendous score for wind instruments to which strings are merely added *ad libitum*. This is because it was written for open-air performance, and its music, therefore, is planned on very broad lines, and has practically none of the subtleties of Berlioz's more normal style of instrumentation. But the third, *Roméo et Juliette*, described as a *symphonie dramatique*, is the greatest of Berlioz's works to which he gave the name of symphony, and the least like a symphony in the normal acceptation of the term. In form it is a curious mixture of the cantata and the symphonic poem. Solo and choral voices are introduced, but rather in order to give some explanation of the musical intention than dramatically. The orchestra is throughout the main means of expression.

It was with the production of these works that Berlioz at last reached to a recognized position in Paris, and almost immediately upon his success he began to look for means to carry his work farther. The mention of the year 1840 is the moment to recall the effect of Berlioz upon Wagner. Wagner had reached Paris in September 1839 in time to hear the first performance of *Roméo et Juliette*, and in the next year performances of the *Symphonie fantastique*, *Harold*, and the great performance of the *Symphonie funèbre* with parts of the *Requiem* held on 1 November 1840. He therefore came just in time to see Berlioz's triumph, while he himself was going through much the same state of mental disturbance, struggle, and disappointment through which Berlioz had fought his way nearly twenty years before. In that year Wagner finished *Rienzi* and composed a 'Faust' overture. *The Flying Dutchman*, his first great opera, was still only forming itself in his mind. That Berlioz's extraordinary skill in wielding the orchestra had the greatest effect upon Wagner is clear in spite of the fact that the two were by no means in complete sympathy with one another. There are various passages in Wagner's writings in which he tries to explain the mixture of feelings with which he regarded Berlioz. But he never tries to explain away Berlioz's genius for the orchestra. On the other hand, it is not surprising that Berlioz was not greatly impressed at this time by what little of Wagner's work he had the opportunity of hearing. When Wagner secured a performance of his overture *Columbus* Berlioz was present, and Wagner looked anxiously for a word of encouragement from him, but got no more than a remark that it was hard to excel in Paris, a fact which they both had full opportunity of realizing. Both were in Paris or its neighbourhood through 1841, and in 1842 Berlioz started upon a long tour of travel to conduct his own works in most of the principal towns of Germany. Curiously enough, they were to meet again soon, for Wagner secured his appointment as conductor at Dresden at the beginning of 1843, and almost simultaneously Berlioz arrived at Dresden in the course of his tour, and one of the first duties of the new conductor was to help in the study of the *Symphonie fantastique*, the overture *King Lear*, and parts of the *Requiem* (see pp. 434–5).

The period of Berlioz's travel began at Brussels in September 1842, and was continued until 1848. He not only carried his music all over Germany, but in 1845 he visited Austria, a visit which accounts for his strange introduction of the 'Marche Hongroise' into *La Damnation de Faust* (Berlioz could never resist the fascination of local colour). He next carried his music to Russia, where he was hailed as an apostle of new art by the young composers of the new Russian school (see p. 509). In his autobiography, a book which is as unreliable as to dates and such-like matters of fact as it is delightful as a picture of his own mind and experiences, there are very full accounts of the state of the orchestras which he met, particularly in Germany. He wrote a racy account to Liszt of a rehearsal in a German country town, in which he describes all the excuses of the late-comers and the innumerable details which he had to insist upon and correct.

Berlioz supposes that he has stopped the orchestra and is upbraiding the drummer. He says, 'You are using wooden sticks and you ought to have them with sponge-heads. It is all the difference between black and white.' The *Kapellmeister* answers, 'We don't know what you call sponge-heads, we have never seen them.' Berlioz: 'I guessed as much, so I have brought some from Paris with me; take the pair that I have put on the table.'

This is a very good illustration of Berlioz's insistence upon the niceties of tone which were simply disregarded by the rough-and-ready methods of the ordinary orchestra before his day. In the *Treatise on Instrumentation* he describes carefully the different qualities produced by different kinds of drumsticks: (1) wooden ends—very hard and dry; (2) leather ends—less startling, but still hard; (3) sponge-ends, which produce a 'grave, velvety quality'. What Beethoven began in treating the drum as a serious musical instrument (see pp. 330 and 332) Berlioz developed in his compositions, and insisted upon when he carried his music all over Europe.

In this he was doing his greatest service to the progress of musical art, and it was after these tours that he summed up all his experience of instrumental writing, performance, and conducting in the *Treatise on Instrumentation* to which we have alluded.

After this period he had still much to do; he composed big works, such as his one oratorio *L'Enfance du Christ*, the *Te Deum* composed for the Paris Exhibition of 1855, and his last opera *Les Troyens*. There were also frequent visits to England when he conducted the New Philharmonic Society and shocked people by his orchestral demands, but all this was comparatively of secondary importance. Of course, he continued to be misunderstood by many to the end of his life; there was a famous cartoon in *Punch* of a gentleman emerging from a concert-hall dazed and deafened, and explaining that he had been hearing the work of M. Berlioz, and even today there are those who still think that the chief aim of Berlioz's large orchestra was to create the biggest amount of noise possible.

But the marvels of Berlioz's orchestration are not the *fortissimi* of the full orchestra; they come from his power of putting every instrument in such a place that its tone tells, and the tellingness is most apparent when he is using few instruments, as he very often does through long passages. The 'Queen Mab' scherzo in *Roméo et Juliette* is a most brilliant example of his art in this respect. The harmonics on violins and harps, the delicate touches on woodwind instruments and horns, the *pianissimo* rhythms for the drums, all contribute; there is only one *fortissimo* in a score of some sixty pages, and that *fortissimo* is produced without the help of any brass instruments save the horn. The whole effect depends upon the perfection of the playing, and that is so true of most of Berlioz as to account for the fact that his music is beloved by great conductors far more than by the general public.

PROGRAMME MUSIC

As Berlioz's orchestration was a revelation to Wagner, so his other ideas about music bore fruit elsewhere. The fact that he always thought of music in connexion with some human story or mental picture fostered the idea of 'programme' music as opposed to music which exists, so to speak, in its own right. The idea of 'programme music' was no new thing. Couperin in France, Kuhnau in Germany, had worked upon it a hundred years before Berlioz was born (see pp. 72 and 89); J. S. Bach was strongly attracted by it, especially by the idea of associating a certain figure of melody with a certain state of feeling; and in a more general way both Haydn, in the titles which he gave to some of his symphonies (see p. 262) and Beethoven, in the Pastoral Symphony (see p. 318) had been drawn to it. But the mere fact of whether a work is given a descriptive title or not does not make the distinction between 'programme' and 'absolute' music. We might say that every genuine piece of music has the elements of both in it. No real musical composition can be so entirely isolated that it can be separated from the composer's life; the scenes he has passed through, the people he has known, the joys and sorrows which have made him the man he is, the books which he has read, and even the games he has played, all have their influence on his work.

On the other hand, it is only when some particular influence stamps itself upon his work so strongly that unless you know what it was you can hardly sympathize with the shape and colour of his music that it becomes what we call 'programme' music, that is, music which needs some explanation beyond itself. Berlioz was the first composer with whom this was constantly the case, and the first who adapted to this end all his means of expression, the form of each work, its melodic and harmonic shape and the tones of the instruments uttering it.

After him came Liszt, whose symphonic poems carried farther the principle of using musical ideas, melodies, and harmonies as though they were words which meant things instead of sounds which express feelings. This sometimes carried music in a wrong direction, and Liszt in his symphonic poems for orchestra and elsewhere gives some instances of the wrong direction. He and others like him could be content with musical ideas which were inexpressive because they meant something outside the actual music. Such a contentment is the abuse of programme music.

A sketch of Liszt's extraordinary career will help us to understand both his weakness and his strength, and that must be done in connexion with his own instrument, the piano.

Suggestions for Further Reading and Listening

A CHAPTER that is largely concerned with instruments and scoring, with special reference to the career and music of Berlioz, invites further mention of Berlioz's own *Treatise on Instrumentation.* A classic of its kind, it can be found in larger libraries and is certainly worth dipping into. For general purposes, however, such books as Gordon Jacob's *Orchestral Technique*, Walter Piston's *Orchestration*, Donington's *The Instruments of Music*, and *Musical Instruments through the Ages*, edited by Anthony Baines, all of which have already been cited, will be far more useful.

Berlioz literature is abundant, headed by Jacques Barzun's monumental, two-volume *Berlioz and the Romantic Century*, a title that exactly describes its nature and scope. A work of enormous erudition, it is a brilliant example of a contextual biography. For a shorter and more technical study, Hugh Macdonald's *Berlioz Orchestral Music* ('BBC Music Guide') can be recommended. As readers may know, Berlioz has been more admired abroad than in his own country, but even in England his stature has not been unquestioningly accepted. One of his most redoubtable champions of an earlier generation was Ernest Newman, for many years music critic of *The Sunday Times*. *Berlioz, Romantic and Classic*, writings by Ernest Newman, edited by Peter Heyworth, represents a cross-section of his proselytizing activities. The composer was himself a fluent writer—at one stage in his career he was a forceful professional critic—and his memoirs, translated by David Cairns, make fascinating reading.

The enormous upsurge of scholarly and public interest in Berlioz during the last few decades is mirrored in the copious recordings of his music. Given so much choice, it may be helpful to point out that certain conductors, past and present, have demonstrated a particular sympathy with his scores, notably Sir Thomas Beecham, Pierre Monteux, and Colin Davis.

So closely is Berlioz's orchestral music bound up with the authentic sound of an orchestra that it cannot usefully be studied at the piano. His virtuosity, like that of Rimsky-Korsakov or Richard Strauss, does not bear transcription. The old reproach that Berlioz was over-interested in spectacular effects, as for instance in the *Grande Messe des Morts* or the 'Witches' Sabbath' finale of the *Symphonie Fantastique* has withered away in the light of wider experience of his compositions. He knew how to use big battalions when the occasion called for them, but a much better idea of his methods can be had from, for instance, the 'Queen Mab Scherzo' and the 'Adagio Love Scene' from his *Romeo and Juliet* Symphony.

The final paragraphs about programme music can be supplemented by Leslie Orrey's book *Programme Music*, and can be illustrated either at the keyboard (Couperin and Kuhnau) or from recordings: Beethoven's *Pastoral* Symphony and Elgar's *Falstaff*, not to mention Liszt's symphonic poems, of which a handful are available, all of course call for a gramophone.

CHAPTER 18

The Piano and its Composers

WE have described three new directions towards which music spread its branches at the very outset of the last century: (1) national opera, realized in Weber's *Der Freischütz*; (2) the union of music and poetry in song, achieved by Schubert; (3) the complete adaptation of Berlioz's orchestra to suggest or illustrate poetic ideas in the symphonic poem or kindred forms. All three of them show the musician striving to join hands with his fellow artists, to share in their life and thought instead of remaining aloof. While this was a gain so great that it is impossible to overstate its importance, we have just hinted that it was and is possible to abuse it. Let the musician breathe in poetry and literature and drama and be filled with a sympathetic appreciation of all the joys and woes and struggles of humanity; it is music, however, that he has got to breathe out, and music has a life of its own which must never be lessened by its contact with other and more transient life.

We are about to see that with all this change and ferment in artistic ideals music in the works of the great masters of the nineteenth century did maintain its identity. Though it sometimes looked as though it might become merely the handmaid to poetry or be swallowed up in a 'union of all the arts', it outgrew all such temporary dangers. It emerged enriched, strengthened, and humanized by its experiences, but still itself.

An instrument which had the greatest influence in keeping to the fore the distinctions which separate music from its sister arts was that most familiar of all instruments, the piano. The modern piano was just perfected, just ready to the hand of the composer when those composers who were born in the first decade of the century were growing up. Those among them who made the piano their daily companion, who expressed themselves most fully by its means, were the men who had the clearest idea of the independent life of music. Mendelssohn, Schumann, Chopin, and a little later Brahms, are four salient examples of this, and in the opposite scale we have to put only one, but that an exceedingly powerful example to the contrary, Liszt.

Let us look first at the great exception, the case of the Hungarian-born but thoroughly cosmopolitan FERENCZ LISZT, who was probably the most wonderful pianist the world has ever seen, and yet who in his later years became the strongest advocate of descriptive and illustrative music.

His career is one of the most fascinating interest; in his character a noble generosity towards his brother-artists was contrasted with an invincible egotism in some of the private relations of life. His gifts were so brilliant that, having reached the summit of attainment as a public pianist in early years, he could put that career aside altogether and devote himself for years to conducting and organizing the music of a small town, Weimar, in such a way that its opera and its concerts became the centre of all the most modern musical developments. He could turn from executive work of this kind to the composition of works ranging from the huge 'programme' symphonies on Dante's *Divine Comedy* and Goethe's *Faust*, symphonic poems for orchestra, and oratorios and church music on a grand scale, to piano pieces involving the most brilliant technical qualities, and songs, a few of which, especially when he chose the French language as his text, are exquisite in every detail. His arrangements of music for the piano covered an extraordinary range of choice. There was scarcely a popular opera, from Donizetti's *Lucia* to Wagner's *Meistersinger*, of which he did not make a 'paraphrase' or transcription for the piano. The symphonies of Beethoven and Schubert and the songs of the latter, even Berlioz's *Symphonie fantastique* and Weber's overtures, were helped towards their recognition by the public through his piano arrangements, and the energetic gypsy dances of Hungary were made known to musicians all over the world through his rhapsodies.

Moreover, there was scarcely a musician of eminence who did not at some time or other feel the benefit of Liszt's personal friendship and his championship before the public. Since he gained a European reputation as a pianist at a very early age he was able to exercise a unique influence in these directions. He was eight years younger than Berlioz, yet when the *Symphonie fantastique* was first heard in Paris in 1830 the sight of Liszt applauding the work amongst the audience was the greatest sign of encouragement which Berlioz got. Liszt's performances of *Tannhäuser* and *Lohengrin* at Weimar at a later date showed that after all Wagner's work was not to be put aside; he was among the first to recognize the genius of Brahms, and he held out a hand of friendship to César Franck when Franck's contemporaries in Paris despised him for a pedant.

One could go on multiplying the instances of Liszt's penetration, and it would be pleasanter to do so than to remember that there was another side. But since that other side affected his own composition very seriously we cannot quite ignore it. For the fact is that his temperament, responding early to that sort of applause and adulation which unthinking people shower upon public performers, became so much addicted to it that in almost all his keyboard music the effect of the moment is the prime consideration. The piano for him was not on the whole the instrument for intimate reflection, but a means of public oratory. It could be oratory of a very fine kind, but the point is that his music was essentially addressed to an audience and was not the confession of a personal faith. The smaller and more intimate piano pieces of his later years, however, are no longer the work of the virtuoso intended for public display; and what is more, they often show enterprise in the use of new harmonic devices far ahead of their time. Indeed, this phase of his work exercised an extraordinary influence on much later composers—Ravel, Skriabin, Bartók, and beyond. His orchestral works had already given many suggestions to Wagner.

Liszt rarely played in public in later life, but appeared in London in the very last year of his life (1886), when he was received with overwhelming enthusiasm. There are few people left now who can give first-hand accounts of his performances, but a short quotation will serve here to suggest his extraordinary power of interpretation, and since the occasion described was not a great public function but a 'semi-private gathering' at Leipzig in the early 1870's, it is likely to be the more accurate:

> In one bar the immeasurable gap between him and all other pianists showed itself in a flash; he was the very reverse of all my anticipations, which inclined me, perhaps from the caricatures familiar to me in my boyhood, to expect to see an inspired acrobat. When I heard the amazing tone and colour he produced, without a theatrical gesture, sitting like a rock at the instrument, full of dignity and composure, I and my rather punctilious companion were so carried away that we waited at the door to cap him as he came out.[1]

This will show why Liszt was an exception among the great composers upon whom the piano exercised the strongest influence; for him the piano was primarily the means of expression; for Mendelssohn, Schumann, and even Chopin it was primarily the means of registering impressions.

Before we study their piano music and its effect upon the art in general we must look rather closely into the circumstances of their lives and both compare and contrast them. These three were the closest contemporaries not only in the beginning but in the end. Liszt, who was two years younger than Mendelssohn and lived until 1886, saw and took part in all the big musical developments of the century, culminating in the production of *Parsifal* at Bayreuth in 1882. Mendelssohn, Schumann, Chopin, on the other hand, all belong entirely to the first half of the century, for Mendelssohn died in 1847, Chopin survived him by only two years, and though Schumann lived till 1856, his last years were so clouded by illness and mental collapse that his active life was very little longer than that of the other two.

[1] Sir Charles Stanford, in an article 'Reminiscences of Leipzig, 1874–5', contributed to the *R.C.M. Magazine*, vol. viii, no. 1.

MENDELSSOHN AND SCHUMANN

In the early lives of the two German-born members of this trio, Mendelssohn and Schumann, we have a contrast not unlike those which we drew between Handel and Bach (Chapter 4) and Mozart and Haydn (Chapter 9).

JAKOB LUDWIG FELIX MENDELSSOHN-BARTHOLDY was born at Hamburg on 3 February 1809, the eldest son of Abraham Mendelssohn, a Jewish banker, who, like so many of his race, was not only commercially prosperous but a man of cultivation who possessed a keen interest in art and literature. Abraham's father, Moses Mendelssohn, had acquired some fame as a scholar. In the early years of Felix's life the family moved from Hamburg to Berlin, where the father founded a well-known banking firm, and there the family, four in number, amongst whom the eldest sister, Fanny, is most important for her constant companionship with Felix, was brought up. Notice, as an indication of how very close together our musical dates lie, that Mendelssohn was born just four months before Haydn died (see p. 210), and that this was the year in which Beethoven wrote the 'Emperor' Concerto (see p. 319).

When Felix was seven years old (1816) his father was sent to Paris on business, and since Felix began his education as a pianist there, this visit was in a sense the beginning of his cosmopolitan musical career. Mendelssohn's father was not, like Handel's, anxious to keep his boy away from music, nor, like Mozart's, was he anxious to thrust him into it. There was never any question either of thwarting his artistic inclinations or of exhibiting him as an infant prodigy, but from the first it was determined to educate and develop every side of his character, and when eventually it appeared that in spite of brilliant abilities in many directions music was the strongest thing in him, music was allowed to become his life.

One hears of him playing the piano at a concert in Berlin when he was only nine years old, but such public appearances were only occasional. We hear much more of the quiet music-makings in the Mendelssohns' home, of Felix's early compositions, which began when he was about eleven years old, of the musical parties held at home on Sunday mornings at which many famous musicians congregated, and where Felix's boyish works were played and discussed and placed beside the mature works of great masters. Along with all this, general education, especially the knowledge of classical literature, Greek and Latin, was carried on, and the life was varied by a certain amount of travel, including a tour of Switzerland and a visit to Weimar, where Mendelssohn met Goethe and played to him. All these experiences were seized upon with vivid responsiveness by Mendelssohn. That is perhaps the most salient feature of his character; everything had interest for him; he sketched the scenery of Switzerland in water-colours; he found music for the poetry of Goethe, and from time to time in the intervals of his busy life he produced elegant translations of classic poetry. Experiences appealed to him more vividly than deeply. Wherever he met with sympathy he was at his best, but his life had to be lived in the sunshine.

Both the outward circumstances and these qualities of temperament give us the measure for the contrast between him and Schumann.

ROBERT SCHUMANN was more than a year younger than Mendelssohn. The son of a bookseller in the small Saxon town of Zwickau, he was born on 8 June 1810. His father's was a typical example of the old German life of the middle classes. Himself the son of a clergyman, he lived amongst his books, and knew them not only as objects for sale, but in their contents as well. Robert was brought up on books, and formed his own tastes by browsing amongst his father's collection, but music was not amongst the interests immediately put before him. Yet it was so strongly ingrained in him that he was early allowed some lessons from the town organist, and when Weber was appointed *Kapellmeister* at Dresden the father took steps to try to procure him as a teacher for his son, though Robert was then only seven years old, and the distance between Zwickau and

Dresden, some forty miles, was not as easily traversed then as now. Perhaps on this account the project fell through, and the only big experience which came in Schumann's way as a child was a visit to Karlsbad, when at the age of nine he heard Moscheles play the piano and was even then deeply impressed by the event. In the next year he entered the Gymnasium at Zwickau, where his school studies were continued for eight years, during which time music fell into the background.

If we compare Mendelssohn and Schumann in the year 1826 we see at once the great difference in the speed of their development. By this date Mendelssohn had composed several of the works by which he is known today; among them is the Symphony in C minor, No. 1, the Capriccio in F sharp minor, Op. 5 for piano, the trumpet overture for orchestra, the string Quintet in A, Op. 18; and in the summer of this year, when he entered the university of Berlin, one of the most brilliant of his orchestral works was written, the overture to *A Midsummer Night's Dream*. Schumann, on the other hand, had practically nothing to show as a composer. In this year his father died, and his mother, who became his guardian, was much less inclined to consider his artistic proclivities. In the following year he began setting some of his own poems to music, and it was then that he formed his lifelong devotion to romantic poetry and literature.

Schumann was nearly eighteen when he matriculated at the university of Leipzig, and before joining the university he was allowed a tour in Bavaria, during which, at Munich, he met Heine, and paid a visit to Bayreuth in order to meet the widow of his literary hero, Jean Paul Richter. It was at Leipzig that his musical life really began. Curiously enough, his university studies were to be devoted to the law. There seems to be some sort of fate by which parents try to distract their children from music by turning them into lawyers, and the attempt has the result of driving them to a decision. Handel and Schumann are conspicuous instances.

The choice of Leipzig as the scene of his legal studies was an exceedingly rash one, for nowhere in Germany was there so much musical distraction. Almost at once Schumann made friends with the musical circle of Leipzig, amongst whom Friedrich Wieck, pianist and teacher, was a leader. To him Schumann went for piano lessons, and there he met not only the musicians of Leipzig and the musical visitors to the town, but Wieck's little daughter Clara, then a child of nine, who was already beginning her training under her father as a pianist. In the following year the mistake of choosing Leipzig was realized, and Schumann was dispatched to Heidelberg, but without producing the desired change in his interests. At Heidelberg he still worked diligently at the piano and still neglected the law, and in 1830 the situation had become so acute that Wieck was called upon to decide between Schumann and his mother, music and the law. The decision eventually was passed in Schumann's favour, and in the summer he left Heidelberg for Leipzig and music study under Wieck.

It was then that his misdirected enthusiasm for perfecting his technique led him to improvise physical exercises which ended in disaster. He permanently strained his right hand, so that his hope of becoming a public pianist was shattered. At first the accident seemed disastrous to his career, but it was soon turned to advantage; instead of studying the gymnastics of the hand, Schumann took up his pen and began to compose vigorously. The variations on the letters of the name ABEGG were his Op. 1, and the choice of the theme records the name of a young lady for whom at the age of twenty-one he had a passing enthusiasm. He was spending the winter of 1832 at home at Zwickau when Clara was brought there to give an orchestral concert. One movement of an early symphony by Schumann was included in the programme, and in the following year various compositions for piano appeared, namely, the 'Papillons', 'Impromptus for the piano on a romance by Clara Wieck', the Sonatas in G minor and F sharp minor, and the Toccata in C, Op. 7.

The record of these years, 1828 to 1832, is still a small one when placed beside Mendelssohn's activities during the same time. Schumann's travels between Leipzig, Heidelberg, and Zwickau are varied only by a holiday trip to northern Italy in 1829.

MENDELSSOHN'S TRAVELS

In the same year Mendelssohn made his first momentous visit to England, and though this was planned as a general educational tour it was the beginning of his professional career. He reached London on 21 April where he was received by Moscheles, whose reputation as a pianist was at its height in this country. At the introduction of Moscheles, he was invited to conduct his Symphony in C minor at the Philharmonic Concert; he was received everywhere, plunged with enthusiasm into all the events of a London musical season and captivated every one by his brilliancy and charm. When the season was over he started upon a tour through England and Scotland. He visited Holyrood, where he made a sketch for his Scotch Symphony. He went on to the Hebrides, and the visit produced the first impressions which eventually resulted in the poetically romantic 'Hebrides' Overture. The west coast, Ireland, and Wales were all visited. He stayed in country houses and delighted in all the pleasures of English country life, returning to Germany in November. In the next year, 1830, his journeys took a different course; he went in the summer to Nuremberg and Munich, and thence through the Salzkammergut to Vienna. In October he saw Venice for the first time; he spent the winter in Rome, and in the spring of 1831 he wandered through the region of the Italian lakes to Switzerland. There he wrote the Scotch and Italian Symphonies and the 'Hebrides' Overture, then returned to Munich, where the piano Concerto in G minor was written for a concert, and before the end of 1831 he arrived in Paris. There he found many musicians, among them Chopin, Liszt, Meyerbeer, and Habeneck the conductor, who was Berlioz's arch-enemy. But Paris was not congenial to Mendelssohn, and in the spring of 1832 he left it for his second visit to

London, where again he was received with open arms, and made his chief public appearances at the concerts of the Philharmonic Society. One of the fruits of this visit was the publication with Novello of the first book of *Songs without Words*, at first called only 'Original Melodies for the Piano'.

In 1833 the seal was set upon Mendelssohn's abilities, first by the invitation to conduct the famous Lower Rhine Festival, held that year at Düsseldorf, and afterwards by the appointment for three years as musical director at Düsseldorf. So at the age of twenty-four we find him established as a musician of European reputation, while Schumann, living quietly at Leipzig, is producing works for the piano and seizing on the few opportunities for performance which the concerts of his personal friends afforded. In 1834 Mendelssohn's activities included the conducting of the Lower Rhine Festival, this time at Aachen, where again he met Chopin, and the beginning of the composition of his first oratorio, *St. Paul.* That year was hardly less eventful for Schumann in a more quiet way, for in the spring his desire to express himself fully both in music and in words led him to make a great venture: he founded the *Neue Zeitschrift für Musik* (*New Musical Journal*), with himself, Wieck, and two other musicians as editors. Schumann's writings were no cut-and-dried, didactic criticism. An immense enthusiasm for everything real, new, and daring appeared in his writing about music as fully as in his own composition. A love of the picturesque and of making stories of everything connected with his life and his art came out as fully in his articles as in his music for the piano. He imagined the existence of a society which he called the 'Davidsbündler', a group of young artists who, strong and vigorous like David in the Bible story, slung their stones at the false giant of the Philistines. Everything which was dull, pedantic, or pretentious in art was represented by the Philistines, and one David was not enough to overthrow them. He would write first under one signature, then under another; Florestan and Eusebius, whom we know in the delightful pieces called 'Carnaval', which he wrote in this year, were his two favourite pseudonyms. And his musical friends were described under other names and enrolled in the society whose views the *Neue Zeitschrift* represented.

All this, with musical composition, brought Schumann for the first time into the full tide of his powers, and in 1835 he had become sole editor of the *Neue Zeitschrift*, when Mendelssohn was offered the conductorship of the famous 'Gewandhaus' concerts in Leipzig. Mendelssohn came in the autumn, and though this was not actually his first meeting with Schumann, it marked the beginning of their firm and lasting friendship. It was at first rather one-sided. It was only natural that Schumann should sit at the feet of the brilliant director of the Gewandhaus; it was equally natural that Mendelssohn, who had mixed with all the great artists of Europe, should see in Schumann only a young man who had written some promising piano music. Also, the fact that Schumann was editor of a musical paper was not immediately a recommendation to Mendelssohn's friendship. He had no more fondness for criticism than most composers have. Mendelssohn was sparkling and animated in company; Schumann was quiet and reserved. It necessarily took some time for them to understand each other equally, since Schumann was immeasurably the greater in his powers of understanding.

CHOPIN'S EARLY CAREER

We have already mentioned Chopin's chance meetings with Mendelssohn, and since he too came to Leipzig at this time and was received into this circle of friends, we may here look back to see what his career had been up to this point.

FRÉDÉRIC (FRYDERYK FRANCISZEK) CHOPIN was just three months older than Schumann. He was born on 1 March 1810. His birthplace, Zelazowa Wola, is about twenty miles from Warsaw, but though he was a Pole by birth he was of French extraction, for his father was a native of Nancy who had settled in Poland as a book-keeper in a business house. The circumstances of Chopin's early life were not specially calculated to bring music from him, but the extraordinary aptitude which he showed made his father send him for teaching to the head of the Warsaw Conservatory. When he was fifteen he played in public part of a piano concerto by Moscheles, perhaps the most technically advanced music of the time, and also published his own first work for piano, the Rondo in C, Op. 1. He was kept at school for two years longer, and on leaving (1827) he produced a very remarkable work, a set of variations for piano with orchestral accompaniment on the theme of the duet 'Là ci darem' in Mozart's opera *Don Giovanni*. This, with other works, including a piano sonata, Op. 4, a Nocturne, and three Polonaises (published after his death as Op. 71), showed the unusual quality of his genius.

At the very beginning of his career Chopin's writing for the piano is quite different in the character of its melody, its ornament, and its harmony from any other music then existing. He had, so to speak, sprung out of the soil; the scales and cadences and pointed rhythms of Polish national song and dance form one part of his vocabulary, the ornament of the Italian aria style another part. The example of a few writers of piano music, such as John Field (1782–1837), an Irishman who spent much of his life in Russia, suggests certain characteristics of his form, but no one of these things nor all of them taken together will account for the peculiarly personal character of Chopin's music. And, further, we must notice that that character appears at once; one may see a certain development in his treatment of form as a whole, but take any single passage of Chopin and it would be hard to say whether he wrote it in the year 1827 or just before his death, little more than twenty years later. With this in mind one can see the justice of Schumann's famous phrase, written in a review of the variations on 'Là ci darem', 'Hats off, gentlemen, a genius!'

In 1828 Chopin was given his first journey abroad and taken by a friend who was visiting a Congress of Physicians in Berlin. The following year included a visit to Vienna, where he played the 'Là ci darem' variations in public with success, and he also composed the piano Concerto in F minor. In 1830, which was also Mendelssohn's great year of travel, Chopin began in earnest his career as a pianist, and toured through many German towns on his way to Paris. He was at Stuttgart when he heard of the taking of Warsaw by the Russians, and the Étude Op. 10, No. 12, built on a rushing figure in semiquavers over which a brave melody sweeps forward to a defiant cadence, is his patriotic comment on the event. He settled down in Paris to the career of playing, teaching, and composing, and, as we have seen, it was there that he came across Mendelssohn in person and numbered amongst his friends all the most important musicians of the time from Cherubini, still the head of the Conservatoire, to Berlioz, who had conquered that institution by carrying off the 'Prix de Rome', and Liszt, the only musician of the piano whose fame was able to surpass his own. Chopin as a pianist was primarily the interpreter of his own music, Liszt was the interpreter of all the great music of the world.

Chopin's delicate health made him retire from the career of a public performer in the year 1835, in which he paid this passing visit to Leipzig, and though in after years he frequently came out of his retirement and paid several visits to England as well as to other places, he definitely turned his back upon the wide public fame to which his gifts entitled him.

SCHUMANN AND MENDELSSOHN IN MID-CAREER

Schumann and Clara Wieck had known each other since he first came as a student to the university and she was a child of nine. By the time she was sixteen, carefully trained by her father, she had made more than a local reputation as a pianist, and she had greater qualities than those which one generally associates with what is called 'an infant prodigy'. Schumann was in love with the young artist beside whom he had grown up, and two years later he made his proposal of marriage, to which, however, the father refused his consent. The years between 1835 and 1840 were far from happy ones for Schumann. It is true that Clara returned his love, but marriage was impossible while the father refused his consent, and the difficulty was only settled at last by the result of a painful lawsuit which went in the young people's favour. And yet in these years we get the very best of Schumann's piano music; the *Kinderscenen* and *Kreisleriana*, the majestic 'Fantasia' in C (Op. 17), the *Novelletten*, and the *Faschingsschwank aus Wien* all belong to these years, and the name of the last recalls the one other incident of the period which needs to be mentioned. In 1838 Schumann went to Vienna with the hope that he might be able there to carve out a career for himself and provide a home for Clara. It was his wish to transfer the publication of the *Neue Zeitschrift* to Vienna, and he went to discover the possibilities. The project did not result in anything, but two other things happened. Schumann's admiration for Schubert led him to call on Schubert's brother, who showed him the pile of manuscripts which had lain undisturbed since Franz's death in 1828. Schumann picked out from amongst them the score of the great Symphony in C major, and arranged to have it sent to Mendelssohn for performance at Leipzig, from which moment that symphony started upon its career in the world at large.

The other event was Schumann's presence at the carnival in Vienna, which led to the merry musical scenes of the *Faschingsschwank*. At that time the 'Marseillaise' was forbidden in Vienna, and the prohibition accounts for the amusing way in which Schumann has let a fragment of the tune slip in incidentally among the many melodies of the first movement.

During these years Mendelssohn's career was one succession of public musical events in which he was the central figure. The concerts at Leipzig, the Lower Rhine Festivals, which he conducted year by year, and at which he first produced *St. Paul* in 1836, visits to England (*St. Paul* was given at Birmingham in the following year), the first performance of Schubert's Symphony in C at Leipzig in 1839, the composition of the *Lobgesang* (Hymn of Praise) for a festival at Brunswick in 1840, again produced in England, at Birmingham, in the same year, are the chief events. He had married Mlle Cécile Jeanrenaud in 1837, and in this as in his music it seemed that Mendelssohn's career was as preordained to smoothness as Schumann's was to difficulty.

Schumann's difficulties, however, were conquered at last; he was married to Clara on 12 September 1840, and the happiness of his first years of married life is shown in the wonderful outburst of song-writing which marks a new phase of his development.

MENDELSSOHN'S LIFE AND CHARACTER

Curiously enough, almost at this moment Mendelssohn's difficulties began; he was persuaded to give up Leipzig and become director of a new Academy at Berlin. It was just the giving up of freedom and the acceptance of control under royal command which was most irksome to Mendelssohn's nature. Organization and efficiency were already the watchwords of the Prussian capital, and schemes of education, including the composition of music to various Greek plays, were forced upon Mendelssohn. His music to *Antigone* is the most important result of this part of his career; during the rest of his life, which lasted only seven years, he was perpetually negotiating to regain his freedom. He did regain it so far as to be able to keep up his connexion with Leipzig, and to secure the establishment of the famous 'Conservatorium' there in 1843; and he made flying visits to England, the last of which took place in 1847, when he came to conduct the revised version of *Elijah* at a concert of the Sacred Harmonic Society. The first performance of that work had taken place at Birmingham a year before (1846), on 26 August.

On his return from his last visit to England he received the news of the death of his sister Fanny, and this caused a shock from which he never recovered. He had persistently overworked, had used his marvellous energies to the full in every direction, and when suddenly a severe strain was put upon him he had no reserve of strength to meet it. He was completely broken down, the buoyancy of spirits on which he had lived deserted him, and a holiday in Switzerland did little or nothing to restore him. Though he returned to Leipzig, and began painfully to take up the threads of his work, there was no more spirit in him, and he died suddenly on 4 November 1847.

In the circumstances of Mendelssohn's early death we see what was the one weakness in his armour. He could not bear reverse as strong men bear it, as Schumann and Berlioz, for example, bore it and conquered it many times. He was never forced to win his way through any uncongenial surroundings; until the time when the King of Prussia caught him and chained him to his chariot wheels at Berlin he was always able to avoid unpleasantness by the simple process of going elsewhere. When he could no longer do this he chafed and wore himself out with work and worry, and when a great sorrow from which there was no escape came upon him he was overwhelmed by it.

This must be noticed because it explains something in his music acknowledged now by all the world. It is not so much a defect as a limitation. It stops short before a certain barrier, which it never passes. We love it for its grace and beauty, admire it for its brilliancy, honour it for its skilful workmanship, but nowhere does it give us that feeling which all the greatest things give us of deep calling unto deep. We have already placed some of his songs beside those of Schubert (see p. 374); we shall find the same stoppage when we place his piano music beside that of Schumann and Chopin, and if we turn to the orchestral music we find Mendelssohn always at his best in moments of gaiety and brightness. The elfin gambols of the overture and scherzo from the music to *A Midsummer Night's Dream* and the sunny glow of the Italian Symphony never fade. Wagner, who was by no means a sympathetic or even always a just critic of Mendelssohn, spoke of him as a 'landscape painter of the first order', and one realizes the truth of this as soon as one places the Italian Symphony and the 'Hebrides' Overture side by side. Never was there a stronger contrast of atmosphere in the music of one man. The blue sky of Italy and the grey sea washing the northern islands, the vine-clad plains and the stern rocks encircled by the flights of sea-birds, take what images you will to represent the two countries and you will find them typical of the contrasts of melody and orchestral tone existing between these two works. Mendelssohn caught the feeling of a scene or a fairy story unerringly; it was the human story which he could not quite unravel because he could only face it in its more genial moods. Even as one says that one expects to be asked, 'How about *Elijah*; is not that a deep and moving human story?' Certainly it is in a sense, and yet if we look at *Elijah* dispassionately we find that it is most moving in its representation of dramatic scenes. Mendelssohn poured out music to sacred words in two oratorios, *The Hymn of Praise*, and settings of numerous Psalms, at a time when most of his contemporaries hesitated to commit themselves to such ideas, and perhaps his very confidence is a sign that neither life nor religion represented to him a difficult path.

SCHUMANN'S LATER LIFE

We left Schumann at the moment of his marriage with an allusion to the songs which immediately followed it. After what has been said of Schumann's songs in Chapter 16 (see p. 376) it will be understood that the mere ecstasy of happiness is by no means the only impulse at the back of his songs, though the ecstasy was there ready to burst out in such a song as 'Widmung' (Dedication) or 'Die Rose, die Lilie' (No. 3 of the 'Dichterliebe' cycle) whenever the poet gave the signal for it. But in the deep sympathy with all phases of human feeling which is the leading characteristic of Schumann's song, we find the happiness which has come through sorrow and anxiety and has faced things out. Schumann is a disciplined soul in a way that neither Mendelssohn nor Chopin could be. Mendelssohn handled every kind of music at once and was immediately successful in each; Chopin spent his life at his piano discovering one treasure of beauty after another and never needing any other means of expression than the keyboard and his own two hands.

Schumann definitely set himself to extend the range of his art.

So far the piano and song had occupied him. In the year 1841 he devoted himself to symphonic music; the Symphony in B flat, now called No. 1 since the early Symphony in G minor (see p. 407) has disappeared, came early in the year, and that in D minor, now known as No. 4, an 'Overture, Scherzo, and Finale', as well as the first movement of the famous piano Concerto, were all written at this time.

Next came a period of chamber music, which includes the three string quartets, dedicated to Mendelssohn, the quintet for piano and strings, the quartet for piano and strings, and a trio (1842); and then choral music, including *Paradise and the Peri* and some of the music to *Faust*, was engaged upon.

During these years the only breaks in the round of quiet home life and composition were the tours which Clara undertook in order to pursue her career as a pianist, and these served also to carry some of her husband's work abroad. One of the most important was a tour to Russia at the beginning of 1844, when the Symphony in B flat was performed, and this took place a little before Berlioz made a similar excursion. No two foreigners subsequently had as much influence upon the new Russian school of composers as Berlioz and Schumann, and no two were less alike in character.

But 1844 was also the year in which Schumann's health began to suffer, and in order to stave off the illness which threatened him the *Neue Zeitschrift* was sold, and he with his wife and family left the many interests of their life at Leipzig to find greater quiet at Dresden. Wagner was now occupying the position of *Kapellmeister* at the Dresden Opera, and immediately Schumann's many-sided sympathy was turned towards the problems of opera. He was profoundly interested by the production of *Tannhäuser* in 1845, and his own only opera *Genoveva* was the result of his sojourn in Dresden. In 1846 he was well enough to undertake another trip to Vienna.

The year 1849 was the centenary of Goethe's birth; it was also the year of the revolution for his part in which Wagner was banished from Germany. Both events are marked in

Schumann's career. The first was the occasion for the performance of his music to *Faust* in Dresden, Leipzig, and Weimar; the second caused him to leave Dresden, not as a fugitive from the law, like Wagner, but in order to avoid the disturbances which the revolutionists were creating there.

In this year, too, Chopin died after a life of wandering, of illness, of transient happinesses, followed by disillusionments and disappointments. Of the three whose lives we set out to trace Schumann alone remains in 1850, and the last years of his life are years of decline. It was in this year that he accepted the position of musical director at Düsseldorf, which Mendelssohn had held years before, and wrote the splendid symphony in E flat called the 'Rhenish' for the Lower Rhine Festival. But though Schumann took up these new duties with enthusiasm he was not successful in them. He had none of that love of orchestral detail which made the mere handling of an orchestra a joy to Berlioz, nor had he the quick precision and untiring energy which gave Mendelssohn his success as a conductor.

The time at Düsseldorf was broken by a visit to Leipzig in the early spring of 1852, and the fact that this visit was the occasion of a festival of Schumann's own music shows how thoroughly his position as a composer was now recognized. But ill health was gaining upon him, and his dissatisfaction with his work at Düsseldorf helped to increase the melancholy which now began to cloud his life. In the autumn of 1853 occurred the last incident in Schumann's life which was of wide public importance: a young man came to his house with an introduction from the violinist Joachim and a portfolio of music. A piano sonata, some songs and chamber music were in the portfolio, and when these were taken out and played their remarkable qualities, as well as the evident strength of character which their composer showed, so impressed Schumann that for the first time for nearly ten years he undertook the writing of a critical article in their praise. The young man was Johannes Brahms; the sonata and the songs were those now known as Opp. 1 and 3, and the article with the title 'Neue Bahnen' ('New Paths') was published in Schumann's old paper, the *Neue Zeitschrift*. Needless to say, it roused a good deal of opposition; it brought Brahms more enemies than friends, and there were plenty of people to ridicule Schumann's critical acumen. It did not, however, do Brahms the only real harm which such praise would have done to a lesser nature; neither then nor at any time in his career did Brahms set himself up as a prophet or suffer from that form of human frailty appropriately called a 'swelled head'. For many years he was to work on with a quiet concentration before he again attracted such public notice.

The climax of Schumann's illness came early in 1854, when in a fit of depression he threw himself into the Rhine and was rescued by some fishermen. The last two years of his life were spent in a private asylum near Bonn. There were intervals when his mind was perfectly clear and when he could even compose, but the intervals grew fewer, and he died on 29 July 1856.

THREE MASTERS OF THE PIANO

It is time to sum up this portion of our story by more detailed reference to the piano music of the masters whose characters we have outlined. This can best be done by a few direct comparisons and contrasts. But in the first place let us glance over the general extent and character of their works.

Chopin's contribution is the largest, perhaps the most far-reaching, but, as we have seen, his piano music represents practically his sole output, which was very far from being the case with either Mendelssohn or Schumann. Chopin's more important works may be summarized as follows:

1. Two concertos for piano and orchestra (in E minor and F minor), with a number of other 'concert pieces' written originally with orchestral accompaniment, such as the variations on 'Là ci darem' and the 'Krakowiak'.

2. Three sonatas for piano (in C minor, Op. 4, B flat minor, Op. 35, and B minor, Op. 58). The first has been overshadowed by the two later ones. Op. 35, containing the Funeral March, is

for that reason the most famous. With them may be classed the four scherzos and three rondos, which have the character of separate sonata movements.

3. Four Ballades, four Impromptus, the Fantaisie in F minor, the Barcarolle, and other pieces, with the series of twenty nocturnes and a set of twenty-four preludes, are all works in which the form is not bound to any established method.

4. Pieces founded on dance forms: 16 polonaises, 19 valses, and 60 mazurkas.

5. Twenty-seven Études (twelve in Op. 10, twelve in Op. 25, and three written for Moscheles's 'Méthode') are intended primarily as means of technical study, but raised the study from the prosaic standard set by Czerny and Cramer to an exquisite form of art.

To classify Schumann's piano music under headings without making a list of titles is a more difficult business. We may put his only piano concerto (in A minor, completed in 1846) at the head, and the Introduction and Allegro (G major) with a Concert Allegro (D minor) beside it, as works for piano with orchestra. The second class is easily filled up by the mention of three sonatas (in F sharp minor, G minor, and F minor), but then the difficulty of classification begins. His first twenty-three opus numbers are all filled with piano music, and almost every opus has a different title since almost every one is founded on some episode of his life or romance of his imagination. The titles sometimes refer directly to these episodes or romances, *Theme on the name 'Abegg', with variations* (see p. 407), *Davidsbündlertänze* (see p. 409), *Carnaval*, and so on; sometimes the references are hidden under more general descriptions, such as *Fantasie* or *Novelletten*, but this does not make them fall more definitely into any one category. Later in his life the descriptive titles are fewer, but so are the compositions for piano. We have a recrudescence of piano music about the year 1850, which includes four fugues, the *Waldscenen* (Woodland Scenes), *Bunte Blätten* (Coloured Leaves), three

Phantasiestücke (Fantastic Pieces), and two *Albumblätter* (Album Leaves). The most that an attempt to classify Schumann can do is to show us its impossibility taken apart from his life, and for that reason we have dwelt with special minuteness upon the circumstances in which his work, especially his early work, was produced.

In Mendelssohn's case the classification is not very difficult, but it is also not very necessary. Beginning with the classical form of the sonata (in E, Op. 6), he practically laid the piano sonata aside and reserved the use of that form for his concerted chamber music and the orchestral symphony. Throughout his piano compositions there are many called 'Capriccio', beginning with the one in F sharp minor, Op. 5, which may be taken as typical, and the title generally means a piece which moves swiftly and brilliantly, and is full of Mendelssohn's quick birdlike energy. Preludes and fugues were another favourite form with him because they recalled Bach, the hero whom he most worshipped, and amongst his works of this kind the one in E minor from the set of six, Op. 35, is an excellent example. His gift for embroidering a theme with graceful ornament is shown in his variations, of which the set called *Variations sérieuses* is the finest.

But when we have mentioned these things and remembered that Mendelssohn wrote two concertos (G minor and D minor) for piano with orchestra, there remains one form of piano composition which puts all his others in the shade, the series of the most lovable little pieces, four dozen altogether, which are known as *Songs without Words* (see p. 409). These were his musical diary in the way that the *Phantasiestücke* and the *Carnaval* were Schumann's. But the diary was continued at intervals through his life. A happy day in the country, a talk with a friend, a game with children, would bring one from him. Sometimes, but rarely, he gave them titles such as the 'Venetian Gondola Song'; more often he was content to let the circumstance which brought the music from him be forgotten, and often those who have loved the songs have made up fancy titles, some of them rather silly ones, such as 'The Bee's Wedding', to describe them.

If we take the *Songs without Words*, the *Phantasiestücke* (Op. 12) of Schumann, and the Préludes of Chopin, we get a perfectly simple means of placing the three composers together under the microscope. Here we can view them apart from the technical difficulties which make the larger works, at any rate those of Schumann and Chopin, exceedingly hard to play, and we can be quite sure that we are getting at the men themselves in their most intimate thoughts.

The first numbers will give us an instructive contrast, and by taking the first of each we avoid the snare of selected evidence. Mendelssohn's first 'Song without Words' (E major) is a lovely melody introduced above an accompaniment of smooth arpeggios supported on a bass moving generally in crotchets. It exactly reproduces the idea of a simple song with an accompaniment for the two hands at the piano, save that the pianist has to play the song melody and accompany it at the same time. The movement is in a ternary form, the traditional form of song (see pp. 54–55); the first section modulating to the dominant is repeated, its middle section culminates in an impulsive cadenza, and a delicate coda is added to round off the whole with a reflection of the melody. Perfectly clear in form, it has a single purpose, the expression of the melody. The accompaniment emphasizes this, but arouses no conflicting interest.

Schumann and Chopin are equally simple in the outlines of their forms, but both are very complex in their texture. Schumann's 'Des Abends' ('In the Evening') is indeed a sort of extension of the ternary form, for the middle section is repeated before the coda, but that adds no real difficulty of comprehension. His, too, is a song melody accompanied, but you have only to look at the first few bars to see what is meant by a complex texture. The melody is in triple time; the accompaniment is duple time, which the signature shows to be the fundamental rhythm of the piece, so that the whole is a most delicate study in what is called cross rhythm:

Ex. 72

Ped. * Ped. * Ped. *

Ped. *

The form of the left-hand arpeggios, too, spread over wide intervals and, interlacing with those of the right hand, draws an attention to the accompaniment which Mendelssohn refused.

The first bar of Chopin's Prélude looks even more complicated:

Ex. 73

Fundamentally, however, it is less so than Schumann's piece, for there is no real cross rhythm. All parts conform to the duple time, in his case also expressed by the signature $\frac{2}{8}$. But when you first look at it you ask: Where is the tune? The music looks like the four parts of a string quartet compressed into a piano score. Consider it as that, and you will find the tune is in the viola part. Here is the beginning of it, and we choose the viola clef because it then lies on the stave:

Ex. 74

It is just one sweep of melody without any modulation or other element of contrast to divide it into sections or make it analysable into binary or ternary form. It is as clear as daylight, and you see that what we may call the violoncello and second violin parts accompany it with arpeggios, while the first violin reinforces it on the second beat of each bar. But though we have used the names of the instruments of the string quartet for purposes of illustration this is essentially piano music, and it and Schumann's 'Des Abends' give examples of one thing which they had in common, a love of intertwining parts which, played by a pianist whose fingers are trained to give due emphasis to the slightest detail and who understands the art of phrasing by the use of the sustaining pedal, can all be made clear and yet all merge into a consistent whole.

In the music of Schumann and Chopin we find the pedal for the first time used as one of the intrinsic resources of the piano. We have seen that it was invented quite late in the eighteenth century (p. 175). Beethoven's deafness prevented him from exploiting it to the full; Schubert wrote too hastily to trouble much about it. It is recorded that Mendelssohn in actual performance used it very sparingly, but to Schumann, whose favourite phrase 'Sehr innig'[1] heads this piece, and to Chopin, who lived his life through the piano, it was the very life-breath.

[1] Scarcely translatable except as 'very intimate'.

Its use enabled them to use counterpoint on the piano not merely as an intellectual interest but for the purposes of what is called colour. When Mendelssohn is most contrapuntal, and he was a master of counterpoint, he is least emotional. For this reason he is never very seriously contrapuntal in the *Songs without Words*. When Schumann feels most deeply his parts divide themselves into many contrapuntal strands producing constantly shifting colours through their conflicting rhythms which can only be compared to the colours of shot silk. In Chopin the same methods are often seen, not always so much as an outcome of deep feeling as of his sheer delight in the beauty of the colour. You see it in the Préludes Nos. 5 and 8, more strongly in the cross rhythms of the Études, Op. 10 No. 10, and Op. 25 Nos. 2 and 3, and in the Valse, Op. 42, where a melody in duple time is accompanied by a valse rhythm.

We can afford to emphasize this side of Chopin's art, because the other side, in which he delights in one long strain of delicious melody accompanied by a delicately devised background of flowing harmony, is so familiar that there is not the least fear of its being forgotten. The series of nocturnes give us one example of it after another. The one in E flat (Op. 9 No. 2), that in F sharp (Op. 15 No. 2), and the most famous of them all, the Nocturne in D flat (Op. 27 No. 2), live constantly in mind. Their tunes, springing as water springs from the fountain to fall again in cascades of rainbow-coloured drops, have nothing to compare with them in all music. We know, of course, that neither Mendelssohn nor Schumann nor any one else ever ventured into that enchanted realm.

But leaving Chopin aside for the moment, let us take another comparative view of the other two, placing the *Variations sérieuses* and the *Études symphoniques* together. We might bring in Chopin here with his variations on 'Là ci darem', but we will not, because that work, though it shows his genius in flashes, has a good deal of the character of a pianist's 'show piece', whereas the other two are here treating the form of variations on a melody from a more serious standpoint, as the titles suggest. Here we see Mendelssohn's contrapuntal vigour in a way in which he never allows it to appear in the *Songs without Words*. In each number of the seventeen variations the general form of the theme, with its striking harmony, is preserved; one never has the least difficulty in recognizing it as the basis of each variation. At the same time each number introduces some new figure which plays round the main form of the theme with infinite skill and variety.

Schumann, on the other hand, treats his theme more airily. He almost seems to wish us to lose sight of it as soon as it has been announced, for the very first variation introduces an entirely new idea, and it is not until the fifth bar that we are shown that this new idea moves in counterpoint with the theme. The second variation, too, has a new melody to which the theme forms a bass, and by the third number, which is not called a variation, the actual outline of the theme has disappeared altogether, and its influence is only felt in the fact that the general scheme of harmonic progressions is the same.

Trace the influence of the theme through all the numbers and you find that the most that can be said is that it is always offering some new suggestion to the composer's fancy. Sometimes it is a melodic quotation to be treated in canon (Étude IV), sometimes it is a new melody growing out of a quotation (Étude VI), but new ideas are so fruitful that the melody of the original theme becomes enveloped in them so that you may lose sight of it. The only constant quantity is the main structure of the binary form made clear by its harmonic cadences, while the details of the harmony are as freely varied as are those of the melody.

Mendelssohn approaches this freedom in variations X and XI, but he restrains himself, and almost immediately after (Var. XIII) gives a clear presentation of his melody in an inner part, decorating it with those staccato ornaments which Joachim has told us gave peculiar charm to his touch at the piano.

Mendelssohn's, then, are variations primarily upon the

melody; Schumann's are on the whole structure of the theme in all its bearings of melody, harmony, and form, and in this one discovers the greater depth and 'inwardness' of his music. Étude XI is a peculiarly beautiful instance of Schumann's coloured counterpoint. It is a duet in which the two parts combine in a melody directly derived from the theme. They treat it imitatively, and all the while a rich accompaniment is supplied by the rapidly moving harmonies of the bass part. Schumann here considers very little the limitations of the human hand. The right hand must stretch and leap to convey the movement of the two parts of the duet, the left hand must be supple indeed to produce the smooth murmuring effect required from the accompaniment. In this way Schumann's polyphonic style extended the pianist's technique immeasurably; Mendelssohn, who always wrote well within what would lie neatly under the pianist's hands, left the technique of the piano very much where he found it. A comparison between this duet and the lovely 'Duetto' in Mendelssohn's *Songs without Words* (Op. 38 No. 6) will illustrate this point clearly.

One more point arises here for notice, and that is the great increase in harmonic range which is so conspicuous in the music of both Schumann and Chopin. Many of the passages in their work which present curious conglomerations of notes and look bewildering to analyse are simply the result of adding ornamental passages to a perfectly plain structure. The *appoggiatura*, which may be described as the use of one note to suggest another note, is as old as music itself, and when you get as many parts as the fingers of two hands upon the keys can represent moving with great rapidity through a series of such ornaments, the actual chords on which they are based may look almost unrecognizable, though to the ear, which takes in not only the note played but the note suggested, the passage represents no harmonic difficulty.

There are, however, some passages where the main progressions of harmony are, or were when they were written, startling. Those in Schumann and in most of the great German writers of the nineteenth century are chiefly the result of that discovery which we saw appeared early in Schubert's songs, the discovery of the possibility of sudden and abrupt modulation of key (see p. 363). Schubert, Schumann, and Wagner all used this resource with electrifying effect; Mendelssohn was less attracted by it.

In Chopin's case, however, there is often another explanation to be found in the fact that his melody itself is not based upon the scale system of the major and minor modes with their fixed contrasts of tonic and dominant harmonies. Those contrasts are the very foundation of all German harmony and much other music of Western Europe, well into the twentieth century, but, as we saw early in our study (Chapter 1), they only represent one out of many possibilities. The old church music up to the age of Palestrina, and the folk music of all countries, including our own, were based upon many and various scale systems. Look through Chopin's Mazurkas, which are the direct outcome of the folk music of Poland, and you will find innumerable melodies which suggest the older modes or other scale progressions which sound strange to ears steeped in the major and minor modes of modern music. Here is one simple example from the Mazurka, Op. 6 No. 2:

Ex. 75

Obviously such tunes suggest very different harmonic relationships from those of what had come to be accepted as the normal scale, and Chopin's most subtle harmonic progressions will be found to be the result of applying modern instrumental harmony to such melodies. Symptoms of the same process appear in all the young national schools of the nineteenth century, all those, that is, who founded their style anew by the application of modern harmony to a traditional folk melody. Grieg in Norway, the Russian composers beginning with Glinka, Dvořák in Bohemia, and later on certain composers in Spain, Hungary, and England have worked upon similar lines, taking the traditional music of their own countries as the starting-point for a new development of both melody and harmony. Chopin's genius, however, nowhere appears more astounding than in this, that at a time when the relations of the scale seemed immutably fixed to all cultivated European people, he was able to render them so flexible that he could weave his national folk melody into a scheme of modern harmony and produce a perfectly consistent impression by means of his extreme sensitiveness to all the attributes of beauty.

Suggestions for Further Reading and Listening

RECOMMENDED biographies of Liszt, Mendelssohn, Schumann, and Chopin are named at the end of Chapter 15, and most of them will come in handy in connection with the present chapter. They can be supplemented by *Franz Liszt, the Man and His Music* (particularly the essays on his keyboard works by Louis Kentner and John Ogdon), by *Frederic Chopin, Profiles of the Man and the Musician*, and by *Schumann, the Man and his Music*, all of which are edited by Alan Walker. (These three volumes are symposia, made up of contributions from teams of specialists.) For an analysis of *Chopin's Musical Style*, pithy, stimulating, and unpedantic, Gerald Abraham's short study could not be bettered.

In conjunction with the various books listed above, Kathleen Dale's *Nineteenth-Century Piano Music* should be consulted. Here the subject is discussed under categories rather than composers, but there is an index of composers and works, which enables you to pinpoint at once, say, Mendelssohn's *Variations sérieuses*. *Men, Women and Pianos*, a social history by Arthur Loesser, covers a period from about the turn of the eighteenth century until the present day, and, although it may not count as primary reading, it contains an enormous amount of information, and repays a leisurely browse.

A good deal of the music mentioned in this chapter may be too difficult for the average, amateur pianist, but even players of modest technique can enjoy Chopin's mazurkas, Mendelssohn's *Songs Without Words*, some of Schumann, and two or three of those strange, bare, final pieces of Liszt. The nocturnes of John Field are worth looking at, partly for their own sake, partly because of their connection with Chopin's nocturnes, and partly because they are relatively easy.

Reference is made on page 401 to Liszt's operatic paraphrases or fantasias. They are extremely difficult, but they occasionally crop up in recitals, and a number of them are available on record. Once very popular and then spurned, they are now coming back into favour; and they tell you much about Liszt, about a certain kind of rather flamboyant keyboard technique, and about popular taste in the middle of the last century. They may also provide some unexpected insights into the opera in question.

CHAPTER 19

Wagner and the Opera

BEFORE we pursue the story of pure instrumental music to the stages which it ultimately reached in the latter half of the century, we must get some notion of the most complex musical mind of the time, Richard Wagner, and see how, devoting his many-sided energies to the problem of opera, he brought about a revolution which was not so much musical as mental. It amounted ultimately to a complete change of the standpoint from which music and its association with other forms of art was regarded.

A rapid sketch of Wagner's chequered career will suffice to give us the necessary basis of fact from which we can discover some of the main ways in which he effected his revolution.

WILHELM RICHARD WAGNER, the youngest of a large family, was born at Leipzig on 22 May 1813. He was therefore the contemporary in age of all the composers whose work we have been considering in the last chapter, but the original character of the work before him made him comparatively slow in development, so that he is far more a composer of the second half of the century than any of them save Liszt.

His mother, left a widow a few months after Richard's birth, soon married again an actor named Geyer; the event caused a removal of the family to Dresden, where Richard was put to school at the age of nine. His cleverness soon asserted itself. It is recorded that at the age of thirteen he translated the first twelve books of the *Odyssey* out of school hours. Poetry of all kinds attracted him immensely. He wrote voluminous verses, read Shakespeare in German translations and learnt enough English to attempt some translation on his own account, and stimulated his fancy by trying to write tragedies partly modelled on the Greek drama, partly on Shakespeare.

In these years Weber was at Dresden (see p. 346), and was on friendly terms with the Geyer family. He became a hero to the young Wagner, who knew *Der Freischütz* by heart. Soon after Weber's early death the family moved back to Leipzig, and there Richard added to his limited musical experiences his first hearing of the symphonies of Beethoven and the music to *Egmont*. He immediately determined that poetry and drama, even the great tragedy which he had designed to write, would be barren without music of the heroic Beethoven-like kind, so he resolved to write such music, and got hold of a book on harmony from which to learn the few technical facts which he thought it necessary to know. In this incident one sees Wagner in a flash. What he willed to do he was quite certain that he could do; he brushed aside every impediment. With supreme self-confidence everything and everybody throughout his life was made to conform to his will, and he never doubted the rightness of his will.

Needless to say, the great tragedy and the great music to it came to nothing, but this much came out of his enthusiasm that some definite musical teaching was procured for him. He was now fifteen, his schooling went on at Leipzig, and he was taught music by Theodor Weinlig, who, as Cantor of the 'Thomasschule', was a successor of Bach. He entered the university in 1831 and wrote music, including a Symphony in C major, with a good deal of diligence; but all the time, even though he allowed himself to be guided by Weinlig into the regular forms of instrumental music, he was inclined to revolt against them. It was in 1833, when he was twenty years old, that his career as a musician began with an engagement as chorus master at the small theatre of Würzburg in Bavaria. Here he wrote an elaborate opera *Die Feen* ('The Fairies'); both words and music were his own composition, and the story, considerably altered, was taken from an Italian play by Gozzi. Though this opera was put aside for many years, and has only been published since Wagner's death, there is a good deal in its melody and in its imaginative treatment of the fairy story which suggests his own style. In some ways it is more characteristic than the later and better-known *Rienzi*.

From this time began the period of more or less transitory theatrical engagements, tentative compositions, continuous difficulties largely made by himself, which lasted until his resolve to go to Paris in 1839. Another opera, *Das Liebesverbot* ('Forbidden Love'), founded on Shakespeare's *Measure for Measure*, belongs to this time. Among his many moves from place to place the appointment as conductor to the opera at Magdeburg, where he met and married Minna Planer, is the most important. The difficulties were largely connected with money. Wagner was always getting into debt because of his rooted assurance that what he required he must have, that if he could not get it for himself other people ought to supply it for him.

This does not give a very agreeable picture of Wagner's character, and many phases of it were far from being agreeable; but it must be remembered that his extreme egotism rested on the conviction that he had the ability for great things. He never saw that other people could not be expected to take him at his own valuation until he had given proof of the justness of that valuation. The better side of him may be compared to Beethoven in his early days in Vienna (see p. 302); one can see now that he no more than Beethoven was playing a gambling game when he claimed to be given a chance to express himself freely. Like Beethoven, he only needed time to justify his artistic claims; but, unlike Beethoven, he made large material claims upon those about him while he was gaining time, and he had no scruples in pressing those claims to the detriment of others.

EXPERIENCES IN PARIS

In 1839, having got nothing but small theatrical appointments in Germany, which chiefly meant the duty of producing other composers' operas, Wagner determined upon a great bid for fortune. He planned a visit to Paris, where he hoped to get a new opera performed by securing the good offices of Meyerbeer, then one of the most popular operatic composers of Paris, and one whose word would carry weight with the directors of the Paris Opéra. Again he was doomed to disappointment, but this Paris visit, nevertheless, had a great effect upon his career.

Wagner, his wife, and a huge Newfoundland dog (at that time his constant companion) all shipped on board a sailing-vessel bound for London at the port of Pillau on the Baltic, and on the voyage he had his first experience of the sea and an exceedingly severe one. In the storm which they encountered the legend of the 'Flying Dutchman', which he had read as Heine told it, was graphically brought to mind, and his impressions became subsequently translated into music in the overture which remains one of the most vivid sea-pieces ever written for the orchestra. They landed in London and stopped there a week, but, quite unknown, did little beyond wandering about the streets. Thence they went to Boulogne, where Wagner met Meyerbeer, obtained the introductions which he wanted and proceeded to Paris. Meyerbeer's introductions did little for him, and during the two years spent in Paris hopes of a performance on a large scale were continually held out to him and as continually fell through. He went on with his work and finished *Rienzi*, scoring it boldly for a large orchestra in the manner popular with Paris audiences. He tried all sorts of means of getting work to support himself; some songs written to French words include the charming 'Dors, mon enfant'. He did a quantity of journalistic work both for French and German papers; for the former he wrote on the nature of German music, for the latter various reports on the music which he heard in Paris. He undertook to make piano arrangements from operatic scores, especially from the popular operas of Halévy, and was even reduced to arranging suites of pieces for the cornet from operas.

Painful as such work was for a man of genius, his genius enabled him to gather a good deal of useful experience from it.

There was much which he could learn from the orchestras of Paris even apart from the example of Berlioz. Certainly, he learnt to know how operas were made; technique, which as a boy had seemed to him a trivial matter, became the groundwork on which he was to build. Moreover, in Paris he met both Liszt and Berlioz, and though he began by falling foul of Liszt for being a successful virtuoso, the foundations of a friendship which later was to be of immense value to him were laid at this time. He could not fail to be impressed by Berlioz's extraordinary command of instrumentation (see p. 394).

DRESDEN AND AFTER

As his prospects in Paris became more hopeless, Wagner began to press for the performance of his opera *Rienzi* in Dresden, and when at last he heard of its acceptance he determined to leave Paris and return to his own country. The acceptance of *Rienzi* was soon followed by his appointment as conductor to the opera at Dresden, and it was here that Wagner had his first successes in the performances both of *Rienzi* and *Der fliegende Holländer* ('The Flying Dutchman').

Here in 1842 he settled down to work with a consistency and enthusiasm which the opportunities called out. He came across a number of folk-tales in simple German versions—the story of Tannhäuser and the contest of song; legends of the knights of the Grail, including stories of Lohengrin, Titurel, and Parsifal, and these soon worked upon his imagination. He began to mould them into material for drama with music, writing his own poems as usual, choosing from the stories those incidents which appealed to him, altering details in order to make the story consistent with his philosophic and ethical theories. For Wagner could never see a work merely as an artistic production; it always had to represent to him, and through him to his audience, some part of his philosophy of life—the redemption of Tannhäuser by the devotion of Elizabeth, the failure of Elsa to trust completely in the moral grandeur of her knight Lohengrin, in these things Wagner had a moral purpose which to him seemed the very essence of artistic expression. He is almost if not quite the solitary instance of a great artist in music who viewed his art primarily from the preacher's point of view. In every department of life he was convinced of his own mission as a teacher. That fact in itself was enough to make his enemies (and no one ever had more enemies than Wagner) ready to point to discrepancies between his teaching and his life.

Tannhäuser was completed in 1844, and followed *Der fliegende Holländer* on to the stage at Dresden in 1845. It is interesting to notice that these years at Dresden included at least the beginnings in Wagner's mind of all the big music-dramas of his life. *Lohengrin* was the next one to occupy him fully, and we have seen that it and *Parsifal*, the last to be actually written, began to germinate in his mind soon after his leaving Paris. The idea for a comedy on the subject of a contest of song as a sort of counterpart to the tragedy of *Tannhäuser* also suggested itself to him, and was eventually fulfilled, though again many years later, in *Die Meistersinger von Nürnberg*. And it was in 1848 that he first began to dramatize the myths of the Nibelungen Saga which materialized subsequently into the great trilogy *Der Ring des Nibelungen*.

But none of these projects save *Lohengrin* got fully shaped at this time, and the production of that work was checked by other preoccupations. He actually finished his score in the spring of 1848, and having done so he allowed himself to be drawn into the political disturbances which ended in the revolution of the next year. It has been pointed out that Wagner's speech to the political club called the 'Vaterlands-Verein' in June 1848 was by no means so violently seditious as it might have been, and some of his admirers have taken pains to discover that he was not really incriminated in the riots of the following year at all, that the order for his arrest was a mistake, and that it really referred to another man of the same name. But the latter part of this defence is quite untenable. Though in his autobiography, written many years later, Wagner was able to make out a case for his innocence, there is not the least doubt of his active part in the revolution, and it was a part of which at the time he had no cause to be ashamed. He had stood for reform in politics as in art, but the powers against him were too strong; his post, held directly under the king, was of course lost to him, and more than that, he was exiled from Germany. He had first escaped to Weimar, where Liszt was then engaged in preparing for the performance of *Tannhäuser*, and in the following year Liszt still kept his work alive by giving the first performance of *Lohengrin*. Meantime Wagner took up his abode in Switzerland, and from that time onwards until the year 1861 Zürich was his headquarters. Not that he remained there all the time; he came to London in 1855 to conduct the Philharmonic concerts, he visited Paris more than once, and in 1860 revised *Tannhäuser* for performance there—a performance upon which he built great hopes, and which was one of the bitterest disappointments of his life. Its production met not only with active opposition, but with an amount of intrigue against its acceptance which made it necessary to withdraw the work after three performances.

THE THEORY OF MUSIC-DRAMA

But before the events of Wagner's second failure in Paris much had happened to contribute to his development. It was natural that, in the years immediately after his executive post as a conductor was at an end, he should return again to literary work, and many of his essays date from this time. It was in 'The Art-work of the Future' and 'Opera and Drama', written a year later, that he developed his theory of what opera should be with a fullness which makes these essays as memorable as Gluck's preface to *Alceste* (see p. 283). But Wagner's theories had not the simplicity of Gluck's. Their exact purport is difficult to unravel, but some of their leading characteristics may be summed up as follows:

1. In the 'Art-work of the Future' he outlines what for him was the ideal form of art. In the three principal means of

expression, gesture, poetry, and sound, he finds an art which expresses all the faculties of man; these he insisted must all be fully unfolded, and must be decorated by the plastic arts of painting and architecture.

2. In opera the expression of these various forms had always been lopsided. Gesture and poetry had been put in the background by music.

3. The poet should not restrict himself for the sake of the music, nor the musician for the poetry; each must intensify the other.

4. What was wanted to achieve the new music-drama seemed to be, first, 'a fellowship of all the artists'; secondly, a new public who would treat art not as an amusement but as a serious preoccupation.

The soundness of Wagner's ideal has been proved in his own work and its ultimate acceptance. The unsoundness in his theories is chiefly due to his constant habit of generalizing from himself. He saw a great thing to do, therefore that thing must be 'the art-work of the future'. He had no inclination to write music apart from what he called 'its fertilization by poetry', therefore he asserted that music by itself was a dead thing. It is a strange irony that he himself should have proved the livingness of music alone in the tremendous finale of *The Ring* when, the drama over, the orchestra soars to a height of expression which it never reached in company with 'gesture and words'.

FROM *THE RING* TO *PARSIFAL*

After this outburst of theory Wagner settled down in 1852 to the work which more than all others was to prove both the truth and the untruth existing together in his ideas. The text of *The Ring* was written in a curious alliterative form of verse which he found susceptible to musical treatment, and the music of its first two parts, *Rheingold* and *Die Walküre*, went forward in the following years. The latter was interrupted by his visit to London but was finished in 1856, and he was well on in the composition of *Siegfried* when another disturbance took place.

For years he had been a trying husband to his prosaic and uncomprehending wife. How much right and how much wrong there was on both sides in the growing quarrel which ultimately separated them it is not necessary to decide, but to read the correspondence, since published, between them is to realize that Minna Wagner was a creature very much to be pitied. Possibly the worst of Wagner was that he did pity her, and always from the lofty standpoint of the teacher, which is so hard to bear with in ordinary life.

At any rate the home at Zürich was broken up, the composition of *The Ring* was checked, and instead Wagner turned to the passionate setting of the love-story of *Tristan und Isolde*, the only one of his music-dramas which seems to have seized him with a sudden impulse and to have been written in one outpouring of unflagging enthusiasm. The first sketch of the drama was made in August 1857, the poem was completed in the following month, and though it was two years before the score was actually finished, anyone who has a notion of the immense labour merely of writing such a score can realize that they were two years of unremitting work. After the completion of *Tristan* came the revision of *Tannhäuser*, which included the rewriting of a great part of the first act, making the overture pass without a break into the first scene, and the texture of the music more closely woven in the manner which had now become habitual to him. Then came the disaster of its production in Paris, and close on that public failure the private one of Minna's final break with him.

His fortunes were at their darkest. It must be remembered that he had heard no one of his great works performed since *Tannhäuser*. He had been debarred from hearing *Lohengrin* when Liszt gave it; *Rheingold*, *Die Walküre*, half of *Siegfried*, and the whole of *Tristan* existed only on paper and in his imagination. That fact alone shows the tremendous strength of his genius. It is only surpassed by the case of Beethoven, who was cut off by deafness from ever hearing his greatest works.

In 1861 Wagner heard *Lohengrin* for the first time, when it was given in Vienna, and soon after the cloud of his ill-fortune was further lifted by the withdrawal of his sentence of exile from Germany. These events were the forerunners of better times, and with his fuller freedom of action he started buoyantly upon the composition of that most lovable of all his works, the comedy planned long since, which now became *Die Meistersinger von Nürnberg*. This, however, was not, like *Tristan*, written straight away. It was dovetailed in with further work upon *Siegfried* and some sketches for *Parsifal*.

The accession of Ludwig II to the throne of Bavaria was an even more decisive turning-point in Wagner's fortunes. That Wagner, the rebel against every established institution, the unruly *Hof-Kapellmeister* and political agitator of the forties, should after a decade of exile return to become the protégé of a king seems one of the strangest reversals of history. But as far as Wagner himself was concerned the change was as human as it was illogical. A king who entertained liberal views towards art and who showed his liberality by dispatching a secretary to find out Wagner and invite him to his capital to finish his work, who followed up this step by endowing him with a pension and inviting him to supply a scheme for new musical education at Munich, naturally placed the idea of monarchy before the rebel in a most favourable light. Wagner began to see opening before him the possibility of realizing the dream of his life, nothing less than the firm establishment of a home for his art free from the cramping conditions of the ordinary opera-house, a place where he might found that 'fellowship of all the artists' and draw together his new and appreciative public.

One of the immediate results of Ludwig's generosity was the first performance of *Tristan* at Munich in 1865, conducted by Hans von Bülow. Afterwards the composition of *Die Meistersinger* went forward rapidly; a group of musicians gathered round Wagner and became inspired by his ideals of performance. Among them was Hans Richter, who was ultimately to become the greatest conductor of Wagner's music. The score of *Die Meistersinger* was finished in the autumn of 1867 at Triebschen, on the lake of Lucerne, where in these years Wagner made his home. Here Richter spent much time with him and copied the score of *Die Meistersinger*. Minna Wagner had died in 1866, and the complications of Wagner's private life at this period, which ultimately ended in his marriage with Cosima, the daughter of Liszt and formerly the wife of Bülow, are too unedifying to be entered into here. The birth of their son in 1869 is a landmark in Wagner's artistic life; that too occurred at Triebschen. *Siegfried*, the third part of *The Ring*, was completed three months after his son was born, and the boy was named Siegfried after the hero whose fortunes Wagner had had so much difficulty in tracing through his great work. The event was further celebrated by the composition of the beautiful orchestral piece known as the 'Siegfried Idyll', a piece in which leading themes from the opera of *Siegfried* mingle with an old German cradle song and are delicately scored for a small orchestra. It was a birthday serenade for Cosima. Richter got together a band of local musicians, taught them their parts, himself played the trumpet part, and a private performance, conducted by Wagner, was given at their house.

At last the great project of *The Ring*, a drama occupying four whole evenings in performance, was nearing completion. *Götterdämmerung*, its final section, went rapidly forward in the year 1870, the more so because some of its music had been planned years ago under the title of *Siegfrieds Tod* (Siegfried's death).

THE FOUNDING OF BAYREUTH

And now at last the musical world at large was sufficiently alive to the importance of what Wagner was doing for its more enterprising members at least to attempt an active share in the project of building a house for the work. Wagner societies began to be formed as tributes of admiration and also to help in the prosaic duty of raising funds. In 1872 a place was found for the theatre: Bayreuth, a quiet Bavarian town off the main lines of traffic yet large enough to be a place where people could gather, a royal residence, but otherwise in size and surroundings like our smaller English country towns, such as Taunton or Ludlow for example, was admirably fitted for the purpose. Wide undulating hills crowned with far-reaching woods lie about the town, and a spot was found on the slope of the hill where the woods begin, a mile or so beyond the houses.

Here, on Wagner's fifty-ninth birthday, 22 May 1872, the foundation-stone of the 'Festspielhaus' (festival playhouse) was laid. Everything which could concentrate the attention upon the drama and its music was thought of down to the smallest details.

The auditorium, instead of being built in the old fashion of circular galleries, is fan-shaped, sloping upwards from the stage at the narrow end in regular tiers which reach in a slight curve from side to side of the building. This plan gives a maximum of seating room, and also has the advantage of giving to every spectator a clear view of the stage, which is practically identical from every part of the house. The rows of doors on each side of the fan make it possible for the audience to reach their seats without a crush. The orchestra, placed between the stage and the auditorium, is sunk below the level of both and is screened from view by steel shields. This has a very appreciable effect upon the tone of the orchestra, it softens the outlines of phrase and blends the instruments into a sonorous whole. The result is a great beauty of tone with, however, some diminution of strength. The conductor behind the outer shield sees both the stage and his players but the audience cannot see him, and this is perhaps one of the greatest advantages of the plan. Everyone who has seen an opera knows the distraction caused by the waving arms of the conductor between the stalls and the stage.

The stage itself was planned to accommodate the most elaborate scenery, machinery, lighting, and other arrangements according to the most modern ideas—most modern, that is, before electric power was in general use. By the middle of the twentieth century, of course, this equipment had in turn grown old-fashioned, but a thorough renovation was undertaken under the direction of Wagner's two grandsons.

At last, in 1876, the 'Festspielhaus' was sufficiently finished for use, and the first festival, that is the first performance of the whole of *The Ring*, conducted by Richter, took place there from 13 to 17 August. The famous violinist Wilhelmj led the orchestra. A remarkable company of singers came together and studied their parts in music and drama with enthusiastic devotion. Amalie Materna was the Brünnhilde; Franz Betz was the first Wotan. Musicians from every country in Europe congregated there to hear *The Ring*, and at last Wagner's highest ambition was fulfilled. It is worth while to notice here that this was also the year in which Brahms's first Symphony was produced at Carlsruhe.

The problems were not quite solved yet, however. There was a large deficit on the balance-sheet of the festival, which made the most strenuous efforts necessary if the Bayreuth theatre was to become an established institution. Like many German musicians, Wagner turned to the country most able to supply funds. A visit to England, including festival concerts of his music at the Albert Hall, was his next venture, but some mistakes in management nearly made the venture increase instead of lessen the debt. The situation was saved by some extra concerts, which provided a fairly substantial sum. These concerts, however, did much to give English people a juster view of Wagner's art than they had had before, and with them the general notion that Wagner's music consisted of a noisy orchestra drowning the singers and setting melody at defiance began to wane; it took many years to die.

Only one more event need be mentioned: the second festival at Bayreuth in 1882, when *Parsifal*, his last work, was produced. Wagner called this a 'Bühnen-Weihfestspiel' (a dedicatory festival drama). It was the only one of his operas written for the Bayreuth stage, and he determined that so far as he could ensure this it should be confined to Bayreuth. There his ideal audience could gather in a mood to take in what he felt to be his last and most serious work, and it was the exclusive possession of *Parsifal* which brought pilgrims from all parts of the world to Bayreuth until the year 1914, when it became no longer legally possible to prevent its performance elsewhere. Wagner died at Venice on 13 February 1883, leaving the Festspielhaus to the care of his widow. Under her direction the festival was repeated not every year but for a month or so every two or three years until 1914, when it was cut short on 28 July by Germany's declaration of war, when the audience, coming out from witnessing the death of Siegfried, the end of the gods, and the enveloping of earth and heaven in flame and flood, heard the news which put an end to the Valhalla which Wagner had raised. The festivals were revived in 1924, under the direction of Wagner's son Siegfried, to whom Cosima had handed over the reins in 1908, and after his death in 1930 his widow, Winifred, an Englishwoman by birth, continued the work of administration. Her sons Wolfgang and Wieland resumed activities in 1951, after another interruption in 1944, towards the end of the Second World War.

WHAT WAGNER ACCOMPLISHED

To return, however, to Wagner himself, we have to ask: What did he accomplish? Did he realize that ideal union of the arts and that 'fellowship of all the artists', and did he establish the direction of 'the art-work of the future' by his own mighty achievements in music-drama? We may give the answer 'no' on all these three points, and yet say emphatically that his life's work was a unique and triumphant achievement.

In the first place, his union of all the arts was limited by the fact that his genius was infinitely greater as a musician than as a poet or a dramatist. A master of tone, he was only a very skilful workman with words, and he was unable ultimately to control the third element in his scheme, gesture, which necessarily rested with the interpreters.

Moreover, his overmastering conviction of the moral importance of his ideas made him insist upon explaining himself at every crucial point, and explanation is fatal to drama. He never outgrew this habit. In the first act of *Parsifal*, Gurnemanz seats himself in order to explain at great length, ostensibly to the young knights of the Grail but really to the audience, how the Order was founded, how it fell into decay, and why the wound of Amfortas cannot be healed until the pure knight, a fool in all earthly things but wise in sympathy, shall appear.

Explanations such as these are constant in *The Ring*, where the whole of the complex story has an allegorical meaning; in *Die Meistersinger* they give way to a tendency to harangue the multitudes on principles of artistic criticism; in *Tristan*, save for King Mark's monologue, they are much less insistent, and the fact together with the simplicity of the story brings that work nearest to the ideal union which he had asserted ought to be found. The story itself is poetry, the drama is not cumbered by elaborate scenic effects such as bring *The Ring* at times, and even *Parsifal*, perilously near to the distractions of popular pantomime. If you would realize the fullest extent to which Wagner reached his goal in this direction you should see an intelligent performance of *Tristan* after first carefully reading the poem.

It will be scarcely necessary to give equal preliminary study to the music. Wagner did not write his music to be analysed, nor for that matter did any of the great musicians, though a careful analysis of it may be very helpful. But a careless analysis, particularly that kind which consists of picking out a dozen or more leading themes, fitting each with a name or a character, and 'spotting' them every time they recur, is not helpful. There are people who go to hear Wagner armed with little books of themes, and spend all the time delighting in discovering the appearance of the ring, or Wotan's spear, or Siegfried's sword. They never get much farther in understanding what is going on. It is true that there are themes connected with these and a hundred other things in *The Ring*, so that the process of identification is possible, if unprofitable.

But in *Tristan* the process is scarcely possible because there Wagner is not concerned with 'things' at all, but with what he called 'states of the soul'; and the themes used to express these states are merged into one another and carried forward upon a flood of feeling expressed in music which justifies itself to anyone who knows the poem, and listens with open ears and a sympathetic heart to its unfolding by voice and orchestra.

WAGNER'S MUSICAL PROGRESS

It is time to look more closely into Wagner's development of this strongly individual style, and to do so it is necessary to go back to the first of his distinctive works, *Der fliegende Holländer*. Much has been said by Wagner himself, and by all who have studied his work in the light of what he wrote about it, of his reforming opera on the basis of Beethoven's symphonic music. If, however, we take *Der fliegende Holländer* as his starting-point, we see that song, as it had been developed by Schubert, exerted at least as strong an influence upon him as the symphonic style of Beethoven. The ballad which Senta sings in the second act[1] is the musical core of the whole drama, and if you place that ballad beside the dramatic songs of Schubert, such as 'An Schwager Kronos' and 'Gruppe aus dem Tartarus' (see p. 361), you see at once the likeness of style. In both we get the sweeping declamatory phrases for the voice, in both the illustrative accompaniment,

> Wie saust der Wind,
> Wie pfeift's im Tau!
> (How the wind howls,
> How it whistles through the rigging!)

You can hear it all in the rushing, chromatic passages of the strings and the strident chords of the wind instruments. In the ballad are two personalities. There is the grim, weather-worn seaman condemned to ride the storm year in, year out; there is

[1] A narrative ballad sung in the course of an opera in order to tell the audience what happened before the action begins was a favourite device of French romantic opera. *The Flying Dutchman*, side by side with much that was new and individual, still contains much that follows the operatic conventions of the era immediately preceding it, in the German as well as the French school.

the woman who can save him and bring him rest through her love, and the two are contrasted musically:

Ex. 76

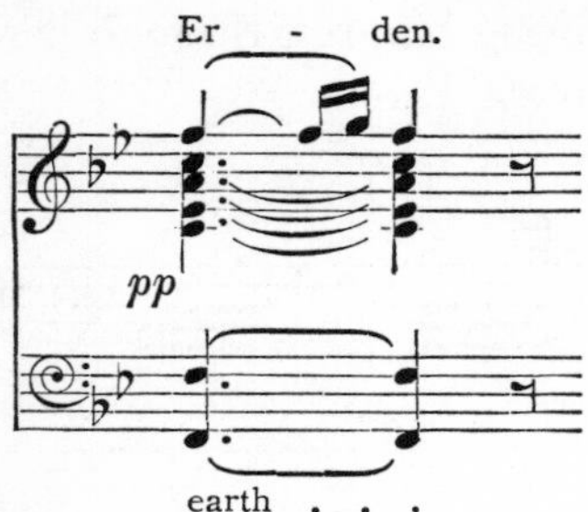

From these two personalities spring, therefore, the leading themes (*Leitmotive*) associated with the characters of the Dutchman and Senta; but realize once and for all that these leading themes are not mere phrases with a label attached to them: they spring spontaneously out of the emotional contrasts of the drama.

The more real Wagner's characters became to him the more constant was his use of the melodies associated with them. In the two works following *Der fliegende Holländer*, *Tannhäuser* and *Lohengrin*, there are still a good many passages where the characters as expressed in the music drop into the background and the progress of the opera is carried on by more conventional means, in the manner of the older forms of opera. Elaborate ensembles, in which all the characters are singing together, are found in these comparatively early works (see, for example, the end of Act I of *Lohengrin*), and in such moments clear characterization is much less definite than in Mozart's great concerted pieces. A general musical effect is all that Wagner aims at; the singers on the stage have more or less to abandon their position as characters to become musical performers.

Later Wagner gave up the employment of such ensembles to a very large extent, and the fact that they were foreign to his style is shown by a comparatively late example, the quintet in the third act of *Die Meistersinger*, which is a high light of the opera, but suspends the action in a way that does not accord with his theories of music-drama. He based his later style more exclusively, so far as the singers were concerned, on dramatic song, and with his firmer grip of the orchestra he raised the illustrative accompaniment to the position of a continuous musical commentary upon the characters, their actions, thoughts, and feelings.

The opening prelude to *Das Rheingold*, a hundred and thirty-six bars all based on a single chord of E flat major, shows the idea of the illustrative accompaniment carried to its farthest point. It is to introduce a scene at the bottom of the Rhine where the Rhine-maidens guard their treasure, the gold from which the ring is afterwards forged. The music is to give the hearers the groundwork of the whole story. Deep beneath the water the forces which are to move the actions of gods and heroes are waiting for their destiny, and the theme first outlined by the horns is one which may be associated with the flow of the river or with the inevitable force of the world. Nothing is more striking in the development of the music of *The Ring* than the way in which its ideas are linked with one another, are actually transformed and grow in musical importance as the drama develops.

Take, for example, one clear instance from *Das Rheingold*: at the end of this first scene, when Alberich the dwarf has seized the gold from the Rhine-maidens and carried it off to forge from it the ring which will give him power over the world, this phrase lingers in the orchestral commentary:

Ex. 77

The textbooks will tell you that this is the motif of the ring. In a sense it is, but it is much more. What it suggests to the mind is not a circle of gold but a sense of hopeless longing; it does not picture an object, it conveys a human feeling. The longing may be the covetous desire of Alberich for power or the sighing of the Rhine-maidens for their lost treasure. Its purport remains undefined, but presently the theme itself is transformed with changes in its intervals, a fuller harmony, a richer orchestration, and a more decisive rhythm; and we hear for the first time a theme to which again the textbooks give a concrete name, the theme of 'Valhalla', the home of Wotan and the gods:

Ex. 78

We see that the two are really one, and from the drama it soon appears that Valhalla itself is the realization of the longing of the gods.

In the gradual extension of an idea we get what may be called by an analogy with symphonic form the principal subject of Wagner's drama, and here comes in the justice of his claim to have remodelled the opera on the basis of Beethoven. For while the four parts of *The Ring*, with all their immense range of character, are on a scale which would be impossible to pure instrumental music, one yet realizes that a wide process of symphonic development is carried through them. Play side by side the first statement of the Valhalla theme by the orchestra as it appears in the twenty bars preceding the second scene of *Rheingold* and the last twenty-eight bars of *Götterdämmerung*, and the process of symphonic development must be clear once and for all.

It was this colossal power of musical development which made it impossible for Wagner to fulfil his theory of the union of the arts. He could not restrain his music from outrunning its companions, poetry and gesture. Musicians may feel that he did something far bigger and far better than the fulfilment of his theory, and they do feel that taking *The Ring* as a whole, when every redundant passage and every tedious repetition has been noted and allowed for, there is such overwhelming force in the musical treatment of the legend that what would be glaring faults according to Wagner's own theory in any smaller work become mere spots in the sun.

The continual progress of musical development from *Rheingold* to *Götterdämmerung* is the more amazing when one recollects the long interruptions which we have seen occurred in the course of the composition of *The Ring*. It is roughly known that the point in the second act of *Siegfried* where Wagner abandoned it in order to compose *Tristan* is somewhere during the hero's soliloquy under the tree, but there is no internal evidence to show it.

Most people will agree that the second act of *Götterdämmerung* is a comparatively weak one, that the chorus of vassals and the trio of Brünnhilde, Hagen, and Gunther with which it ends is a partial return to the old ensemble style which Wagner had put behind him. But that is probably the result of his desire to use up the material of his early scheme for *Siegfrieds Tod*, a lapse which is obliterated by the third act, where the music of *Die Walküre*, *Siegfried*, and the fundamental ideas first shadowed in *Das Rheingold* are summed up and welded into an overwhelming finale.

Neither the subject of *Tristan* nor that of *Die Meistersinger* required anything like the wealth of musical material necessary to *The Ring*. We have spoken of *Tristan* as coming nearest to the theory of union of the arts, and of *Die Meistersinger* as the most lovable of Wagner's works. The natures of the subjects explain both. The delightful character of Hans Sachs, the shoemaker-poet of Nuremberg, his genial views of life, his sympathy and unselfishness, make him unique among Wagner's heroes. Almost everywhere else Wagner's heroes are tainted with his own egotism; what they will is right, and they conquer by their self-assertion. Hans Sachs conquers by his humility, he does not champion his own work but another's, and the whole of the music of *Die Meistersinger* is influenced by the character of Sachs. Except for the places where Wagner cannot resist homilies on art and criticism it is freed from the fetters of his own personality. He is here far more willing to let the listeners take his work in their way rather than in his. One may find in it merely a delightful picture of the old German life of the sixteenth century. The antiquary will find it full of truthful allusions to medieval customs from those of the city guilds to those of musical tablature. The musician can revel in the skill with which three or four melodies develop contrapuntally in the overture. The lover of romance delights equally in the songs of Walther and Eva, the picture of the old street in the moonlight with the watchman droning his call as he goes, and the sunlit festival of St. John's Day. The lover of comedy finds satisfaction in the street brawl and Beckmesser's rough handling by the apprentices. And again, notice that the strength of all these impressions is a musical one. All Wagner's means are perfectly at his command; he never wrote a broader or more firmly knit melody than the 'Preislied', or designed a more vivid and wholly appropriate ensemble than the chorus of the street brawl, or one of greater musical beauty than the quintet.

One might expend many pages in examining the planning of the orchestral commentary, the power with which it bursts into the most vivid prismatic colouring or retires to form a gently suggestive background to the voices.

Enough has been said to show that if we answer the question whether the Wagnerian synthesis of the arts was a success with a negative it is simply because Wagner's powers as a musician were so much greater than those as poet or dramatist that his musical splendour swamps all other considerations.

WAGNER AND OTHER COMPOSERS

Long delayed as Wagner's influence was (it made little impression before the seventies), when it did come it was tremendous and for the time being staggering. Only the very strongest spirits could maintain their individuality against it. Bizet in France and Verdi in Italy were such spirits, and it is quite untrue to say that they succumbed to Wagner, merely because they both used something like the *Leitmotiv*, which indeed they did only to a very moderate extent. A single one is used in Bizet's *Carmen* and in Verdi's *Rigoletto*, for instance, the former associated with Carmen's evil influence on Don José and the latter with Monterone's curse pronounced on Rigoletto. In Verdi's later works (e.g. *La forza del destino*, *Don Carlos*, *Otello*) a greater number of recurrent themes are used, and in *Aida* the heroine has a motif of her own, but these things are reminiscences used in a more purely musical way than in Wagner. Later still Puccini, although clearly intending to imitate Wagner, extended Verdi's rather than Wagner's practice.

It was the second-rate composers in every European country who became more thoroughly 'Wagnerized'. He taught so much, he showed so many possibilities of orchestral sound never before realized, he had so dominating a way of expressing himself, that weaker spirits could not resist the temptation to copy him. But all the composers whose work has lasted, and whom therefore we are to study in the following chapters, resisted the temptation; and the one great follower, Richard Strauss, who began by imitating Wagner's methods closely in *Guntram* and *Feuersnot*, soon learnt to use a closely woven thematic texture in a way of his own. The crowd of Wagnerian operas which were poured out by various composers in Germany amounted to very little of real importance. Of the young composers who gathered round Wagner in his later years, and owned him as a leader, only one, Engelbert Humperdinck (born 1854), need here be mentioned. His delicious children's opera *Hänsel und Gretel* is indeed moulded on Wagner's style, but the style is so differently applied to the simple folk-story of the children lost in the wood, the whole is so fresh in its melody, so apt in its orchestral commentary, that it stands alone. The actual sound of Humperdinck's score is unmistakably Wagnerian, but the simple, popular material is entirely different; so that when for once Wagner uses an artless little German lullaby in the *Siegfried Idyll*, his music in turn sounds for a moment like Humperdinck's.

GIUSEPPE VERDI (1813–1901) began his long career as a

writer of Italian operas in the traditional manner of recitative, aria, and ensemble numbers, which he inherited from his countrymen of the first part of the century. An extraordinary power of depicting a graphic situation in a vocal melody was from first to last characteristic of him, and in the greater number of his operas that power was all-sufficing for his needs. Many of his works, such as *Il trovatore*, *La traviata*, and *Rigoletto* (none of these is among his earliest ones), have an irresistible grip upon the imagination by their sheer force of melody, and *Aida*, written in 1871, is a unique example of a romantic story told entirely in a series of broad and intensely expressive tunes.

Certainly, there could be no doubt about Verdi's individuality, and his reputation at the time he wrote *Aida* was far wider than Wagner's own. Sixteen years followed before he wrote another opera. Wagner's great works had become worldwide possessions, and all the musical world had gone after him, spurning Italian opera, and Verdi amongst it, as a plaything with which *prime donne* amused their admirers, when Verdi produced his *Otello* and followed it with *Falstaff*. A tragedy and a comedy, both founded upon Shakespeare, with finely written libretti by Boito, a literary man and himself a composer of no mean order, suggested a new fellowship of the artists, and one coming not from Germany but from Italy. It was said at the time that many lessons from Wagner were embodied in these works: the plots were developed in continuous music through the whole scene, the musical style was made flexible to the dramatic situation in the way that Wagner advocated. But it was the same Verdi, the same man of eloquent melodies, without desire to preach or to teach, merely anxious to express what was in him. His art had always been free from contemporary influences, though not, in his earlier career, from those of his immediate Italian predecessors. He studied few scores and possessed even fewer, and living retired in his country house of Sant' Agata, rarely visited the larger towns, where he occasionally heard some new opera or another, usually by an Italian composer. He had known *Lohengrin* ever since its performance at Bologna in 1871, but that work contained next to none of the elements that were supposed to have affected *Otello* and *Falstaff*, and with the later Wagner he was only very vaguely familiar. On the other hand he had long ago made use of thematic reminiscence and even of something like leading motifs (e.g. the Curse theme in *Rigoletto*), certainly without so much as thinking of Wagner as a model.

What was really new in these last two Shakespearian masterpieces, and indeed to a great extent already in *Aida* and such other mature operas as *Simon Boccanegra* or *Don Carlos*, is entirely and individually Verdian: a richer and much more eloquent orchestration, which surprisingly often relegates the voice to a subordinate function for a moment, and an ever more resourceful and original use of harmony. And in *Falstaff* Verdi is seen to have finally arrived at a refinement that had certainly not been one of his virtues earlier in his life even in the eyes of his greatest admirers. He had often not so much transgressed against good taste as simply refused to recognize it as a desirable quality; but in *Falstaff* it seems impossible to lay one's finger on a single incident, from first to last, that could give offence even to the most fastidious critic. There is also, in both Shakespeare operas, a new kind of poetical quality, expressed by music of the most exquisite beauty—poignant in the extreme in *Otello* and enchantingly tender or fairy-like in *Falstaff*. Verdi's harmonic originality, which produces a flavour quite unknown in any other composer, is just a matter of letting quite ordinary chords progress in a very uncommon way, as in *Aida*, for example:

Ex. 79

At other times it can be so novel as to anticipate considerably later music—Elgar in *Falstaff* (very appropriately):

Ex. 80 *Allegro.*

and even Delius in *Otello*:

Ex. 81 *Andantino.*

French opera also developed independently of Wagner where it remained most truly itself. Where the influence did assert itself, as for example in Chabrier's *Gwendoline*, and in works by Vincent d'Indy, Alfred Bruneau, Ernest Chausson, and others, it remained an alien intruder. Debussy's *Pelléas et Mélisande* makes use of leading themes, but is nevertheless at the opposite pole from Wagnerism. Bizet's *Carmen*, a quarter of a century earlier, was, as Nietzsche said, the ideal 'Mediterranean' music, and it was in fact the chief cause of that philosopher's alienation from Wagner's work, which he had begun by admiring as ardently as he was personally devoted to the composer against whom he afterwards turned his keenest literary shafts.

Two masters of opera who began their careers at the end of the nineteenth century had better be mentioned here, although their work belongs to the twentieth: GIACOMO PUCCINI (1858–1924) and RICHARD STRAUSS (1864–1949). Their operas vary considerably in quality and meet with very different critical judgements, even at their best; but they are the only two composers of their time who have held the stage of every country that cultivates opera as purveyors of repertory works enjoying the widest possible popularity. Puccini is, of course, most assiduously cultivated in Italy, and Strauss in German-speaking countries; but although elsewhere there are always opera-goers who do not care for their work, their success has been very little inferior to that which their favourite works enjoy at home. These are, in Puccini's case, *La Bohème* (1897), *Tosca* (1900), and *Madam Butterfly* (1904), and in Strauss's *Salome* (1905), *Elektra* (1909), and *Der Rosenkavalier* (1911).

These two were in many ways entirely different musicians: while Strauss was also an eminent orchestral and song writer, Puccini was all but exclusively devoted to opera. The German was also a more profound thinker, who approached his technical problems with a great awareness and responsibility, choosing his subjects with literary discernment and his librettists, including the poet Hugo von Hofmannsthal, with extreme care.

The Italian was a much more instinctive artist, happier with subjects of a sensationally theatrical nature. On the other hand they resembled each other in being ruthlessly exacting in their demands on their librettists; in writing music of a broad effectiveness that often serves opera admirably where it would seem crude in absolute music, or even in programme music (as it sometimes does in Strauss's); in a certain lack of refinement in taste or consistency in style; and above all in an unfailing sureness in the handling of dramatic situations. Strauss has a great gift of delineating stage personages, even down to characteristic turns of speech, whereas Puccini's all sing more or less the same kind of music; on the other hand the latter excels in matching the atmosphere of any scene, even the time of day and the temperature, with music that wonderfully enhances it.

The early works of Puccini, except *Manon Lescaut* (1893), and two after *Butterfly* are not in the current repertory, but two of the one-act operas in the *Triptych* (1918), *Il tabarro*, and the comedy *Gianni Schicchi*, are perfected masterpieces of their kind; and in his unfinished *Turandot* (prod. 1926) he made use in his own high-handed way of many modern devices which in the hands of others had been mere experiments, and achieved a sumptuousness of orchestration not inferior to and more subtle than that of Strauss at his best. Strauss maintained his astonishing technical skill to the last, but did not often reach the same level of inspiration as he had still done in *Ariadne auf Naxos* (1912, rev. 1916), perhaps his best and certainly his most original work for the stage.

Suggestions for Further Reading and Listening

DESPITE the passage of time, Ernest Newman's monumental *The Life of Richard Wagner*, in four volumes, remains the standard biography. The reader coming fresh to Wagner would, however, be well advised to defer tackling it until he has digested any of the many shorter biographical studies, and in fact the survey printed in Chapter 19 fills the bill admirably. At that point, he could embark upon Newman's concise *Wagner as Man and Artist* before undertaking *The Life*. Wagner himself was a compulsive writer as well as composer, and those with leisure can grind their way through his *Prose Works*. Of these, by far the most significant is his 'Opera and Drama', the contents of which have been skilfully summarized by Gerald Abraham in his *A Hundred Years of Music*.

For a closer look at the operas themselves, Newman's *Wagner Nights* (which omits the earlier lesser known works) is a sure recommendation. *The Ring* is a special case, subject as it is to endless reinterpretation: the best guide to the whole cycle is Aylmer Buesst's *The Nibelung's Ring*. (It goes without saying that Bernard Shaw's quirkily enthusiastic encomia on Wagner have lost little of their point and pungency.) Three other recent books deserve mention. John Culshaw's *Reflections on Wagner's 'Ring'* consists of a series of interval talks, by-products of a recording of the operas in Vienna during the 1960s. Another is Bryan Magee's thoughtful *Aspects of Wagner*. *Wagner's 'Ring' and its Symbols* by Robert Donington looks forbidding, but this post-Jungian analysis of the cycle is not only absorbingly interesting but also accessible to all.

As for the other composers mentioned towards the end of the chapter, Dyneley Hussey's and Francis Toye's books on Verdi have their merits, but they are superseded by Frank Walker's biography and Julian Budden's two-volume scrutiny of Verdi's operas. On the other hand, Spike Hughes's *Famous Verdi Operas* may be more suitable for quick reference. Mina Curtiss's *Bizet and his World* is unchallenged as a straight biography, but for the best and most up to date evaluation of the man and his music see Winton Dean's *Bizet* in the 'Master Musicians' series.

The leading authority in English on Puccini is Mosco Carner, and the writings on Richard Strauss include Michael Kennedy's critical biography in the 'Master Musicians' series, Norman del Mar's three-volume account of Strauss's life and works, and William Mann's study of the operas. The composer's own *Recollections and Reflections* are available in English, as is his correspondence with Hugo von Hoffmansthal. Recordings of operas are nowadays furnished with copious documentation, including librettos, and Kobbé's *Complete Opera Book* answers most of the questions that devotees of opera are likely to ask.

CHAPTER 20

Chamber Music and the Symphony

THERE is no surer sign of a musically cultivated people than their forwardness in the production and performance of concerted chamber music. Look back through history and you will realize the truth of this. The madrigal is the first instance (see p. 14). Springing into life in the Netherlands, among what was then the most musically cultivated people, it won its way in Italy in the sixteenth century and then in England, because its very existence depended upon the association of a number of people in a common interest, and in those countries many shared the interest of music. You can test the temper of a people by discovering what they do when they meet together for social intercourse. They talk politics, or they play games, or they make music. In the England of Queen Elizabeth II it is generally one of the former; in the England of Elizabeth I's reign, though politics were fully as absorbing as they are today, the educated classes of society occupied themselves very largely with concerted music, first the madrigal, then concerted instrumental music for viols (see pp. 44–5). At that time a distinctive form of English concerted music—chamber music, as we now call it—came into being and was widely practised both by professional and amateur musicians.

The very name 'chamber music' suggests its chief condition. It is the music which flourishes not as part of a public function, such as a concert or an opera performance, but in the home. You do not judge of a man's literary taste by the books which he keeps in handsome bindings in a room he uses only on great occasions; you get at the shelves in his private den and pick out the volumes which are worn and shabby with use. So with a country's music. Any nation can keep up an appearance of musical taste by a succession of public concerts and operas, but when you find its people practising quartets and other concerted music, vocal or instrumental, for their own pleasure in their own homes, then you know that a real musical life is there. That was the musical life of England in the seventeenth century, and it has begun again in the twentieth where the radio and the gramophone have not reduced it entirely to passive listening.

But the general practice of instrumental concerted music means a higher state of musical cultivation than concerted vocal music implies, for to enjoy that you have to be able to think in terms of music itself, apart from its association with words, and further, it means a more advanced technical education. People can sing to a certain extent by the light of nature; it requires comparatively small training to enable any one with a good natural voice to sing well in a madrigal, but even Doctor Johnson, that most unmusical of Englishmen, saw that the case is very different with a stringed instrument.

> There is nothing, I think, in which the power of art is shown so much as in playing on the fiddle. In all other things we can do something at first. Any man can forge a bar of iron if you give him a hammer; not so well as a smith, but tolerably. A man will saw a piece of wood, and make a box, though a clumsy one; but give him a fiddle and a fiddlestick, and he can do nothing.

So concerted music for stringed instruments flourishes wherever the musical perception is not only strong, but technically developed. It is found in the seventeenth and eighteenth centuries in the violin schools of Italy from Corelli to Tartini (see pp. 170–3), then in the string quartets of Viennese society developed under Haydn's influence (pp. 178 et seq.), a great movement, the greatest which this form of art has ever known, in which Mozart, Beethoven, and Schubert all shared.

MENDELSSOHN AND SPOHR

Mendelssohn's upbringing surrounded him with chamber music. At those Sunday parties in his father's house, every kind of music for instruments was played by the artists who came there week by week (see p. 405). His own first three opus numbers consist of quartets for piano and strings, and many of his best early works are for some combination or other of solo instruments. Amongst them is the Octet for strings which was written in 1825, the year in which Spohr, one of the greatest violinists of the time, visited the Mendelssohns.

Louis Spohr (1784–1859), besides being a great player, was a most prolific composer. His reputation was then at its height, and his visit to Berlin was for the performance of his most successful opera, *Jessonda*. But though he made himself famous on the Continent as a composer of opera, and in England as a composer of oratorio, his violin music was his point of real distinction. His concertos are still studied by violinists because they are models of style in the art of instrumental phrasing, and he also carried his faultless violin style into the quartets and double quartets which are his most important contribution to chamber music.

The great solo player is not the man, however, who most readily produces great concerted music. Spohr so frequently thought of the first violin as a solo part accompanied by the other instruments that his works of this kind have a rather lop-sided effect. We have seen how Haydn developed the polyphonic equality of the members of the string quartet (pp. 178 et seq.), and that equality is the first principle of all good quartet writing. Spohr had a considerable influence on Mendelssohn, who learnt much from him as to effective writing for the violin. The lessons were never forgotten, and they bore fruit years afterwards in that wonderful clearness of phraseology which makes Mendelssohn's violin concerto one of the great masterpieces of musical literature. The Octet, however, especially in its first movement, gives instances of the tendency to think of the top part first, which is a less profitable result of Spohr's example. Only in the Scherzo, a movement of exuberant gaiety handled with exquisite delicacy, does Mendelssohn's genius appear perfectly at ease, and, as we have already seen

(p. 415), that was the type of movement which flowed most directly from his nature.

All through his life Mendelssohn continued to compose music for strings with or without the piano. The series of string quartets was begun with that now known as No. 2 in A, in Berlin, 1827; No. 1 in E flat, having a peculiarly fresh and charming melody as a principal theme which recurs again at the end of the Finale, was written in London in 1829; and three more quartets, published together as Op. 44, were written in Berlin (1837–8). Just before his death, during that last sad visit to Switzerland, he tried to bring himself back to life by the composition of a string quartet (in F minor) which was published after his death as Op. 80.

This last fact may be taken to emphasize the peculiar intimacy of quartet music. It is the one of all the means of musical expression in which the composer's thought is delivered most directly to his listeners. Without the advantages of strong contrasts of tone such as orchestral music naturally possesses, or of personal interpretation such as is always a powerful element in solo piano music, it does not lend itself to illustration of literary ideas as both the orchestra and the piano do. The listener to a quartet asks simply, 'What has the composer got to say?' and the more he has to say the more he turns to this ungarnished way of saying it.

SCHUMANN'S CHAMBER MUSIC

Schumann, as we have seen, came to chamber music comparatively late in his career, and his three string quartets were all composed together and dedicated to Mendelssohn, whose example he followed in writing them. There were many things in Schumann's habit of mind which disposed him more naturally to this sort of music than Mendelssohn was disposed. The *Innigkeit* (inwardness) which led him to that richly polyphonic style in his piano music is just, one would think, the quality of the great quartet writer, and many evidences of it appear especially in the last of the three, the beautiful work in A major.

But Schumann's mind was so formed by the piano that he could never think with equal freedom away from it, and, moreover, his music is always most at ease when it is couched in concise and clearly cut forms. *Carnaval*, with its quick succession of character studies, the *Études symphoniques*, in which each idea is worked out at once and left for another one, all the sets of short piano pieces, whatever their form or their title, have this in common.

In the quartets as in the piano sonatas, fine as they are, one comes across places where the development of the thought is not quite continuous, where a new idea is introduced a little abruptly or impatiently, or where an old one is reverted to because the form requires a repetition. Schumann's chamber music is at its happiest, and flows most smoothly where the piano is combined with the strings, in the trios (particularly those in D minor and G minor), in his one Quartet for piano and strings in E flat, and most of all in the noble Quintet for piano and strings in the same key. In such works he is completely at home with his means of expression; the piano supplies the groundwork most congenial to him, and the strings suggest innumerable flights of fancy which carry his imagination forward without a check. They are full of the glowing spirit of romance, yet the spirit expresses itself easily in the well-balanced form of the sonata.

It was this same capacity which Schumann perceived in the early work of Brahms and heralded with his famous article. He found a musical nature as deep as his own, but expressed with a craftsmanship which had been quite impossible to himself at the age of twenty years. Brahms seemed to have all the advantages of Mendelssohn's skill without the disadvantages of Mendelssohn's facility. And how had all this come about?

LIFE OF BRAHMS

JOHANNES BRAHMS was born at Hamburg on 7 May 1833, and was the son, not of a prosperous Jewish banker, but of a German musician who was anything but prosperous. Johann Jakob Brahms, the father, played two instruments—the horn and the double-bass; and though it is recorded of him that as a young man he had run away from home in order to devote himself to music, there is nothing to suggest that he was a musical genius in the real sense of the term. We have seen so many instances of geniuses who flouted parental authority for the sake of their art, that it is just as well to realize that it is quite possible to flout parental authority without being a genius. In fact, if we could collect the names of all the young people who insisted on becoming musicians in spite of their parents' wishes, we should realize that those who have afterwards justified themselves by gaining lasting distinction have been very few.

The elder Brahms himself became nothing more than an undistinguished player in the theatre orchestra at Hamburg; but he also became the father of Johannes, and he knew enough of music to give his son such education as was possible. If Brahms had written nothing more than the horn Trio we should still be thankful that his father was a horn-player. Throughout his life, whenever he wrote a passage for the horn it was with an intimate knowledge, one might almost say an affection, which was rooted in the memory of his father's playing. Perhaps this is accountable for his persistent clinging to the old natural brass instruments and his dislike of the valve horns.

There is nothing of special moment to record in Brahms's early life. The family was always poor; he got excellent piano teaching from Marxsen, a well-known teacher, but he had to earn a living as soon as possible, and the only possible way he could find of beginning to do so was to undertake work as pianist at a very rough and rather dubious café, a resort of sailors, where the atmosphere was anything but favourable to the formation of an artist. But his character took no harm, apart from a certain uncouthness of manners he always retained; and when he got rare opportunities of appearing in public as a pianist he chose the music which he really cared for —Bach, Mozart, and Beethoven—and he made no attempt to startle the multitudes by a brilliant performance, as he might have done, for his powers as a pianist were of the finest.

Not long before his meeting with Schumann, however, his prospects began to open out. He had a chance of touring as accompanist to a clever Hungarian violinist called Reményi, and in this capacity he travelled to a good many of the towns of northern Germany. The connexion first brought Brahms into touch with Magyar or rather Hungarian Gipsy music, and that in itself would be a sufficient outcome to make the tour important, when we remember the sets of Hungarian dances which he arranged soon afterwards for piano duet, the last movement of the Quartet for piano and strings in G minor, which, like that of Haydn's first Trio, is a Gipsy rondo, and the rhythm of the Finale to the violin Concerto.

But other consequences followed, for it was on this tour that he came across Joachim at Hanover, and, as we have seen, it was Joachim who sent him to Schumann. Joachim has told us what it was that first showed him the immense possibilities of Brahms's genius. Brahms carried a number of his compositions with him and worked at them assiduously, though there was little possibility of their being heard at such concerts as Reményi cared to give. Some were shown to Joachim, among them the beautiful song 'Liebestreu' ('True love'), and its deep and searching melody impressed him at once.

A student cannot do better than begin his knowledge of Brahms with that song. In it you find an epitome of everything which is most characteristic of him. A deep stirring emotion, not violent or passionate but intensely strong, is the chief feature. Brahms's melodies frequently soar over wide-sweeping arpeggio figures, as this does in its first phrase,[1] and the reflection of the melody in the bass of the piano as though one saw it mirrored in deep waters, a suggestion which the words supply in this instance, gives that rich sonorousness which was generally more dear to him than vividness of colouring.

We may feel sure that this song was uppermost in Schumann's

[1] See also 'Weit über das Feld', Op. 3 No. 4.

mind when he spoke of 'songs, whose poetry one would understand without knowing the words, though all are pervaded by a deep song melody'.[1] Schumann also speaks of 'sonatas, more like veiled symphonies, single pianoforte pieces, partly demoniacal, of the most graceful form—then sonatas for violin and piano—quartets for strings—and every one so different from the rest that each seemed to flow from a separate source'.

In this account we can identify the piano Sonata, Op. 1, which with its extraordinarily full writing in many parts is almost more than the two hands of any ordinary pianist can be expected to compass, and may well be described as a 'veiled symphony'; also the Scherzo in E flat minor, Op. 4, which probably suggested the epithet 'demoniacal'. But the early violin sonatas and string quartets have vanished, torn up or burnt by their composer, who had a short way of dealing with whatever of his music seemed to him immature. In the circumstances it is surprising that the Sonata for piano and the Scherzo survived. Their early publication probably saved them. Once published it was too late for second thoughts, but neither strikes us now as fully representing the mature Brahms. The latter is so like Chopin's second Scherzo in B flat minor (Op. 31) in its chief theme[2] that it is worth while to put the two side by side, and to do so shows that Chopin's is far superior in grace of style and understanding of piano effect, though Brahms's has a certain sturdy strength which is foreign to Chopin.

EARLY PUBLICATIONS

A glance at the works published in 1853–4, the time when Brahms's friendship with Joachim and the Schumanns was forming itself, will help to fix in mind some more of the main characteristics of his art. They include the three piano Sonatas (in C, F sharp minor, and F minor) with the set of Variations

[1] The quotations are from the English translation of Schumann's article given in Miss Florence May's *Life of Johannes Brahms*, vol. i, p. 127.

[2] Brahms afterwards said that he did not know Chopin's scherzo when he wrote his own.

on a Theme by Schumann, dedicated to Clara Schumann, with eighteen songs (Opp. 3, 6, and 7).

Brahms was anything but the abstract musician that many people have supposed him to be. There is a story at the back of all his great works, but it is a personal story, not a dramatic one like the stories of Berlioz or Liszt, and it is told only in music. This accounts for the curious contradictions of the early criticisms of Brahms's music. At one time he would be described as a romantic dreamer, at another as a classical student whose art consisted in attaining a well-calculated balance of form. He was both and he was neither. He could dream, but he could also study, and he had a passion for making his dreams come true in his music, that is, for giving them form and substance; but he was no more entirely devoted to form for its own sake than he was to dreams for their own sakes. At first in the piano sonatas you may find a certain amount of struggle going on between the two artistic needs; in the years immediately following their production, when he settled down to the composition of chamber music, they became, as it were, the complement of one another.

DEVELOPMENTS IN CHAMBER MUSIC

The next few years of Brahms's life after Schumann's death were spent in a variety of activities partly at his father's home in Hamburg, and partly at Detmold, the capital of a small state between Hanover and Westphalia, then ruled by a Prince, Leopold, who, with his family and small court, was devoted to music of the finest types. An appointment there to teach and play provided the ideal surroundings for Brahms's progress in chamber music, surroundings which, though on a smaller scale, were not unlike those in which Haydn himself had developed the quartet at Esterház (p. 194).

One might almost say that the small courts of Germany were the making of chamber music, and that their subsequent obliteration in the German Empire destroyed it. At any rate, at this time we see Joachim at Hanover and Brahms at Detmold the one as violinist, the other as pianist, developing their art by means of the support which these institutions afforded them. At Detmold Brahms took part in all the great chamber music then existing, and in particular deepened his knowledge of Mozart and learnt to know Schubert thoroughly for the first time.

The Sextet for strings in B flat (Op. 18) gives clear examples of the influence of both these great masters upon him. Its slow movement, a theme with variations, ought to be compared with the 'Tod und das Mädchen' variations in Schubert's Quartet in D minor. The theme itself has a Schubert-like cast of melody and harmony, and the variations, though more complex than Schubert's, bear out the resemblance.

A glance at the final rondo and a little attention to the way Brahms plays with the cadence figure of the principal theme will show how he absorbed Mozart's methods of development (cf. pp. 245–6), and yet all through the work there is something which is unmistakably Brahms, that breadth and earnestness which we found in the first of his songs and sonatas, and which, however much it may be softened by a supple grace of movement, never leaves his thought.

The two Quartets for piano and strings (Op. 25 in G minor, and Op. 26 in A major) were further products of these years, Brahms took part in the first performance of the G minor Quartet at Detmold in 1859; that in A was first played at Hanover two or three years later. To appreciate the truth of what has been said of the personal story behind Brahms's music, you have only to listen to one or other of these works.

Take, for example, the two middle movements of the Quartet in G minor. One is called 'Intermezzo'; the other has no title save its direction of tempo, 'andante con moto'. The Intermezzo is long, with a trio which purposely presents no strong contrast of mood, and after the trio there is a full repetition of the first part with a coda. The violin is muted, the direction 'una corda' is found in the piano part; incessant triplet figures of quavers pervade one part or another, all the melodies contain prominent drooping figures. The whole of the music in fact is in a dim light; the parts interlace delicately like the overhanging branches of trees.

To pass from this subdued beauty to the first melody of the Andante is like coming from the depths of a wood into the uplands of the open country. The violin and violoncello lead off with a broad melody in octaves which the viola enriches with middle harmonies. The piano part expands into a rolling counterpoint, also in octaves. But this is not the only contrast. The movement stirs, becomes more agitated, more vocal. Notice the incisive string figures above rapid piano arpeggios. Then a new rhythm like the tramp of marching feet comes in the piano part, and soon we find ourselves in the full swing of the march. The tide of human life and energy advances, and though that too passes, it leaves a permanent mark. We cannot return to the complete calm in which the movement opened, and the repetition is scored with a fullness which makes it more vital than the conventional repetition of ternary form.

See how completely free from the conventions as distinct from the principles of form these movements are. One expects at their point in a quartet a slow movement and a scherzo, Brahms gives us neither. The 'Intermezzo' is marked allegro, but its subdued feeling makes its emotional place in the scheme nearest to that of the slow movement, while all the qualities of pulsing life which we associate with the idea of a scherzo are found in the middle of the Andante, literally the movement at a walking pace.

Brahms was in fact particularly fond of breaking away from the conventional distinctions of style in his middle movements. He rarely writes a regular scherzo in triple time, such as the one in the first sextet; he constantly either chooses some less usual rhythm (such as $\frac{2}{4}$, $\frac{4}{8}$, or $\frac{6}{8}$)[1] for his scherzo movement, or else alternates two moods producing an entirely new kind of design, as in the second string Quartet (Op. 51 No. 2), the string

[1] See Quintet for piano and strings, Op. 34, string Quartet, Op. 51 No. 1, piano Quartet in C minor, Op. 60.

Quintet in F (Op. 88), the clarinet Quintet.[1] In the first three of his four symphonies an allegretto movement of infinite graciousness replaces the scherzo.

With the two piano Quartets and the great Quintet in F minor for piano and strings (Op. 34) he had definitely moulded his musical outlook with the help of his experiences at Detmold, and at the same time he had composed a large quantity of songs and other vocal pieces. The appearance in the list of his works at this time of a number of concerted pieces for women's voices recalls another of his occupations. At Hamburg he conducted a choir of ladies, for whom he wrote the four songs for women's voices with accompaniment for horns and harp, the 'Marienlieder' ('Songs of Mary'), and other things. And he took particular pleasure in this work.

But his public career was not progressing rapidly. He had made staunch friends in the musical world, and had made some enemies, partly through his own rough carelessness of behaviour. Some of his music had received a good deal of comment, and his Concerto for piano in D minor, his only big orchestral work so far, had been paid the compliment of abuse. It was time for him to undertake some bigger executive work, and to get some wider experience than merely that of musical life in North Germany.

FIRST VISIT TO VIENNA

He was in his thirtieth year when, in the autumn of 1862, he paid his first visit to Vienna. This visit, like Schumann's, was an experiment, but he found more of a welcome than Schumann had found, and indeed he had more to offer. He did not propose to write about music; it is noticeable that Brahms, unlike most of the great men of the nineteenth century, had no leanings towards criticism or essay writing. The one written document to which he put his name produced such unfortunate results that

[1] The middle movement of the Sonata in A for violin and piano (Op. 100) is perhaps the simplest example of this habit for purposes of illustration.

it naturally confirmed him in his determination to make music rather than words about it.

This document appeared about two years before Brahms's visit to Vienna and deserves mention, for it has some historical importance. It was in fact a manifesto against the *Neue Zeitschrift für Musik*, which by this time was a very different paper from what it had been in Schumann's day. It was employed in supporting the ideas of programme music with which Liszt was specially identified, and in so doing it went so far as to assume that practically all musicians of any consequence gave their allegiance to those ideas. This was too much for Brahms and Joachim, whose views, as we have seen, were of a very different kind, and they drew up a short protest, which they invited others to sign with them. Their action helped to foment a sort of party warfare which became a deplorable feature of musical life in Germany. People talked as though 'programme' music and 'classical' music were necessarily opposed, and as though to admire one must be to despise the other. However, we have seen that music is not necessarily interesting because it illustrates some other idea, nor necessarily admirable because it is in sonata form. It is the spirit behind both that matters.

Brahms, once he had learnt not to talk but to act, made it one of his first actions in Vienna to offer his own piano-playing and the Quartet in A major. He stayed there through the winter, and the impression that he and his music created is summed up by the fact that he returned there in the autumn of the next year to take up the post of conductor of the 'Singakademie', one of the chief choral societies of Vienna. This was the beginning of the permanent change of home from North Germany to Vienna, in which Brahms's career is a parallel to Beethoven's, and, as in Beethoven's case, it is almost the only event of salient importance apart from his work itself (cf. p. 307). Though he did not hold the conductorship for very long he became rooted in Vienna, which he soon learned to love, and had it not been for the existence of railway trains which carried him easily back to Germany for concerts and other musical functions, or to

Switzerland and elsewhere for holidays, he would probably have become as immovable as Beethoven did.

CHORAL WORKS AND SYMPHONIES

It is time to say a word about Brahms's symphonies. We have seen him developing through the early piano music to concerted chamber music. When, his friends wondered, would he go a step farther and, as Schumann had said, 'sink his magic staff in the region where the capacity of masses in chorus and orchestra can lend him its powers'. In the years after he reached Vienna, he went on producing one fine chamber work after another. The strongly poetical horn Trio was played for the first time in 1865, and the first of the three existing string quartets was composed the next year. At about this time he also began to turn to choral composition on a larger scale than the early works for women's voices. His mother died in 1865, and the composition of the Requiem, parts of which had long been in mind, was definitely undertaken. The Rhapsody for alto voice, men's chorus, and orchestra to words by Goethe, the *Schicksalslied* ('Song of Fate') for mixed choir and orchestra, and the *Triumphlied* followed in fairly rapid succession. The last, for double chorus, solo voices, and orchestra, was composed to celebrate the victories of the Franco-Prussian War and the establishment of the German Empire under William I. Alone of Brahms's larger choral works it has found no favour in England.

Still Brahms delayed to write anything of consequence for the orchestra alone. A letter which he wrote before his first visit to Vienna tells us that he was even then engaged upon the Symphony in C minor, but that was fourteen years before it was actually produced. He was always tremendously conscientious about his work, sometimes inclined to become conscience-ridden over it. Majestic and splendid as the first Symphony is, one cannot help feeling that he allowed himself too much reflection in the shaping of it. The first movement has some of the struggling insistence upon themes which made the piano Concerto in D minor seem incomprehensible when it was first written. One grows up to the admiration of both works, but neither has the clear spontaneous style which makes the first movement of the second Symphony immediately lovable.

And here we may notice that having achieved one symphony with apparent difficulty, Brahms almost immediately wrote another with the utmost ease. His works often appear in pairs. The two piano Quartets (Opp. 25 and 26), the two string Quartets (Op. 51), the two overtures called the 'Academic' and the 'Tragic' are other examples, and the pairs are always strongly contrasted. In no case do they represent a wish to repeat a success or to say the same thing over again, but having used a form for one purpose, the experience quickly suggested something else which might be done with it.

The symphonies of Brahms grow as naturally out of his style in chamber music as Haydn's symphonies grow from his string quartet. They are not, like the symphonies of Berlioz, the outcome of the elaborate technique of the modern orchestra. Certain passages, it is true, belong undeniably to the instruments which play them. Compare the two allegretto movements of the first and second symphonies and you find that the tune of the first belongs as unmistakably to the liquid tone of the clarinet as that of the second to the plaintive chirp of the oboe. Imagine the instruments interchanged and you see that both would be spoilt. But in these and similar instances Brahms is using the instruments individually just as they would be used in chamber music, as he did in fact use the clarinet in the quintet, the trio, and the two sonatas which he wrote later for it.

In passages for the full orchestra or for many instruments the qualities of sound are much less closely considered. The sound of the orchestra was not his main object; sometimes he could be almost careless about it so long as the lines of the melodic development were clearly expressed. Wherever an instrument is acting as an individual it is sure to be perfectly disposed in Brahms's scores; when it is one of a crowd its place may not be so appropriate. Berlioz and Wagner both managed their orchestral crowds perfectly, and so, placed beside them, Brahms's orchestration seems elementary. But Berlioz's idea of a symphonic design seems far more elementary when it is placed beside Brahms's, because Berlioz had never had the opportunity which chamber music had given to Brahms of thinking purely and simply in musical terms.

The first Symphony raised almost as much discussion as the early piano Concerto had done. Unfortunately by this time the terms classic and modern were considered to be incompatible, and Brahms was looked upon as the champion of the former against the latter. While one side thought the Symphony a masterpiece the other would see no good in it, and some of its friends in a misguided wish to praise it to the skies christened it the 'tenth symphony', meaning, of course, that it was a successor to Beethoven's ninth. It is only necessary to put the principal tune of the Finale of Brahms's first Symphony beside that of the Finale of the choral Symphony to see that the two are much alike. Brahms himself said, 'Any fool could see that', but also anyone who is not a fool realizes that his is an absolutely distinct creation. Though Beethoven's works were among the strongest and most abiding influences in Brahms's life he never reproduced their manner or their matter in his own music. This very movement is the strongest example of the free hand Brahms could give himself when he chose in the matter of form. A conventionally minded musician would have blazed this tune out in a final recapitulation for full orchestra; Brahms uses it only as a starting-point, and the ecstatic climax reached in the coda merely alludes to its rhythm without repeating it formally. The whole movement, from the mysterious introduction with its solemn horn call and the agitated pizzicato passages for strings, to this climax, has the vividness of graphic programme music, but its features are welded into an ideal shape. Again we feel the human story at the back of the music.

In the years after the production of the first two symphonies Brahms's life only altered in the fact that the wide recognition of his choral and orchestral works brought him more into touch with the outside world. These years were filled with big compositions. There was the violin Concerto written for Joachim and first performed by him at Leipzig, and the violin Sonata in G (1879), and he also launched out into a new phase of music for the piano alone in the Capricci and Intermezzi published as Op. 76 and the two Rhapsodies (Op. 79).

The third and fourth Symphonies (No. 3 in F and No. 4 in E minor) form another pair a few years later, and again they offer a very remarkable contrast of design. No. 3 leaps into existence with a tremendous exuberance. Like the month of March it comes in like a lion and goes out like a lamb. In its last movement it sinks away in a *diminuendo* to a *pianissimo*, and this quiet ending is definitely connected with the exuberant first movement by the use of a quotation from it.

Ex. 82

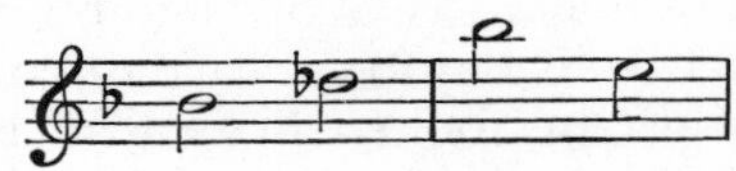

The fourth Symphony, on the other hand, opens with almost repressed quietude, using only a small orchestra, which is increased in the later movements much as Beethoven's orchestra was increased in the fifth Symphony (see p. 333). It ends in a majestic passacaglia, or ground bass (see pp. 70, 81–82, 120), summing up all Brahms's tremendous power of varying and decorating a simple but powerful theme.

There have been many people who have complained that this last of Brahms's symphonic finales is 'dry'—a return to an old-fashioned form made for the sake of showing what can be done with it. The complaint is possible only if the movement is separated from its context; taken in connexion with the mysterious first movement, the brooding tenderness of the slow movement, and the jovial outburst of the scherzo, its stalwart splendour is found to be the necessary complement of these various phases of emotion.

That is the main thing to be learnt about Brahms. His works must be heard as wholes. He rarely insisted upon the fact by making the movements continuous or quoting ideas from one movement in a later one, though the third Symphony, the violin Sonata in G, and the clarinet Quintet give instances of such quotation. But however various the ideas might be they were always parts of a whole wide range of expression. The details of his style are often so interesting intellectually that they tempt one to analyse his music, but it is only safe to begin to do so when you have first grasped something of the whole trend of the work.

We have said nothing in detail of the concertos, of the later chamber works, including two quintets for strings, the trios and sonatas for stringed instruments with the piano, and the series of works for the clarinet with strings, inspired by the playing of Mühlfeld, the fine clarinettist of the Meiningen orchestra. The object of our study, here as elsewhere, has been to get an idea of the distinctive place held by the composer in the musical development of his time, and this is harder in the case of Brahms than in that of Berlioz, whose work was bound up with a certain new type of expression, or that of Wagner, who revolutionized another type. Brahms was neither a pioneer nor a revolutionary; he was, like Bach, merely the most mighty wielder of the forces which his time had inherited. When he died, on 3 April 1897, a great period of music came to an end. He had held to an ideal of his own, which in many respects ran counter to the ideals of his most powerful contemporaries; but he had entirely justified that ideal in his long series of concerted works which closed with the clarinet Quintet, because he had proved that to be true to it was the only way for him to say what it was in him to say. The personal story at the back of his music remains to the last, and in the clarinet Quintet, the last piano pieces, songs, and particularly the set of organ chorales published after his death, one finds a spirit of restful gravity, the spirit in which a man having finished his life's work prepares to lay down his tools.

CÉSAR FRANCK

We will turn to another of our list of music's strong men (see p. 339), one whom so far we have not considered at all. It may have been a surprise to some to find César Franck in a list which included neither Grieg nor Dvořák. If it is remembered that this list represented not so much its members' own achievements as their influence upon others the surprise vanishes. Certainly none of Franck's teachers or contemporaries at the Paris Conservatoire were disposed to magnify his abilities; no Schumann trumpeted his coming at the age of twenty to a surprised world. Indeed, at that age there was nothing to trumpet about; all that happened was that Franck quietly left the Paris Conservatoire, having completed a serious course of study and won some prizes, but without even competing for the famous Prix de Rome, which Berlioz in his day had won so hardly.

César Franck was born at Liège on 10 December 1822, that is to say, rather more than ten years before Brahms, and less than ten years after Wagner was born. He came of a family of Belgian artists who traced their connexion with the art of painting back to the middle of the sixteenth century, and his father, seeing that his son had talent in another direction, fostered the talent and had him educated in music first at home, then in Paris. He entered the Paris Conservatoire, which still had Cherubini at its head in 1837, and worked there for five years, so that he was a music student through just those eventful years when Berlioz's big works won public recognition (see p. 394), when Liszt was at the height of his reputation as a public pianist, and Wagner was there longing for his chance and staving off starvation by arranging cornet solos. Franck must then have been impressed by the orchestration of Berlioz as well as by the brilliant piano style of Liszt. The dedication of an early trio for piano and strings 'à son ami Franz Liszt', composed in 1842, shows that not only Liszt's music but some personal kindness earned Franck's regard. On leaving the Conservatoire, however, Franck went home for a time, and for two years was away from the main streams of musical life. During this time a good many compositions, chiefly for the piano, but some of them for piano and stringed instruments, were written, none of them works by which he has become permanently known.

In 1844 he returned to Paris, where practically the whole of his subsequent life was spent. Again the date is significant; by this time Berlioz had started on his journeys through Europe, and Paris was for the time being relieved from his campaign for modern music. The death of Cherubini, on the other hand, had broken the link with the older classical ideals. One might suppose it to be the right moment for the expression of a new voice, but Franck was by no means ready to step into any position of authority. His music was still small in amount, and still tentative in purpose. An oratorio, *Ruth*, was composed and performed for the first time in 1846, the same year in which Mendelssohn's *Elijah* was produced at Birmingham. It is important only as the beginning of a new phase of French oratorio in which Franck excelled at a later time with a greater work, *Les Béatitudes*. But throughout the next twenty-five years his life was as uneventful as any active musician's life could well be. In 1858 he became organist of the church of Sainte-Clotilde, and this post he held for forty-two years until his death in 1890. Almost all his works written between the time of his appointment and 1870 are organ music or church music for voices with the organ.

The year 1870 is as critical a date in the fortunes of Franck as it was in those of his adopted country. Probably the Franco-German war was directly responsible for the fact that in that year he was naturalized as a French citizen. How far it was responsible for the fact that from then onwards appeared all the works of chamber and orchestral music which made him the apostle of French art one cannot say precisely, but the influence of politics upon the reception of his music has certainly been great. In 1871 the Société Nationale de Musique was founded for the purpose of promoting the work of living

French composers, who were then sadly neglected in Paris, not to mention the French provinces. It was in 1870 that Franck wrote *Les Béatitudes*; two years later he became first organ professor at the Conservatoire, and another work for chorus and orchestra, *Rédemption*, followed in 1874. His richest period of composition began with *Les Éolides*, a symphonic poem for orchestra after a poem by Leconte de Lisle (1876). The Quintet for piano and strings in F minor (1878–9) was followed by *Le Chasseur maudit*, a symphonic poem for orchestra after Bürger (1882); *Les Djinns*, another symphonic poem, after Victor Hugo, with a solo part for the piano, and the *Prélude, Choral et Fugue* for piano, appeared in 1884, and *Hulda*, an opera in four acts, with the *Variations symphoniques* for piano and orchestra, were completed in 1885. Still his activity increased: the Sonata for violin and piano, and the *Prélude, Aria et Final*, a companion work to the *Prélude, Choral et Fugue*, belong to the year 1886, when he began the Symphony in D minor, which was completed two years later. One more large chamber work, the string Quartet in D, was written in 1889, and these last years contain also a number of vocal and organ works.

Vincent d'Indy, foremost amongst Franck's admiring pupils, spoke of him as 'the genius of improvisation', and that seems to be the first principle of Franck's music. He wrote down his musical thoughts as they occurred to him, and whether they occurred as the result of impressions created by a poem, or as purely musical ideas such as those of the Sonata and the Quintet, made little difference to his attitude of mind. His music seems at once reflective and impulsive, but this did not prevent his exercising a great deal of thought over matters of form and expression. While he improvised he still took pains to correct his impressions so as to present them with complete clearness. D'Indy drew another picture of him, sitting before his music paper with a pencil in one hand and a piece of india-rubber in the other. It seems exactly to represent his method of work. The pencil enabled him to put down his thoughts with an unpremeditated spontaneity, the india-rubber allowed him the privilege of second thoughts whenever they came to him. In this his way of working was very much the same as that displayed in the sketch-books of Beethoven, save that he most frequently obliterated his discarded ideas instead of leaving them for the instruction of students.

FRANCK'S TREATMENT OF FORM

Before we draw direct comparisons between the music of Franck and of Brahms, a few words about Franck's treatment of musical form are necessary. In approaching the composition of pure music, that is to say, music apart from drama and words, Franck was neither guided nor hindered by established traditions to the extent that German musicians necessarily were. He had not behind him the same influence to urge him to the direct continuance or extension of sonata form. The music of Paris was in the middle of the nineteenth century almost completely the music of the opera save for the sudden ebullition of descriptive orchestral music for which Berlioz was responsible. Orchestral concerts were few, chamber music scarcely existed. Franck as an organist knew his Bach well and revelled in the depths of his polyphony; he studied the scores of Beethoven, and was particularly attracted by the last quartets in which Beethoven himself breaks away from his own older standards of balance displayed in the earlier sonatas, quartets, and symphonies. Clearly, he felt, something else is possible. A richly polyphonic style might be evolved in which melodic ideas should be varied, extended, and decorated without necessarily displaying the features of exposition, development, and recapitulation, or dwelling upon definite contrasts of key.

His first Trio, for piano, violin, and violoncello, begins with a movement which never definitely modulates at all; it merely changes its mode from the minor to the major and back again. He had a natural love of melodies which circulate round a single note, as the following one from his first Trio does:

Ex. 83

And, consequently, modulation of key, which means the contrast of one tonal centre with another, was a secondary consideration to him. In the instance just given his melody circulates round the note F sharp diatonically, that is to say, using it as the keynote and making the intervals of the tune move through those of the scale of F sharp. In his later works he more frequently made his melodies circulate chromatically, involving a temporary modulation. But this modulation comes in as an incident rather than as an essential part of his design. The following example from the Quintet gives a typical instance of his melody circulating chromatically round a single note (E flat):

Ex. 84

Franck built up his larger forms chiefly by showing other relationships than those of key between his melodic ideas. He very constantly reintroduces the themes from one movement into a later one, sometimes altering their rhythm, as the writers of programme music of his time constantly did, but more often preserving their form very much as it first appeared while showing some new and subtle connexion between melodies freshly introduced and those from which he started.

If you analyse the Sonata for violin and piano you will find a constant recurrence of melodies through its four movements, and in the last those which occur prominently in the earlier ones are summed up by their connexion with the broad and splendid tune which both instruments play in canon. The same kind of treatment is found in both the Quintet and the Symphony, and though the main features of sonata form are preserved in all three, those features are not really their basis of design.

FRANCK'S CONTEMPORARIES AND SUCCESSORS

Among the composers of French opera in the mid-nineteenth century too numerous for mention here, one, CHARLES GOUNOD (1818–93), may be taken as typical, because two of his operas, *Faust* and *Roméo et Juliette*, with certain choral works such as *The Redemption*, *Mors et Vita*, and the *Messe solennelle*, reached extraordinary popularity in England at their time. Born in Paris, Gounod was contemporary with Franck at the Conservatoire, and went to Italy as holder of the Prix de Rome. It was the *Messe solennelle* which first brought him to England (1851), and certain of his choral works, including *The Redemption* produced at the Birmingham Festival (1882), were written for the English public, and influenced by the prevailing taste for sacred choral music in this country. A strong reaction against the cloying sweetness of his style was felt in the later and more robust taste of both France and England. The opera *Faust* (1859) still holds the stage, however, and is likely to do so, for in its way it is a masterly piece of musical dramatization. It may be taken as typical of the ideals of French opera before either the influence of Wagner was felt in Paris or the stiffening of the national temper against that influence re-asserted itself in the works of a younger generation, of which such works as Alfred Bruneau's *L'Attaque du Moulin* (1893) and Gustave Charpentier's *Louise* (1900) were the outcome.

One of the greatest of French operas, *Carmen*, which belongs to this period—it was produced in 1875—has already been mentioned (see p. 453); but its composer, Georges Bizet (1838–75) must here be singled out as one of the most distinctive figures in French music, though little has remained of his large operatic output and only a handful of his other works have endured, such as the delightful C major Symphony of his adolescence, the *Jeux d'enfants* suite for piano duet (orchestrated later) and above all the incidental music for Daudet's tragedy *L'Arlésienne*, which wonderfully evokes the atmosphere of the Provençal setting of the play.

Bizet stood entirely apart from Franck and his school, which however affected the rebirth of French instrumental music even in composers not directly connected with it, such as Édouard Lalo (1823–92) and Camille Saint-Saëns (1835–1921), who both produced symphonies at almost the same time that Franck produced his. The latter wrote music in every form for instruments with a profusion which Franck never reached. Judged by quantity Saint-Saëns would certainly have the first place amongst the French composers of instrumental music of the nineteenth century, but varied and highly polished as his works are, they have not the strength of individuality which made Franck's work one of the big forces in the growth of music.

Among the Franck pupils the outstanding figure is that of Vincent d'Indy (1851–1931), a noble composer still unduly neglected even in France itself, perhaps because his veneration for Bach and Beethoven and a superficial adherence to Wagnerian principles in his dramatic works made him appear too Germanic at a time when the general tendency was towards a return to the pure Frenchness that was found in the work of Gabriel Fauré (1845–1924), a master with equally lofty ideals but of an entirely different artistic character. But it was overlooked that d'Indy, on the one hand, was greatly interested in the folk-song of his native southern mountain region of France and introduced it into much of his music, sometimes literally and sometimes in spirit; and that Fauré, on the other, by no means withheld his admiration from the German classics.

Fauré is one of those composers who appear at their greatest in their smallest works. He wrote little on a large scale except the opera *Pénélope* which, though full of lovely music, is dramatically rather ineffective. His *Requiem* is lyrical and much smaller, and he was so little interested in the orchestra that he did not even score all his works himself. But his chamber music (2 piano Quartets, 2 piano Quintets, a piano Trio, a string Quartet, 2 violin and 2 cello Sonatas) are works of great subtlety, while his very numerous piano pieces (mainly barcarolles, nocturnes and the like) and his many song settings of the finest French poetry belong to the loveliest things of their respective repertories produced at any time or in any country. The flavour of Fauré's shifting chromatic harmony is not only entrancing, but so individual as to be immediately and unmistakably recognizable.

Paul Dukas, of whose small output the orchestral scherzo *L'Apprenti sorcier* is best known, was never a direct pupil of Franck, but nevertheless showed a little of his influence. Henri Duparc, Ernest Chausson, and the Belgian Guillaume Lekeu, on the other hand, all came under Franck's teaching and, though they wrote fine music, never achieved real independence. But Duparc's fifteen songs—he wrote little else on account of an early breakdown—are among the finest in the French repertory of the period. Indirect followers of the Franck school, who were taught on that master's lines at the Schola Cantorum founded by d'Indy as a rival to the Conservatoire, which then still took the Gounod-Massenet line, remained under the Franckian domination, and some also followed d'Indy in his addiction to folk-music, which turned them often into attractive but small-scale regional composers (e.g. Déodat de Séverac, Guy-Ropartz, Rhené-Baton). The one disciple of the Schola who was to grow into a distinctive personality and a sizable master was Albert Roussel (1869–1937), who exercised his gifts in all the important categories of music—dramatic, symphonic, choral, chamber, down to the small forms of instrumental pieces and songs.

A 'character' in French music at the time was Emmanuel Chabrier (1841–94), who was brilliantly original and had the rare gift of fun which was totally lacking in the Franckians. This, indeed, anticipated a characteristic of twentieth-century French music, which lies outside the scope of this chapter.

The symphony, with which this chapter has been largely occupied, developed during the later nineteenth century in the hands of some composers to be considered in the following chapter as representatives of national tendencies in different countries. But it also continued to be cultivated in Vienna, which still remained its centre at that time, thanks not only to Brahms but also to two other composers: Anton Bruckner (1824–96) and Gustav Mahler (1860–1911). Brahms was antagonistic towards Bruckner all his life and towards Mahler at any rate early in that composer's career; but both found adherents of their own and succeeded in having their works performed within the sphere of their partisans' influence. After their deaths their music gained ground on a less restricted territory, though it still remained firmly rooted locally and threw out strong offshoots only where it had aroused the interest of some cultivators to whom it happened to have made a special appeal. Thus Mahler found a champion in Holland and Bruckner became relatively familiar in the United States mainly through the influence of Central European settlers.

Bruckner, though also an important composer of Catholic Church music, is a true symphonist in the sense that he was capable of inventing material that could be satisfactorily developed only in orchestral music on the largest scale. Everything in his symphonies is big—his detractors object that everything is merely long—and he is indeed a composer of large stature, faults and all. His chief defect is his weakness in the art of transition; so that if one considers the great interest of symphonic writing to lie in the ways and means of getting from one structural feature to another, Bruckner's stopping and starting again appears clumsy. He is also reproached with having been incapable of making up his mind about the definitive shape of a symphony, or at any rate of maintaining his decision against criticism. There is still much argument about the authenticity of various versions of his symphonies. He was always willing to revise, cut, or re-orchestrate them on the advice of conductors and other experts, which perhaps he was too weak or too amiable to disregard, but may, on the other hand, have thought really valuable. About the magnificence of the actual material of Bruckner's symphonies there can be no doubt. They give the impression of vast mountain landscapes populated by a race of noble supermen, awkward and devoid of grace, but with a fine, clean beauty and not without touches of tenderness. Wagnerian scenes on a grand scale are often brought before the hearer, and indeed the rich orchestration suggests Wagnerian scenery, but there are no dramatic developments: everything is fundamentally simple and straightforward.

Mahler is an entirely different figure as a symphonist. He was essentially a song-writer, and although he regarded his symphonies as by far the most important part of his output, they are very much affected by vocal music ranging from folk-song and lyrical song to conceptions like large choral cantatas. Five out of his nine symphonies (there is an unfinished tenth) contain vocal parts, the huge No. 8 as many as eight for solo voices in addition to a double chorus and a choir of boys. The symphonies strike one as consisting of song material inflated to make works of an enormous size, so that, being what they are, it is by no means out of place to regard his best work, *Das Lied von der Erde*, as yet another symphony.

One of the greatest conductors who ever lived, Mahler knew the art of orchestration intimately and applied it to his own works in a highly original and most interestingly varied way. But the musical material also varies most disconcertingly in the symphonies, so that no consistency of style may be looked for, and side by side with striking ideas may be found much that is sentimental or downright common. Strains in a folk-song vein ring false because they are felt to be the expression of a very sophisticated artist's hankering after innocent simplicity, and they do not accord with the bitter outpourings of the self-centred egotist concerned with his own woes while he pretends to voice those of the universe, which is what Mahler's symphonies chiefly convey to the hearer.

Being sadly deficient in taste, Mahler is met with distaste by a great many people who are not in some way prejudiced in his favour by national or personal considerations. But he also has numerous ardent admirers, and one thing that cannot be denied by anybody is that his symphonies are quite extraordinarily interesting, at least as much so for their defects as for their qualities of striking originality and unfailing technical mastery.

Suggestions for Further Reading and Listening

As a number of books about Mendelssohn, Schumann, Brahms, and Franck have already been listed, this instalment of suggestions for further reading follows the sequence of topics as they arise in Chapter 20. For a start, Mendelssohn's chamber music can be followed up in John Horton's 'BBC Music Guide', while Spohr's life may be scanned in Dorothy Moulton Mayer's short biography. This many-sided and enormously active musician also found time to produce a long but very readable autobiography, which is to be found in larger libraries.

Schumann's chamber music is amply covered in the various recommended Schumann studies (Chapters 15, 16, and 18), and the same applies to Brahms. Here, however, Ivor Keys's *Brahms Chamber Music* and John Horton's *Brahms Orchestral Music* ('BBC Music Guides') should be consulted, as should the first volume of *The Symphony* (Penguin), edited by Robert Simpson. It covers, composer by composer, the period from Haydn to Dvořák, and includes César Franck and Bruckner (an outstanding contribution by Deryck Cooke).

For amplification of the material on Franck and his successors, Martin Cooper's *French Music*—from the death of Berlioz to the death of Fauré—is an obvious choice, though it can be supplemented by the first part of Rollo Myers's *Modern French Music*. (Readers surprised by the omission of Debussy and Ravel in Chapter 20 will discover them in the next chapter.)

With regard to individual French composers, the most useful books are as follows: *Saint-Saëns and his Circle* by James Harding, biographies of Fauré by Charles Koechlin and Norman Suckling, Sydney Northcote's *Songs of Duparc*, and Basil Deane's *Albert Roussel*. In addition there are first-rate chapters on Fauré and Roussel in Mellers's *Studies in Contemporary Music*, and on Fauré and Duparc in Laurence Davies's *The Gallic Muse*.

The concluding section of Chapter 20 is concerned with Bruckner and Mahler, composers who, readers may feel, did not immediately recommend themselves to Colles. (Their popular following in this country, particularly that of Mahler, is indeed of relatively recent origin.) Formerly squeezed into a single 'Master Musicians' volume by Hans Redlich, they have now graduated to a book each in that series, *Bruckner* by Derek Watson, and *Mahler* by Michael Kennedy.

Mahler has also come in for searching scrutiny in two large-scale biographies, by Henri-Louis de la Grange and Donald Mitchell. While the former examines the minutiae of the composer's day-by-day life, the latter subjects his music to an exceptionally thorough analysis. The general reader, however, may find it easier to start with Bruno Walter's short and affectionate study of Mahler and go on from there to *Gustav Mahler, his Mind and his Music*, by Neville Cardus, the fruit of a lifetime's devotion. *Gustav Mahler, Memories and Letters*, by Alma Mahler, paints a marvellously vivid picture of the composer and of Vienna at the start of the century; it is all the better for Donald Mitchell's annotations, amplifications, and corrections.

CHAPTER 21

National Ideals

We have now dealt at some length with nine out of the ten men whom we took as typical figures in the music of the nineteenth century. Tchaikovsky is separated from the others by belonging to a country which until his day had never exerted any distinct influence upon the music of Europe as a whole. It was through Tchaikovsky's work that Russia began to impress herself on the West, and that is why we have taken his name as representative of the Russian school of composers, though others are more specifically national figures.

But before we begin to consider Tchaikovsky and his compatriots a few words about the idea of national music, illustrated by the work of one or two of its chief exponents outside Russia, will be helpful. There is scarcely any subject connected with music which is more in need of clear thought at the present day, but it is quite easy to understand it if you turn to the historical facts. Misleading arguments about it come from two opposite points of view, and are all the more misleading because both have an element of truth behind them. On the one hand, it is said that music must speak in the language of the country where it was born; on the other, it is urged that the language of music is common to at least all European countries, so why be at such pains to distinguish between them? The two seem to be direct contradictions, but that is due to using the metaphor of language wrongly. The real distinction between the music of different European countries is not one of language but of thought and feeling showing itself in a different use of the same musical language.

Take a simple illustration, not from music but from the speech of the people of these islands. They are practically all used to talking the same language, but an Englishman, an Irishman, and a Scotsman talk it in very different ways. If they are simple folk they will differ so much in the actual expressions used that they will hardly be able to understand one another. If they are educated people actual differences of expression in the construction of sentences will hardly appear, but their differences of thought become more marked. Ask an Englishman, an Irishman, and a Scotsman for a piece of information, and you generally find that the Englishman will tell it to you shortly and expect you to understand it whether he puts it clearly or not; the Irishman will put his answer quite neatly, but will not care very much whether you grasp it or not; the Scotsman will take great pains to make you understand, as much on his own account as on yours. That is because in each case you are dealing with a different kind of mind, and similar differences of mind appear in the music of different nations, even though they are all using the same musical language.

The place of folk-melody in cultivated music is very much like the use of dialect expressions in speech. A more or less primitive people naturally begins to develop its music out of its native song. It uses the actual phrases and rhythms of such melodies because they most naturally express the people's way of thought. As it grows up it sheds these provincialisms, but it does not lose its characteristic way of thought. Of the modern French composers mentioned at the end of the last chapter, for example, only a few, and with the exception of d'Indy only minor figures, show any influence of folk-melody at all, but the others are no less distinctively French on that account. It only becomes more difficult to lay a finger on the exact quality in their music which is French; in fact, it is not a matter of language but of tone of mind.

DVOŘÁK AND GRIEG

In Dvořák and Grieg we get two clear examples, one in the east and the other in the north of Europe, of composers who set themselves consciously to express their national tones of mind.

To do this they had to begin by reverting to what may be called a musical dialect.

EDVARD GRIEG was born at Bergen in Norway in 1843, and he studied music at Leipzig from 1858 to 1862. He was therefore very fully grounded in the German tradition of music as it had been carried on by Mendelssohn and Schumann. There were, however, influences nearer home: the poetry and drama of Ibsen, to whose *Peer Gynt* he supplied incidental music which has become one of his most popular works, did for him very much what the German poets did for Schumann; moreover, like Chopin, he belonged to a country which possessed a very distinct kind of folk-music of its own, and the intervals and rhythms of Norwegian folk-melody were to him a native dialect which pervaded his whole imagination.

If you compare Grieg's lyric pieces for the piano with Schumann's short piano pieces you will find certain very strong likenesses of style, the first of the lyric pieces, for example, might almost have been written by the composer of the *Kinderscenen* and *Fantasiestücke*; but whenever Grieg ventures upon a more decisive melody the likeness of general form and style to Schumann goes into the background. The *Ballade* (Op. 65 No. 5) and its companion *The Wedding Day* (Op. 65 No. 6) represent him in two quite different moods and each of them quite foreign to any music of the Leipzig school. The kind of melody, as we saw in the case of Chopin, at once induces new kinds of harmonic movement. In *The Wedding Day* you will find such chords as the added sixth, the augmented triad, and various positions of the chord of the ninth insisted on strongly, and, as the following example shows:

Ex. 85

they are the result of combining melodies. In such things Grieg is anything but free from foreign influence, and it is practically impossible for any music of the present day to be free from the influence of its predecessors and contemporaries, whether native or foreign. Such influence, however, to composers who have their own point of view based on the tradition of their country's thought and feeling is real education; when it is used by composers who have not that foundation, it becomes merely superficial teaching. In this example, Grieg's musical idea, a repetition of a short syncopated phrase, seems elementary, and his music on the whole has a suggestion of provincialism from his way of insisting strongly upon his native turns of musical speech. He contrasts with Chopin in this, for Chopin welds his suggestions from Polish melody with an art which brings it into consonance with the forms and manners of a larger world.

What Grieg did for the music of Norway, Dvořák did with greater directness for the music of Czechoslovakia. In his case the development of a distinct national style in music was part of a social reaction against the swamping of Bohemian nationality by Austrian imperialism. Dvořák was not the first apostle of his country's music. Bedřich Smetana (1824–84) had preceded him, and by the time that Dvořák was growing up, a national opera-house, under Smetana's direction, had been founded in Prague. It is Smetana, in fact, who is the outstanding representative of the nationalist musical movement in Czechoslovakia. His operas, of which only *The Bartered Bride* is universally known, and his cycle of six symphonic poems, *My Country*, which deal with various Bohemian historical and geographical subjects, are full of music of a delightful freshness. But by no means all his work 'travels' well, and those of his compatriots who uphold his claims as the greatest home-grown composer against Dvořák's overlook the fact that the latter is more universal, and therefore greater. If Dvořák is accused of having deferred too much to the dictates of the German classical forms, it must also be recognized that part of his greatness lies precisely in his masterly handling of those forms.

Antonín Dvořák was born in 1841 and was given some schooling first at Zlonice, and afterwards at a German school at Kamenice. His early life in some ways was like that of Haydn, for his father was comparatively poor, and the education that he got was only of an elementary kind. He entered the organ school at Prague in 1857, however, and while he was there supported himself by playing the viola in a town band. A few years later, when the Bohemian theatre was opened, his band was employed for occasional music, and in 1866, when that theatre became a regular opera-house under Smetana's direction, Dvořák became a member of its orchestra. His compositions in early years were rather divided between his enthusiasm for national music, stimulated by Smetana's example, and his admiration for Wagner, whose style he tried to emulate in at least one opera. But he soon saw the truth that Wagner's style was the result of his own genius, and that what he could learn from it was the lesson of self-reliance.

Dvořák's intimate acquaintance with the orchestra as a player gave him a wonderfully sure hand in writing for it, and he had written several symphonies, some music for strings, and chamber music before his powers received any public acknowledgement. The event which most brought him into the light was his entry of compositions to compete for a grant from the Austrian government.

It is interesting to remember that Brahms was concerned in the award, and that although Brahms was not particularly ready in his appreciation of music with other ideals than his own he quickly saw the genius of Dvořák's work. It was due to him that Simrock, the publisher, accepted Dvořák's music and asked for more; in response to that request the Slavonic dances for piano duet were written, and gained a popularity almost as great as Brahms's Hungarian dances. Brahms also used his influence to suggest to Dvořák the study and composition of chamber music. So in Dvořák's quartets and other chamber works one finds again a certain strong foreign influence, but a thoroughly healthy one. The general form of the sonata type which the Germans had developed is adopted by Dvořák, but, as in the case of Grieg, the type of melody and the texture of the harmony come from his own national spirit.

These two bars from the first movement of the string Quartet in E flat, Op. 51, give a glimpse of Dvořák's style:

Ex. 86

The second violin and viola are playing in octaves a tune which has already appeared as the second subject of the movement in regular sonata form. The violoncello accompanies with a strong figure which is obviously derived from the tune itself, and above, the first violin trips along with a dancing tune in a rhythm which is very prevalent throughout the movement. The counterpoint itself is ingenious, yet it is so simple that it requires no mental effort to appreciate it. It has the genial ease of Haydn.

This Quartet is one of the instances where Dvořák used the word 'dumka'[1] to describe the slow movement. The word is

[1] The Dumky Trio, Op. 90, for piano and strings, is composed of a series of such movements.

best translated as 'lament', and, used in the music of his country, it means a short piece of a persistently sorrowful kind.[1] The drooping melody of this 'Dumka', with the accompaniment thrummed on the strings of the violoncello, suggests a dirge sung by a peasant singer to the accompaniment of a guitar or similar instrument:

Observe that the 'Dumka' alternates with a vivace, and that the merry tune of the latter is a transformation from the sad theme of the 'Dumka':

[1] Compare the old English 'Dump', a melancholy slow movement frequently found in Elizabethan instrumental music, and alluded to ironically by Shakespeare, *Romeo and Juliet*, Act IV, Sc. v.

This method of contrast seems to be taken from Brahms's example (see p. 470), but again the influence from outside appears only in the manner and not in the matter of the music. Another title and manner of expression which he adopted from his country's music was the Furiant (nothing to do with 'fury'), a fast dance with the rhythm 1.2, 1.2, 1.2, 1.2.3, 1.2.3, which in his hands became a scherzo of an exceptionally unfettered and vigorous kind. Both the Dumka and the Furiant can be studied in those written for the piano alone (Opp. 12, 35, and 42).

Everything which Dvořák had to say was said with that simple clarity of expression which turns readily from one strong emotion to another without apparent premeditation. When he combined contrasting rhythms, as he often did, it was without intellectual questioning which both Schumann and Brahms bestowed on such things; it was done for beauty of colour or sheer charm of effect. He could pour out his heart in a phrase of melody, such as the second theme of the beautiful violoncello Concerto, without either reserve or affectation, and perhaps no one of the nineteenth-century composers came so near to that childlike attitude of musical devotion which belonged to the composers of the older world. That was partly because Dvořák remained through life a simple Bohemian peasant in spite of travels abroad.

His most popular symphony, 'From the New World', the Quartet in F, Op. 95, and the Quintet in E flat, Op. 94, were products of his visit to America. In 'The New World' Symphony Dvořák caught the flavour of the half-merry, half-mournful Negro melodies of America. He strenuously denied that he had actually quoted any of them, though you will often see i stated in print that it is more or less made up of borrowed tunes of the kind. If 'The New World' Symphony is not the best of Dvořák it is still very good, and it happens to be the work with which most people in England begin their knowledge of him. The Scherzo is most characteristic of him in its vigorous use of short and impulsive rhythmic phrases.

Dvořák's last works were some orchestral ballads on folk

legends, but it is interesting to notice that the greater part of his instrumental music claimed no reference to a story of any kind, as one might naturally expect from a composer whose sympathies were so intimately bound up with the scenes and legends, the art and the poetry of his native country. The existence of the national opera-house in Prague was probably the cause of this. When he had a story to tell, the stage was there to tell it for him in the unmistakable way which music alone can never achieve. He wrote nine operas, and most of them have been frequently given there, but not elsewhere. His choral works and songs, such as his first cantata *The Heirs of the White Mountains*, *The Hymn of the Bohemian Peasants* (4-part chorus with accompaniment), the set of duets (soprano and contralto) on Moravian folk verses (Op. 32), and the Gipsy songs (Op. 55), also gave him scope for the expression of the racial spirit of his music in conjunction with poetry.

We have dwelt rather closely upon Dvořák because, in spite of the ready recognition which his music gained during his lifetime (he died in 1904), there has been very little attempt since his death to spread the knowledge of more than a few favourite works. Yet he established a style which is national in its origin strong enough to appeal to all the world. That, it must always be remembered, is the aim of the national ideal in music. It is not or should not be urged that the members of a nation should shut themselves up to talk their own dialect among themselves, but by developing their own way of thinking in music they should contribute something distinctive to the world's thought; and because music is ultimately a common language a nation's contribution in music can go forth more directly than a nation's thought expressed in poetry can do.

DEBUSSY

A composer as great in his own way as Dvořák, and more important as an influence, began to make his mark towards the end of the nineteenth century: Claude Debussy (1862–1918). He too was in a sense a nationalist, for although he was hardly at all affected by folk-music, he became more and more consciously an upholder of the French traditions. It was difficult at first even for his compatriots to believe this, because on the surface his music seemed to defy every rule and upset every convention. It was certainly not conventional, and after some early works that might have been ascribed to any elegant and decently skilled French composer of no great seriousness, he respected no laws of harmony or form that did not happen to suit his purpose. He had gone through a normal schooling and knew the rules he chose to break, but like his fellow-artists, the impressionist painters and the symbolist poets, he aimed at creating an idiom for his personal expression that should achieve its object by forming a discipline of its own, in its way no less exacting and certainly no less idealistic than that which he often defied. The means by which he realized his aims were sometimes retrogressive rather than progressive: a passage quoted earlier (see p. 7) has already shown that he would not hesitate to revert to twelfth-century *organum* when it suited him; but he also invented much that was entirely new, especially in the matter of harmony and of pianistic sound-effects, while his forms were deliberately kept so fluid as to strike his contemporaries as mere shapeless meandering until he had succeeding in persuading them that he knew very well what he was doing. Once it was understood that the vagueness of his music was as deliberately produced as the nebulousness of Turner or Whistler in painting and that the unexpected combinations and progressions of his harmony resembled the new manipulations of words for sound as much as for sense of Baudelaire or Mallarmé, Debussy was acknowledged to be one of the great creative artists in music. That he was more than a mere innovator has been shown by the permanence of the best of his work. Nothing is easier in music—or in any art—than to experiment with ways and means untried before, and no art grows old and stale more quickly than that which relies on nothing but novelty; but the fact that after half a century and more the best of Debussy's works have kept their places as undisputed masterpieces as certainly as the best painting of Manet or Renoir have done proves his very individual procedures to be right, not for everybody, but for himself, because they were arrived at by means of an artist's instinct leading to greatness by a route of his own choosing and making.

THE BRITISH NATIONAL REVIVAL

The revival of folk-music began in Great Britain towards the end of the nineteenth century. Various causes made the more cultivated people realize the existence of Scottish and Irish folk-song before they were aware of English folk-song. English people were inclined to be careless of their own artistic possessions. Charles Villiers Stanford (1852–1924), born in Ireland, though his family belonged to the English settlement there, saturated himself in Irish folk-song; and the Edinburgh-born Alexander Mackenzie (1847–1935) sometimes introduced Scottish folk material into his works where the chosen literary material (stage adaptations from Scott, poems by Burns, &c.) or his fancy dictated. He wrote three Scottish Rhapsodies for orchestra, Stanford five Irish ones. The latter did much serious work of restoration by making countless arrangements of Irish folk-songs which played their part in moulding his own style of song composition very much as the Russian folk-song arrangements of Tchaikovsky and Rimsky-Korsakov moulded their melodic types. The supreme beauty of Stanford's numerous songs is not so much the feeling for the measure of the English language as the capacity for discovering a musical thought which chimes perfectly with the poetic thought of each lyric he undertook to set.

English folk-music had no great influence on composers until the twentieth century was on the way; but other forces were at work during the later years of the nineteenth century which are now clearly seen to have pointed forward to a renewal of production that has made the present age a fourth creative period in English music comparable to the phases dominated by Dunstable in the fifteenth century, by Byrd in the sixteenth and by Purcell in the seventeenth. These masters, outstanding as they were, are no more isolated figures of eminence in their period than Elgar, who takes up a similar position in the phase we are now approaching, is in his own time.

Elgar developed late and so does not come within the scope of this chapter; but apart from Stanford and Mackenzie, three men older than he must here be mentioned as representing as many different classes of music, each important in its way in the English music of the time. To think of the church music of Samuel Sebastian Wesley (1810–76), the choral music of Hubert Parry (1848–1918) and the comic operas of Arthur Sullivan (1842–1900) is to realize that our country's music was anything but stagnant in the nineteenth century.

Throughout his life S. S. Wesley, a grand-nephew of the great evangelist, in his compositions and in his executive work as a church musician, was the champion of a type of church music which, while it preserved the dignity of the older cathedral music, was free from any archaic pose. He poured scorn upon those who thought that church music must necessarily be written in breves and semibreves; he laughed at the attempt to revive plainsong while that attempt was founded upon very imperfect knowledge of the characteristics of the old music. His melody and his harmony for voices with organ accompaniment could be daringly modern in its progressions; yet it always preserved the character of church music. In his later works, especially the two anthems for eight voices, 'Let us lift up our hearts' and 'O Lord, Thou art my God', he cultivated a massive style of contemplative church music, and in the magnificent unaccompanied psalm 'In exitu Israel' one sees clearly the influence of Bach's choral style. His anthems trace their descent back to Orlando Gibbons (see pp. 42–4), and his treatment of language in melody had the strongest influence upon Parry, an influence which shows itself even more strongly in Parry's later church cantatas for the Three Choirs Festivals than in his earlier works.

Parry's choral music, whether for the church or the concert-room, is always the outcome of the English language; he ranged much more widely than Wesley, and the poetry of Milton in *Blest Pair of Sirens* and *L'Allegro ed il Pensieroso* was as much his groundwork as the language of the Bible. To find how thoroughly his choral music is rooted in English traditions, place his setting of Pope's *Ode on St. Cecilia's Day* beside Purcell's of the ode by Brady, particularly the chorus 'Soul of the World' (No. 5) in the latter. You will not be likely to make the mistake of supposing that Parry's choral music reproduces Wesley or Purcell or Gibbons; it simply suggests the same growth of style which we have found developed in so many instances throughout our study of musical history, and by this stage it is hardly necessary to point to the fact that originality is consistent with continuity.

Original as Parry was, he was not strongly creative, though extremely productive. He had an extraordinary facility for writing technically unexceptionable music with an unfailingly good texture (his basses are as mobile as Handel's), but his very ease led him to write too much, almost as though from habit, and his invention is always apt to flag. He very often began a work most promisingly—the opening of *Blest Pair of Sirens* is truly magnificent and stirring—but inspiration was rarely kept working at full pressure for long. There is no doubt, however, that it was chiefly Parry's example to which we owe the continuance of the splendid English choral tradition: Wesley might have kept it confined to the Church alone, and it might well have collapsed after him but for Parry's interest in it. He saved it for greater men to work at a generation after him.

To turn from the church music of Wesley and the choral works of Parry to the comic operas of Sullivan may seem a somewhat violent change of standpoint; but they have this in common—their dependence on and their admirable treatment of language. Sullivan produced a unique and typically English form of operetta as a result of working hand in hand with a unique and typically English humorist, W. S. Gilbert. Sullivan's art as an illustrator of words in sound was the precise counterpart of Gilbert's in verse, often based on quips of language, skilful rhymes, metrical ingenuities which Sullivan matched with even greater resources of rhythm, and allusions to current events, such as the aesthetic movement satirized in *Patience*, which he further spiced with his inimitable gift of musical parody. But although, without Gilbert, Sullivan never achieved anything to secure him immortality, he brought to the Savoy operettas an extraordinary superiority of musicianship, which he exercised with supreme skill without ever showing it off for its own sake. His orchestration is always highly effective as well as charming, he could combine melodies of different rhythm or character in admirable counterpoint, and he was able to produce a perfectly written fugal passage when it was appropriate, as at the entry of the learned Lord Chancellor in *Iolanthe*. In the same character's nightmare song he produced a piece of fantastic orchestration worthy of Berlioz.

If we look at the instrumental music of our countrymen it is much less easy to point decisively to any continuous growth of a national style. The composers of the nineteenth century had no direct link with their country's past history in instrumental music. A century and a half had passed between the death of Purcell and the time when composers such as Parry and Stanford began their work. And during that time this country had lived almost entirely on foreign instrumental music. The problem was by no means so simple for our composers as it was for Grieg or Dvořák or the Russians, because the primitive types of folk-music in England had been largely smothered and forgotten by the more cultivated classes of society. Glinka had little difficulty in recalling to his mind his country's folk-music, because it was associated intimately with his childish days; but the folk-songs of England had been long relegated to country inns and cottage homes, and it was not until a campaign was instituted to rediscover them quite late in the last century that ordinarily musical people had any notion of their real characteristics of melody. We see now that it was too late for them to become the basis of a national form of music comparable to the nineteenth-century Russian school, for example. But we need not regret this, for other and more vigorous influences have worked towards the shaping of a new British school of composition of an abounding richness, as we shall see in the last chapter.

RUSSIA'S POSITION IN ART

With our thoughts clear upon the principles of national music we may turn to the history of Russian music in the last half of the nineteenth century. Here we are dealing not with a simple self-governing country such as Norway, nor yet with a conquered people like the people of Bohemia strenuously anxious to reassert their individuality in the face of an imperial power which threatened to obliterate it, but with a great people united indeed under the government of the Tsar but containing a number of different and often conflicting interests and traditions. Until the beginning of the eighteenth century Russia had been very much isolated from the rest of Europe. It was Peter the Great—the Tsar whose name was perpetuated in the capital, St. Petersburg, now Leningrad, which he founded—who insisted upon closer intercourse between his empire and the nations of Western Europe, and his policy had its effect upon the arts in general and music in particular by opening the way for the importation of foreign artists of every kind. Italian opera spread to St. Petersburg in the eighteenth century and took possession of the stage very much as it spread to Vienna and London. Composers such as Sarti and Paisiello wrote operas in Italian for the court of Catherine the Great just as Handel and Bononcini had written them for the courts of the first Georges in London, and this artistic domination from without lasted into the nineteenth century. One fashion succeeded another, and in the early part of the century French opera, Méhul and Cherubini, as well as the music of Vienna, came to Russia. But along with it native music persisted. After all fashionable life is a small part of any nation, and it was an infinitesimal part of a great empire such as Russia. Peasant songs and ballads were the daily life of millions of people who had never seen an opera. The Russian church, cut off from communion with western Christianity either catholic or protestant, preserved its own music and its own tradition of unaccompanied song unimpaired. Yet all the time musical life was growing and strengthening amongst the Russian peoples.

The man who first gave to this life an unmistakable voice was MIKHAIL IVANOVICH GLINKA. He was born in 1804, that is a year after Berlioz, and was brought up in the surroundings of a cultivated family who would no more have thought of music as a suitable career for a young man of birth and breeding than any English family of the upper classes would have thought of it at that date. At the age of twenty Glinka entered the Civil Service, and the enthusiasm which he had felt for music since he was a child found vent in his attending the opera and taking part as an amateur in all the music which came in his way. It is interesting to notice that the event which made him turn seriously to the question of his country's music was his leaving the country. He had composed a good deal of music, both for voice and instruments, though chiefly as a hobby, when in 1830 he started on a prolonged journey to Italy. His health was bad, a warmer climate was needed, but a passion to visit the land from which so much music had come also urged him to the visit. When he was there he discovered for the first time that Italian opera was what it was because it sprang from the life of the Italian people. He realized that what was natural to them was affectation should he attempt to reproduce it. If he was to do anything worth doing he must be natural, and for him nature was expressed in the tunes which as a child he had heard the Russian bandsmen play at home.

GLINKA AND RUSSIAN OPERA

When he got back to Russia in 1834 he determined upon a great project, the composition of an opera in the Russian language with a story drawn from national history, such a story as would stimulate all his love of his country's legend, song, and poetry. The project was actually fulfilled in the opera known as *A Life for the Tsar*, which was performed in the presence of the Tsar himself in November 1836.

The occasion is as memorable a landmark in the history of Russian music as the production of *Der Freischütz* had been in German opera (see p. 346). There are in the music some things which remind one of Weber's style, a sign that Glinka's grasp was not yet quite certain, but it was sufficiently characteristic to show the possibility of a new ideal. Its nationality is no mere matter of quotation from folk-songs; the evidence is found in Glinka's own melodies, rhythms, and harmonies. The overture gives a practical example of Glinka's style, and a comparison with Weber's operatic overtures will show both the likeness and the difference.

Glinka followed up this with another opera, *Russlan and Ludmilla*, which takes its subject not from history but from legend. While the motive of *A Life for the Tsar* is directly patriotic, the story of a peasant who ventured his life to save that of his sovereign from treacherous enemies, *Russlan and Ludmilla*—the names are those of hero and heroine—appeals to that delight in the story of true love which never 'runs smooth' until the last scene or the last chapter, a delight which is so inherent in human nature that it is expressed in every phase of literature from the folk-tale to the modern novel and stage play. The evil genius who impedes the love of Russlan and Ludmilla is a magician who carries away the bride from the wedding feast, and it is worth while to notice, in view of what has occurred since in modern music, that Glinka describes the magician and his sinister art by the use of a descending scale in whole tones in the bass:

Ex. 89

That scale, obliterating the distinctions of key and the ordinary processes of melody founded on arrangements of tones and semitones, no doubt seemed to him an apt way of suggesting the defiance of nature which belongs to the arts of magic. It gives a good instance of Glinka's attempt to express character by exceptional musical devices. Another example may serve to show what magical touches he could apply by harmonic progressions which, though quite simple, were in his time daringly novel and original:

Ex. 90

There is a similar device in an opera, *The Stone Guest*, by Dargomizhsky (1813–69), who played a large part in the movement to found a distinctively Russian type of opera. His *Roussalka* (Water Nymph), founded on Pushkin, is the most strongly national in its treatment of Russian folk-legend. *The Stone*

Guest is a version of the story of Don Juan which Mozart had made famous, and the use of the whole-tone scale in the episode of the statue accepting the hero's flippant invitation to supper is one instance among many of Dargomizhsky's desire to lay emphasis upon the dramatic purport of the story. Dargomizhsky in fact laid more stress upon the truthful expression of the drama by the use of unusual harmonies and a close attention to the verbal accent of his vocal parts than Glinka did, though much less professionally, and it was he more than Glinka who began that intimate association between the Russian language and its music which we find later, particularly in the songs and operas of Mussorgsky.

In *The Stone Guest* Dargomizhsky took as his text the poem by the great Russian poet Pushkin, and set it to music without cutting it up to make a conventional operatic *libretto*. It is impossible to over-estimate what the musicians of Russia owe to their national poet. His stories and poems form the basis of many of their finest works, and the widespread knowledge of him among the people at large has given to the composers an immediate point of contact with their audiences.

From what has been said it will be clear that the new Russian music founded upon folk-music, and furthered by poetry, first got its development most naturally in opera. Symphonic and chamber music were to come later. The latter, we have seen, always indicates an advanced state of musical cultivation, and Russia offers an example of this sequence of events as conspicuous as that shown in the story of France.

After the opera the next step was the fuller development of the orchestra. Glinka was instrumental in bringing Berlioz to St. Petersburg on his first visit of 1847 (see p. 395), and on that occasion a great deal of Berlioz's music was heard at concerts given both there and in Moscow. But Glinka died (1857) in the interval of twenty years which separated Berlioz's two visits, and when he came again (1867–8) a new generation of musicians, working in very different conditions from those in which Glinka had begun, was there to welcome him.

THE RUSSIAN NATIONALISTS

About 1860 there came upon Russia an enthusiasm for education which affected music by the foundation of various institutions and academies, including the Conservatory at St. Petersburg. Anton Rubinstein, whose fame all over Europe as a pianist became only second to that of Liszt, was its director, and under him education was pursued very much on the lines of the conservatories of western Europe, such as those of Paris and Leipzig. The knowledge of music, not the development of a national form of music, was its aim, and the policy, while it had certain advantages, had corresponding disadvantages. Rubinstein was perfectly right in seeing that Russian music could not flourish in exclusion; foreign influences are not to be avoided, nor, as we have seen, is it desirable to avoid them; but the group of young composers who had inherited the ideals of Glinka and Dargomizhsky had some fears lest they should be swamped by the adoption of habits and rules imported from without.

Mily Alexeyevich Balakirev (1837–1910) was the only one of this group, five in number, who from the beginning of his career was devoted to music. Living in the country, he was brought up upon the folk-music of Russia, and when quite a young man came to St. Petersburg in time to get into personal touch with Glinka. He gathered round him four others, César Cui (1835–1918), an engineer, Modest Mussorgsky (1839–81), an officer in the army, Nicholas Rimsky-Korsakov (1844–1908), a naval officer, and lastly, Alexander Borodin (1833–87), a scientist and lecturer on chemistry, and these, all of them men of remarkable musical talent, with only Cui falling short of genius, were fired with a single-hearted enthusiasm by Balakirev's example. One more member of the group who was not a composer, but who aided the 'five' by his great literary ability and his critical insight, was Vladimir Vassilievich Stassov.

When Berlioz arrived on his second visit he was met and welcomed by the whole of this group. No doubt his reputation, as from his youth an enemy of academies, made his welcome the warmer. Cui, whose position amongst them was stronger as a writer and propagandist than as a composer, wrote an enthusiastic article in the *St. Petersburg Gazette* on the *Symphonie fantastique*. Berlioz's music was listened-to and studied by them all, and his influence is very apparent in the instrumentation as well as to some extent in the form of Rimsky-Korsakov's symphonic poems *Sadko* and *Antar*, and the suite *Scheherezade*.

Rimsky-Korsakov was the first among the Russians to produce a symphony, and was the most prolific composer of this group; he produced a large number of symphonic works for orchestra, a dozen operas, and some chamber music in the course of a long life. Borodin, a much slower worker, whose instrumental works include two symphonies, two string quartets, and only one complete opera, *Prince Igor*, probably left a stronger mark upon his country's music because of the direct purpose and strength of his works. Mussorgsky, with more genius than any of the others, accomplished less in bulk than Rimsky-Korsakov, partly because he excluded from his work more rigorously than any of them the influence of foreign music, and partly because when he left the army, poverty and ill health, the latter increased by drink, preyed upon him, and he died early, leaving a number of wonderfully imaginative songs, a little piano music, one great opera, *Boris Godunov*, finished, and a number of works unfinished. It requires some knowledge of the Russian language to appreciate thoroughly the intimate connexion between poetry and music existing in Mussorgsky's songs and in *Boris Godunov*, but with the aid of translations some idea can be gained of his dramatic truthfulness and of his readiness to use any musical means which will express character.

So devoted was Mussorgsky to the expression of character by vocal phrase, simple rhythm, and striking harmony, that he was long regarded as having cared very little about orchestral colour, and his works were largely edited and re-scored after his death by Rimsky-Korsakov. But it is now recognized that he knew very well what he was doing.

TCHAIKOVSKY

PETER ILYICH TCHAIKOVSKY (born 7 May 1840) came of a family which had shown no strong artistic leanings. He is one more example of the great composer who was first intended to be a lawyer. Like so many of his Russian contemporaries whom we have just discussed, his first interest in music was that of an amateur. He was twenty-one when he began to study music seriously, and two years later he gave up his post, that of a first-class clerk in the Ministry of Justice, in order to enter the new St. Petersburg Conservatory. Here he came strongly under the influence of Rubinstein, for whom he had an unbounded admiration, and under whose guidance he began to compose. He was not amongst the group of young composers who welcomed Berlioz on his visit in 1867. By that time he had migrated to Moscow, where another Conservatory had been founded under the direction of Rubinstein's brother Nicholas. Tchaikovsky was engaged as a teacher of harmony, and for some time he lived in the same house with Nicholas Rubinstein, who was an able musician though less famous than his brother.

These circumstances are sufficient to show the distinct line which separated Tchaikovsky from his contemporaries who, half playfully, half in earnest, called themselves 'the invincible band'. The name itself was enough to arouse opposition in anyone who was not included in it, and since 'the invincible band' opposed itself directly to the influence of Rubinstein it was natural that Rubinstein's admirer should hold aloof. In these two groups we get something of the same kind of antipathy which existed in Germany between Liszt and Wagner on the one hand and Brahms and Joachim on the other. Yet if Tchaikovsky was inclined to be inimical to the 'band', he was big enough to appreciate the powers of some of its members. The fact that his fantasy-overture *Romeo and Juliet* is dedicated to Balakirev and that *The Tempest* is dedicated to Stassov shows this.

Tchaikovsky's life was a difficult one. He was fortunate in

getting many of his works produced as they appeared, through the influence of Nicholas Rubinstein, yet neither his fame nor his fortune made rapid progress. The opera and the orchestra were from the first his chief means of expression, though amongst the list of his works fifty Russian folk-songs arranged for piano duet are worth noticing. Two symphonies, the fantasy-overture *Romeo and Juliet*, and three operas were works of the period which culminated in 1875 with the piano Concerto in B flat minor and the third Symphony in D. The struggle of these years told seriously on his health and spirits, but in 1876 he was able to leave work for a time, to travel, and incidentally to be present at the first Festival at Bayreuth when *The Ring* was produced. Some of his works also travelled: *Romeo and Juliet* was performed in Vienna and in Paris, though not with any great success.

The peculiarities of Tchaikovsky's temperament are stamped strongly upon his work. His vividness of imagination and openness to impressions show themselves in the daring designs of the symphonic poems *The Tempest*, *Romeo and Juliet*, and *Francesca da Rimini*. It was an imagination which had in it the seeds of morbidity, and that quality grew upon him throughout his life. It was, to some extent at any rate, the warmth of his imagination which led him into his unfortunate marriage in 1877. There was a strain of morbidity in his failure to make the best of the situation which he had brought about. A complete breakdown and prolonged illness separate the works we have mentioned from those of his later life which, with a few exceptions, have become the most famous. After this illness, too, a change in his fortunes was brought about by the disinterested friendship of a woman, Nadezhda von Meck, who, some years his senior and a widow with a large family, took so great an interest in Tchaikovsky's art that she made him an allowance in order that he might be able to live where he liked, to travel when he would, and devote himself to composition. The curious fact about this friendship is that Tchaikovsky and his benefactress never met. They corresponded constantly, Tchaikovsky telling her about the progress of his works, his ideas for future ones, his hopes and his difficulties in carrying them out. The fourth Symphony (F minor) was dedicated to her, and with it in the year 1878 appeared Tchaikovsky's best-known opera, *Eugene Onegin*, and the violin Concerto.

The opportunity for travel brought to him by the generosity of Madame von Meck helped considerably in the spread of Tchaikovsky's music outside Russia; it also did something to break down the reserve, the dread of publicity, and the fear of associating with others, which were symptoms of his extreme sensitiveness of disposition. Reserve is the last quality which most people knowing Tchaikovsky's music would attribute to his character. There is a boldness and a blatancy in some of his musical ideas which make people of fastidious taste shrink from him. The swaggering tune with which the piano Concerto in B flat minor opens shows no diffidence, and his habit of battering out the tunes of symphonies in great orchestral climaxes has earned him the reputation of a composer who wears his heart on his sleeve without fear or shame. But his art was his outlet of communication to the world, and it is notorious that none is so bold as the naturally reserved man who throws his reticence to the winds in a moment of confidence.

Italy, Germany, France, England, and America were all included in Tchaikovsky's travels. Some of them were undertaken for pleasure or health, and the *Italian Capriccio* for orchestra records impressions received on one of these visits to Italy. Others were undertaken to superintend performances of his symphonic works, but whenever he returned to Russia he would slip away into a quiet country life in which he could work with comparatively little disturbance. When his friend Nicholas Rubinstein died in 1881 he might have taken his place as the director of the Moscow Conservatory, but he could not bring himself to face the prospect of tying himself down to such work. In the following winter, spent in Rome, he wrote the fine elegiac Trio for piano and strings in A minor in memory of his friend.

The eighties were much occupied with operas, including

Mazeppa, which, like *Eugene Onegin*, is based upon a poem by Pushkin; the music to *Manfred*, orchestral suites, including 'Mozartiana', an orchestral arrangement of some pieces by Mozart, and church music. In 1888 he undertook a big concert tour through Europe, which brought him to London for the first time, and in 1889, the fifth Symphony being completed, he made another tour, partly for the purpose of introducing that work.

TCHAIKOVSKY AND THE ORCHESTRA

Tchaikovsky's orchestral music is a curious blend of the two attitudes represented by Berlioz and Brahms. In his symphonic poems he set himself to illustrate a story as frankly as Berlioz himself did. The popular *1812 Overture*, depicting Napoleon's invasion of Russia and his repulse, is the most positively pictorial of them all, and, planned for open-air performance, it may well be compared with Berlioz's *Symphonie funèbre*. His own remarks about it show that Tchaikovsky was conscious of the limitations of such music, and in his symphonies he rejected the idea of direct illustration. Yet some kind of programme is present in each of the later ones. We spoke of the story at the back of Brahms's works, and that, too, is true of Tchaikovsky's symphonies, and is made far more obvious in them. In none of the last three great ones can the story be said to remain in the background. In the fourth and fifth Symphonies the striking motto themes which begin them and cut across the course of each movement give evidence of this. Brahms, too, we have seen, used such a motto in the third Symphony, but the casual hearer may listen to that symphony several times before he realizes the fact. He cannot do that with Tchaikovsky.

In the case of the fourth Symphony Tchaikovsky tried to put his story into words in a private letter to Mme von Meck in order that she might sympathize the more closely. But the effort was not very successful. He was able to do little more than describe the moods of the themes and movements, which are so clearly evident in the music itself that the verbal comment seems halting and unsatisfactory by comparison. He describes the motto theme as fate, 'a power which constantly hangs over us like the sword of Damocles'. Sorrow, hope, joy, dreams are all subject to its influence, and in the last movement, the principal theme of which is a Russian folk-song, he suggests that the only escape from fate is the unthinking life of a primitive people. In all this one sees the personal story of his own life, the strong impulses and vivid imaginativeness haunted by a morbid depression, from which he could never escape for long.

At the end of the letter he says: 'Naturally my words are not clear, nor are they exhaustive enough. Therein lies the peculiarity of instrumental music, that you cannot analyse its meaning.' These words are very significant. They lead up to the conclusion that there is no actual dividing-line between programme music and absolute music. All good music has elements of both; it may be described in words, but it contains far more than words can convey; it may be analysed into its musical features, but it is the expression of something more than its outward features of sound.

The last of Tchaikovsky's symphonies, called 'The Pathetic', is the most distinctly autobiographical of them all. It is unnecessary to lay stress upon the gloom which pervades it from its opening theme to the long *diminuendo* of the slow movement which forms its Finale. The very fact of ending a symphony with such a movement stamps it with its peculiar character. Three out of its four movements end *pianissimo*, and only the third, an original mixture of the scherzo and the march, contrasts in a sort of reckless hilarity with the pervading atmosphere of disillusionment. Even the second movement, famous for its gracious melody in five-four time, is broken in upon by a middle section in which a drooping and sorrowful theme is played over a continuous pedal bass (that is, the key-note constantly repeated). This device of a throbbing pedal also adds poignancy to the last pages of the Finale.

There was no sorrow of outward life to account for this increasing gloom. The last years of Tchaikovsky's life were marked by such success at home and abroad that he had strong inducements to happiness. All sorts of stories have been built round this Symphony, but it certainly had nothing directly to do with his death. When he was planning it in 1892 he wrote hopefully to his brother about the work and his own future. Its composition, too, followed closely upon the production of one of the brightest of his works, the fairy ballet called *Casse-noisette*, well known in its subsequent form as an orchestral suite. Its general mood was in fact simply the outcome of that tendency to depression with which Tchaikovsky had been afflicted at intervals and with increasing force through his life. But it is the most forcible expression of a purely personal characteristic which the art of music can show. Its personal characteristics prevented its immediate success when it was heard at St. Petersburg in October 1893, but once fully realized its acceptance by the public all over Europe, and especially in England, became excessively enthusiastic. Tchaikovsky, however, did not live to see the immense popularity of his 'Pathetic' Symphony; he died on 6 November 1893.

Tchaikovsky was widely accepted, particularly in England, as a typically Russian composer, yet, as we have seen, he definitely put aside the conscious effort to evolve a national style. What he did was to evolve an exceedingly personal style, and because he was a Russian by birth, upbringing, and outlook upon life, his personal expression included many elements typical of his nation. Though he often drew upon Russian sources for his melody, sometimes using actual folk tunes or church tunes, for example in the slow movement of the string Quartet in D, the Finale of the fourth Symphony, and the *1812 Overture*—elsewhere his melody without actual quotation suggests the rhythms and intervals of Russian folk-song—there are many other influences of foreign origin almost equally strong. There is a suavity, one might almost call it a sentimentality, in Tchaikovsky's melody which none of the nationalist composers, Mussorgsky, Rimsky-Korsakov, or Borodin, would consent to cultivate. His love of Italy and her music may account for this to some extent, as his great admiration for Mozart certainly accounts for that dexterity of workmanship which gives charm to the smaller movements of his symphonies and suites. What he most shares with his contemporaries is simplicity of melodic outline combined with emphatic expression of his ideas, heightened by richness of orchestral colouring.

Tchaikovsky's persuasive way of expressing himself carried his music abroad at a time when the austerities of Mussorgsky would not have been tolerated by any audience not previously interested in Russian ideals; and the coming of Tchaikovsky to western Europe therefore prepared the way for the coming of others of his nation.

Suggestions for Further Reading and Listening

THIS chapter surveys the late nineteenth-century school of Russian composers, as well as Grieg, Smetana and Dvořák, Debussy, and the British National Revival. For further reading on Grieg, John Horton's volume in the 'Master Musicians' series is the first priority. Grieg's particular brand of nationalism is, on the whole, more strongly in evidence in his later works, and can be studied most easily in the last of his *Lyric Pieces* for piano and, more specifically still, in his *Slaater*, transcriptions for piano of country dance tunes originally played on the fiddle.

The standard book in English on Dvořák is by John Clapham, though Alec Robertson's biography in the 'Master Musicians' series is still valid. Dr. Clapham has also written an excellent 'Master Musicians' study of Dvořák's predecessor, Smetana, and there is a full-scale biography by Brian Large.

Literature about Debussy is copious, headed by Edward Lockspeiser's 'Master Musicians' contribution, and also by his *Debussy, his Life and Mind*, a much fuller treatment in two volumes. *Debussy Orchestral Music* and *Debussy Piano Music* are succinct 'BBC Music Guides' written by David Cox and Frank Dawes respectively. For a short, clear-headed, and clearly expressed analysis of Debussy's Impressionism, see Roger Nichols's monograph in the 'Oxford Studies of Composers' series. As its title indicates, Christopher Palmer's *Impressionism in Music* has a broad scope, embracing most of the composers and topics mentioned in Chapter 21, including the Russian Nationalists.

The 'British National Revival' can be explored in more depth in Chapter XI of *A History of Music in England* by Ernest Walker, revised by J. A. Westrup, and in the first part, 'Gestation', of Frank Howes's *The English Musical Renaissance*.

As regards Russian music, Gerald Abraham's various books are essential reading. They include his *Masters of Russian Music* (with M. D. Calvocoressi), *On Russian Music*, the selection of essays *Slavonic and Romantic Music*, and his completion of Calvocoressi's *Mussorgsky* in the 'Master Musicians' series. There is a study of Glinka by David Brown, and this particular period may also be read up in the first volume of Gerald Seaman's *History of Russian Music*.

Inevitably Tchaikovsky looms large in all writing about late nineteenth-century Russian music, but for a close-up view readers are recommended to Edward Garden's book in the 'Master Musicians' series, to John Warrack's beautifully illustrated biography and also, on a pocket-size scale, to Warrack's *Tchaikovsky Symphonies and Concertos* ('BBC Music Guide').

Most of the music referred to in Chapter 21 is available on record, including a fair representation of Parry and Stanford, of Glinka opera (*Life for a Tsar* and *Russlan and Ludmilla*), of Balakirev, Mussorgsky, and Rimsky-Korsakov. As it happens the text specifies no particular music by Debussy, perhaps because of its ubiquity. Those wishing to trace the evolution of this composer's thought and style could for instance compare his *Petite Suite* with his *Nocturnes* and then with *Jeux*. Alternatively, in terms of the piano, they could move from the *Deux Arabesques* to *Images*, and then on to his *Twelve Studies*.

Index